A ROAD TO STONEWALL

Male Homosexuality and Homophobia in English
and American Literature, 1750–1969

TWAYNE'S LITERATURE AND SOCIETY SERIES

Also Available

Imagining Columbus: The Literary Voyage
Ilan Stavans

Epidemics in the Modern World
Joann Peck Krieg

Literary Aftershocks: American Writers, Readers, and the Bomb
Albert Stone

Tales of a Working Girl: Wage-Earning Women in American Literature, 1890–1925
Laura Hapke

Vietnam in American Literature
Philip H. Melling

A ROAD TO STONEWALL

Male Homosexuality and Homophobia in English
and American Literature, 1750–1969

Byrne R. S. Fone

TWAYNE PUBLISHERS • NEW YORK
MAXWELL MACMILLAN CANADA • TORONTO
MAXWELL MACMILLAN INTERNATIONAL • NEW YORK OXFORD SINGAPORE SYDNEY

"Episode of hands" and the lines from "Voyages, V" are reprinted from *Complete Poems of Hart Crane*, edited by Marc Simon, by permission of Liverwright Publishing Corporation. Copyright © 1933, 1958, 1966 by Liverwright Publishing Corporation. Copyright © 1986 by Marc Simon.

The poetry and prose of Walt Whitman quoted in the text is reprinted with permission of the New York University Press.

Twayne's Literature and Society Series No. 6
A Road to Stonewall: Male Homosexuality and Homophobia in English and American Literature, 1750–1969

Byrne R. S. Fone

Copyright © 1995 by Twayne Publishers

Twayne Publishers
Macmillan Publishing Company
866 Third Avenue
New York, New York 10022

Maxwell Macmillan Canada, Inc.
1200 Eglinton Avenue East
Suite 200
Don Mills, Ontario M3C 3N1

Library of Congress Cataloging-in-Publication Data

Fone, Byrne R. S.
    A road to Stonewall : male homosexuality and homophobia in English and American literature,
1750–1969 / Byrne R. S. Fone.
        p. cm. — (Twayne's literature and society series ; 6)
    Includes bibliographical references and index.
    ISBN 0-8057-8856-5 — ISBN 0-8057-4534-3 (pbk.)
    1. English literature—History and criticism. 2. Homosexuality and literature—Great Britain—History.
3. Homosexuality and literature—United States—History. 4. Gay men's writings, American—History and
criticism. 5. Gay men's writings, English—History and criticism. 6. American literature—History and
criticism. 7. Homosexuality, Male, in literature. 8. Homophobia in literature. 9. Gay men in literature.
10. Homophobia—History. I. Title. II. Series.
PR408.H65F66 1994
820.9'35206642—dc20   94-17118
                                                                                                      CIP

The paper used in this publication meets the minimum requirements of American National Standard for
Information Sciences—Permanence of Paper for Printed Library Materials, ANSI Z39.48-1984.∞™

10 9 8 7 6 5 4 3 2 1 (alk. paper)
10 9 8 7 6 5 4 3 2 1 (pbk.: alk. paper)

Printed and bound in the United States of America.

For Richard

CONTENTS

ACKNOWLEDGMENTS

When I began this book I was teaching a seminar in gay studies at the Graduate Center of the City University of New York, and the following term I taught another graduate seminar at the City College of the City University of New York. Our discussions—often acrimonious, often heated, sometimes painful, more often enjoyable and stimulating—were of immense help to me as I wrote. Therefore I want to thank my students in both courses, for this book is very much from them and certainly for them.

I also want to acknowledge some writers without whose recovery of some of the hidden materials of our history, or without whose speculative work, I could not have begun or finished this book. Chief among them, and due my special thanks for the place he holds in the very creation of the field of gay studies, is Jonathan Ned Katz, whose *Gay American History* (1976) and *Gay/Lesbian Almanac* (1983) provided access for me to rare texts that I have woven into my narrative. Katz has reclaimed a massive archive of texts useful for viewing both the growth of homosexual and gay consciousness and the presence of homophobia in society. His annotations and commentary are thought-provoking in the best traditions of scholarship. I would not have been able to pursue my writing about, and collecting of, texts in gay American fiction without Roger Austen's ground-breaking and wise book, *Playing the Game: The Homosexual Novel in America* (1977); Robert K. Martin's *The Homosexual Tradition in America Poetry* (1979); and Thomas Yingling's *Hart Crane and the Homosexual Text* (1990), a profound evaluation of homoerotic aesthetics.

For English nineteenth-century and early twentieth-century texts, Timothy d'Arch Smith's *Love in Earnest: Some Notes on the Lives and Writings of English Uranian Poets from 1889 to 1930* (1970), Brian Reade's *Sexual Heretics: Male Homosexuality in English Literature from 1850 to 1900* (1970), Louis Crompton's *Byron and Greek Love: Homophobia in 19th-Century England* (1985), Jeffrey Weeks, *Coming Out: Homosexual Politics in Britain from the Nineteenth Century to the Present* (1977), and Richard Dellamora's *Masculine Desire: The Sexual Politics of Victorian Aestheticism* (1990) have shaped my work. Useful for my earliest period has been Kent Gerard and Gert Hekma's *The Pursuit of Sodomy: Male Homosexuality in Renaissance and Enlightenment Europe* (1989), in which immensely informative essays by Randolph Trumbach, G. S. Rousseau, Dennis Rubini, and Stephen O. Murray provided additional primary materials to help construct my narrative of eighteenth-century English sodomitical history.

In addition, I want to thank Gabriel de la Portilla, with whom I have had many hours of useful discussion on the varied subjects of this book. His own work in this field has helped to focus mine. My special thanks goes to Barbara Sutton, whose practiced eye and ear saved me from editorial disaster, and who so professionally helped to tame my manuscript. I want to thank Southern Illinois University Press for permission to include in this book material that, in a somewhat different form, appeared in my *Masculine Landscapes: Walt Whitman and the Homoerotic Text* (1992). I want also to acknowledge the New York University Press for permission to reprint material from *The Collected Writings of Walt Whitman* and the Liveright Publishing Corp. for permission to reprint material from *The Complete Poems of Hart Crane*.

Finally, I want to acknowledge here a debt of friendship, and that to the late Richard Hall, to whom I dedicate this book. Richard died before the book was finished, yet his support sustains every page. Over nearly two decades he was to me not only a dear friend but an example of what a writer ought to be and could be. His own work—in fiction, in criticism, in drama—illuminates our times. I miss him.

Byrne Fone
May 1994

INTRODUCTION

"Stonewall" is the emblematic event in modern lesbian and gay history . . .
that moment in time when gays and lesbians recognized all at once their mistreatment and their solidarity.
                                                    —Martin Duberman, *Stonewall* (1993)

When in June 1969 riots broke out at the Stonewall Inn, a gay
bar in Greenwich Village, in response to a police raid on the bar, many there
dismissed it as an unsavory but minor rebellion against authority by a freakish
minority, while some who were there and who were homosexual condemned
the violence and feared that it would destroy the "hard-won" right of homosexuals to assimilate with straight society and endanger their right not to tell
if they were not asked. For some it was a giddy and intoxicating street event;
certainly it was street theater and one of the most successful gay dramas yet
produced.[1] Others, however, suspected that there was something far more,
though many were not sure to what that something more might lead.

The *Village Voice* reported the event with the headline "Gay Power
Comes to Sheridan Square." According to *Voice* reporter Lucian Truscott,
"As the patrons trapped inside [the Stonewall Inn] were released one by one,
a crowd started to gather on the street. . . . Suddenly the paddywagon arrived
and the mood of the crowd changed. Three of the more blatant queens—in
full drag—were loaded inside. . . . [A] cry went up to push the paddywagon
over. . . . [T]he next person to come out was a dyke, and she put up a struggle. . . . It was at that moment that the scene became explosive. Limp wrists
were forgotten."[2] Howard Smith later reported in the *Voice*: "The door is
smashed open again. More objects are thrown in. . . . By now the mind's eye

has forgotten the character of the mob; the sound filtering in doesn't suggest dancing faggots anymore. It sounds like a powerful rage bent on vendetta" (Fone 1979, 322). Three nights of rioting followed. Ten years of radical change followed that.

When the New York police raided the Stonewall Inn they expected no more than the usual response to such raids: some snide remarks, campy bitchery, and acceptance, usually indifferent, sometimes sullen, of the verdict of the law. But that night, instead of disappearing into Village streets to find other bars, the patrons remained outside the bar. The crowd grew larger and increasingly defiant. Bitchy remarks became jeering shouts; hostility grew. A bottle was thrown, a window broken, a paddy wagon arrived. Blows were exchanged, arrests made, and suddenly a riot exploded. Stonewall was born and history made. Things were never to be the same. For the first time in American memory, gay people refused to accept the verdict of the law—a verdict that indicted them as second-class citizens, as sick, perverted, and criminal, as undeserving of the protection of the law as they were of the compassion of the righteous. Instead someone shouted "Take your hands off me!"

After that night old certainties were no longer secure in America: stereotypes about fairies, faggots, and pansies; old myths about butch dykes and effeminate men; the old notions about limp wrists, hairdressers, and ballet dancers; and the old fears about perverts and child molesters had to be seriously questioned. After that gay people were no longer lonely men who lived down the street, were no longer "unmarried" uncles, "spinster" aunts, or "peculiar" cousins; they were suddenly America's sons and daughters, husbands and wives. After that night "coming out" was the watchword, liberation the cause, "Gay Power" the battle cry. Gay people were no longer content to accept arrest and the loss of job, career, and dignity as the penalty for being what they were. They were no longer content to hide, to lead double lives, or to suffer in fearful silence as their rights were trampled on or ignored. Gay people began a decade of activism characterized by marches and public demonstrations, by legal and political battles, by increased visibility in the arts, business, and professions. And the idea became a certainty that "coming out" was not only a declaration of independence but an affirmation not of what one has become but of what one is.

Historian Martin Duberman considers Stonewall "synonymous over the years with gay resistance to oppression. Today, the word resonates with images of insurgency and self-realization and occupies a central place in the iconography of lesbian and gay awareness. The 1969 riots are now generally taken to mark the birth of the modern gay and lesbian political movement."[3] Stonewall, therefore, marks the incendiary beginning of a quarter-century of exhilarating activism and pride and sexual celebration among lesbians, gay men, and bisexuals. We have been shattered by and now courageously confront the horror of AIDS. We have entered a decade in which we have cause both for celebration and apprehension.

We can celebrate our increased general visibility, our greater organization in public life, the queer effrontery, subversion, and remarkable *difference* of our style and our politics. We can celebrate the recognition that we must avoid not only the anxious urge to assimilation that marked the pre-Stonewall years but the equally anxious urge to locate in and define ourselves solely by the boundaries of the sexual and stylistic ghettos constructed by the high and mannered excesses of 1980s clone culture. In the 1990s homosexuals have deployed in life and in texts our most valuable asset: difference. We support it with militancy, with a formidable library of lesbian and gay writing, and with our other most valuable tool—that distanced, knowing, dead-on and laser-sharp ironic queer humor that punctures the spirit, as activist queers assault the body, of homophobia. Who other than a group of queers would stage a demonstration at a mall in the heartland with the chant "We're here, we're queer, we're going shopping"?[4]

Since 1969 gay literature has been a vocal and supporting partner to the activism that has been the primary mark of the movement for lesbian and gay rights. Much of the most remarkable gay and lesbian history of the last 25 years can be located in battles fought on the streets and in the courts, in demonstrations and marches, in the formation of organizations and the creation of political initiatives. Much of this history has been recorded, sustained, and mythologized by our texts; by the extensive, rich, and varied production of lesbian and gay novels, poetry, and plays; and by political, literary, critical, theoretical, and historical texts that have appeared since 1969.

Literature and social action since Stonewall have been two equally powerful forces working toward the single goal of gay and lesbian visibility and social equality. In this sense, then, since 1969, our history has been both textual and social. Many may consider the greatest achievements of the post-Stonewall period to have been those accomplished by social and political action. Still, an argument surely can be—perhaps ought to be—made that these achievements may also have been initiated by our texts and that they have been made possible in a climate in which social action is supported by a rich fabric of "homotextual" culture.

Today our novels, poetry, and plays are published under many imprints and with high print runs; our contributions to the documenting and critiquing of culture from a homosexual perspective are shaped and supported by the presence of lesbian and gay studies in the academy. Gay and lesbian studies courses are being taught in a remarkable number of major universities. Lesbian and gay scholars are rewriting canons, theory, and textual evaluation and are thus righting wrongs perpetrated against homosexuals and their books by a heterosexist and often homophobic literary and historical criticism, and are as well renegotiating the very construction of lesbian and gay "identity."

Celebration is clouded by apprehension. Apprehension is simple though deadly: it is named AIDS. It has not been conquered, and homophobia, an equally virulent disease, has not been defeated or even weakened. "Family values" in some quarters is still a code word for bigotry and hate. A 19 July 1993 letter to *Newsweek* shows how far we have yet to go. Commenting on an informative and positive cover story on lesbians in America—a remarkable media breakthrough—a woman from St. Louis wrote, "Homosexuality is abnormal behavior. In no way, shape, or form is it a moral equivalent of heterosexuality. If this makes me a homophobe, I wear the label with pride." *Newsweek* assures us in its summary of other outraged responses that the writer is not alone in her pride in the label she has chosen to wear.

In eroticized America, homosexuals and bisexuals wage a battle for jurisdiction over the body with political conservatives and the religious right, with any number of "moral" minorities that declare their intention to erase the culture of gay people, deny the validity of their desire, and make their lives invisible. I do not think this deliberately separatist and perhaps baroque insistence too extreme, for I write in an America where gay-bashing increases daily, where homophobia is virulently present not only in the streets but on television, in newspapers, and in church pulpits.

Stonewall was a beginning, but it was also a culmination, and that is the subject of this book. Stonewall happened because homosexuals of all races revolted against an act of official oppression. But Stonewall does have a past as well. To borrow Duberman's term, it is the "emblematic" culmination of the work of gay activists in the 1960s who staged demonstrations against social oppression, who organized groups of gay people to fight for civil rights, who founded gay magazines and newspapers to educate the public about gay culture. It is the culmination of the work of homosexual rights advocates in the 1950s who founded groups like the Mattachine Society and the Daughters of Bilitis. It inscribes the work of writers like Donald Webster Cory, who in his pioneering 1951 book, *The Homosexual in America*, warned that if the homosexual "does not rise up and demand his rights, he will never get them."[5]

Stonewall reflects not only social activism but an incredible explosion of gay and lesbian literature that appeared between 1930 and 1969. These books helped to change the face of American writing and speculated about and invented different versions of gay identities. They were a textual reflection of the American psyche where fears about sex, difference, and definitions of masculinity circulated darkly as novels tried to discern how the "he-man virility of our young country" and the "staunch masculine or commendably feminine characteristics" of Americans ought to be portrayed. These quotations are from sex texts of the 1930s that warned that there were "ten million male and female queers in this country"—a fact that the writer found "terribly sinister" and "decadent."[6]

Stonewall owes its symbolic power to the American textual construction of homosexuality and homosexual lives and identities undertaken by homosexual writers after 1930. There is also a debt to be paid to the writings of some remarkable homosexual pioneers of the beginning of the twentieth century. To a more distant past a greater debt is due, since therein lies the origin of an American ideal of homosexual liberation and the most powerful and profound construction of American homosexual identity as an inseparable and potent element in American political and social life. I speak of course of the writings of Walt Whitman. His textual definitions of his homosexuality and his search for men with "blood like mine" circulating in their veins established homosexuality (what Whitman called comradeship, adhesiveness, and manly love) as one of the great and informing texts in American letters.

When in 1860 Whitman announced his intention to "tell the secret" of his nights and days and "celebrate the need of comrades" he was heard more clearly by European writers than by American. Stonewall therefore has origins in Europe too. In English texts published between 1850 and 1900 writers like John Addington Symonds and Edward Carpenter theorized homosexuality, identified homophobia, and insisted that homosexuals must rise up and secure their rights. Other authors, not yet considered by a largely homophobic medical discourse as "homosexuals" but sometimes calling themselves "inverts" or "Uranians" (while society called them "effeminate," "diseased," "perverted," or "insane"), sometimes directly advocated and celebrated in their texts the love of men for men, sometimes conveyed such love in coded and indirect ways, and occasionally translated homosexual love into subversive texts enacting forbidden sexual desire. In the late nineteenth century homosexuality was said to have been called the love that dared not speak its name. But in Europe and especially England between 1850 and 1900, the unnamed love was spoken about with increasing frequency in texts and in public.

In the early nineteenth century, however, homosexuality rarely spoke at all and certainly had no name save for those society gave it: sodomy, sin, and crime. Only one English writer anonymously but bravely announced, in terms that would have been cheered at Stonewall, that he was no longer willing to hide his desire or to assimilate himself into a society that not only despised him but that would kill him. These radical sentiments appear in the poem Don Leon (1833), the first homosexual liberationist text written in England, the first imaginative fiction to positively portray a homosexual—

"sodomitical" is the term appropriate to the period—identity. It is also one of the first texts in English to advocate the decriminalization of homosexuality and the social acceptance of homosexual love and desire. *Don Leon* answers eighteenth- and early-nineteenth-century texts that condemn sodomy as a crime against God and nature committed by monsters and effeminate men who nevertheless lightheartedly called themselves "mollies." Mollies questioned rigid gender definitions and hinted at a new fluidity in sexuality. In their cross-gendered masquerade they initiated transgression against social and sexual roles as the function of sexual difference, reflecting the process that was inventing the modern homosexual.

Though the many roads to Stonewall have been constructed by lesbians and gay men, the road I want to mark crosses masculine landscapes only. The landmarks at which I pause are surprisingly numerous. I have surveyed literature forecasting the lives of gay people from the mid-eighteenth century to the eve of Stonewall. Before 1969 there were no marches, few political initiatives, and only a handful of organized groups. The text is what dominates—books examining aspects of homosexuality in, say, literary history or social structures, written arguments for social equality or novelistic portrayals of homosexual lives. In a very exclusive and particular way the pre-Stonewall history of men who love men is the history of the word, though a word ever yearning to be made flesh.

This is not to say that these texts make no reference to the culture that produced them or that there is no history of same-sex love outside of texts. But texts—many of them "literary"—are the primary historical materials of male same-sex desire. A large generalization might see them as responses and resistance to homophobia, and the texts that construct homophobia are as much a part of this history as texts written by homosexuals. All of these texts perhaps can be seen as historical "events" that have contributed to the construction of homosexual identities and have created a climate that helped to initiate some of the defining moments of the modern fight for gay and lesbian rights.

The social activism of our own time is mirrored and even originates in the homoerotic and polemic texts of the nineteenth and early twentieth century, and speculations as to who we are and what and why are finally the primary text as well as the essential subtext. In a broad and of course dangerous sense, these texts are all "coming out" stories, and they write themselves as opposition to the social requirements of concealment. They are all keys to the closet door. It is largely the essentialist presumption of most of these texts that the art we have created, the music we have written, the books we have produced, and the many roles we have played in society are indelibly tinged with what we have at this moment in the twentieth century come to believe is the single most vital and salient fact of identity: sexuality. An early seventeenth-century sodomite might likely be puzzled by this seeming obsession or fail to understand it entirely. The texts I analyze herein increasingly presume that sexuality is the central fact of human life and the central ingredient of identity, that homosexuality is what Whitman described as that which "contains all the rest."

These texts were written by men whose fascination with homosexuality is fueled not only by desire but by its opposite: the conscious suppression of desire prompted by a terrible awareness of the restricting and destroying power of homophobia, even though "homophobia" was a term they would not possess any more than they would possess "homosexual" as common currency until well into the twentieth century. The love they championed was in public described by those who legislated against it as the love not to be named among Christians. Even in private it was painfully felt that it dared not speak its name. While Michel Foucault has made it clear that silence was the very last thing the invention of sexuality implied or desired, these texts were nevertheless powerfully affected by those who were obsessively concerned to situate homosexuality medically or morally, legally or dogmatically within one sphere or another of social and linguistic control and definition. These texts attempt to break the tyranny of socially regulated and defined speech about (homo)sexuality and thus to speak about homosexuality in another way and to transfer its definitions from proscriptive medical, moral, legal, and dogmatically religious discourse into positive literature and polemics.

Homophobic texts were never silent about homosexuality, but homosexuals had been silent about themselves. By the early nineteenth century, however, homosexual writers asserted that not only was homosexuality not a sin but that it must be named among Christians and that the dictum that homosexuality dared not speak its name was indeed a dare to be risked. But these texts also insisted that naming was only one aspect of larger and more complex identities. Homosexual texts began the work of bringing homosexuals into being—of inventing ourselves—and freed readers and writers to speak a multitude of other names and to attempt to define and construct equally various identities. Indeed, it is in these texts that the very concept of homosexual identity is invented. These texts were written because those who wrote them courageously believed that silence equals invisibility. They thus prepared a textual ground on which our dictum that silence does indeed equal death could figure with potent resonance. They enacted textual dramas aimed at the liberation of homosexuals from oppression, and they thus forecast what Stonewall would come to mean and what the movement it ignited would try to achieve.

In discussing male "homotextuality" in this study I have sought neither to dogmatically assert nor deliberately deploy any mechanism of "theory" or even to construct special categories of or positions about what homosexual texts are or ought to be—and I do not offer these texts in order to canonize them. I offer a meditation on relevant readings that have especially interested me—a meditation informed by other scholars' meditations about homosexuality in texts and homosexuality generally that have often influenced, changed, angered, or delighted me. I have chosen texts that have articulated homosexual identities over time. The cultural space represented by homoerotic textuality has allowed Uranian poets, homosexual polemicists, and gay novelists the chance to enact in texts not only justifications for homosexuality but inventions of it, records of it, and forecasts of what it might be. Thus the texts I have chosen also contribute to the origination of certain historically resonant literary and social gestures that pertain specifically to homosexuality in texts and as text, to the development of certain historical and critical imperatives that define homosexual and homoerotic texts, and to the use of these texts as increasingly eroticized resistance to homophobia.

Because textual articulations of homosexual identities and the impact of homophobia on these identities is my primary concern, I can only make a gesture here to a reading of texts that deploys the vital critique founded in analyses of race, class, and gender. It is obvious, of course, that uneasy collisions as well as the tentative renegotiations between race and homoerotic desire are apparent in the texts of Langston Hughes, James Baldwin, Charles Wright, Hubert Selby, and John Rechy, to name a few of the writers important in the last part of the period I cover. There is also no doubt that these collisions occur in the texts of earlier American writers like Bayard Taylor, Herman Melville, Charles Warren Stoddard, and Whitman, all of whom enacted in texts fantasies and wrote speculative dramas about desire between men of color and white men—although these texts are filtered through the privileged but distorting lens implied by the fact of their race. Junctures of race and sex need to be constantly critiqued in both English and American texts, and some of the texts I discuss do explore that terrain.

Similarly, in nineteenth-century American and especially English writing questions pertaining to class as the often troubled companion of homosexual desire may be an equally disturbing theme. Though certainly germane to the later writers I mention in American texts, class is also a vital issue in several possible readings of Whitman as it is in E. M. Forster's *Maurice*, a novel that confronts the fatal sexual allure of social and class inequality. That allure is as much an obsession in the work of Symonds, who wrote 60 years earlier, and it was surely nearly fatal in the life of Oscar Wilde. Indeed, class is often the inverse text of those works by Wilde that also question heterosexual social norms and all sexual orthodoxies.

Many of the texts I have chosen are neither the most significant nor even the most representative. Many of them, indeed, may seem insular, referring to the seemingly etiolated concerns of a special class or a single race, though indeed they are all projected within a discourse that questions presumptions about gender. As to gender, the third in that sometimes politically sensitive

triad, and the analyses of gender particular to feminist theory and the homo-
eroticization of it still being richly enacted in gay and queer theoretical speculation, I can only suggest that, in the polemical speculations and subversive
poems of both nineteenth-century British and American writers and in the
rich fiction of early twentieth-century American homosexual writers, theory
may discover a sometimes unlooked for—perhaps unexpected—and original
source. There, theorization of the multiple articulations of gender and sexual-
object choice coexists with attempts to fragment "homosexual identity" and
to construct it into a very modern concept of "homosexual identities."

Some of the texts and writers I have read are unacknowledged or
unknown, some now even scorned because of what they inescapably were.
What they attempted to become is sometimes consigned to a reading that
renders them quaint, antique, irrelevant, or sometimes racist, classist, or anti-
feminist. The perplexed exploration of racism, classism, and anti-feminism is
surely the life blood of current reevaluative cultural discourse, and the inter-
play of all these with complications of difference and desire has quickened
our own lives and writings. These are serious questions and deserve a book of
their own. There surely are books to be written about race, class, and gender
that can be constructed out of the materials I discuss here. But no materials
are exclusive enough to produce only one book, and homosexuality has still a
thousand unwritten texts. In this book, while I attend to these questions
when it seems important, I do not reject texts or writers because *they* do not
attend to them.

My fairly single-minded purpose is to read certain homosexual texts—
texts that seem to me to be crucial in developing a homosexual and homoeroticized critique of homophobia, of homosexual oppression and repression;
texts that intertextually construct, before Stonewall, a "liberationist" and
even activist reading of homosexual identities. The writers I deal with are
white, middle class, and male. These men surely were as entangled in the
racial, class-bound, and gender-specific mythologies of their times as, for
example, we are. But no matter what failings the lens of our own political
sensibilities may discern when it is trained on them, what we cannot ignore
is that in writing about what they were, they courageously contributed to the
creation of what we are becoming.

Many of the texts I discuss are unavailable to readers save in private collections or in some larger libraries. Many are out of print, rare, or inaccessible. Many are inaccessible now because they were inaccessible then,
privately printed in a few copies; many of those made publicly available were
then seized and destroyed. Their past inaccessibility is founded on the same
reason as their present rarity: they are homosexual texts written by homosexual
writers.

Many of these texts may seem to be minor ones as well as disqualified ones
since, as some critics insist, they speak only to the "narrow sensibility" of a

few, to use a favorite criticism of homoerotic texts. Critics have denigrated them as art and dismissed their authors as mediocre writers whose purpose is to specially plead for the immoral and the indefensible; their subject matter has been rejected as immature, marginal, minor, narrow, and often obscene. Discussing homosexual novels of the 1950s, John W. Aldridge wrote, "The homosexual experience is of one special kind, it can develop in only one direction, and it can never take the place of the whole range of human experience which the writer must know intimately if he is to be great. Sooner or later it forces him away from the center to the outer edges of the common life of his society where he is almost sure to become a mere grotesque, a parasite, or a clown. The homosexual talent is nearly always a precocious talent, but it must necessarily be a narrow one, subject to all the ills of chronic excitation and threatened always with an end too often bitter and tragic."[7]

Aldridge invokes every cliché that the psychoanalytic science of the 1950s enshrined in its pantheon of attempts to explain and "cure" homosexuality: homosexuality moves its "victims" ever further into the darkness of the outer edges of society where the homosexual's once exciting and precocious talent narrows, his life becomes exaggerated, socially worthless, and effeminate, and loneliness and death is inevitable. Aldridge's critique of homosexuality could well pass as the plot of one of those novels of the 1940s and 1950s in which homosexuals inevitably shoot themselves at the end after leading lives of lonely promiscuity.

The critical response to Whitman's homosexuality and the homoeroticism of his texts gives a kind of organizing shape to and an example of the more general strategies of homophobic criticism. After Whitman's death some critics denied his homosexuality, feeling that it was a blot on the purity of the legend. Others attempted to "de-homosexualize" the celebrations of the text by forceful denial, ingenious misreading, or, as in the instance of one critic who changed the pronouns of an original Whitman manuscript from masculine to feminine, textual tampering.[8] Even if the homoeroticism of the texts was grudgingly admitted, critics recoiled at the possibility that what art implied biography might ratify.

In 1906, for example, Bliss Perry, one of Whitman's earliest American biographers, asserted that "as far as I know there has never been the slightest evidence that Whitman practised homo-sexuality." In his conversations with those who knew Whitman well he insisted that he had "never heard the slightest hint of the charge" that Whitman was homosexual.[9] Half a century later G. W. Allen felt that the *Calamus* emotions were "not yet pathological" and doubted that "actual perversion" was likely between Peter Doyle and Whitman.[10] Some recent critics have suggested that Whitman's homosexuality and homoerotic texts are not worth talking about. In 1985 William White conceded that a few scholars in the 1980s had written an "article or two, or a chapter in a book, on the subject of Whitman's homosexuality" and that most critics were not "sidestepping the issue," he pointed out that "for some of us it is simply not an issue since there is no real evidence that Whitman was a practicing homosexual." White seems to feel that without practice there is no homosexuality. Hence it is not a subject worth discussing, since, as he says, even though "writers in gay magazines" feel that Whitman was one of them, most "contributors to periodicals prefer dealing with other subjects." White's comparison between apparently "serious" heterosexual "scholars" in serious journals as opposed to frivolous gay "writers" in even more frivolous gay magazines further suggests some of the more egregious condescension of nonhomosexual critics.[11]

Some critics, like David S. Reynolds writing in 1988, are not willing to come "to a firm conclusion about Whitman's sexual preference." Reynolds argues that Whitman "wanted to avoid the deceit and artificiality, the amorality, that he associated with the heterosexual love plot" and that a way of "avoiding the love plot was to emphasize adhesive love," which "in the phrenological terms of the day was not associated with homosexuality."[12] It is true that Whitman drew his term *adhesive* from phrenology; it is true that he was appalled by sentimental plots about heterosexual love. But that did not stop him from writing sentimental stories about veiled homoerotic relationships between men and boys, and most of his poems in *Calamus* are, after all, love plots dealing with relationships between men.[13]

Both early and recent discussions of Whitman's sexuality tend to deny the possibility of homosexual acts or the validity of homosexual feelings; they use language powerfully charged with disapprobation and dismiss the question as relatively unimportant, as Perry's, Reynolds's, and White's examples demonstrate. Some writers find homosexual feelings so repugnant that their presence in text seems almost to invalidate that text. Such a position was taken by Mark van Doren in 1942, when he described Whitman's "manly love" as "deficient and abnormal love," and by Edwin Miller, who suggested that Whitman's "deviancy" and "absence of [heterosexual] experience" are barriers to a mature art. This position admits the homosexuality but insists, as Robert K. Martin observes, that homosexuality contributed to his art in no way "except to flaw it" (Martin 1979, 6). So John Snyder speculates that the "lover in *Calamus* . . . fails because failure is the given end of homosexuality" and thus implies that because of that double failure the text fails too.[14]

In 1989 David Leverenz bluntly announced that Whitman's homosexuality and homoeroticism "make me, as a heterosexual male, recoil."[15] In each instance can be heard the echoes of Aldridge's method—one that ignores the text and fixes on and judges the sexuality of the writer. Finding that sexuality distasteful—immature, flawed, an emotional "failure," deviant, abnormal, deficient—the text itself is no longer assessed critically but, rather, the writer and text are judged from a platform built on unexamined socially constructed moral repugnance, fear, and bigotry.

Gay theorists have begun to suggest that homophobia is a necessary ground for straight constructions of identity and perhaps even a useful part of critical discourse since it sets in train fecund speculation about the place of homophobic prohibition in current thought about any text—homosexual or nonhomosexual. It also allows a critique within the compass of not only a writer's self-evaluation but of the aesthetic, historical, and political situation of texts as homophobic or anti-homophobic discourses. The deep questions are thus implied in such an emotionally charged word as "recoil"—the raw reaction of homophobia—or raised by asking why it is, as White says, that critics "prefer dealing with other subjects" than homosexuality—the intellectualization of that raw response.

When a critic compares homosexual to heterosexual experience and finds it wanting because he does not share it or because he fears it and founds a critique on that fear, when homosexuality is trivialized by the critical assertion that "it is not an issue," this bespeaks a fatal inability on behalf of nonhomosexual critics to make the dangerous leap and the vitally necessary critical distinction between difference and its manifestation in the word. In the 1950s Aldridge had decided that homosexuality and "racial conflict" (!) were "simply minor issues. They cannot be other than minor subjects for a kind of writing that operates only on one level" (Aldridge, 104). Thirty years later the judgment that homosexuality "is not an issue" because no one knows if Whitman actually had sex with men is as naive and dangerously reductive.

It may well be that some American critics in the 1950s and 1960s believed that those texts and writers that constitute fully a third of the "great books" of any canon they might have constructed are indeed marginal to the full "human" experience of "normal" heterosexual life. Who would believe, however, that in 1993 the homophobia that makes Aldridge's book so repellant might be discovered again? Reviewing Brad Gooch's *City Poet: The Life and Times of Frank O'Hara*, Joan Acocella takes Gooch to task for "dwelling on O'Hara's homosexuality":

> How long will we wait for the Synthesis, the time when homosexual artists will be treated like heterosexual artists? It will not serve the cause of justice for an artist of O'Hara's general, human appeal to be put forth as a "gay poet." Gooch does not apply that label, but the accumulation of sexual detail does it for him. And, in case you're thinking that this material, however excessive, might nevertheless be fun to read, forget it. Larry Rivers describing exactly what he and O'Hara did in bed, who put what where, who did what then—there's something grim about it, something dogged.[16]

There is something not only grim but stunning about this smug homophobia. One hopes that the "Synthesis" Acocella looks for will be a long time in coming since homosexual poets are not "like" heterosexual poets, in part because, just as she says, heterosexual critics have erased and "glossed over" homosexuality "even when it was crucial," as it is with O'Hara, as it is with any homosexual writer. If Gooch does not label O'Hara a gay poet, it is not the accumulation of sexual details, however much they may make critics like Acocella or Leverenz recoil, or however much she distances herself from them with a trendy new-journalistic style, that is the vital marker. Instead it is the force, weight, the nuances and enactments, and also the silences of a homoerotic text or any text by a homosexual writer that would allow that label to be applied. It is a label that O'Hara would have worn proudly. As Thomas Yingling suggests about O'Hara: "To read O'Hara as a 'straight' poet is to devalue the historical significance of his work and requires that one bring a flat ear to his text, missing almost all the nuance, humor, and insight of it. It also means missing—if this is possible—some of its most direct references."[17] Current lesbian and gay criticism will, one hopes, provide a sufficient corrective to commentary such as Acocella's, but one also hopes that essays like hers are not trial shots in a new barrage of critical homophobia.

Fortunately gay and lesbian critics have begun to renegotiate the historical and critical perceptions of homosexual texts and to reclaim a heritage. In Martin Duberman, Martha Vicinus, and George Chauncey's 1989 collection of essays by gay and lesbian scholars, *Hidden from History*, and in several full-length studies, this heritage is being recovered from a narrow interpretation that does not or will not recognize that difference, not a specific sexual practice, is the essence of homosexual textuality. George Chauncey's *Gay New York: Gender, Urban Culture, and the Making of the Gay Male World, 1890–1940*, a book that appeared just as my work was in galleys, extensively surveys gay social and material history and suggests that the varieties of erotic difference that texts describe was ratified by life. Chauncey describes a rich and complex gay male society that existed in New York City half a century and more before Stonewall—a society that is mirrored in many of the texts I discuss in the last section of this book. Difference—sexual, social, political— ranges itself against the compulsory heterosexualization of texts that Acocella advocates when she abjures "gay" status for O'Hara and thus erases difference from texts in favor of an aesthetic that seems to be based on a grim and dogged notion about what is or ought to be "fun to read."

I do not for a moment mean to suggest that homosexual sex is not as important and vital a part of homoerotic texts as are other markers of homosexuality. Whitman—who in his texts certainly put everything everywhere in a thousand brilliant variations on cocksucking, fucking, coming, and jerking off, to be grim and dogged about it—translated such sexual enactments, "however excessive" they may seem for nonhomosexual critics, into a poem that is not only fun to read but is the greatest spiritual text America possesses. One wonders sometimes that if a text had the names changed to protect the innocent sensibilities of the reviewer whether the reviewer would still be so shocked by what he or she had to review and whether it would still sound like this: "In case you think this material, however excessive, might nevertheless be fun to read, forget it. Constance Chatterley describing exactly what she and Mellors did in bed, who put what where. . . ."

While homosexual texts have changed radically and impressively over time, it is chilling how little the language of homophobia has changed. The mission of gay and queer criticism now is to resist such incursions and misreadings as I have just outlined and establish a criticism in which such homophobia can have no honored place. The mission of the texts I discuss in this book was to open a space where such resistance is possible. Over time we have invented ourselves and articulated identities, communities, and desire in texts. Thomas Yingling argues that those engaged in reclaiming the literary and social history of those articulations would now "insist that male homosexual articulations of desire are materially different from other sexual articulations." He goes on to say, "Western patriarchal culture has overwhelmingly solicited heterosexual rather than homosexual desire as the key to sanctioned social and legal identities" (Yingling, 29). As queer theory resists such notions of identity and seeks to redefine nearly every victory won and every assumption so painfully wrought out of the battles of Stonewall, every presumption about how lesbians and gay men are defined from both the outside and the inside—indeed, about the continuing utility of terms like *gay*, *lesbian*, and *queer*—it today founds its critique on ground long prepared.

It is to Stonewall, an especially American moment, that my comments lead, and the English and American texts I discuss resonate against that moment in a particularly relevant and special fashion. No single homosexual literary or social plot, no history or set of texts can adequately map the road—the many roads—to Stonewall or to our own moment in the history of gay times. This book is one map only, and tentative and roughly drawn at that—one that has as much, perhaps more, to do with my own travels in erotic literary landscapes as it has to do with any attempt to set a course that will chart every landmark or negotiate every trail opened by criticism or theory, no matter how luminous may be the goals to which such pathways lead. Taken together, the texts I discuss do in a sense tell a "story" and indeed are persuasive as well as inventive—in them we invent ourselves. Surely what more persuasive and inventive moment in gay history than that June night in 1969.

I want to tell this story not so much for the seasoned scholar as for those for whom the idea of gay literature is intriguing or perhaps even new, and for whom Stonewall may not even be a memory. I write for the student who comes to this literature with eagerness and curiosity to discover in books what he has found or may suspect in himself. This book is also for those who are skeptical of the elision of "gay" with "literature" or for those who had not imagined that it was possible even to construct such a term. I want to show that sodomite, homosexual, or gay means more than sex, yet that what men did or desired can have a significant place in what they wrote. Sex is the text, but once it is the text it becomes so much more. The landscapes of homoerotic desire, of homosexual books, gay texts, queer stories, are richly scenic and full of wonders. There is much mapping left to do, and we must all be cartographers.

The Punishment of Sodomites, by Nicholas Hogenberg (seventeenth century). Bibliothèque Nationale, Paris.

chapter 1

CRIMINAL BODIES: SODOMITES AND MOLLIES, 1700–1833

I think there is no crime in making what use I please of my own body.
—William Brown on his arrest for sodomy (London, 1726)

   In Paris in 1725 a man named Deschauffours was burned at the stake for sodomitical crimes. In 1733 a satiric pamphlet was published in Paris that suggested that the author saw Deschauffours as a member of a special and persecuted minority. Declaring Deschauffours a martyr, the anonymous writer described the event anagramatically: "Fourchuda [Deschauffours] a celebrated inhabitant of Spira [Paris] who in his zeal in defending a large army of Eugabors [Bougres-Buggerers], was taken prisoner in the struggle, was condemned and thrown into the fire."[1] Nominating Deschauffours as defender of an "army" suggests that Deschauffours, and perhaps the author of the pamphlet, presumed that the sodomitical Eugabors rather than being isolated individuals were instead a persecuted minority united not only by their persecution but by their desires. Deschauffours's "zeal" defending them marks him as an advocate for them, an early activist resisting social and political oppression.

  That the author of the Deschauffours pamphlet can talk about an "army" of sodomites suggests at least that the idea that sodomites might be in some sense a community was not an invention of this text alone. Indeed, in 1724 another commentator feared that if sodomites are spared punishment society would be disrupted and "there will be great disorders" and "all kinds of people will take off their masks, believing everything is permitted, and they will organize leagues and societies" (quoted in Rey, 134). Leagues, societies, and armies of marching sodomites become fearful specters associated in these texts with the disruption of society itself. Another possible interpretation of the Deschauffours text as satiric of the unlikelihood of a manly or militant sodomitical organization suggests that effeminacy in its sense of unmasculine weakness was now firmly associated with sodomites. But even this does not mitigate the fear that haunts these texts—the fear that the social structures and the class system may be vulnerable to disruption by sodomy.

It is unlikely that Deschauffours was an aristocrat, a social group with whom sodomitical practices had traditionally been associated. Indeed, evidence suggests that at the beginning of the eighteenth century it was the general and popular belief that sodomites were found only among the aristocracy. Writing in 1720 about some young French noblemen who, instead of more capital sentence, like burning, were condemned to exile as punishment for sodomy, Marshal de Richelieu echoed this belief: "As this vice is unknown among the people, one [needed] a punishment that afforded no scandal" (quoted in Rey, 134). By 1784, however, Moufle d'Angerville in his *Memoires secret*, writing about the prevalence of sodomitical acts and the presence of "pederasts" in Paris, suggests a shift in opinion: "This vice, which used to be called the beau vice because it had only affected noblemen, men of wit and intelligence, or the Adonis, has become such a fashion that there is no order of society, from dukes on down to footmen, that is not infected" (quoted in Rey, 134). D'Angerville's choice of "infected" to describe homosexuality is telling, for, like a disease, it was believed that sodomitical vice infected those touched by it, and like the victims of nineteenth-century vampires, homosexuality could infect and convert a populace.

For this reason social control of sodomites was coming to be seen not solely as a subject for ecclesiastical jurisdiction, and sodomy as a sin dangerous only to the immortal soul; it was considered a danger to society and was the state's responsibility to survey and control. A Parisian document discussing sodomy reports that the "police discover dangerous inclinations in certain souls which may promptly lead them to misdeeds. Such a character already turns to crime; it is time to sequester him from society" (quoted in Rey, 145). Among these "misdeeds" are sodomitical acts and among the "certain souls" are sodomites who can be sequestered from society, this text suggests, without respect to rank or status in society. By 1738 in fact, in Paris police records, the term sodomite—as indicating the perpetrator of a specific act—begins to be replaced instead by "pederast," a description of a type of person with special "inclinations" who is presumably a member of a special "league and society" that admits anyone without reference to class or status who shares similar desires.

Sodomites prosecuted in the eighteenth century came from all classes. That homosexual subcultures crossed social boundaries is firmly supported by police and court records. In Paris, for example, between 1723 and 1749, 53 nobles and bourgeois, 212 merchants and artisans, 129 domestic servants, and 40 others of no special rank, were arrested for sodomy (Rey, 135). Trials in the Netherlands in the 1730s saw all social levels brought to trial, and contemporary accounts of the trial and punishment of sodomites in London in the early nineteenth century show a similar broad social range (see Gerard and Hekma, 263ff, 407ff).

It is true that most cases "are united by the common factor of belonging to sections of society subject to the full workings of the legal system" and that "few had access to the immunities which grew with ascent in the hierarchical establishments."[2] This is supported by the case of the exile—rather than imprisonment or death—being imposed on the aforementioned young French noblemen, and by the fact that some influential Englishmen in the early nineteenth century were able to escape physical punishment—though not social ostracism—only by voluntary and sometimes by enforced exile. Yet it became increasingly difficult, especially in England, for even the influential or socially prominent to escape some kind of public humiliation or punishment.

Whatever the class, punishment for sodomy in Europe after 1750 became more and more common, and homophobia became more and more evident. Shifts in gender roles and the hardening of gender expectations and stereotypes—coupled with increasing anxiety about sexuality itself and about sex as an arena for crime—led to a public awareness of the presence of a specific group of what were thought to be dangerous sexual deviants, "perverted," as an eighteenth-century pamphleteer insisted, "in body and mind" and with the dangerous ability to infect society with their desires.[3]

It became increasingly believed that such men—for women were rarely mentioned as being so "perverted"—were demarcated by special signs. D'Angerville in 1784 associated the "beau vice" with "men of wit and intelligence, or the Adonis." This formula sets homosexuals apart because of special abilities or appearance. It also forecasts concepts that came to be encoded within homophobic public perception and later nineteenth-century homosexual apologia: namely, that homosexual ranks contain a disproportionate number of men of wit and intelligence, and that it is the unusual physical attractiveness of homosexual men that is a mark of their sexuality and a factor in their devastating ability to lure innocent men to sexual ruin. Curiously, these perceptions about sodomitical power seemed to tally without fear of possible contradictions with the general perception of weak effeminacy. All of these perceptions, of course, acted as a marginalizing social force.

THE SODOMITE AND "EFFEMINACY"

From the Middle Ages to the early seventeenth century, religious and legal opinion tended to conceive of sodomy as an act that, though contrary to nature, anyone could commit. The sodomitical act was, strictly, anal penetration, but broadly it could apply to any act not aimed at procreation, thus it was associated with any number of nonprocreative sex acts including bestiality and homosexuality. Sodomites were, therefore, people who had committed this unlawful sexual act and were not necessarily thought of as either a particular group with special predilections for sodomy, nor as people who were inevitably unmanly or effeminate. Instead, the sodomite could be a heterosexual who had broken the law, or a provocative libertine who intended to defy the law and social convention. The "beau vice"—by which d'Angerville certainly intends homosexuality—was most often included under the general prohibitions against sodomy and, if named at all, was spoken of as the crime not to be named among Christians.[4]

Such libertine rakes as the Earl of Rochester, whose 1660 poem *Sodom; or, The Quintessence of Debauchery* praises equally the sexual use of whores and boys, suffered relatively little social disapprobation, nor is it likely that he was thought of as effeminate or conceived of as a separate and subversive species that might organize "leagues and societies." Nor would many in England, France, or the Netherlands prior to 1700 subscribe to any definition of the sodomite as congenitally afflicted by a desire to engage in sodomitical acts.

By 1784, however, when d'Angerville asserted that people are "infected" by sodomy, the perception of sodomy seems to have changed. The growing linkage between sodomy and effeminacy, which becomes more evident after 1700, encouraged a public perception that the sodomite was not simply a fallen heterosexual who took the active role with either sex as a demonstration of manliness. Instead the sodomite had become a male who took the passive role in sex with other men and who had "sacrificed" manliness and virility, expressing this sacrifice not only in his sex role but in the conduct of his life as well by adopting effeminate ways and even wearing women's clothing.

As early as 1734, for example, a Dutch publicist, Justus van Effen, described sodomites as "hermaphrodites in their minds" and "effeminate weaklings," while a pamphlet attacking sodomites described them as having a "feminine mind in a man's body" (Boon, 246). In 1749 an English anti-sodomite pamphlet, *Satan's Harvest Home*, detailed the "Reasons for the Growth of Sodomy in England" and offered the opinion that the "men of a tender Constitution" are likely to be sodomites and suggested that "the Effeminacy of our Men's Dress and Manners particularly their Kissing each other" was both cause and symptom. Indeed, the pamphlet went on to say, these "enervated and effeminate animals" had "sucked the Spirit of Cotqueanism [cotquean: a man who acts like a woman or housewife] since infancy," suggesting—as nineteenth-century medical theory would later assert—that sodomites are born, not made.[5]

By the early 1800s the sodomite had become firmly pictured in the popular mind as an effeminate species, a depraved denizen of a sexual underworld, with a special language and signs, and possessed of a voracious sexual appetite and predilection only for his own sex. Sodomites were imagined to be seducers of the innocent young, responsible for the ruin of innocent married men and of the perversion of marriageable bachelors from their proper course. Despite this ambitious program accorded them, sodomites were nevertheless still believed to be exclusively the weak and passive recipients of the sodomy act. What had once been an unhappy error in individual judgment had now become a group effort.

These anti-sodomy perceptions need to be read in relation to the increase in legal persecution of homosexuals after 1700. More men were persecuted for sodomy between 1700 and 1850 than at any other time in the previous 600 years. In Holland a series of persecution beginning in the 1730s marked "the dividing line between the image of the sodomite as an actor, a criminal, or a sinful 'heterosexual,' and the view that sodomites (the plural) constituted an interrelated network, a virtual 'fifth column' of profligates, the devil's henchmen, a vital threat to sanity, reasonableness, and purity" (Boon, 242). Before 1730 in that country there are no known convictions for sodomy; between 1730 and 1732 numerous sentences were handed down against men convicted of sodomy, of which more than 200 resulted in execution.[6] In Prussia between 1700 and 1730, 43 males and one female were charged with involvement, either as witnesses, accomplices, or participants, in sodomy; torture was used to obtain confessions, and the punishment of execution by the sword was followed by burning the corpse.[7]

There are few records of either trials or execution for sodomy in Tudor England or in that country in the seventeenth century. The earliest successful prosecution of adults for sodomy did not come until 1631, and there were few for the rest of the century. But in 1726 "a great number of these Wretches were convicted and three put to death" for sodomy, and between 1749 and 1804 executions averaged one every 10 years. Between 1806 and 1839, however, 60 men were hanged by the public executioner and another 20 under the auspices of the navy (Crompton, 16–18). As Randolph Trumbach observes, "It is likely that Early Modern Europe experienced a sodomy paranoia paralleling the witch burning craze," and in England that paranoia reached its height in the eighteenth and early nineteenth centuries.[8] Most of Europe repealed the death penalty for sodomy by the end of the eighteenth century, and the imposition of the Napoleonic code eliminated entirely any penalty for sodomitical acts in countries subscribing to the code. England, however, did not eliminate the death penalty until well into the nineteenth century, and homosexual acts remained criminal there into the twentieth, as they remain in America in many states today.

Public anxiety about sodomites led not only to more prosecutions but also to attempts by authorities to entrap sodomites and to discover their meeting places to increase the prosecutions. Anxiety fueled public fascination with and demand for knowledge about them. Newspapers pandered to people's desire to participate vicariously in the persecution and punishment of homosexuals by giving daily accounts of the trials, convictions, and executions of defendants, who were almost always described as "miscreants," "wretches," or "monsters" and practitioners, as Blackstone's Commentaries say, of the "sodomitical, detestable, and abominable Sin called Buggery, (not to be named among Christians)" (quoted in Crompton, 15). During the Dutch trials and executions newspapers offered daily "Accounts of the Proceedings against the Sodomites of that Country," and in England at mid-century, during a single two-year period, newspapers published more than 2,000 reports of trials, arrests, and speculations concerning convicted and alleged sodomites.

Death could be by burning, drowning, or strangling, though in England hanging was the favored method of execution. More often than not the execution was preceded by confinement in the pillory and exposure to an angry mob that hurled dung and rock at the accused. An 1810 pamphlet describes the punishment of the so-called Vere Street Coterie that had been apprehended in London's White Swan Tavern:

> The gates of Old Bailey Yard were shut and the miscreants brought out, and placed in the caravan. . . . [T]hey all sat upright, apparently in a composed state. Directly the church clock went half-past 12, the gates were thrown open . . . a grand sorties of police was then made . . . the caravan went next. . . . The first salute received by the offenders was a volley of mud, and a serenade of hisses, hootings, and execration, which compelled them to fall flat on their faces in the caravan. The mob, particularly the women, had piled up balls of mud to afford the objects of indignation a warm reception. . . . Before the cart reached Temple Bar, the wretches were so thickly covered with filth, that a vestige of the human figure was scarcely discernible. . . . Some of them were cut in the head with brickbats and bled profusely. . . . Before any of them reached the place of punishment, their faces were completely disfigured by blows and mud, and Before they mounted [the pillory] their whole persons appeared one heap of filth. Upwards of fifty women were permitted to stand in the ring, who assailed them incessantly with mud, dead cats, rotten eggs, potatoes, and buckets of blood, offal and dung. (quoted in Crompton, 166)

That the authorities were not content with regulation only but created situations to entrap victims is attested to by the London press. As one newspaper reported, "Two persons, James Bryan and Frederick Symonds, who were recently apprehended in St. James park for indecent practices, were yesterday tried. . . . It was proved that the police disguised themselves on the occasion."[9] Indeed, entrapment was seen as an appropriate response to the presumed crime, and the police used the very youths who were deemed to be victims of the "disgusting practices" of such men: "a lad who alleged he had been tampered with in the streets, for the gratification of what is called abominable lusts, was taught how he should deliberately lead his seducer into a snare, which was to be set for him, and how, just when his seducer's breeches were unbuttoned, he was to make the signal, by which the police officer, planted for the unworthy purpose, was to take him in a state of unequivocal delinquency" (*Don Leon*, 58).

Entrapment, prosecution, and the punishment of the pillory were so horrendous that many apprehended sodomites took their own lives. One man accused of indecent assault on a boy was overcome by a mob who "smeared his face with tar, gave him severe blows on the head with fists, sticks, etc., until he fell down. Whilst undergoing this persecution, the unhappy man, in the open street, drew a penknife from his pocket, and inflicted a severe wound in his throat. He was immediately conveyed to a hospital . . . but the nervous excitement under which he laboured, and the blows which he had received, producing fever, he gradually sunk and expired" (*Don Leon*, 93–94).

MOLLIES AND MOLLY HOUSES

Popular perceptions, at least about the existence of a homosexual underworld, were in fact correct. In Italy and Spain sodomitical subcultures seemed to be flourishing by the fifteenth century; in London, the Netherlands, and France strong evidence for the existence of such fully formed subcultures appears in the late seventeenth century. Most evidence supports the probability that a distinct homosexual subculture had existed in many large European cities by 1650. By 1700 in London, Amsterdam, and Paris such subcultures could claim defined meeting places—parks, latrines, public arcades and certain taverns. Trial records indicate sites in The Hague and in other Dutch cities frequented by homosexuals. Several areas in Amsterdam—among them the town hall, certain taverns, public toilets, and parks—were known to be sites of homosexual liaisons, as were the houses of known sodomites, such as Willem Van Schalen, government employee.[10] At the Universities of Utrecht and Leiden a homosocial club may have been documented, this one seemingly consisted "primarily of British students and their tutors in the two Dutch universities."[11]

In England in the 1720s the activities and publications of various Societies for the Reformation of Manners—groups concerned about the laxity of public morals—had revealed in the press the meeting places of sodomites: coffeehouses around the Royal Exchange, the piazzas of Covent Garden, the latrines of Lincoln's Inn, Birdcage Walk in St. James's Park, the so-called Sodomites Walk in Moorfields. Such public sites required sodomites to use special codes for recognition and special signs and gestures to identify and to indicate sexual interest in one another (Trumbach 1989, 408). English sodomites made themselves known by a variety of signals: "If one of them sits on a bench he pats the back of his hands; if you follow them, they put a white handkerchief through the skirts of their coat, and wave it to and fro; but if they are met by you, their thumbs are stuck in the armpits of their coats, and they play their fingers on their breasts."[12] In the Netherlands Jacobus Hebelaar in 1764 describes similar customs: "A person who met another man [in the front of City Hall], whom he thought to be a sodomite, looked the other stark in the eye and put his hands on his hips, which was answered by the other in the same way, after which they gave each other a nudge with the elbow. And the signals used at the back of City Hall were such, that if someone doubted, he went to make water. The other did the same and having known one another in that way, the one went into the public toilet, where the other followed immediately."[13]

Homosexual subcultures—networks of men (almost never of women) involved with one another for social and for sexual reasons—were active and reasonably complex in London and other large European urban centers by 1830. The existence of such subcultures and of special private meeting places in London is documented by raids on sodomite establishments in 1698, 1707, 1726–27, 1763–65, 1776, 1798, and 1810 (Trumbach 1989, 409). These meeting places, called molly houses, were generally private clubs, though sometimes they were taverns in which a back room was reserved for the use of special patrons. The word "molly" may have been imported into English from the Greek New Testament "malakoi"—men who engage in passive homosexual acts—that had been translated into English as "effeminates." It first appears in English as "molles" (the translation of "malakoi" in the Latin Vulgate) in Richard of Devize's Chronicle of the Times of King Richard the First (1192), where it seems to refer to men who are described as weak or "effeminate" and mentioned in a context that includes reference to sodomites and catamites.[14] By the early nineteenth century the public considered a "molly" an effeminate male who preferred sex with men and the passive role in anal intercourse and whose social life was spent in a homosexual subculture dominated by transvestism and role reversal.

Molly houses provided men with a safe place to meet and have sex with one another. They may have served as a clearinghouse for procuring boys and young men for sexual purposes and as sites of social rituals that involved the adoption of feminine roles and sometimes dress. We should not assume, however, that effeminacy was the primary code of homoerotic social interaction. Trumbach argues that outsider descriptions of this subculture have always emphasized its effeminacy, yet it is hardly surprising that the popular and legal emphasis on effeminacy as a condition of the sodomite came to be a description fulfilled by those it intended to describe. With their effeminate mannerisms the mollies imitated or even parodied what they imagined to be aristocratic manners. The pseudo-aristocratic names—"My Lady," "Princess Seraphina"—they adopted suggest that a source for their mannerisms lay in the spectacle of court, just as the adoption of female personae, whether by eighteenth-century mollies or contemporary drag queens, is not only a tribute to but a burlesque of received expectations about gender roles. As Trumbach implies, heterosexual respectability was as much the object of molly travesty as was that travesty an attempt to imitate female roles and social mannerisms.

On the Continent the effeminate manners and social rituals of Philippe, Duc d'Orleans, the brother of Louis XIV, and his entourage have been well documented and suggest widespread homosexual practices (see Oresko). While less evidence of this kind is available for the otherwise very extensively documented homosexual subcultures of the Netherlands, witnesses in trials of the period attest to such effeminacy "because of the way sodomites spoke to one another and the nicknames they have to one another. Nicknames were often the feminine equivalent of the sodomites' male names" (van der Meer, 292). Considerable evidence is available to show the nature and extent of the effeminate rituals of London's sodomites. Samuel Stephens, a constable who infiltrated a well-known molly house in 1725, reports: "I found between 40 and 50 Men making Love to one another, as they call'd it. Sometimes they would sit on one another's Laps, kissing in a lewd Manner, and using their hands indecently. Then they would get up, dance and make Curtsies, and mimick the voices of Women. . . . Then they'd hug, and play and toy, and go out by Couples into another Room on the same Floor, to be marry'd, as they call'd it."[15]

Fashion and style of dress was imagined to be one of the distinguishing hallmarks of the sodomite. In Holland, as Boon suggests, "effeminacy expressed itself through clothing, and the Dutch, once renowned for their simplicity and austere mode of life, now dressed in grand style and extravagant attire. Through unmanly French fashions, sodomites could display their perverse attitudes openly and unrestrained" (Boon, 241). The attempted linkage that mollies made between themselves and the aristocracy—and the blurring of the distinctions between what was perceived to be aristocratic behavior and what was perceived to be unmanly or effeminate behavior—is mirrored not only in verbal forms but in extravagant fashions.

The reaction of the populace to fashionably dressed nobles was, however, often quite different from its reaction to fashionably dressed sodomites: "to people of the lower classes, a noble—powdered, pomaded, refined—was both elegant and effeminate," but "if someone on a lower scale . . . assumed this costume . . . not only did he betray his social condition, but in addition, his effeminacy, by losing its accepted associations with elegance and the upper class, became an indication of the wearer's real effeminacy" (Rey, 189). In England, as Trumbach points out, "if the public was convinced that all sodomites were effeminate and misogynist, it believed as deeply and as erroneously that sodomy was a fashionable vice—the final corruption of the aristocracy. But again the evidence of the trials does not bear this out. The men in the London sub-culture were drawn from the middle and lower classes" (Trumbach 1977, 19). The true aristocracy was largely not involved in the general activities of these groups; rather, those leagues and societies were populated by men like J. Baron, a Paris brewer who invited several fellow sodomites to his tavern, where "the others approached us, embracing and saying, 'Hello Mesdames.' Baron arranged his hair with a woman's headdress, which was black, like the hairdo of a woman at court" (quoted in Rey, 186–89).

Of course not all homosexual men were mollies; indeed, probably most were not. Many, as trial records show, were married—a status many used as a defense, since "it was part of the 18th century stereotype to believe that if a man were married he could not be a sodomite" (Trumbach 1977, 18). Many also rejected effeminate practices and role-playing as did one man, a painter, who in 1748 "withdrew from these gatherings [of mollies] because they were too scandalous. Several members imitated women and made gestures which showed what they were." The painter admonished them, "Can't you adopt men's mannerisms rather than women's?" (Rey, 188).

Sex, however, was what drove the molly houses and the subculture. The notorious Vere Street molly house and other taverns and private clubs were certainly sites of homosexual seduction. Sex between men, between men and boys, between exclusive sodomites and nonsodomites, is fully and specifically documented in journals, court records, and literature. Sexual activities between men seem to have involved masturbation, anal penetration, and intercrural intercourse, and, to a lesser extent, fellatio, and increasingly kissing, which in the seventeenth and early eighteenth century had been a common form of greeting between men but which by the late eighteenth century had become a sign of sodomitical tendencies (Trumbach, 428, n27). Sex occurred in pairs and in groups; boys were procured for men, and male prostitution flourished, as did blackmail and physical attacks on homosexuals. Men also lived in long-term relationships, however, and practiced monogamy, as did apparently Jan van Weert, who in 1802 was tried and convicted in part on the evidence of a letter from his friend: "Jan, write me if your heart is still worthy of mine . . . thou art faithful to me until death; who will separate us, nobody but the will of the Heavenly father, and we are tied in love forever" (van der Meer, 289).

LITERARY TRANSFIGURATIONS

Sodomite subculture flourished despite widespread homophobia, which was expressed not only through legal prosecution and persecution but as literary satire, biased reportage, and in the form of journalistic or moralistic attacks on sodomites. Few text published between 1700 and the early nineteenth century portray sodomites in any light that could be described as sympathetic or positive or that sites sodomy in a context that is social rather than exclusively sexual. If the social and legal prohibitions constructed a version of the sodomite that made him both monstrous and contemptible, novels, broadsides, poems, and moral essays produced an equally laughable and equally horrifying figure.

Homosexuals in literature were also depicted in the same divided, even schizophrenic, manner: on the one hand they were weak and on the other hand dangerous. If weak and effeminate, they were then the legitimate prey of homophobic violence and the object of scorn and derision. But when practicing their infectious vice they were seen as dangerous monsters whose existence undermined morality and social stability, and whose uncontrolled sexuality threatened to destroy all virtue and corrupt all innocence. In short, the depiction of the homosexual in early modern texts is stereotypical and parodistic, conforming no doubt to some social reality but also making a potent contribution to this social reality, for such exaggerated and distorted characterizations of homosexuality were accepted by society as real and used by homosexuals themselves to construct the materials and rituals of their subculture.

The literary presence of homosexuality is hinted at by the title of a 1729 pamphlet that will serve to represent many: "A Hell upon Earth, or, the Town in an Uproar. . . . Occasion'd by the late Horrible Scenes of . . . Sodomy." As G. S. Rousseau points out in what is the best survey to date of eighteenth-century literature occasioned by homosexuality, "Except for Smollett's detailed representations [in *Roderick Random* and those not sympathetic] this homosexual subculture was not realistically represented in *literary* texts, except as targets for abuse" (Rousseau, 143). The aforementioned newspaper accounts suggest the popular level of homophobia, and the rhetoric in Edward Gibbon's *Decline and Fall of the Roman Empire* (1776) demonstrates the virulent disapprobation. As Gibbon says, "I touch with reluctance and dispatch with impatience, a more odious vice, of which modesty rejects the name, and nature abominates the idea." Gibbon then, as Louis Crompton points out, "in two long paragraphs . . . finds space for at least a dozen opprobrious terms—'odious vice' and 'abomination' are succeeded by 'infection,' 'degeneracy,' the 'indelible stain of manhood,' 'unmanly lust,' 'sin against nature,' 'licentiousness,' 'impure manners,' 'disease,' 'corruption,' and 'mortal pestilence'" (Crompton, 23). Gibbon's terms constitute very nearly a history of the changing attitudes toward homosexuality, ranging from the "abomination" of biblical texts to the eighteenth-century moral and social disapprobation seen in "indelible stain of manhood," "unmanly lust," and "impure manners" to a forecast of nineteenth- and early twentieth-century assertions centering on the medicalization of homosexuality as a "disease" and "infection"—indeed, as a form of mental illness, the consequences of which are "degeneracy."

RODERICK RANDOM

In no text is there presented such a full-scale picture of the popular conception of a sodomite as in Tobias Smollett's *Roderick Random* (1749). There Lord Strutwell and Captain Whiffle represent not only the effeminacy and evil imagined to be associated with homosexuality but also demonstrate that the social spectrum is "infected" by such men. Roderick's first encounter with English sodomites comes on board ship as a new commanding officer, Captain Whiffle, arrives. Whiffle, together with Simper, his surgeon, and Vergette, his valet, are full length portraits of stereotypical homosexuals. Indeed, as Rousseau observes, Whiffle's description is so "stereotypical that it must have been archetypal in the 1740's," and "it may represent the first authentic description of the enduring male homosexual stereotype in modern culture" (Rousseau, 147). Whiffle arrives in "a ten-oared barge, overshadowed with a vast umbrella."[16] He is a "tall, thin young man," dressed in extravagant and dandyish—hence effeminate—fashion: "His hair flowed upon his shoulders in ringlets, tied behind with a ribbon." He wears a coat of "pink-colored silk lined with white" that "by the elegance of the cut retired backwards" and a "white satin waistcoat embroidered with gold, unbuttoned at the upper part to display a brooch set with garnets" (221).

The luxurious fabrics—silk and satin as opposed to the customary home-spun seaman's garb—the unmanly pink of the material, the wanton and coy ringlets (again, hardly the style of a seaman), and the suggestive cut of the coat (revealing more of his physique than is decently allowable and pointing not only verbally—"backward"—but actually to the supposed site of his sexual pleasures), together with the unbuttoned waistcoat that reveals a distinctive item of feminine adornment, a brooch, leave little room for doubt—if fashion indicates sexuality as Smollett clearly intends that it does—as to what Whiffle is. But if doubt remains, "the most remarkable parts of his furniture were a mask on his face and white gloves on his hands, which did not seem to be put on with the intention to be pulled off occasionally, but were fixed with a curious ring on the little finger of each hand" (221).

One such absolutely archetypical "pinky ring" immediately indicates effeteness, but two suggest even worse perversion, while the gloved hands—never bared in honest manly labor—indicate an effete luxury. The mask—a stylish item often worn by women engaged in assignations and associated also with libertine masquerades at which sodomites were alleged to engage in "matters not fit to be mentioned"—places him entirely beyond the pale of masculinity (Rousseau, 155, n88). Because satire depends not only on exaggeration but on recognition—on the creation of stereotypes—it is likely that Whiffle must have been recognizable to readers in 1749 as an example of what Smollett clearly sees as a crisis of masculinity.

A 1703 pamphlet addresses this crisis so closely associated with sexual deviance: "The Men, they are grown full and Effeminate as the Women: we are Rivall'd by 'em even in the Fooleries peculiar to our Sex: They Dress like Anticks and Stage Players, and are as ridiculous as Monkeys: they sit in monstrous long Periwigs. . . and esteem themselves more upon the Reputation of being a Beau, than on the Substantial Qualifications, of Honour, Courage, Learning, and Judgement."[17] The pamphleteer's comparisons firmly situate these men as sodomites, just as Smollett's transcription of Whiffle's effete comments to Simper—together with the name Simper—gives verbal evidence of Whiffle's sodomitical tendency: "O! my dear Simper! I am excessively disordered! I have been betrayed, frighted" (224). Such linkage between verbal and physical mannerisms is made by Ned Ward in *The London Spy* (1709) when he describes London's sodomites "as a particular gang of sodomitical wretches in this town who call themselves mollies and are so far degenerated from all masculine deportment or manly exercises that they rather fancy themselves women, imitating all the little vanities that custom has reconciled to the female sex, affecting to speak, walk, tattle, and scold, and to mimick all manner of effeminacy that has even fallen within their several observations, not omitting the indecencies of lewd women, that they may tempt one another by such immodest freedoms to commit those odious bestialities that ought for ever to be without a name" (quoted in Kimmel, 115).

Whiffle's appearance conforms with this diatribe. His thinness suggests the weak constitution and his attire the gender confusions attributed to sodomites. Presumably such a creature could not be concerned with the manly and presumably nonsodomitical subjects of "Honour, Courage, Learning." Whiffle's appearance suggests that he is as vain as the men skewered in *Mundus Foppensis; or, The Fop Displayed* (1691), who "Far must more time . . . trifling Wast / E'er their soft bodies can be drest / The Looking Glass hangs just before / And each o' th' Legs requires an hour" (quoted in Kimmel, 113). Not only is Whiffle a picture of what Ned Ward despises, but he is also surrounded by a crowd of attendants who share their master's "disposition," a crowd indeed recalling the "gang of sodomitical wretches" in Ward and the "leagues and societies" of sodomites so much an anxious feature of popular texts.

When one of the ship's crew seeks an audience with Whiffle, the captain is found "reposing on a couch with a wrapper of fine chintz around his body and a muslin cap bordered with lace about his head," a domestic and indeed effeminate picture. He reacts to the mate's entrance and appearance and apparently also to his rather gamey smell by screaming in horror, "I am betrayed," and calls him a "monster." Then Whiffle "sunk down upon the settee in a fit; his valet de chambre applied with a smelling bottle, one footman chaffed his temples with Hungary water" (222). Whiffle's reaction to the rough true-blue Englishman is precisely that of a stereotypical hysteric woman so commonly portrayed in the plays of the period, whose virtue is threatened and whose honor "betrayed" by the imagined advances of barbaric men intent, so it is implied, on rape.

The mate, incensed, seeks out Random and delivers himself of a tirade against Whiffle that recalls the language of the anti-sodomite pamphlets: "I do affirm . . . that I have no smells about me but such as a Christian ought to have, except the effluvia of tobacco . . . as for my being a monster, let that be as it is: I am as Cot [God] was pleased to create me, which, peradventure, is more than I shall aver of him who gave me that title, for I will proclaim it before the world that he is disguised, and transfigured, and transmogrified with affection and whimsies, and that he is more like a papoon [baboon] than one of the human race" (223).

If there was any doubt as to Smollett's intention in this portrait, there can be no doubt now, for, like Gibbon's tirade, this by the mate is replete with anti-sodomitical rhetoric. The mate is a decent Christian who, like manly men, smokes tobacco. He is no monster, but Whiffle is, and "monster" here echoes that appellation of monstrosity conferred on all sodomites. The mate is "just as God made him," but the captain is an ungodly and hence unnatural creature, who in donning disguises transmogrifies himself from male to female by the use of "affectation and whimsies," traits associated with coquettish women. Indeed, Whiffle is so much a monstrosity that he is a baboon—that is, no man at all, but instead a creature whose animality suggests indiscriminate and uncontrolled sexual desire.

In this passage Smollett ranges the true-blue Englishman—rough, healthy, and sexually correct—against the deviant sodomite—diseased, effeminate, and masked. The actual mask that Whiffle wears represents the disguise the mate accuses him of donning and suggests a major theme both in homophobic and homoerotic discourse, for this is the same charge that Queensberry will make against Oscar Wilde when he accuses him of "posing" as a sodomite. In 1889 the poet Mark André Raffalovich adopted the pose as a badge of pride and transgressive distinction when he urged that he and his friend "put on" the pose of "languor which the world frowns on, / That blamed misleading strangeness of attire." The mask that Whiffle wears, here a fashionable mark of his sodomite status, forecasts the appearance of the mask as a far more complex symbol in homoerotic texts, for it becomes the mask that homosexuals wear—sometimes must wear—at once to conceal and proclaim difference.

Whiffle's valet, Vergette (whose name Rousseau suggests is a pun on the French *verge*: a very small penis), and his surgeon, Simper, appear as confederate sodomites. Simper, a "young man gaily dressed, of a very delicate complexion, with a kind of languid smile on his face, which seemed to be rendered habitual by a long course of affectation" (that languor of which Raffalovich speaks), enters, and "the captain . . . flew into his arms, crying, 'O! my dear Simper, I am excessively disordered.'" Simper diagnoses this disorder as "entirely nervous" (224). The very word "disordered" again recalls a thousand instances of neurotic female complaints portrayed on the London stage and forecasts the medicalization of homosexuality. The captain then prohibits access to his cabin to anyone save Simper and his servants—a perfumed entourage—thus establishing an exclusive community of sodomites in the midst of the ship's larger nonsodomite community. In doing so he creates just the sort of exclusive league inveighed against in the pamphlets and gives ship's gossip the opportunity to "accuse of him of maintaining a correspondence with the surgeon not fit to be named" (225). Of course sodomy is meant, that vice not to be named among Christians.

Whiffle's appearance may recall both the Restoration rake and the dandyish beau. With none of the masculine swagger associated with the rake, everything about him, like the beau, is excessive. But the beau boasts and prattles as much about (hetero)sexual conquest as about fashion.[18] If Whiffle is neither precisely rake nor beau, he is not exactly a molly either, for his habits of dress, at least those that Smollett lets us see, are not transvestial but only suggestive, though his adoption of a chintz wrapper and lace cap would appear to hint that in private moments he may adopt even more effeminate attire.

The appearance of the mollies as very nearly a third sex represents a "transition from one sexual system to another—from a system of two genders of male and female to a system of three genders of man, woman, and sodomite."[19] Whiffle may not be a molly, but he is certainly a sodomite. He is the newfangled sodomite who does not seek out boys but men, and not nonsodomite partners but, in the person of Simper, his own kind. He accepts the equally foppish and sodomitical attentions of Simper, who is his mate in age and in sexual desire. His portrait suggests that Smollett—along with numerous other homophobic pamphleteers—had already noticed what Michel Foucault suggested two centuries later: that homosexuals had become a species.

Random's next encounter with sodomitical culture comes when he is urged to seek out Lord Strutwell who, he is told, will help him with a position or preferment. Smollett's depiction of Whiffle and his servants as men of similar "dispositions" allows him also to suggest that this disposition to a certain extent levels social distinction. His portrayal of Lord Strutwell adds aristocracy to the social mix, and Strutwell's attempted seduction of Random displays just how desire within sodomitical subcultures could, at least for the temporary purposes of sexual satisfaction, cross social boundaries.

Whiffle offends, in Smollett's eyes, by his style and by his pose—his disguise. But because he is portrayed as weak, he is also laughable and hence is trivialized at the same time he is satirized. But Strutwell is different. He may appear on the surface to be all of the things Whiffle represents, and his effete surface style may seem to be as laughable and open to trivializing satire as Whiffle's. But he is also what Whiffle is not: he is the sodomitical monster, representing both incarnate evil and dangerous intelligence. Though Strutwell displays more elements of the old libertine rake than Whiffle, he also represents another new sodomitical kind: the sodomite apologist and activist who tries to seduce not only by attempts to arouse sexual desire or by offers of material advantage but by perversion of the intellect as well.

Strutwell is not only a practitioner of sodomitical acts but a spokesman for a homosexual life-style.

On meeting Random, Strutwell immediately identifies himself as a member of a sodomitical coterie, for "he frequently squeezed [Random's] hand." In *Satan's Harvest Home* readers are warned that "tho many Gentlemen of Worth, are oftentimes, out of pure good *Manners*, obliged to give into" squeezing the hand, "yet the Land will never be purged of its *Abominations* till this Unmanly, unnatural Usage be totally abolish'd; for it is the first Inlet to the detestable Sin of Sodomy" (Rousseau, 150). Strutwell immediately offers Random the possibility of employment, and Random is so affected that he "could not help shedding tears at the goodness of this noble lord" (337). Strutwell, perhaps taking them as a sign that Random too shares his inclinations, or at least as an opportunity for close physical contact, "caught me in his arms, and hugged and kissed me with a seemingly paternal affection." Random describes the kisses as paternal but almost immediately rejects the paternal interpretation of Strutwell's kisses and is "confounded at this uncommon instance of fondness for a stranger" (337–38). Strutwell, certainly psychologically savvy, has taken the opportunity of tears to make a sexual advance. Random is confounded by this and "remains a few moments silent and ashamed," aware perhaps that kisses between men and especially between strangers are, in the newer social dispensations of mid-century, no longer the innocent demonstrations that they might have been a generation before.

The next day, and after more physical expressions of esteem, Strutwell continues his campaign of seduction, this time not sexually but intellectually, flattering Random by speaking to him as an intellectual equal and appealing not to lust but to letters: "Among other topics of discourse, that of Belles-lettres was introduced" (338). Despite its location in a homophobic text, Strutwell's disquisition is nevertheless an early example of the deployment of what would eventually be appropriated as pro-homosexual polemic. His text, and his use of it, is a familiar sexual ploy. By treating sodomy as a historical rather than sexual fact, Strutwell defuses the sexual threat but allows the introduction of sodomy into a discourse that is nevertheless intended to be seductive. Once introduced, the lure of the forbidden and the very presence of sex in the discourse creates a kind of sexual atmosphere that Strutwell knows well how to turn to advantage, especially if, as Strutwell apparently believes about Random, the subject shares similar though perhaps buried inclinations.

Citing antique virtue and invoking a host of the great who were practitioners of this morality, Strutwell attempts to justify homosexuality. A similar course of seduction was used by one Captain Rigby who in 1698 tried to seduce a young man and offered similar justification and examples: "He asked the boy if 'he could F[uck] him.' The boy asked 'How can that be?'"

Rigby replied: 'I'll show you for its no more than was done in our forefather's time.' He continued: 'The French king did it, and the Czar of Muscovy made Alexander, a carpenter, a prince for the purpose'" (quoted in Trumbach 1990, 109).

Strutwell, using the same strategy, gives Random a copy of Petronius Arbiter's *Satyricon*, in which homosexual lovers play a major role. Random's comment that the work is "lewd and indecent" can only be a response to the homosexual component of it. Strutwell immediately counters with a disquisition that is at once satiric and serious. He echoes the popular objections to sodomy yet turns them to his own use and uses them in the defense of sodomy. *Satan's Harvest Home*, published one year after *Roderick Random*, when read against Strutwell's apologia, shows how both in some aspects engage the same sort of polemical approach to sodomy. But Strutwell's purpose is patently different from that of the author of *Satan's Harvest Home*, who asserts that sodomy is a "Damned Fashion! Imported from Italy amidst a train of other unnatural vices." He sees it as a foreign import and insists that in England "till of late years, Sodomy was a Sin in a manner unheard of in these Nations." He plays on both the fear of homosexual conspiracy and the increase of homosexuality: "We have much Reason to fear, that there are Numbers as yet undiscover'd, and that this abominable Practice gets Ground ev'ry Day" (quoted in Crompton, 55–56).

Strutwell uses similar arguments, touching on the foreign origins of sodomy, its increase in England, its effects on family virtue and marriage, and on the deteriorating manhood of England. He uses the same materials but to a quite different end. Strutwell asserts instead that the condemnation of sodomy by both law and social opinion is founded on "prejudice and misapprehension." But unlike the pamphleteer who accuses sodomitical practice of being in opposition to the principles of reason, Strutwell reverses the argument and asserts that it is the lack of "true reason and deliberation" on the subject of sodomy that is in violation of the principles of reason and thus leads to prejudice. Though his intent is to win Random's assent to sodomy and hence to sex, his discourse is at the same time an early, unusual, and powerful assertion of a position that was hardly prevalent at that time and would not begin to be publicly voiced for nearly another century.

Strutwell then advances two arguments for sodomy—the first based on the practices of the past and of illustrious men, an argument that in later apologia like the anonymous 1833 poem *Don Leon* or John Addington Symonds's "A Problem in Greek Ethics" will assume the status of a polemical trope; the second based on the incidence of it in modern times: "The best man among the ancients is said to have entertained that passion; one of the wisest of their legislators has permitted the indulgence of it in his commonwealth; the most celebrated poets have not scrupled to avow it. At this day it prevails not only in the East but in most parts of Europe; in our own country it gains ground apace, and in all probability it will become in a short time a more fashionable vice than simple fornication" (339).

The second argument is an obvious echo of the anti-sodomitical pamphleteers, but again it is turned to Strutwell's use, for he supports it by arguing from utility. Sodomy is a socially desirable practice since it incurs no increase in and rather militates for the reduction of population, prevents infanticide, and incurs on the state no cost for the support of illegitimate children who are deserted "to the utmost want and wretchedness, or bred up to prey upon the commonwealth" (339). Of even greater moment is that the practice of sodomy "prevents the debauchery of many a young maiden, and the prostitution of honest men's wives, not to mention the consideration of health, which is much less likely to be impaired in the gratification of this appetite than in the exercise of common venery, which, by ruining the constitutions of our young men, has produced a puny progeny that degenerates from generation to generation" (339).

Here, too, Strutwell has turned the anti-sodomitical arguments cleverly against the pamphleteers. Like them he invokes virtue and the health of the populace and the sanctity of marriage, but by using and reversing popular arguments against sodomy, Strutwell asserts that sodomy is in fact useful and valuable to the commonwealth. His arguments from utility, interestingly, anticipate the arguments Jeremy Bentham would make in his 1785 essay "Paederasty," in which he offers similar assertions about the utility and social innocence of sodomitical acts. They foreshadow also the same arguments that appear in *Don Leon* in 1833.

Strutwell's final argument derives from the proposition that sodomy is useful because it provides pleasure: "I have been told that there is another motive, perhaps more powerful than all these, that induces people to cultivate this inclination, namely, the exquisite pleasure attending its success" (339). This justification by pleasure is almost flippant, yet it cunningly asserts a significant set of principles. It is desirable because the irresistibility of the pleasure principle justifies the attempt, while the pleasure obtained is "exquisite." "Exquisite" situates this pleasure in an area bounded on the one hand by the curious, the bizarre, and the forbidden and on the other by a world of precious effeminacy in which gender transgression is a powerful subtext. Thus success is almost always attendant on it because the moral strictures against sodomy constructed by a few are in practice ignored by the many, who delight as much in transgressing the law as in engaging in the act.

Smollett may have been using the transposition of anti-sodomite arguments into a pro-sodomite polemic as satire, and perhaps its effect was based on what Smollett and his readers must have felt was its absurdity. Still, Strutwell's arguments that the laws against sodomy are too severe and irrational, that they are derived from prejudice and misunderstanding rather than from justice, and essentially ineffectual against a natural desire, since "notwithstanding the severity of the law against offenders" the practice is growing rather than decreasing, are a first salvo in a discourse valorizing sodomitical rights. Finally, Strutwell's argument—and Strutwell's character—is firmly founded in a particular and emerging view of what the sodomite is—a species, not an accident of nature. Whereas the author of *Satan's Harvest Home* described sodomy as a "fashion," Strutwell, more modern, sees it as an "appetite" and an "inclination," situating sodomites in discourses appealing to the medical and social, not the legal and moral, to nature not nurture. Strutwell, despite his class and effete and rakish manners, is in some ways a modern activist homosexual who conceives of his identity in terms of sexual desire, identifies sodomites as a discrete and even self-identified group, and in his polemical pro-sodomitical discourse advocates social tolerance and legal reform of the proscriptions levied against them.

Random's response to Strutwell's polemic is predictable for so true-blue an Englishman: he is at once obtuse and appalled. Not really understanding the point of Strutwell's attempted seduction nor the wiles of his text or even the identity Strutwell constructs, Random, in an intense moment of homosexual panic, fears that Strutwell might take him for a sodomite: "I began to be apprehensive that his lordship, finding I had traveled, was afraid I might have been infected with this spurious and sordid desire abroad. . . . Fired at this supposed suspicion, I argued against it with great warmth, as an appetite unnatural, absurd, and of pernicious consequences, and declared my utter detestation and abhorrence of it" (339). To cap his attack, Random quotes the "lines of the satirist"—lines of course written by the satirist Smollett himself: "Eternal infamy the wretch confound / Who planted first the vice on British ground! / A vice! that, 'spite of sense and nature, reigns, / and poisons genial love, and manhood stains" (339). Smollett has put in Roderick's mouth lines from his first published work, "Advice," a satire in verse that is in large part an attack on sodomites—lines that usefully summarize the homophobic discourse of the period that charges that sodomy is an un-English foreign vice that, despite the prohibitions of natural law and the dictates of reason, has nevertheless infected English society and destroyed both the institutions of marriage and manhood.

Random has heard neither Strutwell's text nor his subtext, for the poem Roderick quotes is a reverse recapitulation of the very arguments Strutwell has just advanced. Random does not—or will not—realize that Strutwell is a sodomite, nor does he understand the ingenuity of Strutwell's argument, taking it for a test of sexual orthodoxy rather than a strategy of sodomitical seduction. Random represents the blind and prejudiced bigotry of the anti-sodomitical pamphleteers and of the average Englishman. His response uses all the legal and social terms of disapprobation—*unnatural, infected, abhorrence, absurd, detestation*. What is more, in slavish deference to Strutwell's class and hoping still for the "advancement" that Strutwell might effect, Roderick worries about what Strutwell imagines him to be. By misreading Strutwell's intentions and desire, and by denying that he might be what

Strutwell hopes he is, Roderick effectively and comically forecloses all hope of Strutwell's help.

Strutwell urbanely retires from the attempt at seduction and says that he is glad to find Random's opinion "so conformable to his own," thus wickedly pointing up Random's naïveté. Though Strutwell has not seduced Random, he has shown him up as a fool and has intellectually bested him and thus, at least to his own satisfaction, demonstrated the intellectual superiority of sodomites over their persecutors. He demonstrates also that he is no weak effeminate but rather a wily and dangerous foe. His triumph is not only over Random but over the anti-sodomitical forces that sustain moral and social bigotry and persecution. Strutwell has had his revenge, not only against Random's attack on sodomy as something "absurd" but for his gratuitous quote of the satirist's lines. The true satirist is Strutwell, and the object of mockery is Roderick Random, not sodomy. Though Smollett may have intended Strutwell to be a monster, the effect of the discourse is anti-homophobic; the text rewrites intention, suggesting either that Smollett's sympathies undermined his own homophobic text, or that conceptions of discrete sodomite identities and the growth of positive advocacy concerning them was already becoming a distinct discourse powerful enough to influence texts.

JEREMY BENTHAM'S INQUIRY

In the eighteenth century a considerable body of writing addressed itself to sodomy, constructing it as a danger to society. Quite differently, however, certain other texts can be seen that begin to construct a tradition, however fragmentary, of protest against homophobia, radically negotiating a space for sodomy as a possible alternative life-style, a sensibility, and as a legally and morally blameless act. Though this latter position can be found specifically in only a small body of writing, its effect can be traced subversively even in presumedly homophobic texts.

Between the publication of Smollett's text in 1749 and the writing of *Don Leon* in 1833, perhaps the most significant document advocating reform in social and legal attitudes is the essay "Paederasty" by the utilitarian philosopher and advocate of law reform, Jeremy Bentham. Though written in 1785, with an elaboration of his position in notes written in 1816, the text was not published until the twentieth century. Bentham argues against the traditional homophobic charges against sodomy: he advocates the decriminalization of sodomy and insists that it poses no threat to marriage or manhood. He theorizes the causes of sodomy and also of homophobia, suggesting that antipathy to and fear of sexual pleasure is the root cause of homophobia. He supports his argument by reference to ancient Greek practice and with an appeal to the principles of utilitarian philosophy, arguing that the "ethical value of an act" is to be tested by whether it "increased pleasure and diminished pain"—precisely the test, by the way, that Strutwell applies to sodomy.

But Bentham also expresses fear of the possible consequences to himself of writing about sodomy, thus illustrating the homophobic climate of the times. He writes, "I am ashamed to own that I have often hesitated whether for the sake of the interests of humanity I should expose my personal interest so much to hazard as it must be exposed to by the free discussion of a subject of this nature." To write about homosexuality exposes the writer to as much danger as the practice of it, for "when a man attempts to search this subject it is with a halter about his neck. On this subject a man may indulge his spleen without control. Cruelty and intolerance . . . screen themselves behind a mask of virtue."

Louis Crompton, whose study of Bentham's essay is the most compelling and most complete, suggests that Bentham's "opinions on homosexuality do not seem to have had any effect in England."[20] While this is true in a direct sense, what he advocates but hesitated to publish in "Paederasty" in 1785 can be discerned forthrightly in *Don Leon* in 1833 and discerned also in a textual and even social climate of protest and critique of homophobia evident in texts and material life at the end of the eighteenth and at the beginning of the nineteenth century, even though, if anything, as Crompton says, the condition of English homosexual had by then worsened.

By the time *Don Leon* appeared in 1833, not only was there a distinct sodomite subculture in most cities of Europe but also what might be called a distinctly literary sodomitical subculture that provided a network of contacts across Europe, as well as an epistolary network of equally fascinating proportions. I think of Lord Harvey's letters to his alleged lover, Stephen Fox, of Horace Walpole's correspondence with Horace Mann, of William Beckford's diaries and correspondence, of the correspondence of the poet Thomas Gray with his friend Bonstetten. There is every reason to suppose that Walpole and numerous of his male correspondents such as Mann may have formed a group—sophisticated, highly literate, familiar with the world, and well read in the homoerotic areas of classical texts. Allusions in this correspondence suggest that there was a growing if generalized homosocial and homoerotic discourse increasingly available in the late eighteenth and early nineteenth century.

Lord Byron and his friends Charles Skinner Matthews and John Cam Hobhouse, as Crompton shows, were one such group of homosexual friends, and their correspondence suggests that "in a sense these three share what would today be called a gay identity, based on common interests and a sense of alienation from a society they must protect themselves from by a special 'mysterious' style and mutually understood codes" in their letters (Crompton, 129). It is in one of these letters to Byron in Turkey that Matthews notes that Byron can there, for a small fee, have whatever homosexual experience he wants, but in England "what you get for £5 we must risque our necks for; and we are content to risque them" (quoted in Crompton, 161).

While the molly houses, despite legal harassment, continued to flourish as sites of sexual organization, homosocial groupings at the great universities can also be discerned. Rousseau has identified such a group through the activities and correspondence of the homosocial academic club participated in, Rousseau suggests, by the writers Mark Akenside, John Wilkes, and Andrew Baxter. Phallic clubs detailed in Ward's homophobic *History of the London Clubs* parallel such sites of a generalized homoerotic ambience as the villa of Cardinal Albani in Rome, the court of Frederick the Great, the atelier of the Comte de Caylus in France, which were private centers where, as Rousseau says, "homosexual aesthetes" could find their "artistic and erotic sides conjoined" (Rousseau, 155).

Travel books explored not only exotic lands but detailed the erotic and sometimes homoerotic landscapes of these places, while the Gothic novel in the hands of Walpole, Beckford, and Monk Lewis display exotic and homoerotic if not homosexual ambience, especially in Beckford's *Vathek* (1786), in which the beautiful youth Gulchenrouz becomes the object of the Caliph's desire and the dreadful Giaour delights in devouring beautiful boys. That *Vathek* was recognized as a homoerotic site—if only by association with its author, whose life and reputation were blasted by accusations of sodomitical acts with the young Lord Courteney—is suggested by lines Byron had intended for *Childe Harold* in which he describes Beckford as "unhappy Vathek" who was smitten with "unhallowed thirst / Of nameless crime, and thy sad day must close / To scorn, and Solitude unsought" (quoted in Crompton, 120).

This new homoerotic aestheticism was also powerfully reflected in Johann Wincklemann's studies of Greek art—which Walter Pater would later identify as being in part informed by a sensitivity to the beauty of young men—and in the publication of Richard Payne Knight's study of phallic symbolism, *The Worship of Priapus* (1785). Texts like these suggest a joining of homoeroticism and the application of that eroticism to the interpretation of texts and art. Even the (presumably) sexually orthodox Percy Bysshe Shelley turned his attention in 1818 to the subject of sodomy in his "Discourse on the Manners of the Ancient Greeks Relative to the Subject of Love," in which, while seemingly disturbed at the notion of actual physical sodomy, he is not unsympathetic to the eroticization of male friendships. This text, like Bentham's, remained unpublished until the twentieth century.

As Rousseau has suggested, there is little literature—defined in the broadest sense to include not only the usual genres but also pamphlets, travel literature, and religious and philosophical writings—that was in the eighteenth and early nineteenth centuries any sense sympathetic to sodomy. Despite this and despite public disapprobation and legal strictures and punishments, what we might think of as a form of modern homosexual style and practice seems to have found some ground for growth during this period. Homophobia seems to have existed in tandem with and quite possibly to have fueled the growth and formalization of two subcultural constructions. The first is the growth in the latter eighteenth and early nineteenth century of the sodomite molly sexual subculture. The second—though perhaps slower, more cautious, and more hidden—was a growth among middle-class and aristocratic (i.e., literate) sodomites of an awareness of a special homoerotic identity. Coupled with this, also slow and cautious, was the foundation of a distinct homosexual literary and artistic culture that, as Rousseau has shown, was woven throughout the artistic and lettered culture of continental Europe (Rousseau, 156–61).

Such special cultures identify themselves sooner or later in texts, hinting at their own existence indirectly or openly declaring their interests and allegiances in an effort to create a textual mirror of life. If eighteenth-century men who loved men or who admitted allegiance to desires and engaged sensibilities not approved by most of their fellow men made their presence known indirectly in texts, at the beginning of the next century one writer boldly constructed the first open textual advocacy for the love that could still not be named among Christians. It is to this writer I now turn.

This 1762 broadsheet shows a molly in the pillory. The woman on the left offers him a "Buggurme Pear."

chapter 2

NATURAL PASSIONS: *DON LEON,* 1833

Though law cries "hold!" yet passion onward draws;
But nature gave us passions, man gave laws,
Whence spring these inclinations, rank and strong?
And harming no one, wherefore call them wrong?
                                    —*Don Leon* (1833)

An item from the London *Courier* for August 1833 reads,
"Captain Henry Nicholas Nicholls . . . was convicted on the clearest evidence at Croyden, on Saturday last, of the capital offense of Sodomy; the
prisoner was perfectly calm and unmoved through the trial, and even when
the sentence of death was passed upon him. . . . The culprit, who was fifty
years of age, was a fine looking man and had served in the Peninsular war.
He was connected with a highly respectable family; but since his apprehension not a single member of it visited him" (*Don Leon,* 57). The same year
Nicholls was executed the anonymous poem *Don Leon,* alleged to be by Lord
Byron, advocated the decriminalization of sodomitical acts. Prompted in part
by Nicholls's trial and execution, the poem argues that such treatment of
sodomites constituted an egregious injustice. It identifies and condemns a
combination of religious, moral, legal, and social structures, all of which, the
Don Leon poet asserts, are founded on ignorance about and irrational hatred
of sodomy.

The *Don Leon* author has, in effect, identified what we now call homophobia as the cause that leads to the unjust persecution of sodomites. Rather
than reading "sodomy" as a broad category indicating a broad spectrum of
prohibited social and sexual acts, the poet seems to define sodomy solely as a
sexual act consequent on the sexual desire of male for male. He argues that

sodomites, far from being isolated and individual sinners, are an identifiable and persecuted minority bound together by a temperament—what he calls a "predilection"—and perhaps even by a sensibility that is intimately founded on and perhaps even defined by their sexual desire. He insists, repeatedly, that the sexual desire of the male sodomite for other males is as natural to them as is the desire of the male nonsodomite for women.

Framing this argument within a first-person account that purports to detail the secret homoerotic life of Lord Byron, the poem describes what we would now call Byron's "coming out." [The Byron who narrates *Don Leon* I will hereafter call "Byron"; the historical Byron I will call "Lord Byron."] The text demonstrates what we might now also describe as an "activist" advocacy of homosexual sex and of a homosexual "life-style." Furthermore, the poem asserts that the emotional and literary manifestations of such desire are worthy of praise and argues for the positive value of homosexual desire in human affairs. In short, *Don Leon* seems to construct homosexuals as a separate species whose desires, acts, and texts ought to be freed from the suffocating strictures with which society, law, and religion have bound them.

The medicalized term "homosexual," not yet having been coined, was not available to the poet; "sodomite" was firmly but negatively inscribed within a proscriptive social and a developing sexual discourse.[1] The idea of sodomy and the term "sodomite" is reinscribed, however, within a positive context in the poem. *Don Leon* is a text that responded to a public and specific event—the execution of Nicholls—and makes Nicholls a martyr. The execution of any martyr is a real event in the chronicles of a persecuted minority, and by creating a martyr *Don Leon* constructs a minority as well. As a text *Don Leon* has become a transgressive event in itself: it is the first in English poetry to intervene against homophobia. As Louis Crompton says, *Don Leon* is "the earliest published protest against homosexual oppression in England that has survived and the first plea for understanding" (Crompton, 361).

Speaking about the nineteenth-century homosexual, Michel Foucault described the birth of the modern homosexual "species" in his now-famous formulation:

> Nothing that went into his total composition was unaffected by his sexuality. It was everywhere present in him: at the root of all his actions because it was their insidious and indefinitely active principle; written immodestly on his face and body because it was a secret that always gave itself away. . . . We must not forget that the psychological, psychiatric, medical category of homosexuality was constituted from the moment it was characterized—Westphal's famous article of 1870 on "contrary sexual sensations" can stand as its date of birth—less by a type of sexual relations than by a certain quality of sexual sensibility, a certain way of inverting masculine and feminine in oneself. Homosexuality appeared as one of the forms of sexuality when it

was transposed from the practice of sodomy into a kind of interior androgyny, a hermaphroditism of the soul. The sodomite had been a temporary
aberration; the homosexual was now a species.[2]

Foucault dates this origin of species to 1870, but the *Don Leon* poet in 1833
spoke of an "idiosyncrasy" prevailing in those whose "predilection was for
males," while Walt Whitman described his love of comrades in 1860 as "the
life that does not exhibit itself yet contains all the rest." The birth date of a
new sexual being and the popular perception of this being can be traced even
earlier than Foucault's date of 1870—a date that is, after all, really only a ter-
minus in a long historical process.

An appeal for the rights of sodomites in an age that accorded them none
and conceived of them as monsters of depravity, the poem is also a ground-
breaking proposal of the new concept that sodomites are not individual
sinners linked only by the commission of the particular act of sodomy but
instead a discrete group within society who differ not because of sin but
because of sexual orientation and sensibility. It is an angry indictment of
anti-sodomitical society and law and of hypocritical sexual morality. In
addition, as a purported first-person account of the growth of a homoerotic
sensibility, *Don Leon* is the first long poem of the nineteenth century that
records candidly the growth of a personal homoerotic self-awareness. It is
thus the initiator of a genre, for as a record of "coming out" it foreshadows
the homoerotic confessional tale of the nineteenth century as well as the
"coming out" story found not only in late nineteenth- and early twentieth-
century homoerotic texts but also in twentieth-century gay fiction.
Confessional genres in homoerotic texts are derived in part from the medical reading of homosexual lives as "case studies." But unlike many of the
later case studies and twentieth-century novels that often capitulated to
the presumption that a homosexual life must by definition be incomplete,
unsuccessful, or end in tragedy, *Don Leon* ends in a burst of homoerotic
humor and in an assertive celebration of sexual freedom and unorthodox
sexuality.

That the poem was not written by Byron seems certain, but who the
author was remains conjectural. George Colman the younger, a minor playwright who was on close terms with Byron, has been offered as a candidate.
Colman was a satirist, and "there are parallels between *Don Leon* and some of
Colman's satires." But Colman died, old and ill, three years after the poem
was written, at the age of 73. If not Colman, then it was perhaps another
intimate of Byron. The poem shows that the author had an intimate knowledge of Byron's life—he reveals information about Byron's homosexuality
that would not be revealed or substantiated until modern biographies began
to examine this aspect of Byron's life. This friend may have been William
Bankes, an antiquarian and collector who was arrested in 1833, the year the
poem was written, for having sexual relations with a guardsman. Bankes was

also a member of Parliament, and the author of the poem displays a minute knowledge of the inner workings of Parliament. What is more, Bankes had visited Byron in Italy after Byron returned from the East and "may have exchanged confidences with him," for much of *Don Leon* details Byron's homosexual experiences in Greece and Turkey (Crompton, 357–58).

Don Leon dramatizes the development of a what we might now describe as a radical homosexual political consciousness. Such a consciousness must include not only an acknowledgment of the desire for same-sex intercourse but also of the political, social, spiritual, and moral consequences of such desires. It must represent and celebrate an awareness that a homosexual act is only an outward sign, to appropriate the definition of a sacrament, of an inward sensibility. If Byron indeed is theorizing sensibility, then he also seems to recognize the radically different imperatives that homosexuality asserts for an interpretation of a spiritual, social, moral, and creative life as an aspect of human natural life. Byron suggests this recognition when he urges later biographers to "be true to nature; paint me as I am," insisting that the example he offers should "let . . . one great truth unfold." This "truth" is, that for those who are sodomites, "foulest obloquy attends the good / Whose words and deeds are never understood."

Appealing to an "ermined judge" to look at his "work," the poet begins with a powerful image of that work: the body of a man hanged on the gallows for sodomy. Byron asks, "What had he done?" The answer is clear when he urges the reader to "ask Beckford and Courteney," who were ostracized by society into exile when their sodomitical affair was made public. This dead sodomite represents all sodomites, but he is also, as the notes to the poem point out, intended to recall Captain Nicholls. This man, Byron insists, had committed no robberies, rapes, or murders, had broken no bonds of "social safety." Indeed, even his gathering places were hidden from public gaze, and he kept his activities secret. But the "secret haunts" are discovered when the judge sends his "myrmidons" to entrap the sodomite in molly houses and places of congregation. Gibbon, despite his homophobic comments, had described accusations of sodomy as "the crime of those to whom no crime could be imputed" (Crompton, 24). Byron echoes this, insisting that it is impossible to describe as just convictions gained by entrapment and sentencing and execution meted out for a "crime" that had violated no social bond or compact.

Because neither the law nor even the healing muse will speak out against this injustice, it remains for him alone to speak out in defense of sodomites. Even though his laureate wreath might wither and torment might "rack my body here"—as would the pillory—"my voice I'd raise insensible to fear." In an uncanny prophesy of the current gay motto "silence = death," he insists that if he does not do so, then "silence now were tantamount to crime." This is the first and most direct challenge yet sounded in English literature to the legal persecution that is a consequence of homophobia. The challenge is also thrown down against the sexual hypocrisy that Byron sees as endemic in England, a "land where every vice in full luxuriance flowers" and "bold-faced harlots impudently spurn / The modest virgin's blush at every turn." While the sexual underworld frequented by nonsodomites flourishes openly, unchecked, and uncensored and among worldly men largely unblamed, "one propensity" that if "left unheeded would remain unknown" is hounded until "the poor misogynist is hung" and his reputation after death destroyed by public revelation of his guilt (60–80).

Byron reminds the reader that society bases its detestation of sodomites on the Bible and on the church's condemnation, which imputes catastrophes to the presence of sodomites in society, citing how "God's tardy vengeance smote Lot's native town with brimstone." But, he insists, the teachings of "mother Church" do not provide adequate evidence that sodomitical acts or desires are perverse negations of "natural" inclination. Byron draws on the very argument the church advances—the argument from nature—and insists that Nature herself proves otherwise, for just as "the tree we plant will, when its boughs are grown, produce no other blossoms than it own," so "in man some inborn passions reign / Which, spite of careful pruning, sprout again" (110–29). This is the first shot in Byron's fusillade against religious, legal, and social arguments that condemn sodomy and the first formulation of his oft-repeated message, which we would now frame as homosexuality in homosexuals is natural.

If this is so, then it is legitimate to inquire "was I or nature in the wrong, / If, yet a boy, one inclination, strong / In wayward fancies, domineered my soul, / And bade complete defiance to control" (129–33). He is not speaking here of self-control, though it is clear that he feels that the overwhelming power of homoerotic desire has nothing to do with rational or conscious choice but instead is associated with social control, for he insists that "the charms of women first my homage caught" not because of desire but because his response was "by early education taught." This may be another unique moment in English literature, for it suggests that homophobia and persecution of homosexuals is a tool for the social control of sexuality and proposes a theory of the social construction of sexualities (135–40). The poet's potent observation that his "youthful instincts, forced to brood / Within my bosom seemed awhile subdued" (134–35) expresses his belief that sodomy is not a sinful act or a crime but a response to instinctual nature.

Byron's acquiescence to the demands of orthodox sexual education led him into unhappy sexual adventures with women, which, when rebuffed, led him to "turn" the course of his desires. Entrance into young manhood provides an opportunity for the release of the passions that had been forced to "brood" within his bosom when he discovers a young worker on his father's estate (165–79). When he looks back from a "riper age" he is aware that in this first encounter with homoerotic desire he was still in thrall to education and still unsure of the implications of his wooing of a "gentle boy." Though Byron had offered caresses to "Mary" and "Margaret," he knew that "decency forbad / The same caresses to a rustic lad." But he is now firmly set on a course that transgresses against orthodox education and sexuality—one that will "inwardly presage / The predilections of my riper age."

Byron knows what he feels: "Love, love it was that made my eye delight / To have his person in my sight." Yet he still wondered "Why did I give gauds to deck they form? / Why for a menial did my entrails warm?" In retrospect the answer is easy: "secret longings" prompted him to "pursue / Those inspirations, which, if books speak true, / Have led e'en priest and sages to embrace / Those charms, which female blandishments efface" (177–82). The grammar is perhaps deliberately vague. It is not female blandishments that efface those homoerotic charms; it is those charms that efface female blandishments. The text recalls here a more ancient biblical text: the love of man for man surpasses the love of man for woman. But no matter how strong it is, Byron recognizes that such love of necessity is a "secret longing," for heterosexual desire needs keep no such secret.

These twin themes—the power of homosexual love to vanquish heterosexual love and its secret estate—are conventional tropes in homosexual literary and polemic discourse. Another aspect—also in a sense part of a larger homoerotic discourse—is marked by the word "menial." As Randolph Trumbach has suggested, age-mate sexuality was by this time very much a feature of homosexual style, but Byron's interests are largely those of his class—old-style pederastic relationships between older and younger men, often of different classes. Here too is another thread that runs from Byron to Wilde: sexual involvement with youths of a different and generally lower social class.

As Byron becomes older he spends his time in "mirth and revels" and laments the absence of his "truant muse." He connects the loss of even his youthful poetic inspiration with the absence of "some kindred mind, where confidence, / Tuned in just unison, might meet return, / And while it warmed my breast, in his might burn" (190–200). Here Byron specifically indicates the sex and temperament of what is surely that archetype of homoerotic desire, the ideal friend. He also makes the connection between homoerotic desire and creative inspiration that suggests another dominating trope in homoerotic texts, the dependence of certain texts for their full realization on the admission of homoerotic desire.

He soon discovers such a potential friend among the choir boys (201–10). He then makes another telling connection—one that, incidentally, will become a considerable minor melody in later British homoerotic literature—when he describes how "lips o'er which no youthful down had grown" had in "full choir the solemn anthem sung." At such moments the "pathos of the strain would soothe my soul." Such religious pathos, or perhaps the sight of what Thoreau in a similar reverie called "succulent" buds of young manhood, may also have soothed his soul and relieved it only temporarily. Not many years later John Addington Symonds daily attended Evensong in order to hear his own beloved Willie Dyer sing solemn anthems, and in the thinly veiled eroticism of John Francis Bloxam's "The Priest and the Acolyte" (1894) in which a priest and a young boy die together in a love-match pledged from a poisoned chalice, there can be heard a lurid and more explicit echo of Byron's pious and quasi-erotic text.

In *Don Leon* the choir boy is named Eddleston. In Lord Byron's life the real John Edlestone was one day to be the posthumous subject of the "Thyrza" elegies. When Lord Byron wrote the "Thyrza" poems he veiled Edlestone's identity beneath the feminine Thyrza. But while Lord Byron was reluctant ever to admit his involvement with John Edlestone, the Byron of *Don Leon* was more than willing to reveal his obsession and its sexual component. His "secret longings" are carefully detailed: "Oh! how I loved to press his cheeks to mine; / How fondly would my arms his waist entwine! / Another feeling borrowed friendship's name, / And took its mantle to conceal my shame. / Another feeling! Oh! 'tis hard to trace / The line where love usurps tame friendship's place" (210–20). The exclamatory generosity of this passage speaks to the intensity of its passion. Byron places a rich freight of erotic association on "friendship," eroticizing thereby the friendship tradition in which descriptions of powerful male affection were presumed to be free of sexual passion. In this text and perhaps in others, friendship is only a mantle to cover something more carnal. Indeed, his use of "shame" may even be an early instance of the encoded text that Alfred Douglas later uses in his poem "Two Loves" (1894), wherein heterosexual love insists about homosexual love that "his name is Shame" and again in a poem called "In Praise of Shame" (1894), wherein he insists "Of all sweet passions Shame is loveliest."[3]

There is surely no "tame friendship" about the passion Byron describes; instead the passion is uncontrollable. Byron confesses that "this youth was my idolatry. / Strong was my passion, past all inward cure." The vital question is, "Could it be so violent, yet pure?" He feels as if some "philter" had been "poured into my veins" (226–29), a chemical aphrodisiac—"an unknown mixture"—that arouses this violent passion. His passion for Eddleston leads the philosophic lover to further inquiry: "What lights this fire? / Maids not boys were wont to move desire." In answer he repeats his founding assumption that it is natural: "What prompts nature to set the trap." His desire impels him to flout society, law, and reason itself in the pursuit of his ardor: "Why truckles reason to concupiscence? / Though law cries 'hold!' yet passion onward draws; / But nature gave us passions, man gave laws" (240–41). In this couplet the old definition of sodomy collides with a new and developing construction of homosexuality: the individual commission of a sodomitical act as opposed to a general response to inborn propensities. Byron recognizes that this dichotomy of interpretation marks and defines the anxiety that homosexuals daily face.

Though the incident with Eddleston is intended as biographical data, it also serves to initiate a full-scale inquiry into the origin and nature, the morality, the history, and the philosophical and literary associations, of homosexual desire: "whence spring these inclinations rank and strong? / And harming no one, wherefore call them wrong?" In reply Byron enters into a justifying discourse, arguing first from utility that these are emotions "harming no one," and second from Christian ethics that homosexual desire is consonant with "virtue's touchstone"—namely, "Unto other do, / As you would wish that others did to you." He then deploys a variant of an image from Plato's *Symposium* in which male friends, having in ancient days been cleft in two and having been forever seeking their lost other half, when reunited exist forever in a transport of love and joy. Byron justifies his love not by its sexual but by its spiritual component when he rings a musical change upon Plato: "Then tell me not of sex, if to one key / The chords, when struck, vibrate in harmony" (240–48). Finally, as a matter of sexual utility and to the good of domestic and social harmony, homosexual acts lead neither to the defloration of virgins nor to adultery. He commits no sacrilege against marriage: "I plough no field in other men's domain," nor does he bring unwanted progeny into the world: "Where I delve no seed shall spring again" (251–52).

Though his arguments seem cogent to him, he is still unsatisfied and determines to find some breath of an explanation in literature. In another convention of homosexual writing he calls on the "volumes of the dead" to explain and justify his passion. His catalog of authorities is a bibliography of homoerotic literature, for he includes Plato and Socrates, Bion, Plutarch, Virgil and Horace, and enlists Shakespeare as one whose "sonnets to a stripling's praise" would "damn a poet now-a days." He then asks, not unreasonably,

> I love a youth; but Horace did the same;
> If he's absolved, say, why am I to blame?
> When young Alexis claimed a Vergil's sigh,
> He told the world his choice; and may not I? . . .
> Then why was Socrates surnamed the sage,
> Not only in his own, but every age,
> If lips, whose accents strewed the path of truth,
> Could print their kisses on some favored youth
> Or why should Plato, in his Commonwealth
> Score up tenets which I must note by stealth? (269–82)

Byron's rhetoric invokes an ancient world in which he believes there was no blame for these desires. The overtones of "absolv'd" and "blame" invoke religious prohibition. Alexis's decision—"he told the world his choice"—offers a public example from the ancients and a choice not available to Byron. The invocation of Plato's *Republic* cites a classical legal precedent against the legal persecutions of his own day. In each of these areas—morality, society, and politics—affirmed participation in homosexual love relegates the lover to a secret and hypocritical status. Byron is powerfully aware of the double life repressive society forces homosexuals to lead. While similar lists of homosexual writers in homosexual texts usually offer only justification by association, Byron uses his list to attack the legal and moral system itself and to score up his tenets against that system. Even as he does so he is publishing new standards.

That homosexuality has been found in the lives and writings of the pagan poets is hardly an original conclusion. Indeed, he admits that everyone knows this for "these are . . . samples musty grown." But in a more transgressive attack he now turns to modern times and seeks out homosexuality in the lives of the powerful and socially significant, among "pious men," kings, saints, scholars, jurists, and captains. All these "found solace in a minion's arms" and were unable to resist the imperatives of a sexually "omnipotent" nature. Indeed, nature, he once more asserts, cannot be ignored or changed by moral or mere legal fiat. The proscription against sodomy is derived not from natural fact but from social prejudice, and it is inconsistent to condemn "wise men . . . whose deeds and sayings history records" because they "ate of the fruit of that forbidden tree / Which prejudice denies to you and me" (290–324). The unspoken modifier of "prejudice" is "alone," and Byron justifies his conclusion by a utilitarian appeal to happiness that is "man's pursuit through life." Happiness has been achieved by the uncriticized and unblemished actions of wise men in both pre- and post-Christian eras who have, despite prohibition, found solace as nature, not law, prompted them to do. His second justification is that the practice exists universally "in every caste and every clime." This argument logically and rationally forbids the denomination of what is both a universal and natural action as criminal.

Byron adds one further radical observation to his text, and that is a denial of the effects of the example of "vice" on innocent minds: "In vice unhackneyed, In *Justine* unread, / See schoolboys, by some inclinations fed: / Some void, that's hardly to themselves confessed" (349–52). This is intended to further buttress his presumption that homosexual desire is inborn and not learned, not an acquired perversion but a natural inclination to which the two youths respond. Byron's boys feel "mutual vague desires" and find "solace in a comrade's breast." They take "lonely walks" through the same emotional fields and forests that prompted Byron when he was younger to seek out Edlestone. The language—"some inclination," "vague desires," "unknown feelings"—marks this text as a homosexual text; it uses indirection and imprecision to directly and precisely indicate that the sin that cannot be named is precisely what is meant. *Don Leon* recognizes the imperatives of sex and records the translation of "unknown feelings" into "closer ties" and specific act: "They love. The mutual vague desires arise. / Perhaps by night they share each other's beds, / 'Till step by step, to closer union led" (356–58). Byron lets no opportunity pass to insist that these desires are natural—"Imperious nature's sensual prickings goad, they own her dictates."

In another remarkable and prophetic passage Byron addresses teachers and parents, urging them to allow "truth" to find the way "through fogs of prejudice" and to "shut your eyes" to the love and sexual experiments of these young comrades. It is far better for young men to engage in homosexual lovemaking than to be infected with diseases contracted from "harlots" with whom they may waste not only their manhood but their health and their fortune. Though he insists that homosexuality is natural, he advances the argument that prejudice against it does not arise naturally but is taught by society. Wedded to the definition of homosexuality as a crime against nature was the presumption that if it was unnatural, then abhorrence of it was the natural reaction to it. This is not so, Byron asserts, for pedagogues like parents are responsible for the fogs of prejudice: "'Twas ye who roused the latent sense of shame, / And called their gambols by an odious name."

He returns to his autobiographical comments and describes his school experience that created torment and discontent: "Feverish fancies floated in my brain. / Longing, yet forced my purpose to restrain, / Upon the brink of infamy I staid, / Now half resolved to plunge, now half afraid" (390–94). His longings and the sudden death of Eddleston impel him to leave college to "ramble and investigate mankind" and search in "distant climes," for "mental freedom's pure Aurora" (415–17). Byron's association of the pursuit of forbidden sexual desire with intellectual freedom forecasts another subtext of homosexual polemic: the assertion that homosexuality is an intellectual as well as a sexual orientation.

Because England offers no hope for the free satisfaction of his desires nor hospitable home for an exercise of mental freedom vis-à-vis this sexuality, he seeks a sexual Arcadia where he can find "clandestine" love, a place where "Cupid's wings were free, / his hands unbound / Where law had no erotic statutes framed, Nor gibbets stood to fright the unreclaimed" (423–27). He finds it in Turkey, where "youths . . . with their blandishments inveigle man, / As does in Christian lands the courtesan." In Turkey, "none can trespass on forbidden ground," for homosexuality is not forbidden. In Constantinople he "sought the brothel where . . . the black-eyed boy his trade unblushing plies." But because he is accompanied by a disapproving companion to whom he dares not describe how these homosexual possibilities attract him, he desists from indulging, and "deep in the dark recesses of my mind / I hid my thoughts." If his recognition of his desires in early youth and in school was the first step toward self-realization, his experience in Turkey, though voyeuristic only, is the second step. Here he can only watch, but the sight of such sexual freedom "touched some inward sense," and he becomes "resolved to do what yet I feared to tell" (458–68).

Though his original intent was to search for "love, love, clandestine love," circumstances begin to convince him that homosexual desire has not only a physical but a social context. Surrounded by presumably heterosexual companions who are shocked by the homosexuality of Turkey, he takes yet another step toward self-awareness when he recognizes the difference between them and himself and the social and emotional consequences of that difference: "I found no kindred leaning in the breast / Of those around me, and I felt oppressed" (469–70). Byron's use of "oppressed" here means emotional not political oppression, but it does suggest the development of a homosexual politics in which sexual and social oppression will be equated, and it further emphasizes Byron's increasing awareness that homosexual desire renders men different in far more realms than merely that of sexual desire.

Emphasizing his recognition of difference by action, he determines to leave his companions, for "mental freedom is to think alone," and he sets out on a "different course." It is to Greece that he feels impelled to go, where he hopes to "lay . . . down beneath the shady plain, / Where Phaedrus heard grave Plato's voice complain. / Another Phaedrus may perchance go by" he hopes and his "fond dreams become reality" (496–500). Of course they do, for here he encounters Nicolo Giraud. He takes the youth as his page and "with culture stirred his mind, and in it choice instruction poured." Giraud becomes to Byron what Phaedrus had been to Socrates, a younger man loved and taught by an older lover. Indeed, Byron emulates with Giraud the relationship that Socrates and Phaedrus had so ardently discussed. Giraud learns choice bits of knowledge while Byron is possessed by the "burning fever of love." Byron describes his sleeping lover: "How many hours I've sat in pensive guise, / To watch the mild expression of his eyes! / Or when asleep at noon. . . / How long I've hung in rapture as he lay. . . . / How oft at morn . . . / I've gazed unsated at his naked charms, / And clasped him waking to my longing arms" (592–604).

That the account of the affair with Nicolo Giraud accurately parallels the events of Lord Byron's life is suggested in a letter written in 1810, in which Lord Byron gives hints to his friend and confidant Hobhouse about the real nature of the relationship: "But my friend as you may imagine is Nicolo . . . we are very philosophical.—I am his 'padrone' and his 'amico' and the Lord knows what else besides." Louis Crompton points out that the philosophical nature of their relationship may be another coded classical allusion, this time to Lucian's statement that "the love of boys is 'more philosophical' than the love of women" (Crompton, 151). But Thomas Moore, Lord Byron's biographer, in 1830 described this relationship in quite other terms in an attempt to defuse any suspicion of homosexuality: "In Greece we find him forming one of those extraordinary friendships . . . in which the pride of being the protector, and the pleasure of exciting gratitude, seemed to have constituted to his mind the chief, the pervading charm. . . . In [Giraud] he seems to have taken the most lively, and even brotherly interest" (quoted in Crompton, 151–52).

Don Leon, however, offers a far more precise explanation for the relationship. His desire for Giraud effects the wedding of inspiration and passionate sexuality: "Oh how the happy moments seemed to fly, / Spent half in love and half in poetry! / The muse each morn I wooed, each eve the boy, / And tasted sweets that never seemed to cloy" (618–21). In a letter to Hobhouse written later the same day as the one mentioning Giraud, Lord Byron reports, "I have employed the greater part of today in conjugating the [Greek] verb [to kiss]. . . . I assure you my progress is rapid" (Crompton, 152).

Despite his success with Giraud and the pleasure it brings, Byron is still unsure about the nature of his desires, and he attempts the presumed curative of heterosexuality and woos three daughters of an aging widow. But he discovers them to be, in comparison with Giraud's "ardent passions," intellectually vapid and spiritually dead: "Felt I their charms? I felt them not." He affirms that the experience taught him that "women as women, me had never charmed, / And shafts that others felt left me unharmed." In comparison his affair with Giraud awakens him to a new life for Giraud's beauty "would unlock the gates of prejudice." The prejudice, of course, is Byron's own lingering doubt—socially constructed doubt—about homosexuality. But the affair gives him the courage to "mock the sober fears that timid minds endure." And as a result of freely engaging in homosexual love he is able at last to combine action with speech, to acknowledge what he desires and act on those desires: "So boldly I set calumny at naught, and fearless utter what I fearless wrought" (676–91).

Only 30 years later Walt Whitman would utter a similar declaration: "I will escape from the sham that was proposed to me, / I will sound myself and comrades only—I will never again utter a call, only their call." Whitman's manuscript version is precise and Byronic: "I will utter the cry of friends." Byron's passage from doubt to certainty and from sexual dubiety to sexual acceptance is complete. The verbal affirmation of his desires—that "fearless utterance"—is the first recorded account of "coming out" in English, as well as the first published assertion that homosexual sex is both a political act and a mark of sexual and social rebellion. But he carries the argument one step further, for he speculates, "Is there an idiosyncrasy prevails / In those whose predilection is for males?" This is, of course, once again an attempt to inscribe homosexuality within rather than outside of nature, for "idiosyncrasy" as he uses it denotes a special temper or a constitution in those in whom this "rooted bent" congenitally exists.

Having done what he had earlier only "resolved to do" and "fearless uttered" what he had earlier "feared to tell," Byron enters into a series of arguments justifying homosexuality. The first is the argument by example: a local and revered magistrate keeps a handsome boy as his lover, while in the entire nation "the self same usage reigns with high and low." If homosexuality can be justified by the example of honorable men and by the practice of entire nations, it can also be justified by those scientific theories that speak to the general welfare of nations—namely, theories concerning the problem of overpopulation. Those "economists who seek the world to thin" should suggest homosexual practice and urge mankind "in sterile furrows" to "sow his seed." Because homosexuality produces no children, to engage in it would in effect "follow the strict Malthusian creed" (733–81).

Byron concludes his arguments for public acceptance of homosexuality by citing a voluminous list of contemporary sexual—largely heterosexual—vice and the consequences of this vice to the state. If homosexuality were the only moral irregularity in England then there might be some reason for social control, but because it is the least harmful of all such sexual practices it is sheer hypocrisy to condemn it. While noble lords are able to engage in the most appalling heterosexual adventures without retribution, Beckford, "caught perchance in some unseemly play," looses his reputation and "years have not served to wipe the stain away." The press delights in such exposé, and "Bow Street bloodhounds" seek out "some poor wight" to ruin and expose. But homosexuality, he argues, is rife in England also among supposedly respectable and heterosexual men, for "the bishop drills the foot guard grenadiers" and soldiers and sailors commonly engage in homosexual acts in barracks and on ship. The teacher delights in seducing his charges: "Ask him of Eton, who if fame speaks true, / Made open boast he all his scholars knew / By their posteriors better than their face" (916–18).

Despite the prevalence of homosexuality in all ranks of life, however, no rank can protect him accused of it, and Byron cites those who have been destroyed because of allegations of homosexual conduct, mentioning the cases of the eminent scholar Richard Heber, who was ruined and exiled for allegations against him; of Lord Stanhope, who hanged himself because of similar allegations; and of Grey Bennet, a member of Parliament who suffered a similar fate. His argument is that the nation's best citizens are destroyed by such convictions and that Parliament is spineless in its defense of such good men. The state is corrupt that does not recognize that "of every crime you punish I descry / The least of all perhaps is sodomy" (1038–39).

That he finally deploys the word after long and careful avoidance only makes its appearance more powerful and more shocking.

Byron ends the poem by retailing to his wife the sexual "wonders I had seen," concluding with homosexuality. To her question "can male then covet male? / Can man with man hold intercourse of love" he responds with a justification from ancient example: "boys strung old Anacreon's lyre . . . boys the sober Virgil's lines inspire" (1131–57). Because his wife is pregnant and unavailable for intercourse, he asks her "to copulate *ex more pecudum.*" In order to convince her to assent to anal intercourse he offers a long paean in praise of it, asserting that it is practiced or at least desired by all heterosexual men. The passage is long and bawdy and has been seen by some as a curious intrusion into the more serious business of the poem—the justification and analysis of homosexuality. By capping the poem with this bawdy but still serious disquisition, however, Byron reduces to absurdity the final argument against homosexuality—that is, that of all the offenses that homosexuality is presumed to commit against nature, anal intercourse is the most abhorrent and offensive.

Though society presumes that anal intercourse is the distinguishing act of the sodomite, Byron's argument shows that sodomy is not the pernicious vice of a few monsters of sexual misconduct but a general practice not only among "heathen" Turks and other foreigners but also of a large segment of the English population of all classes. If presumably "normal" men practice anal intercourse in a heterosexual context, then there is a moral and logical inconsistency in practicing it in one context and condemning it in the other. The final cap to the poem is that Byron's wife consents to the act, and he commits on her—as an act of heterosexual intercourse, albeit condemned also as sodomy—the very act that in homosexual intercourse is prohibited. To conclude a poem justifying homosexuality with an act of illicit heterosexual intercourse is a brilliant strategy since it effectively undermines the validity of any kind of sexual prohibition, and in the bawdy context of the lines it subjects all such prohibitions to the corrosive power of humor and satire.

Byron concludes with a plea to Moore—his biographer to whom the poem was addressed—to "be true to nature, paint me as I am" (1309). Thus, as a homosexual, he places himself within the circle of the natural, outside of which nothing, not even homosexuality or the sodomite—as he has now defined himself—can exist. Because the poem exemplifies the salutary effects of fearlessly uttering what Byron had discovered about his sexual nature, he urges Moore to "let my example one great truth unfold" that there are those "whose words and deeds are never understood," especially if they are guilty in the eyes of the world of sexual deviation.

His real purpose in writing the poem is to offer himself as an example: "I stand a monument, whereby to learn / That reason's light can never strongly burn / Where blear-eyed prejudice erects her throne, / And has no scale for virtue but her own" (1383–86). This statement suggests that it is not, finally, the text that is the most effective attack on homophobic prejudice but instead the person of the poet and the living man. Byron has no intention of being, like Shelley's poet, an unacknowledged legislator. Not only his words but his deeds are the weapons to attack prejudice and destroy it.

In this, as in so much else, Byron—whoever he was—looks ahead to active and personal attacks on socially instituted homophobia. His message is that finally there can be no absolute decision on the morality of sexual acts, for moral codes are socially constructed: "Love . . . has various creeds by various nations made: / One holds as dogmas what the other mocks; / That schism here which there is orthodox" (1405–1408). He concludes with a joke—a play on "end" and "tail"—asserting that "whatever mortals do, / They must keep their latter end in view. . . / Our latter end—what is it but our tail?" But it is a serious joke, for inscribed within the images of "end" and "tail" and their obvious allusion to anal intercourse is the entire complex question he has raised about homosexual conduct and the place of homosexuals in the social and legal system and most especially about the punishments visited on them by a repressive social and legal system. About that dreadful "end" he makes no joke but gives a warning: "at the risk of life, approach it not." As Lord Byron's friend Charles Matthews indicated, however, desire to find sexual release or an ideal friend—a moment of passion or a partner for life—often impelled men like Byron's two youths to "seek solace in a comrade's arms." For which, as Matthews says, "we must risque our necks . . . and are content to risque them."

Thomas Eakins's *The Swimming Hole* (1883) evokes the homoeroticism of much of Walt Whitman's poetry. Oil on canvas, c. 1883–1885. Purchased by the Friends of Art, Fort Worth Art Association, 1925; acquired by the Amon Carter Museum, 1990, from the Modern Art Museum of Fort Worth through grants and donations from the Amon G. Carter Foundation, the Anne Burnett and Charles Tandy Foundation, Capital Cities/ABC Foundation, *Fort Worth Star-Telegram*,

chapter 3

RARE SPECIMENS OF MANHOOD: AMERICAN HOMOEROTIC TEXTS, 1825–1850

The first I conceive of true friendship when some rare specimen of manhood
presents itself.
                    —Henry David Thoreau, *Journals* (1839)

In America as early as the 1840s some texts had begun to contribute to the construction of a homoerotic discourse that was to become a
significant thread—if cautiously encoded—in the transcendental and radical
individualism of the new democracy. When exported across the Atlantic,
specifically by the poetry of Walt Whitman, this American discourse would
have a powerful influence on the development of English homoerotic texts.
But the homophobic laws, customs, and religious belief of England had been
a legacy to the former colonies. What the eighteenth-century English legal
discourse asserted about sodomites, law in America upheld. What English
social custom believed about the iniquity and monstrousness of such sinners,
America ratified. Sodomy in the early colonies was punished by the same
legal strictures as in England.

The colonists saw sodomy as a sin that must be rooted out and as a crime
that endangered the foundation of "normal" morality and sexual practice.
And just as in England, where the crime not to be named among Christians
seemed to have been on everyone's lips, in America in the seventeenth and
eighteenth centuries sodomy, as Jonathan Katz argues, "was not a secret, not
unspoken, not unnamed. Sodomy raised to capital status, was also raised to a
relatively high degree of public consciousness. From almost the first years of
the English settlement on this continent, sodomy was publicly named as one

of the major crimes against the state, one of the few infractions meriting death."[1] Far from being ignored, the early settlers were willing to repeatedly name sodomy in their sermons and in the records of their punishments as a deviation from the laws of God and nature.

In America as in England, social conceptions of sodomy began to change in the late eighteenth century. Anti-sodomitical discourses gradually began the transference, similar to the English process, that moved sodomy from sin toward crime and onward into the realm of unspeakable acts and socially and medically aberrant behavior. This social anxiety and the homophobia it produced was already very much part of the history of proscriptive discourse as early as 1810, when in a case prosecuting an assault for attempted sodomy the offense is described as "that most horrid and detestable crime (among Christians not to be named), called sodomy."[2] At a later appeal of the sentence, one of the judges observed that "the crime of sodomy is too well known to be misunderstood and too disgusting to be defined."

Mid-nineteenth-century American texts began to inscribe sodomitical acts within a sphere that allowed an association of emotional context with the act, making the anxious leap from notions about the individual sodomite to speculations about a species marked by effeminacy and mental instability. Just as dubious commentary about intense male-male friendships played a part in social and literary discussion in England, so in America in the first half of the nineteenth century understanding of just what erotic implications were inscribed within literary portrayals of passionate male-male friendship was very much in crisis. Such portrayals—in the novels of Herman Melville or the poetry of Walt Whitman—could be but were not necessarily read as a definitive site of homoeroticism. It is important therefore, as Robert K. Martin says, to establish just what was "normal" for writers and for society in the mid-nineteenth century.[3]

Male-male friendships had to exist against a background that included the homophobia evident in legal proscription of sodomitical acts—though the death penalty was repealed in many states by mid-century—and against the often hysterical and certainly prohibitive discussion growing out of the moral purity movement that stressed especially the perceived evils of masturbation and its association with sexual perversion and "degeneracy" and increasingly and specifically with effeminacy and homosexuality. In an 1826 letter recovered by Martin Duberman, male-male intimacy is clouded by suspicion of perversion and also by what seems to be a curious dichotomy between the imperatives of intimacy and a somewhat uncertain though troubled sense of just what such intimacy might imply. In the letter Jeff (Thomas Jefferson Withers) writes to his friend Jim (James H. Hammond)—both men are in their twenties—wondering "whether you yet sleep in your Shirt-tail, and whether you yet have the extravagant delight of poking and punching a writhing Bedfellow with your long fleshen pole—the exquisite touches of which I have often had the honor of feeling."

The jocular tone at first suggests that for these young men what they experienced was also enjoyed, free from anxiety about—indeed, perhaps unaware of—sodomitical imputations. Even under his offhand tone, however, Jeff feels the need nevertheless to caution Jim that if he keeps this up there may be "awful results" and that unless such actions are corrected they may result in "devastation, horror & bloodshed." Jeff's use of "devastation" certainly echoes prohibitive texts that attributed the destruction of civilizations to sodomy, while the "bloodshed" that might result suggests the severest legal penalty. Jeff's uncertain if cautionary tone implies that he is torn between personal loyalty and a homophobia that had already been deployed as a facet of public discourse.

Michael Moon suggests that there was an "increasing predominance of homophobia in American society from the 1830s forward."[4] Thus when Walt Whitman's *Leaves of Grass* appeared in America in 1855, it was already possible to construe Whitman's poem as a dubious contribution to what moralists saw as a proliferation of sexually aberrant texts. In a review of *Leaves of Grass* in the *New York Criterion* (10 November 1855) Rufus Griswold left no doubt about what he found in the text. Griswold begins with a general diatribe against writers who disregard "all the politeness and decencies of life" and inveighs against "the tendency of thought in these later years" that allows in texts "a degrading, beastly sensuality that is fast rotting the healthy core of all the social virtues." But he moves Whitman's text into the specific area of condemnation of sexual difference when he associates it particularly with "crime" committed by "monsters" of "vileness": "The records of crime show that many monsters have gone on in impunity, because the exposure of their vileness was attended with too great indelicacy. *Peccatum illud horribile, inter Christianos non nominandum.*" He carries his argument from a general diatribe against immorality in texts into the specific language of homophobic condemnation—language that commonly described homosexuals as "monsters of depravity" and homosexual acts as "vileness." There can finally be no doubt about what he sees this text to be and within what discourse he intends to inscribe it when he resorts to the Latin legal description of sodomy as "the horrible sin not to be named among Christians."

Therefore by 1855 in America anxiety about sodomy was powerful enough and sufficiently deployed to have moved from legal and moral discourse into the pages of journals reviewing the work of a relatively unknown writer. Griswold was no doubt sure that his readers also were as well acquainted with sodomy as the judge in 1810 and as equally disgusted by it when he judged Whitman's text on homophobic rather than critical grounds. Griswold's criticism of Whitman's text as one among those that "may leave a foul odor, contaminating the pure, healthful air" lies within the developing medical model that defined homosexuality as a contaminating disease and that used such words as "inversion" and "perversion" to define the newly constructed "homosexuality" in the medical literature of mental disorder and pathology.

If Griswold saw horrors in texts in 1855, by 1866 homophobia had become a specter haunting society in general. Horatio Alger, whose boys book's can well be said to be one of the founding sources of that part of the American dream that insists that young men can make a success in a capitalist society by enterprise and hard work, often with the help of an older male patron, was accused by the elders of the Unitarian church of Brewster, Massachusetts, where he was a minister, of "the abominable and unnatural crime of unnatural familiarities with boys." The crime Alger committed is "too revolting to think of" and is abhorred by "an outraged community" (Katz 1976, 33–34). In 1885, in a diary also recovered by Martin Duberman, a young man discovers that his friend is "a C—-sucker & that he loves and enjoys that d—d custom so revolting to every right minded person." Yet in another entry he denies that his own practice of hugging and kissing a loving bedfellow—"I loved to hug & kiss him"—was the "least demonstration of unmanly and abnormal passion," asserting that such a thing would be as "revolting" to his friend "as it is & ever has been to me" (Duberman 1986, 43–45). In these texts manly friendship clearly has an erotic component but one that is complicated by social conventions that condemn same-sex intimacy. By 1895 Max Nordau was certain about what such intimacy implied, at least in Whitman's poetry. He describes Whitman as "morally insane" and as "one of the deities to whom the degenerate and hysterical of both hemispheres have for some time been raising altars."[5]

Against this background of homophobia, American writers attempted to identify what same-sex desire implied, to explain what it demanded, and to locate it in literature and society. Of course in the early nineteenth century the word "homosexual" was unknown, and early nineteenth-century readers held a different conception of homosexual acts and emotions from those of the late nineteenth or the twentieth century. What we might now think of as an expression of homoerotic feeling could well have been understood by early nineteenth-century interpreters as falling within the bounds of romantic friendship and in literature as manifestations of what has been described as a literary friendship tradition.

Because the sexualization of conduct and the concept that sex defined the individual was not, in the early part of the century, as yet part of the common discourse, sex was conceived of as an act, not as something that defined individuals. In this sense, as Foucault points out, in the early nineteenth century there were no homosexuals. Therefore men could express their feelings for other men in ways that the late nineteenth or the late twentieth century might find suspect. That having been said, however, sexual encounters between men were still punishable, and by mid-century strong emotional attachments between men had begun to fall between the definition of intense friendship and that of suspect or perverse or immoral behavior.

A literary friendship tradition allowed male-male friendship to be expressed without censure. The Bible itself praised the relationship of David and Jonathan, whose love was "wonderful passing the love of woman," and classical texts were inevitably cited as examples in which intense male friendships were valorized. But these friendships were assumed to be, finally, without a sexual component, and the nature of the affection was asserted to be without carnal desire. Some writers, however, while engaging the language of traditional friendship texts, hinted that their particular expressions of friendship concealed something more passionate. "As to manly friendship, everywhere observed in The States," Whitman wrote to Ralph Waldo Emerson in 1856, "there is not the first breath of it to be observed in print."[6] Whitman was largely correct. Published texts were often cautious in expressing same-sex desire. In private journals, however, such desire could be expressed. Though these private musings could not influence other readers, they are part of a speculative discourse about "manly friendship." Two American writers contribute to this speculation in the privacy of their journals: Emerson and Henry David Thoreau.

EMERSON AND THOREAU

In an 1820 journal Emerson addresses what was for him apparently an anxiety-ridden collision with homoerotic experience. There he describes a passion, inexplicable even to him who had explained Nature itself, for a young man named Martin Gay. This passion both unnerved and fascinated him. His puzzlement echoes in his diary entry asking of Gay, "Why do you look after me? I cannot help looking out as you pass."[7] The friendship, frustratingly, remained distant, and so Emerson transformed what little reality he possessed into a more useful fiction, writing a brief play that he accredited to an invented author. The author is Froedmer; his play is "The Friends." Gay appears in it as Malcolm, and Emerson drew a little sketch in the text, beneath which he wrote as a plea to his friend, "grant me still in joy or sorrow / In grief or hope to claim thy heart." Froedmer/Emerson writes lines even more intense: "Malcolm I love thee more than women love" (Gilman et al., 1: 291–92). Malcolm and Froedmer join hands there with David and Jonathan, whose love in the Bible was described as passing the love of woman.

Perhaps thinking about his own unsettling experience Emerson in 1834 wondered about "the disturbance, the self-discord which young men feel" and concluded that it "is a most important crisis" (quoted in Katz 1976, 461). In the same journal he speculates about a similar feeling he intuits in Shakespeare's sonnets, speculating on Shakespeare's "unknown self." He observes "how remarkable in every way are Shakespeare's sonnets. Those addressed to a beautiful young man seem to show some "singular friendship amounting to a passion" (Gilman et al., 3: 289–90). The singular friendship

Emerson felt for Martin Gay he seems to see reflected in the "passion" of the sonnets. Perhaps he discerns there his "unknown self" and identifies his own crisis—one that he could not or would not resolve.

Speculations about eroticized friendship appear also in journal entries Henry David Thoreau was making in 1839, wherein he meditates on the relation between love and friendship. His "rare specimens" are described horticulturally—like Emerson's and Whitman's leaves—as "young buds of manhood." "By what degrees of consanguinity," he inquires, "is this succulent and rank growing slip of manhood related to me?"[8] The "degrees of consanguinity" of course suggest those limits within which marriage is allowed or disallowed. The sanctified relationships he imagines with these rare specimens of manhood are indeed holy, for in them he can "worship moral beauty" manifest in manly flesh. He is touched by transcendental ecstasy when he sees them, for "they are some fresher wind that blows, some new fragrance that breathes." Nearly divinities, Thoreau's young men create the world he lives in: "they make the landscape and sky for us" (Torrey and Allen, 1: 107–108).

Thoreau's metaphors protest the separation of and work to conflate friendship and homoerotic passion: "commonly we degrade Love and Friendship by presenting them under a trivial dualism" (Torrey and Allen, 1: 107–108). The friendship tradition as practiced by the vast majority of heterosexual writers participated in that dualism by imposing on friendship a misread Platonism and by firmly separating it from the presumed sole legitimate arena of sexual experience, the heterosexual. Such texts expressed capitalized Friendship in terms of male relationships only, as Emerson clearly does in his essay on the subject. This of course could also be a complicit action, for it thus gave writers the chance to engage in extravagant protestations of male-male friendship, which could pass without any imputation of impropriety—either physically or emotionally—though such impropriety may indeed have been implied, intended, or even desired. But Thoreau is willing to theorize a dualism between manly love and other—heterosexual— love: "the rules of other intercourse are all inapplicable to this." "This" intercourse—specifically made different in his text from the "other intercourse"—has special laws and a special site, a divine realm he calls a "parcel of heaven." When we are separated from that "parcel of heaven we call our friend," that separation is "source enough for all the elegies that ever were written" (Torrey and Allen, 1: 107–108).

Thoreau defined friendship erotically in an 1838 poem titled "Friendship." Love is the "connecting link between heaven and earth," and lovers are "kindred shapes" possessing a "kindred nature." Indeed, they are intended "to be mates, / Exposed to equal fates / Eternally." Lovers are like "two sturdy oaks" whose "roots are intertwined insep'rably," anticipating also Whitman's choice of the oak as a symbol of manly love. Thoreau argues wittily that "love cannot speak . . . without the help of Greek, / or any other tongue" (Torrey and

Allen, 1: 40–43). Plato's *Symposium* originates the imagery of kindred lovers, and Greek, as the only tongue in which such love can speak, locates the passion within the homoerotic traditions associated with Greece.

In a January 1840 journal entry Thoreau further explores the associations of Greece with homoeroticism: "History tells us of Orestes and Pylades, Damon and Pythias, but why should not we put to shame those old reserved worthies by a community of such" (Torrey and Allen, 1: 113). He means a community of "such" homosexual lovers and conjures a vision of this erotic Arcadia: "Constantly, as it were through a remote skylight, I have glimpses of a serene friendship land." In this friendship land there is needed one other only: "I would live henceforth with some gentle soul such a life as may be conceived, double for variety, single for harmony,—two, only that we might admire at our oneness,—one, because indivisible. Such a community to be a pledge of holy living. How could aught unworthy be admitted into our society?" (Torrey and Allen, 1: 113). In this utopia there will be nothing "unworthy," and because it is a society of lovers the love that binds them is worthy as well.

Like Byron in *Don Leon*, Thoreau wants to meet an ideal friend: "For many years have I striven to meet one even on common manly ground and have not succeeded." Such a friend might be "as holy a shrine as any God's." His grammar hints that there may have been such a friend who dwells in the "distant horizon as rich as an eastern city" and "seems to move in a burnished atmosphere . . . his house is incandescent to my eye." Whether real or a fiction of desire, this friend is an "apology for my life. In him are the spaces which my orbit traverses."[9] Platonically, love lifts him into "higher walks of being"—indeed, it invents "poetical life." Thoreau's extravagant metaphors ascribe to friendship the very qualities usually celebrated as those obtaining in love between man and woman. In the presence of a friend "I am ashamed of my fingers and toes. I have no feature so fair as my love for him. There is more than maiden modesty between us." What "more" there is between Thoreau and his friend is hinted at in another extravagant and suggestive metaphor that conjures consummation: "He sails all lonely under the edge of the sky, but thoughts go out silently from me and belay him, till at length he rides in my roadsted." Perhaps this friendship, if it existed at all, was like that between Emerson and Martin Gay, fantasized and unrequited, for Thoreau extends his metaphor further, and it echoes Emerson's anguished "Why do I look out at you as I pass?" Thoreau says, "But never does he fairly anchor in my harbor. Perhaps I afford no good anchorage . . . his house is incandescent to my eye, while I have no house, but only a neighborhood to his."

Informing his perception of this friendship is the need for secrecy concerning it. He writes, "I cannot make a disclosure—you should see my secret.—Let me open my doors never so wide, still within and behind them, where it is unopened, does the sun rise and set." His friend is his secret, and the friendship is founded and depends on secrecy: "Does he forget that new mines of secrecy are constantly opening in me?"[10] Thoreau is not willing to reveal his desire in any place but his private journals, where the secret of his friendship can be safely inscribed. That secrecy attends on homosexual relationships is a given just as the fact that the "unmanly" construction that may be imputed to a passion between men demands that there be no revelation. When Emerson confesses his love for Martin, he translates his desire into fictitious drama, and Whitman describes the *Calamus* poems celebrating manly love as texts that "shade and hide my thoughts," though he admits that "they expose me more than all my other poems" (*LG*, 131).

While homoeroticizing friendship, Thoreau's text also defines some of the proscriptions levied against such eroticization. In an 1852 journal entry he comments about this: "Boys bathing at Hubbard's bend, playing with a boat (I at the willows). The color of their bodies in the sun at a distance is pleasing, the not often seen flesh-color. I hear the sound of their sport borne over the water. . . . What a singular fact that . . . men were forbidden to expose their bodies under severest penalty" (Torrey and Allen, 4: 92–93). It is, of course, not the exposition of nakedness that results in the "severest penalty"—death must surely be that penalty—but the desire that accompanies that exposition. Thoreau associates nakedness with desire, and his desire is directed at naked men. Thoreau's seeming overstatement is accurate: sexual desire for men is punishable by death. Thus hiding in the willows by the banks of the stream, voicing his lament that the flesh is "not often seen," Thoreau watches young buds of manhood at their naked sport. He is safe because he is a watcher only; at a distance and voyeuristically he absorbs a scene in which he is fearful to participate, knowing full well what the "awful results" may be. Thoreau's bathing boys scene also looks ahead to a similar scene Whitman will construct in section 11 of "Song of Myself," where 28 young men bath in an ocean of homoerotic implication, and it also forecasts an entire genre of homoerotic texts, mostly English, like Frederick Rolfe's "Ballade of Boys Bathing," in which bathing boys become the focus for desire.

In an entry written in 1840 Thoreau complains how "mean relations and prejudices intervene to shut out the sky and we never see a man as simple and distinct" (Torrey and Allen, 1: 144). The distance he keeps from bathing boys is marked and measured by such "mean relations and prejudice," for it is no longer "simple and distinct" when it becomes hedged about with threats of "severest penalties." Thoreau's yearning sexual mythmaking was written in private and in isolation, in what may well have been, in part at least, a self-imposed sexual exile. Thoreau sought, finally, instead of caresses, the chaste solitude of Walden.

In his journal in 1839 Thoreau lamented that "the nearest approach to a community of love in these days" (Torrey and Allen, 1: 115)—a community he identifies as made up of lovers like the Greek Damon and Pythias and

Orestes and Pylades—"is like the distant breaking of waves on the seashore" (Torrey and Allen, 1: 115). Thoreau was not alone in searching for a kind of friendship that "once certainly existed" both in literature and society. Emerson in 1841, feeling an absence, demanded "spermatic, prophesying, man-making words." While Emerson and Thoreau speculated in the privacy of their journals, Whitman more publicly in the letter to Emerson in 1856 complained about the absence in print of manly friendship, "everywhere observed in The States," and Bayard Taylor in a letter to Whitman in 1866 finds in *Leaves of Grass* what he "finds nowhere else in literature"—that is, "that tender and noble love of man for man which once certainly existed but now almost seems to have gone out of the experience of the race."[11] Whitman was to elaborate that "noble love" in the *Calamus* poems of 1860. While these poems were certainly the most important and extensive nineteenth-century American texts to explore questions about homosexual identities, other American texts cautiously considered some of the implications of the experience of the "tender and noble love of man for man."

HERMAN MELVILLE

Whitman was much taken by a first novel of a young American writer named Herman Melville. The novel was *Typee* (1846), a story of the South Seas adventures of two young friends. In a review Whitman described the novel as a "strange, graceful" book, one to "hold in one's hand and pore dreamily over of a summer day."[12] "Reverie" in nineteenth-century medical theory, "was commonly held to lead to masturbation."[13] Whether the dreamy state invoked by this Arcadian South Seas paradise could be associated with this dangerous reverie I do not know, but Whitman was already fascinated by images of the conflation of male friendship and sexuality and constructed in his texts reveries of friendship and desire.

I do not insist that *Typee* is "about" homosexuality; it is not, directly. But it certainly is imbued with a suggestive amount of homoeroticism, and it is one of the earliest American texts in which a sustained relationship between men, situated in an Arcadian venue, is sustained by a powerful if coded subtext of homoerotic desire. Robert K. Martin reminds us that while for most of its contemporary readers the novel was a travel narrative, it could serve other purposes: "For nineteenth-century homosexuals, in search of both a justification for themselves and a possible realization for their desires, the journey to an exotic landscape offered the possibility of locating a place where there might be others like them, a place where friendship might play its legitimate part in social life" (Martin 1986, 19). Martin sites *Typee* within a genre he calls "the quest for the Golden land," which I have identified as a version of homoerotic pastoral in which an eroticized Arcadia is a safe and erotic haven for homosexual lovers.[14]

Tom and Toby are these friends. Toby is first encountered "leaning over the bulwarks, apparently plunged in a profound reverie." He is, Tom says, "a young fellow of my own age, for whom I had all along entertained a great regard. . . . [H]e was active, ready, and obliging, of dauntless courage, and singularly open and fearless in the expression of his feelings. I had on more than one occasion gotten him out of scrapes into which this had led him; I know not whether it was from this cause, or a certain congeniality of sentiment between us, that he had always shown a partiality for my society."[15]

Toby's fearless expression of feeling isolates him from the common run of men, who observe the obscure if powerful taboo against the unmanly expression of feeling. That Toby is "singular" and that there is a "certain" congeniality between he and Tom indirectly hints at a special relationship. Furthermore, Toby is "a strange wayward being, moody, fitful, and melancholy—at times almost morose" (53). His moodiness and his self-imposed isolation mark him as an outcast separated from society by his willingness to transgress against its laws or customs.

Tom also responds physically to Toby: "There was much even in the appearance of Toby calculated to draw me toward him. . . . Toby was endowed with a remarkably prepossessing exterior. Arrayed in his blue smock and duck trousers, he was as smart a looking sailor as ever stepped upon a deck" (53). The sailor is an icon of considerable erotic resonance in homosexual literature, especially in Melville's texts: in *Redburn*, *Whitejacket*, *Moby-Dick*, and of course *Billy Budd*, where he is an image both central and erotic. Toby is "singularly small and slightly made, with great flexibility of limb. . . . [H]is naturally dark complexion had been deepened by exposure to the tropical sun, and a mass of jetty locks clustered about his temples, and threw a darker shade into his large black eyes" (53). This mixture of boyish beauty and emotional otherness combines mysterious sensitivity with the attributes of the rough and manly sailor. The sum of these parts is erotic and sexually suggestive. As Martin says, "Travel books should also be thought of as a possible Victorian form of genteel pornography," permitting the "exploration of alternate sexuality" (Martin 1986, 19). Tom recognizes the singularity of their attraction to each other and fixes Toby in the special world of male bonding that Whitman would later describe as comradeship. For Tom, Toby is the "very one of all my shipmates whom I would choose for the partner of my adventure." He is the ideal "comrade . . . to divide its dangers" (54).

Toby and Tom jump ship and land on an island that Tom describes in Arcadian terms: "I looked straight down into the bosom of a valley, which swept away in long undulations to the blue waters of the distance. . . . Over all the landscape there reigned the most hushed repose, which I almost feared to break, lest, like the enchanted gardens in the fairy tale, a single syllable might dissolve the spell." This is the happy valley, an enchanted garden, a "capacious and untenanted valley, abounding in all manner of delicious fruit." Tom urges that "we should at once take refuge in it and remain there as long as we pleased" (73–75). This is Thoreau's friendship land, the same hidden Arcadia that Whitman seeks next to the margins of the Calamus pond, and the same happy valley described by Bayard Taylor in his novel *Joseph and His Friend* (1870).

Readers of the novel know that in the land of the Typees, the tribe that shelters Tom and Toby, Tom is given the services of Kory-Kory, whose purpose is to minister to Tom's comfort. Kory-Kory is "twenty-five years of age, about six feet in height, robust and well made." Kory-Kory is devoted to Tom and serves him with jealous efficiency, bathing him, feeding him, carrying him, lighting his pipe, sleeping next to him, and offering, in short, all the intimate services that might be provided by a nineteenth-century wife—or a devoted lover. Tom points up the intimacy of their sleeping arrangements: "the next morning I found Kory-Kory stretched out on one side of me, while my companion lay upon the other" (116). Melville places Tom between the devoted innocence of Kory-Kory and the sexually charged presence of Toby, symbolically placing him between love and desire, and in so doing foreshadows the matrimonial intimacy of Queequeg and Ishmael in *Moby-Dick* in 1850 and Whitman's *Calamus* lyric of 1860, "When I Heard at the Close of the Day."

If Whitman was plunged into dreamy reverie by suggestive scenes of intimacy between men, he may well have been especially captivated by the handsome youth Melville introduces in the person of Marnoo, a homoerotic Adam in this sexual paradise. Marnoo steps out of myth and legend into Melville's erotic mythmaking, for he is an exciting embodiment of sexual promise and homoerotic fantasy:

> The stranger could not have been more than twenty-five years of age, and was a little above the ordinary height; had he been a single hair's breadth taller, the matchless symmetry of his form would have been destroyed. His unclad limbs were beautifully formed; whilst the elegant outline of his figure, together with his beardless cheeks, might have entitled him to the distinction of the Polynesian Apollo; and indeed the oval of his countenance and the regularity of every feature reminded me of an antique bust. . . . The hair of Marnoo was a rich curling brown, and twined about his temples and neck in little close curling ringlets, which danced up and down continually when he was animated in conversation. His cheek was of a feminine softness, and his face was free from the least blemish of tattooing . . . a slight girdle of tappa, scarcely two inches in width, but hanging before and behind in spreading tassels, composed the entire costume of the stranger. (169)

Melville passionately describes the erotic components of Marnoo: sensuously curling hair; feminine cheeks or face yet a masculine and perfect bodily form, an inevitable comparison to classical—hence homoerotic—beauty; and of course nakedness, here tantalizingly presented. Melville elevates the taboo Marnoo—the archetypal beautiful boy, the truly ideal friend, and the very image of Apollo—to near divinity. By eroticizing both Marnoo and Toby, Melville achieves what Emerson desired when he wished that his "friend . . . be different from any individual I had seen." Indeed, Emerson invested Martin Gay "with a solemn cast of mind, full of poetic feeling . . . an idolater of friendship" (quoted in Katz 1976, 458).

Melville constructs a fictional world in which the primary characters are outcasts from the land-locked world of (hetero)sexual morality. In *Typee* he begins a project in which the union of male couples will be shown, as Martin argues, as a possible "strategy for redefining American society" (Martin 1986, ix). In his novels *Redburn* and *Whitejacket* male companionship borders on the erotic, and in what Martin calls the "male marriage of Ishmael and Queequeg" in *Moby-Dick*, Melville radically reorders traditional relationships. With *Billy Budd* he would engage in his most profound meditation on the nature and consequences of eroticized intimacy between men.

BAYARD TAYLOR

In a poem written about the same time Melville published *Typee*, Bayard Taylor eroticizes the sailor: "I pine for something human, / Man, woman, young or old,— / Something to meet and welcome, / Something to clasp and hold." He confesses, "I have a mouth for kisses. . . . I have a heart in my bosom / Beating for nobody's sake. . . . O warmth of love that is wasted!" So powerful is his desire—he too "pines" for love—that "I could take the sunburnt sailor, / Like a brother, to my breast."[16] The Taylor who so homoerotically described a sunburnt sailor appears in one of Whitman's notebook entries in 1854. Whitman says that Taylor's poems "have as attributes what might be called their psychology—You cannot see very plainly at times what they mean although the poet indirectly has a meaning."[17] Whitman was fascinated with the concept of indirect speech. His *Calamus* poems, as he said, "hide and shade" his thoughts and so "indirectly" may well indicate a special literary tongue he detects in Taylor's texts. Certainly "indirectly" defines the experimental discourse that theorizes the implications of manly love that is part of Whitman's special tongue. The indirect meanings and "psychology" that Whitman finds in Taylor's texts mark that same manly friendship Whitman hoped to see mentioned in print. A reading of Taylor's *Poems of the Orient* (1854) shows that Whitman's hints about their "psychology" suggest that he did indeed detect the recognizable air of homoerotic texts.

Taylor dedicates his poems to Richard Henry Stoddard and hopes he can "join . . . hands, / And knit our souls in Friendship's holy bands." Taylor wishes that his friend "were with me" and "couched on [Mount] Tmolus side / In the warm Myrtles, in the golden air." In this pastoral Arcadia, Taylor avers that if Stoddard were with him "little were the need of this imperfect artifice of rhyme" since presumably their companionship—or their love—

would provide music enough. But "I am solitary," Taylor says, "I cannot choose but sing." The songs he intends to sing will display "the unshackled range / Of all experience . . . that my songs may show / The warm red blood that beats in hearts of men." Emerson, in his 1841 essay "On Friendship," had already spoken about the "ruddy drop of manly blood" that flowed in the veins of friends, and Whitman would very soon write about the "blood of friendship hot and red" that flows in the veins of the young men "silently selected by lovers" in a poem that would eventually become "To a Western Boy" in the *Calamus* series.

Taylor's *Poems of the Orient* are sited in an erotically resonant locale. The Orient was seen to be exotic, pagan, and, most importantly, tolerant of homosexuality. As Louis Crompton argues, it was this tolerance that "inevitably drew homosexual or bisexual writers" to oriental themes and led more sexually orthodox writers to reject them (Crompton, 118). It may be recalled from *Don Leon* that it was in Turkey that Byron's orthodox companions were scandalized by the scenes of sodomitical pleasure that fascinated Byron. Like *Don Leon*'s Byron, Taylor continues on to Greece and constructs it as an erotic site. In "A Paean to the Dawn" he praises Greece as a place where "love was free, and free as air / The utterance of Passion." Here "the heart in every fold lay bare, / Nor shamed its true expression."[18] Greece, of course, was enshrined in history and myth as the essential locale for the expression of manly love. In texts the "expression" of heterosexual love was not considered to be shameful, and so Taylor seems certainly to mean that it is homosexual love that has been, since the Greeks, "shamed in its true expression" (Taylor, 37–38).

In Greece, Taylor finds that literary expressions of love inscribe ideal figures who possess a "perfect limb and perfect face," that "surpassed our best ideal . . . the Beautiful was real." The conflation of beauty, physical perfection, and Greece with the "true expression" of love in texts also conflates homosexual passion with aesthetic principles and with the "fearless utterance" of homoerotic desire, to borrow Byron's words from *Don Leon*. Indeed, Taylor insists that in Greece "men acknowledged true desires" and acted on them: "Impulse and Deed went hand in hand." Because he sees Greek sexual freedom as a source of power, Taylor determines to "seek the fountain head / Whence flowed their inspiration, / And lead the unshackled life they led" (Taylor, 38). In this friendship land Taylor can find truth in desire and, like Whitman, will renounce "the World's false life."

Empowered by Greek friendship, Taylor continues his journey, and in "The Poet in the East" he finds another land with which he identifies, for "his native soul was there." He compares what he finds in this native land with recollections of other, more "familiar visions that mocked his quest / Beside the Western streams." Western streams flow through lands in which passion, especially homoerotic passion, cannot be freely uttered. The visions are "visible forms of early and precious dreams," Platonic dreams of idealized homosexual love that Taylor had detailed in "A Paean to the Dawn." He decides to stay "on the lost Arcadian shore: here is the light on sea and land, / And the dream deceives no more." Entering into his Arcadia, Taylor is released from the deceiving visions that "mocked" him "beside the repressive Western Streams," and he discovers, the implication is, that his dreams of manly love can here be made real.

He makes clear, if there is doubt, what associations he wants the reader to make with East and West. The Western streams named in "The Nilotic Drinking Song" are the Schuykill or the Croton. The free eastern waters are those in which "Ganymede dipped for Jupiter." They remind him of Anacreon's stave and the "honeyed lips of Hylas," that handsome youth for whose love Hercules pined (Taylor 38, 56–57).

Taylor concludes his oriental poems with a final intriguing comment. In the East, he says, "I found, among those Children of the sun, / The cipher of my nature,—the release / Of baffled powers, which else had never won / That free fulfillment" (Taylor, 66). There can be little doubt that his references to "nature" and "baffled powers" in the context of the sexual freedom he constructs suggests that, for Taylor, access to homoerotic passion also allowed him access to inspiration.

Taylor may have couched his oriental poems in language both vague and allusive, inscribing his sexual desire in airy metaphor. But in "Hylas" (1850), written a few years before *Poems of the Orient*, he seems to be quite sure in what direction desire lies. When the water nymphs, taken by his beauty, pull Hylas into their sacred pond; Hercules, mad with grief, leaves the Argonauts to search for him, repeatedly calling his name in vain. Theocritus had told the story, and Taylor uses it as his most extended "literary exercise" in homoerotic poetry. Martin suggests that Taylor's "use of the Hylas myth as a poetic subject is part of an attempt at self-definition and also part of an attempt to situate himself in a poetic tradition which will justify his emotional life" (Martin 1979, 101).

Taylor creates a fully eroticized male portrait of Hylas, Hercules' favorite, describing his slow disrobing: "Unfilleting his purple chalmys. . . . Then, stooping lightly, loosened he his buskins." He soon stands

Naked, save for one light robe that from his shoulder
Hung to his knee, the youthful flush revealing
Of warm, white limbs, half nerved with coming manhood,
Yet fair and smooth with tenderness of beauty.

Hylas "dropped the robe, and raised his head exulting." Taylor dwells on the details of his beauty:

the thick, brown locks, tossed back-ward from his forehead, . . .
full the red lips, parting,

Like a loose bow, . . .
His large blue eyes, . . .
Were clear as the unshadowed Grecian heaven;
Dewy and sleek his dimpled shoulders rounded
To the white arms and whiter breast between them.
Downward, the supple line has less of softness:
His back was like a god's; his loins were moulded
As if some pulse of power began to waken;
The springy fulness of his thighs, out-swerving,
Sloped to his knee, and lightly dropping downward,
Drew the curved lines that breathe, in rest, of motion. (Taylor, 73)

The florid diction does not conceal the erotic nature of the portrait. It is as daring and as desirous as Melville's description of Marnoo, as specifically sexual as any description of erotic young men that Whitman was yet to write. No euphemism is present when Taylor looks hard at that intimated point where "downward the supple lines have less of softness." Whitman will later frankly stare at "the masculine muscle" outlined against the tight fabric of a fireman's trousers and sing songs about the "well-hung" rough. Taylor's gaze is as obsessively fixed on Hylas's loins and thighs—not only on the decreasing softness but also upon the rising "pulse of power" that awakens to "springy fulness" and soon becomes "outswerving," dropping breathtakingly to Hylas's knee.

Taylor's baffled homoerotic powers have been well released here. In the aforementioned letter to Whitman, Taylor also spoke about "the awe and wonder and reverence and beauty of Life, as expressed in the human body, with the physical attraction and delight of mere contact which it inspires." When we hear Taylor's description of Hylas and read his testimony to the release of baffled powers, the same release that happens to Byron in *Don Leon* when he finds desire in a lover's arms, Whitman's observation about Taylor's "psychology" seems indeed to be perceptively pointed.

This rakish portrait of Walt Whitman appeared in the first (1855) edition of *Leaves of Grass*.

chapter 4

CELEBRATING COMRADES: WALT WHITMAN, 1840–1860

I feel a hundred realities . . . clearly determined in me that words are not yet formed to represent. Men like me . . . will gradually get to be more numerous . . . then the words will follow.
— Walt Whitman, *The Primer of Words* (ca. 1850)

"THE CHILD'S CHAMPION"

In 1841 Ralph Waldo Emerson wrote of eroticized friendship as "delicious torment": "we seek our friend . . . with an adulterous passion which would appropriate him to ourselves." Emerson will not "treat friendship daintily, but with roughest courage"; he prefers "the company of ploughboys and tin-peddlers to . . . silken and perfumed amity" and attempts to separate friendship from any imputation of effeminacy.[1] In a fluid image highlighting secrecy and intimacy, Emerson asserts that "through thy friendship fair" course "the fountains of my hidden life." It may be no coincidence that in the story "The Child's Champion," written in the same year Emerson penned the preceding words, Walt Whitman also uses the image of the erotically charged fountain to celebrate a passion for a youth: "It is passing wondrous, how . . . we meet with young beings, strangers, who seem to touch the fountains of our love, and draw forth their swelling waters."[2] Not content to complain or merely theorize about the need for a language to express manly love and the homoerotic desire he so powerfully felt and detected in the young men of America, Whitman experimented with it in this early work.[3]

"The Child's Champion" is the story of young Charles, who is saved by a the handsome Langton from the violent attentions of a sailor in a barroom. Charles is all innocence; Langton all sophisticated experience. As a result of Langton's act, their friendship blossoms into love. At Charles's first appearance he is described as "languid," a word that by mid-century will have distinct erotic resonance. A dead father and an intense relationship with his mother hint at a psychological profile even before such facts were thought to signify. When he and his mother part, "each pressed a long kiss on the lips of the other." On the way to his job, with an employer whose cruelty reflects that of his dead father, he chances to look into the windows of a tavern: "In the middle of the room were five or six sailors, some of them quite drunk. . . . The men in the middle of the room were dancing. . . . [I]n short the whole party was engaged in drunken frolic." But "what excited the boy's attention more than any other object was an individual. . . . His appearance was youthful. He might have been twenty-one or -two years old. His countenance was intelligent, and had the air of city life and society. He was dress'd not gaudily, but in every respect fashionably . . . and his whole aspect that of one whose counterpart may now and then be seen upon the pave in Broadway of a fine afternoon" (*EPF*, 71).

One of the drunken sailors sees Charles and literally pulls him through the window into the bar. Taking a "fair view of the boy, who though not what is called pretty was fresh and manly looking, and large for his age" the sailor exclaims, "There my lads . . . there's a new recruit for you. Not so coarse a one either." If the sailor intends to recruit Charles into their dissipated ranks, his response is curious, sinister, and fraught with erotic implication because it is Charles's manly good looks on which he focuses. The sailor offers Charles brandy; innocent Charles refuses. Angered, the sailor forces him to drink, and when Charles refuses again the sailor strikes him. If the text pictures force, the subtext implies rape, for the spurned sailor reacts more violently still and placed "one of his tremendous paws on the back of the boy's head, with the other he thrust the edge of the glass to his lips." Charles resists yet again and the now furious sailor "seized the child with a grip of iron; he bent Charles half way over, and with the side of his heavy foot" gave him a "sharp and solid kick." The eroticism of violence needs no gloss and here the erotic text surfaces from beneath the violent one to elaborate the encoded homosexual rape. Langton, watching and appalled, comes to the boy's rescue. "Assuming, unconsciously . . . the attitude of a boxer" he attacks the sailor and protects Charles, who "now thoroughly terrified, clung round his legs" (*EPF*, 73).

If violence implies desire so that the sailor, literally, tries to bend Charles to his desire, it is also violence that impels Langton to the rescue and out of the sexual excitement of violence grows Langton's conviction that "he should love him." Violence too sets flowing the fountains of love and the swelling waters, and on this torrent of desire Charles and Langton are eventually carried to share a bed at the inn: Charles the languid and dreamy boy has found a protector, and Langton, a dandy transformed into a manly boxer by love, discovers an object to redeem his life from pointless debauchery.

Transformation through love is one of the primary texts of nineteenth-century domestic fiction: fair maiden saved from sexual ruin by the intervention of the handsome hero who she will, inevitably, marry. Here there is the virginal Charles, who is not entirely passive, for it was Langton's good looks that "excited the boy's attention." Langton himself is no paragon (his past sins are implied but suspiciously unnamed), while the choice of a sailor who wants to recruit a handsome boy need not be glossed too deeply to discover the same hints at sexual villainy that Melville explores in *Redburn* and *Billy Budd*.

While I do not propose that Whitman pictured an incident in a gay bar in which a lustful sailor attempts to rape a handsome boy, forcing him to commit an act against his will, yet a subtextual reading can suggest this, for what follows is an unmistakable moment of homosexual eros when Langton and Charles go to bed together. The crux of it all is to be found in the question the text asks: Why should Langton protect the boy, since most of the other denizens of the place "were content to let the matter go as chance would have it" (*EPF*, 73)? Langton voices the question:

> Why was it that from the first moment of seeing him, the young man's heart had moved with a strange feeling of kindness toward the boy? He felt anxious to know more of him—he felt that he should love him. O, it is passing wondrous, how in the hurried walks of life and business, we meet with young beings, strangers, who seem to touch the fountains of our love, and draw forth their swelling waters. The wish to be loved, which the forms of custom, and the engrossing anxiety for gain, so generally smother, will sometimes burst forth in spite of all obstacles; and kindled by one, who, till the hour unknown to us, will burn with a lovely and pure brightness. (*EPF*, 74, n23)

Langton is attracted to Charles because he is a "young being" and a "stranger" and because the "language of the turning eyeballs" is decoded to say both love and desire. Symbolically but clearly the rising fountains and the swelling waters of love bathe the scene in phallic and ejaculatory implication. Whitman would later record the love that can "burst forth in spite of all obstacles" when it is "kindled" by a stranger in *Calamus* 2. Athletic Langton, that protective boxer, bursting with desire for Charles, might read with sympathy *Calamus* 36 in which Whitman would soon warn of "something fierce in me eligible to burst forth." What was eligible to burst forth was his love for "an athlete" who is "enamour'd of me."

The tale now enters the realm of allegorical if oblique homoeroticism and sexual mysticism. Charles and Langton now hold "communion together," sharing a sacrament of love. Langton suggests, since it is late, that the boy spend the night at the inn. Forbidden desires are hinted:

> It was now past midnight. The young man told Charles that on the morrow he would take steps to have him liberated from his servitude; for the present night, he said, it would be best for the boy to stay and share his bed at the inn; and little persuading did the child need to do so. As they retired to sleep, very pleasant thoughts filled the mind of the young man; thoughts of a worthy action performed; of unsullied affection; thoughts, too—newly awakened ones—of walking in a steadier and wiser path than formerly. All his imaginings seemed to be interwoven with the youth who lay by his side; he folded his arms around him, and while they slept, the boy's cheek rested on his bosom. Fair were those two creatures in their unconscious beauty—glorious, but yet how differently glorious! One of them was innocent and sinless of all wrong: the other—O to that other, what evil had not been present, either in action or to his desires! (EPF, 76, n38)

Charles is eager to share Langton's bed since by doing so he will be "liberated" from his servitude, both to his cruel employer and perhaps too a compulsory sexual identity represented by his provincial life. Langton too is filled with amorous speculation: "All his imaginings seemed to be interwoven with the youth who lay by his side!" This scene from the romantic mythology of redemptive love is also a scene rich in homoerotic implication. Charles lies in the arms of the ideal friend and this "glorious" pair become Jonathan and David, Damon and Pythias, Orestes and Pylades.

Though they begin the night side by side, they end it entwined. They are visited by an angel who smiles on "those who slumbered there in each other's arms." The angel kisses Charles, and when a "bright ray of sunlight," presumably from heaven, gives him leave, he kisses Langton also, giving the two his blessing. In each other's arms they are dangerously close, and a scene from Calamus 11 makes a parallel: "In the stillness of the autumn moonbeams his face was inclined / toward me, / And his arm lay lightly around my breast—and that night I was happy." Langton, dreaming of newfound "unsullied affection," is happy too.

The image of two intertwined lovers appears in many transformations in Whitman's later poetry, but perhaps most provocatively in "Bunch Poem" in the 1856 edition of Leaves of Grass (titled "Spontaneous Me" in 1867), in which Whitman realizes a sexually transgressive fantasy: "two sleepers at night lying close together as they sleep, / one with an arm slanting down across and below the waist of the other." These sleepers are the "boy" and the "young man" who engage in a half-waking masturbatory encounter.

The boy "arouses" the young man, telling him an erotic dream. The young man responds, and "privileged feelers" are "intimate" with "the hubbed sting . . . the sensitive, orbic, underlapp'd brothers"—the penis and testicles—and the "curious roamer the hand" grasps and arouses. The pulsing and steady metrical beat, the "pulse pounding through palms" leads to ejaculation, and the young man, though at first "ashamed and angry," is finally purified by the seminal release and concludes the poem "willing and naked" and at peace. The boy who aroused the young man with "pressure" and the excitement of erotic dreams brings him to climax with his privileged roaming hand, releasing in him just as Charles had released in Langton the "swelling waters" of the "fountains of love." In both story and poem forms of custom are metaphorically transgressed, not only by the homoerotic context but by the reversal of expectations when the boy, not the young man, initiates sex.

The ending of "The Child's Champion" invokes a homoerotic utopian dream that not even the intrusion of heterosexual union can destroy. Even though Langton marries, Charles and Langton are to be forever together, and "the close knit love of the boy and him grew not slack with time" (EPF, 79). They live forever in each other's arms, graven on their own Grecian urn, willing to transgress and protect each other from the "forms of custom and the engrossing anxiety" of the "hurried walks of life."

When Whitman wrote "The Child's Champion" he was a largely unknown young writer, still "unremark'd seated in a / corner," waiting for his ideal friend to gloriously appear and speculating on just how he could infuse literature with a breath of manly love. In this early story he cautiously but deliberately begins an exploration of the landscapes of homoerotic desire. Robert K. Martin argues that in the 1840s homosexuality was "indistinguishable" in literature "from other forms of male friendship" (Martin 1989, 181). Whitman's task was to distinguish it, and though the clues are faint and indirect, we ought to heed him when he reminds us, "I meant that you should discover me so by faint indirections" (LG, 135).

LEAVES OF GRASS

Whitman called Leaves of Grass a "language experiment," part of which was his attempt to create a language that would adequately express his feelings about comradeship and manly love and define its place in the new American literature he had announced that he was creating. In a journal of the early 1850s, before Leaves of Grass was published in 1855, Whitman speculated on the relationship between language and manly friendship. This journal he eventually called The Primer of Words. In a manuscript version of this text (I enclose his deletions in brackets), he makes the links between desire and text:

This is to be said among the young men of these states, that with a wonderful tenacity of friendship, and [a manliness] of passionate fondness for their friends, and always a manly readiness to make friends, yet they have remarkably few words [to] of names for the friendly sentiments.—They seem to be words that do not thrive here among the muscular classes, where the real quality of friendship is always freely found. Also they are words which the muscular classes,[and] the young men of these states, [are] rarely use, and have an aversion for;—they never give words to their most ardent friendships.[4]

Though he deleted it in the final text, here "manliness" precedes "passionate fondness" and equals manly love, while the "muscular classes"—those he calls "roughs" in his poems—are firmly identified with "young men" by the deletion of "and." These muscular men have relationships in which the "real quality" of friendship can be found. If "real" suggests the unrealized in friendships, that "real quality" is what most men have never found in friendship: sexual desire. Whitman wants to give these lusty, muscular, young men access to words, to names, to desire and identity. These, he is confident, will one day appear: "When the time comes for them to represent any thing or any state of things, the words will surely follow . . . As for me, I feel a hundred realities . . . clearly determined in me, that words are not yet formed to represent. Men like me . . . will gradually get to be more and more numerous . . . then the words will follow" (*DN*, 3: 745). "Men like me" defines what he means by "any state of things."

The state of things he envisions involves the construction of manly and erotic identities, which will appear as men like him "get . . . more numerous," creating special communities of desire. That he discerns the erotic reality of friendship as something "clearly determined in me" pointedly invokes essential theories and genetic constructions. His assumption that the special language that special friendship requires is not yet available defines also the task he sets himself: to create that language and utter, as he says in 1860, the cry of friends. Whitman eroticized words like men: "Words . . . are showing themselves, with . . . foreheads muscular necks and breasts.—These gladden me!—I put my arms around them—touch my lips to them" (*DN*, 3: 739). In another entry he defines masculine words as "all words that have arisen out of the qualities of mastership, [freedom go] going first, brunting danger first,—words to identify [an erect and athletic] a hardy [an upright] boyhood—[an unstained] knowledge—an [sweet] erect, sweet, lusty, body, without taint—[those where whence all] choice and clear of its [love life] pure power" (*DN*, 3: 739–40).

"Freedom," "mastership," "erect," "upright," "sweet," "lusty": these words read *power, sexuality*, and *phallicism*. They are in constant association in his subtext with the "young men of these states," and they oppose words that point to shamefaced perceptions of desire: "taint" and "(un)stained." Thus they valorize same-sex intimacy and assert that the semen expended in manly love might not corrupt but free the "erect, sweet, lusty, body." The love of "erect" young men equals "pure" phallic power. The conceptual linkage between male-male intimacy and sodomy, debauchery, unnatural vice, and effeminacy is Whitman's target; his achievement is to reclaim manly love both for sex and for purity.

By the time Whitman published the first edition of *Leaves of Grass* in 1855 he had carried his search for homoeroticism in texts into his notebooks and from there into "Song of Myself." In his letter to Emerson in 1856 he prophesied that if muscular words can be found, they will form a language that will make American texts "strong, limber . . . full of ease, of passionate friendliness" (*LG*, 741). The strength and passion Whitman hopes for, of course, are markings of homoerotic texts. But not only will his new language define, but it will also resist. He tells Emerson that the texts he intends to displace are "without manhood or power," texts in which only "geldings" are depicted. In these flaccid texts weak words are like the unaroused penis, "its flesh is soft; it shows less and less of the indefinable hard something that is Nature." Texts reflect their readers and writers, for the literature he deplores is created and read by "helpless dandies" who "can neither fight, work, shoot, ride, run, command" but who are instead "devout, some quite insane, castrated," who can be seen "smirking and skipping along . . . no one behaving . . . out of any natural and manly tastes of his own." These dandies produce texts in which the "lives of men and women . . . appear to have been . . . of the neuter gender . . . if the dresses were changed the men might easily pass for women, and the women for men." This literature makes "unmentionable" the "manhood of a man . . . sex, womanhood, maternity, desires, lusty animations, organs, acts" (*LG*, 736–39).

This attack against literary dandyism and prudery is infused with the same clichés that were developing as definitions of the effeminate homosexual. His use of "insane" and "castrated" predicts medical perceptions of homosexuals, while "smirking and skipping" reflect homophobic clichés of effeminacy. Curiously, Whitman's text accords with a parody of Whitman's poetry written around 1860 in which a "Counter-Jumper," the dry goods salesman who had become associated with effeminacy and homosexuality, is described as "weak and effeminate," depraved and "feeble." But Whitman is not devaluing homosexuality, only effeminacy. Indeed, he is using the very terms that demonize same-sex love in order to redefine the literary basis he feels is necessary to valorize it. In an oblique reference to same-sex affection he insists that there must be a language that can apply to "men not fond of women, women not fond of men" (*DN*, 3: 746). Whitman's opposition to effeminacy in literature is an attempt to recover for American literature a masculine, anti-aristocratic, democratic style that he sites within a homoerotic aesthetic. As he observed in another notebook, "What is lacking in literature can . . . only be generated from the seminal freshness and propulsion of new masculine persons" (*DN*, 1: 223). He does not want to erase manly friendship from American texts, nor its sexual expression. Instead, he hopes to write effeminacy out of texts and out of the language.

The masculinized, eroticized language Whitman called for in 1856, of course, had already been produced in his own *Leaves of Grass* in 1855, especially in the erotic "Song of Myself." His *Calamus* poems, included in the 1860 edition of *Leaves of Grass*, used eroticized language to form the most substantial collection of homoerotic lyrics yet written in America. In an 1876 Preface to a new edition of *Leaves of Grass* Whitman argued that the importance of *Calamus* "resides in its Political significance," for it is by the "fervent, accepted development of Comradeship, the beautiful and sane affection of man for man, latent in all young fellows . . . and what goes indirectly and directly along with it, that the United States of the future, (I cannot too often repeat,) are to be most effectually welded together, intercalated, anneal'd into a Living Union" (*LG*, 753). The "sane" affection of man for man and what goes directly or indirectly along with it is the cure for the "insane" and castrated effeminacy of texts and society. What "goes directly and indirectly along with it" is the sexual expression of affection.

Whitman argued in his 1856 letter to Emerson that literary texts should repeal the "filthy law" that enforces silence about sex. The discourse he wants to construct is one in which "the body is to be expressed, and sex is." Such texts will create sites for the free expression of sexuality among both women and men. If sex is admitted to literature women will "approach the day of organic equality with men" (*LG*, 739). By "organic" he means quite simply an equality in the use of the sexual body—the genital organs. This equality between women and men is a prelude to the realization of male-male genital activity. The greatest triumph of organic equality will be that men will be able to celebrate their own "organic" liberation from heterosexuality, for without organic equality between men and women, "men cannot have organic equality among themselves." "Among"—both inclusive and excluding—defines his context as sexual as well as affectional and defines the "real" emotion he discerns in "passionate friendliness." Organic equality also excludes sexual passivity and, because he seems to conflate passivity with effeminacy, the "unmanly" behavior of the effeminate homosexual.

Whitman elaborates this position in a footnote to *Democratic Vistas* (1871), in which he argued that

It is to the development, identification, and general prevalence of that fervid comradeship, (the adhesive love, at least rivaling the amative love hitherto possessing imaginative literature, if not going beyond it,) that I look for the counterbalance and offset of our materialistic and vulgar American democracy, and for the spiritualization thereof. . . . I confidently expect a time when there will be seen running, like a half-hid warp through all the myriad audible and visible worldly interests of America, threads of manly friendship, fond and loving, pure and sweet, strong and life-long, carried to degrees hitherto unknown—not only giving tone to individual character, and making it unprecedentedly emotional, muscular, heroic, and refined, but having the deepest relation to general politics. I say democracy infers such loving comradeship, as its most inevitable twin or counterpart, without which it would be incomplete, in vain, and incapable of perpetuating itself.[5]

In his letter to Emerson, Whitman urged that if the "United States are founding a literature," then "in poems, the young men of these States shall be represented, for they outrival the rest of the earth." Just as in *Democratic Vistas*, where American political and spiritual health must rest on a foundation of manly friendship, so he theorizes that American literature will not be complete until manly friendship is fully represented in its texts. Whitman outlines his own role in creating a climate for such an inclusion: "everyday I go . . . among the young men, to discover the spirit of them and to refresh myself." These excursions provide more powerful inspiration than any that contemporary literature offers: "I am myself more drawn here than to those authors, publishers, importations, reprints" that make up American texts.

Whitman knew that the construction of sexualities depends as much on language as on sexual act. He argues that because there is no eroticized and defining language there is no literature to express the reality of manly friendship. What is "important in poems" is to name "in specific words" the "main matter" that "is so far quite unexpressed in poems; but . . . the body is to be expressed and sex is." Sex, "avowed, empowered, unabashed" is that on which "all existence, all souls, all realization, all decency, all health, all that is worth being here for, all of women and of men, all beauty, all purity, all sweetness, all friendship, all strength, all life, all immortality depend" (LG, 739–40). In that rush of language the subtle inclusion of "friendship" nestled tellingly between sweetness and strength should be noted, for like all the other terms of his list friendship also depends on sex.

In "Song of Myself" Whitman becomes "undisguised and naked" in order to allow himself free space to confront and change the "forms of custom and the engrossing anxieties" of American sexual life. "Song of Myself" is an American homoerotic epic, and in sections 28 and 29 Whitman is brought "quivering . . . to a new identity" in which he defines the textual meaning of homoerotic desire. The new identity he discovers is both his identity as a poet and his identity as a lover of men—a sexual identity that, he argues, is the inseminating and controlling force of his poetry. He willingly succumbs to an ecstasy induced by homosexual acts. As a result of this experience he is able to create one of the central and significant moments of "Song of Myself." His acceptance of homosexual desire has enabled him to project "landscapes masculine full sized and golden." These are the homoerotic masculine landscapes of his poems.

Perhaps the most valuable gloss on sections 28 and 29 was written by Whitman himself in his notebook versions of these lines. These versions more clearly express homoerotic desire and more explicitly detail homosexual acts than do the compressed final version. Here the erotic muse, Whitman's "fierce wrestler," is truly and erotically present. In the final published version he demands, "Villain touch, what are you doing? . . . my breath is tight in / its throat; / Unclench your floodgates! you are too much for me." These lines compress and censor the powerful rape scene of the notebooks (Whitman's deletions are in brackets):

Fierce Wrestler, do you keep your heaviest [strike] grip for the last?
Gods! [Wrestler] Will you sting me even at parting?
Will you struggle even at the threshold with [gigantic] [delicious] spasms more delicious than all before? [Will you renew this and]
Does [even as you fade and withdraw] it make you ache so to leave me?
Do you wish to show me that even what you did before was nothing to what you can do?
Or have you and all the rest combined to see how much I can endure
Pass as you will; take drops of my life [only go, or is] if that is what you are after
Only pass to some one else, for I can contain you no longer.
I held more than I thought
I did not think I was big enough for so much ecstasy
Or that a touch could take it all out of me. (*NUPM*, 1:77)

The homoerotic violence is enlarged in another manuscript version of this scene:

Gripp'd wrestler! do you keep the heaviest pull for the last?
Must you bite with your teeth at parting?
Will you struggle worst? I plunge you from the threshold.
Does it make you ache so leaving me!
Take what you like, I can resist you;
Take the tears of my soul if that is what you are after.
Pass to some one else;
Little as your mouth, it has drained me dry of my strength.[6]

The experience is homosexual; the speaker is the fantasizing partner/creator in an act of homosexual rape. The result is orgasm, impregnation, and ejaculation. The floodgates are unclenched not now by a single hand only but through mutual sexuality. Masturbation, the solitary vice, has been superseded by a violent yet ecstatic union between the poet and his masculine muse. In "Song of Myself" what remains of the notebook entries is the invocation to "blind loving wrestling touch." But even though the rapist-wrestler has literally disappeared, he anonymously dominates the imagery as the sheathed, hooded, sharp-toothed, uncircumcised penis. The central image is now the sperm that descends like a fertilizing rain on the body and spirit of the poet, whose new identity is nourished by these ejaculations. The lines suggest both oral and anal sexuality and picture both masturbation and mastery. The final lines in section 29 make the leap from sexual passion to inspiration and art. Fertilized by the showering semen the "sprouts take and accumulate." The seeds of art are planted and instantaneously grow, becoming "prolific and vital." The harvest is stupendous and plentiful. As he surveys these fields of phallic stalks, the literally seminal is converted into the metaphorically seminal, the sprouts explode into poems, and his poetry will define and henceforth describe "landscapes . . . masculine full sized and golden."

THE *CALAMUS* POEMS[7]

In "Song of Myself" Whitman defined the word to express manly friendship as "the unfolding word of the ages . . . a word of the modern . . . a word en masse . . . a word of faith that never balks." This word is a "password primeval" and it allows him to speak in "forbidden voices"— voices expressing sexual power that strip away veils and transgress the established boundaries of traditional power. In the 1856 edition of *Leaves of Grass* he announces the word in "Song of the Open Road": "Here is adhesiveness;, it is not previously fashioned, it is apropos." "Adhesiveness" was a term used in phrenology to imply nonsexual friendship. Whitman uses it differently. His use is not a borrowing, for he insists it is "not previously fashioned." It is a new word with a new meaning that signifies manly love. The word is apropos, for it suggests daily experience and the unspoken sexual signs exchanged between strangers: "Do you know what it is as you pass to be loved by strangers? / Do you know the talk of those turning eye-balls?" This "talk" is the language of adhesiveness, and only men like him are fluent in it.

In the *Calamus* poems in 1860 Whitman again takes up the theme of manly love and looks for words to describe it. In "Proto-leaf," which introduced the third edition, he sings the "song of companionship . . . a new ideal of manly friendship" to be enunciated in the "new evangel-poem of lovers and comrades." Here "adhesiveness" is described to a comrade as a "pensive aching to be together" though "you know not why and I know not why."[8] "Adhesiveness" becomes now the "word to clear one's path ahead endlessly." In *Calamus* 1 it is the word that will open to him untrodden paths that will lead him to the Calamus pond, a world where men can love men. In the Calamus garden he can "talk" at last; the word is unloosed. He is "no longer abashed"; he has escaped from the "usual adjustments and pleasures" and now has found the strength to "unbare my breast," "sound myself and love," and "utter the cry of friends" (*Calamus* 2). In the course of the *Calamus* poems he asks many important homosexual questions: "I wonder if other men ever have the like, out of the like feelings?" "Is there even one other like me?"

Whitman makes connections with other older homoerotic literary traditions in the *Calamus* poems. The literature of the past offers examples and prophecies of those lovers in *Calamus* 8: "Long I thought that knowledge alone would suffice me. . . . There I met the examples of old and new heroes—I heard of warriors and sailors, and all dauntless persons." But what most affects him is when he refers, for example, to the "brotherhood of lovers" in *Calamus* 28: "I hear of the brotherhood of lovers, how it was with them, / How together through life, through dangers, odium, unchanging, / long and long, / Through youth and through middle and old age, how unfaltering, / how affectionate and faithful they were."

He also postulates what we might now call a gay community, or at least a sexual fraternity, when he announces in *Calamus* 2 that he will "give an example to lovers." He indicates an awareness of the present and past existence of such people in *Calamus* 1 when he asserts that his songs are to be sung "for all those who are or have been young men." In *Calamus* 23 he is very much aware of the "men in other lands, yearning and pensive" who, "If I could know these men / I should love them as I love men in my own lands." His allusions to a sexual community wherein he can participate in "the mid-night orgies of young men" ("Native Moments") or catch the "frequent and swift flash of eyes offering me love" (*Calamus* 18) are enlarged by his predictions in *Calamus* 34 of a community of lovers—"I dreamed in a dream, I saw . . . the new City of Friends"—and made nearly metaphysical by his suggestion in *Calamus* 42 that there is a physiological connection—"I [can] . . . help him become eleve of mine . . . if blood like mine circle . . . in his veins."

He even intimates in *Calamus* 41 that there is a spiritual and mystical bond between men like himself: "I perceive one picking me out by secret and divine signs . . . I meant that you should discover me so, by faint indirections, / And I . . . mean to discover you by the like in you." The future, he prophesies, promises a new city of friends who "shall finally make America completely victorious, in my name," an America where "it shall be customary in all directions . . . to see manly affection" and where these lovers "shall be masters of the world under a new power." By 1860 he theorizes that love between men is far more than simply a description of a sexual event; this love signifies geographical, historical, national, political, even a spiritual and physiological community.

The first *Calamus* poem, "In Paths Untrodden," was in fact one of the last to be written. Whitman completed it shortly before he took the 1860 edition to the publisher. This poem sums up the results of the investigation that began in "The Child's Champion" and continued throughout the creation of his major texts. After the publication of the *Calamus* poems, Whitman would never produce so extensive a collection of homoerotic texts.

In "In Paths Untrodden" Whitman uses again that significant verb "project" that he first used to describe masculine landscapes when he resolves that he will sing only songs of manly attachment, "projecting" and "bequeathing hence types of athletic love." If section 28 of "Song of Myself" was a private revelation empowered by sexual discovery and announcing something yet to come, the first *Calamus* poem celebrates a public epiphany. It announces a new intention empowered by his recognition that homosexual life is not only sexual but social, defined not only by sexuality but by sensibility—the "substantial life" that "contains all the rest." This life is a lifeline, connecting him to every other man, those living then, those who will read him, those who read him now:

> In paths untrodden
> In the growth by the margins of pond waters,
> Escaped from the life that exhibits itself,
> From all the standards, hitherto published—from the pleasures, profits, conformities,
> Which too long I was offering to feed my Soul;
> Clear to me now, standards not yet published—clear to me that my Soul,
> That the soul of the man I speak for rejoices in comrades,
> Here by myself away from the clank of the world,
> Tallying and talk'd to by tongues aromatic,
> No longer abash'd, (for in this secluded spot I can respond as I would not dare elsewhere,)
> Strong upon me the life that does not exhibit itself, yet contains all the rest,
> Resolv'd to sing no songs today but those of manly attachment,
> Projecting them along that substantial life,
> Bequeathing hence types of athletic love,
> Afternoon this delicious Ninth-month in my forty-first year,
> I proceed for all who are or have been young men,
> To tell the secret of my nights and days,
> To celebrate the need of comrades.

In a twentieth-century phrase this poem records what we call "coming out." Like *Don Leon* it details the speaker's acceptance of his homosexuality and the recognition of a homosexual identity, and again like *Don Leon* it asserts the poet's determination to use his art in the service of the definition and defense of manly love. Whitman speaks from a site found only by walking roads taken by no other poet, leading to what is a hidden and also a sacred precinct by the "margins of pond waters." This is the same pond he will describe in *Calamus* 3, from which he plucks the Calamus root that he will give as a token to lovers. This site is that same Arcadia Byron sought when he went to Greece, a haven far from locales where homosexual love is prohibited. Here Whitman can escape from the heterosexual life he sees as being opposed to the hidden life of homosexuality. The exhibited life has long established "standards"—laws and prohibitions—as well as "pleasures"—accepted forms of sexual desire—and most of all "conformities"—a code of majority social and sexual conduct—that he has for too long unquestioningly followed. Indeed, these have been accepted as the only moral and spiritual sustenance with which "too long" he was "offering to feed my soul."

The standards that proscribe homosexuality and demand conformity to a single code of sexual conduct no longer provide him with meaning or nourishment. He is aware of the impelling need to seek a new world, a new life, and a different kind of sustenance. He transfers the metaphor of spiritual sustenance from its original site in the symbolism and doctrine of Christianity, where sustenance is provided by faith and the holy food of Communion, into the theology of his new homoerotic faith. There the new standards and the soul-nourishing food will be found in the love of comrades. In the 1860 version this is clear, for there "the soul of the man I speak for, feeds, rejoices only in comrades." In this new world there are new "standards not yet published."

He must still deal, however, with homophobic prohibitions. Aware that the desires and the standards he wishes to publish cannot yet safely be announced, he has journeyed to the hidden pond where his doctrine can be fully be expressed "by myself, away from the clank of the world." Society not only forbids his acts but even his words and so he has sought a "secluded spot," where "I can respond as I would not dare elsewhere." In this mysterious grove he hears mystic voices—"tongues aromatic"—the voice of the Calamus itself, and this mystical voice inspires him and gives him a revelatory vision of "the life that does not exhibit itself, / yet contains all the rest." This is the most profound of Whitman's definitions of homosexuality, for in it he invokes one of the dominant themes of homoerotic literature—namely, that homosexual desire is not merely a sexual component of the individual but a profound psychic and spiritual condition that defines and controls the self; it is an identity in and of itself.

Michel Foucault has described homosexuality as "everywhere present in [the man]. . . . It [is] consubstantial with him . . . a singular nature." Whitman's invocation of a "life that does not exhibit itself" recognizes this singular nature and his assertion that it "contains all the rest" is the first modern definition of homosexual identity. The metaphor of feeding dominates here too, for he feeds not only on homosexual life but also on the phallic root. It has become his Eucharistic food, and from it he has derived the power to reject not only sexual and social conformity but also all the other themes of his poetry in favor of the one overriding poetic obsession. He determines to "sing no songs today but those of manly attachment."

But even as he makes this decision to do this "today," he also realizes that there is more to this than immediate utterance. He has a responsibility to history, to "all those who are or have been young men." And so he envisions a sexually charged continuum, extending from himself back into the past and ahead into the future, along which are ranged all the young men who share in his sexual desire. To them he will "project . . . types of athletic love." In the coded world of Whitman's texts "young men" are always icons of homoerotic desire, while "athletic" signifies not only strength and prowess but manly love itself. What he will bequeath them he will project along a "substantial life"—an image that suggests not only a personal but a historical vision. The "types" he will bequeath are his poems themselves. In them he will reveal the secret that dominates him not only in dream, fantasy, and desire but in the active and waking day, in all aspects of his life. Whitman admits proudly what he desires and insists that these desires define not only his actions but the fabric of his soul and that this soul spoke to the souls of others, defining them as a community of lovers and asserting a common identity that might change the world.

Though Whitman was determined to create homoerotic texts, he was also very much aware that such a creation would take place in a hostile climate. As early as 1841 in "The Child's Champion" Whitman had recognized that the "forms of custom" can "smother" the "wish to love and be loved." In the story he hoped that this wish could "burst forth in spite of all obstacles . . . and burn with a lovely and pure brightness" (EPF, 74). By 1860 he had determined "to tell the secrets of my nights and days." But the homophobic specter exemplified by Rufus Griswold's 1855 review still hovered, so much so that in 1870 Whitman could warn another enthusiastic young writer whose tales were also drenched in homoeroticism that homophobia was a powerful and dangerous presence. This writer was Charles Warren Stoddard, who invoked Whitman "In the name of CALAMUS" as he was about to set sail for his own happy valley where he hoped to "get in amongst people who are not afraid of instincts." Stoddard recorded his sojourn there in his *South-*

Seas Idyls (1873), which Whitman had read, describing the book as "beautiful and soothing."

Whitman warns Stoddard, however, that "I do not of course object to your emotional & adhesive nature, & and the outlet thereof [by which he means the sex with men that Stoddard had euphemistically but certainly described], but warmly approve them," yet "do you know (perhaps you do,) how the hard, pungent, gritty, worldly experiences & qualities of American practical life also serve? how they prevent extravagant sentimentalism" (*CWW*, 2: 97). Whitman's warnings to Stoddard in 1870 may reflect disillusionment with the possibility that the free love of comrades might be realized and fear and disappointment that the homoerotic aesthetic he had tried to construct had not only been misunderstood but been labeled perversion. So when the English critic J. A. Symonds wrote to Whitman in 1890 asking directly whether his poems could be construed to advocate homosexual affections and the physical realization of such affections, Whitman's response, at once explosive and cautious, suggests his own fear that his texts will cast a dangerous shadow on his life—a fear that later biographers, eager to absolve Whitman of homosexuality or eager to prove it, have perhaps not taken enough into account. The discomfort imposed by the sexual "conformities" of such a "hard, pungent, gritty" world is of course what Whitman in his *Calamus* fantasy was determined to escape from.

Whitman stood at the beginning of that discourse that Foucault identifies as that in which the sodomite, who had been a "temporary aberration," became a member of a homosexual "species." Foucault dates this category from 1870. Whitman forecast this sensibility and contributed to its identification as early as 1840, describing it in *Calamus* 1 (1860) as the "substantial life" that does not "exhibit itself yet contains all the rest." Whitman seems to be well aware that provocative texts embodying discourse at once secret, forbidden, and necessarily indirect were potent agents for calling into life the very society they hopefully and effectually prophesied. The terms he creates—"manly friendship," "the young men" of the states, and "men like me"—create in their turn a community of desire sharing a sexual, social, and psychological condition and perhaps even a specific historical consciousness.

Speaking "outside of" the world of the common reader, Whitman's coded formulas can be deciphered to read: difference, separateness, and perhaps even awareness of oppression. Here is the conviction that such desire defined even the minor acts of daily life and that the breath of manly love must be translated into the active weapons of words. When Whitman described manly love as "the life that does not exhibit itself yet contains all the rest" he joined that formula to that other definition from

Calamus 6 that forecasts identities and sensibility: "O adhesiveness! O pulse of my life!" The "secret of my nights and days" that Whitman was determined to reveal was immediately recognized by English writers like J. A. Symonds and Edward Carpenter, who were eagerly listening for the announcement of a program in which homosexual love was to be an instrument for spiritual growth, social change, and political reform.

Frederick Leighton's *Study of a Nude* is representative of Victorian England's tastes for art depicting figures from antiquity. The painting's unmistakable homoerotic nature, however, was not part of the cultural dialogue.

chapter 5

WAKING UP ENGLAND: WHITMAN AND ENGLISH HOMOEROTIC TEXTS, 1868

I can't help wishing you should know that there are many here in England to
whom your writings have been as the waking up of a new day.
—Edward Carpenter to Walt Whitman (1874)

English authors of literature that celebrated and romanticized
desire between males were surely on the watch for writers who felt as they
did and were keenly aware of any nuance in a text, however subtle, that suggested empathy with their desires. To find Walt Whitman English writers
may have had to look geographically far, but they did not have to look hard.
Some English readers had already encountered Whitman. John Addington
Symonds read Whitman's poems in 1860 and called it an epiphany. But
more discovered Whitman in 1868 when a selection of his poems appeared
in England, edited by William Michael Rosetti. By the latter part of the century Whitman's name, as Richard Dellamora shows in *Masculine Desire: The
Sexual Politics of Victorian Aestheticism*, had become, for poets like Algernon
Charles Swinburne in the 1860s and Gerard Manley Hopkins in the 1880s, a
signifier for erotic desire between men.[1]

Whitman's homoerotic texts were more immediately recognized and more
influential in England than in America. Symonds, who had read Plato at 18
and described it as a revelatory experience clarifying his sexual desires,
encountered a second revelatory literary experience that was to shape his
perceptions of homosexuality. Symonds had already embarked on a career as
a writer of homoerotic verse, and he would eventually become one of the
major spokesmen for homosexuality in England. But in 1865, at 25, Symonds

was electrified when he first encountered Whitman's *Calamus* lines: "One who loves me is jealous of me and withdraws from me all but love . . . I am indifferent to my own songs—I will go with him I love, / it is enough for us that we are together—We never separate again." Symonds describes the experience in his memoirs:

> This fine poem, omitted from later editions of *Leaves of Grass*, formed part of "Calamus." The book became for me a sort of Bible. Inspired by "Calamus" I adopted another method of palliative treatment, and tried to invigorate the emotion [homosexual desire] I could not shake off by absorbing Whitman's conception of comradeship. The process of assimilation was not without its bracing benefit. My desires grew manlier, more defined, more direct, more daring by contact with "Calamus." I imbibed a strong democratic enthusiasm, a sense of the dignity and beauty and glory of simple healthy men. . . . I can now declare with sincerity that my abnormal inclinations, modified by Whitman's idealism and penetrated with his democratic enthusiasm, have brought me into close and profitable sympathy with human beings even as I have sinned against law and conventional morality.[2]

From the moment he read *Calamus*, Symonds's life would be intertwined with Whitman's. Reading Whitman galvanized Symonds's intellectual and sexual perception of homosexuality. His comments indicate that he sees homosexual desire as more than just a consummation of a sex act; it is a state of mind and a feeling shared by a distinct community of men, a homosexual identity. It is clear that Symonds was bedeviled by his desires—he called them "abnormal inclinations"—and the sense of guilt that went with them. Whether he embraced sexual liberation in general or his friend Roden Noel in particular at that time is not clear, but one positive result did arise from his reading: "The immediate result of this study of Walt Whitman was the determination to write a history of paiderastia in Greece and to attempt a theoretical demonstration of the chivalrous enthusiasm which seemed to me implicit in comradeship" (Symonds, 189). Symonds was then set on a course of work that produced the works he forecast. These were the essays "A Problem in Greek Ethics" (1883) and "The Dantesque and Platonic Ideal of Love" (1893), both of which begin to chronicle homoerotic desire.

Symonds may have been among only a few to discover Whitman in 1865, but by 1868 the poet's name was known in England—at least to those who wanted to know—because of Rosetti's blue volume of selections of Whitman's work, including some of the *Calamus* poems. This drew the attention of a larger following and began the process of canonization by a group of disciples—largely homosexual men—who looked on Whitman as a prophet of sexual freedom and a delineator of a new sexual identity. Rosetti had been introduced to Whitman's poetry in 1856. This came about because, after the almost total failure of the first edition in America, Whitman's publishers sent copies to England to be sold. One Thomas Dixon, a cork cutter working in Sunderland, bought at an auction a remaindered copy of the 1855 edition. Dixon had also founded a school of art and a library. He showed the book to his friend, William Bell Scott, a minor poet and a friend of Rosetti. Bell then sent a copy to Rosetti.

Rosetti was apparently impressed by the work and started to praise it to his friends. Then, in 1866, he received a copy of the 1866 edition of *Leaves of Grass* and a book by Whitman's American friend and disciple William Burroughs, called *Notes on Walt Whitman Poet and Person*. Rosetti read Burroughs and also the new edition that included the *Calamus* poems. In July 1867 Rosetti wrote an article about Whitman in which he described *Leaves of Grass* as comparable to Greek poetry and Shakespeare. By then there was enough interest in Whitman to prompt Rosetti to publish a selected edition of Whitman's work. This he did in 1868, though some of the more sexually explicit or homoerotically suggestive poems, among them "Song of Myself" and most of *Calamus*, were not included. Nevertheless, the little book in blue covers was to win Whitman more fame in England than he had yet achieved in America (see Allen, 382–88).

Perhaps because his friend Symonds had read Whitman or because everyone seemed to be doing so, Roden Noel also had become a disciple. He was so impressed that he wrote the essay "A Study of Walt Whitman" that appeared in an Oxford University magazine, *Dark Blue*, in October 1871. It does not have the distinction of being the first essay on Whitman written in England—several had been written after 1866—but it may have the distinction of being the first written by a man whose desires and practices were actively homosexual. Noel is rumored to have been the man who introduced Symonds to homosexual sex, and perhaps because of Noel's study—or at least at the same time it appeared—Symonds began his correspondence with Whitman, writing his first letter in October 1871 and enclosing a copy of a long poem, dedicated to Whitman, called "Love and Death: A Symphony." The poem begins by observing that Symonds has "too long . . . refrained." It is soon clear that he feels he has too long refrained from speaking about comradeship and homoerotic love, for he envisions a world in which "there shall be comrades thick as flowers," and he invokes as his muse a "friend, brother, comrade, lover!"[3] Whitman refrained from answering until the end of January 1872, but when he did he thanked Symonds for his "beautiful and elevated" poem that "I have read and reread . . . & consider it of the loftiest, strongest & tenderest" (*CWW*, 2: 158–59). Whitman had already written in *Calamus* that he hoped the world would consider him to be the "tenderest lover."

In the meantime the leaven of Whitman's poetry was working. One of those who had read Rosetti's blue book in 1869—and may have been alerted by such titles supplied by Rosetti as "Love of Comrades"—was Edward Carpenter. Carpenter recalls in his memoir, *My Days and Dreams* (1916), that "it was not till (at the age of twenty-five) I read Whitman—and then with a great leap of joy—that I met with the treatment of sex which accorded with my sentiments." Because of that reading "a profound change set in within me . . . what made me cling to the little blue book from the beginning was largely the poems which celebrate comradeship. That thought, so near and personal to me, I had never before seen or heard fairly expressed."[4] Carpenter, who had been ordained an Anglican priest in 1870 and published in 1873 his first volume of poetry, *Narcissus and Other Poems*, which contained minor poetry with homoerotic insinuations, suddenly determined to reject the past and begin a new life.

Whether it was his reading of Whitman's poems or a combination of this and the dim and straitened prospects that lay ahead of him as a clergyman, Carpenter abandoned this vocation in 1874 and a new life devoted to the defense of radical social causes, among them feminism and the acceptance of homosexuality. He began his new life, like Symonds, by also beginning a correspondence with Whitman in 1874. In one of the first letters he told Whitman that "I can't help wishing you should know that there are many here in England to whom your writings have been as the waking up to a new day." He went on to specify just what dawning was at hand: "Because you have, as it were, given me a ground for the love of men I thank you continually in my heart. . . . For you have made men to be not ashamed of the noblest instinct of their nature. Women are beautiful; but, to some there is that which passes the love of women."[5] "That" which passes the love of women is of course homosexuality, and Carpenter would not wait long to carry his message personally to Whitman in America, doing so in 1877.

Out of this visit would come the final impetus for Carpenter's Whitmanesque long poem *Towards Democracy* that he began in 1880 and published in 1883. The publication of this poem contributed perhaps in some ways more than did the publication of Whitman's poetry, for *Towards Democracy* was taken up by a group of young poets who were beginning their own labors in the 1880s. These writers sometimes called themselves Uranians and in their works celebrated homosexual love, between men and between men and boys. They had derived their name from the writings of the German Karl Heinrich Ulrichs, author of numerous pamphlets on homosexuality in which he employed the word "Urning" to denote homosexuality. They also derived a good deal of support from Symonds, whose reading of Whitman allowed him to reach out to other writers who he saw as fellow surveyors of special masculine landscapes.

A reader of Carpenter's Whitmanesque poem was the sex researcher Havelock Ellis. Though not himself homosexual, Ellis was to become nevertheless fascinated by homosexuality, in part on account of his lesbian wife, in part perhaps because of the increasing presence of it in medical discussions, among them Richard von Kraft-Ebing's German language *Psychopathia Sexualis* (1886), on which Ellis would in part model his *Studies in the*

Psychology of Sex (1897). In 1889 Ellis wrote an essay on Whitman that he included in his book *The New Spirit*. Though not directly dealing with Whitman's homosexuality, the essay did draw the attention of Symonds, who wrote to Ellis and brought up the subject of homosexuality. Though the two men never met, their correspondence, occasioned by Whitman, did lead to an agreement in 1892 to collaborate on what would become volume 2 of Ellis's *Studies*, an inquiry about homosexuality called *Sexual Inversion* (1897). Symonds, one of the first to use the word "homosexuality," published in 1891 "A Problem in Modern Ethics"—a result, as he pointed out, of Whitman's fertilization of Symonds's mind. Appearing in only a few privately printed copies, this essay is the first in modern times to summarize the most progressive—and hence sympathetic—views of homosexuality, and to argue for a change in the laws that by then had criminalized the very existence of homosexuals.

Over a 20-year period Symonds had continued his correspondence with Whitman in an attempt to get him to commit himself to a personal statement about his homosexuality. Symonds would puzzle over whether what he felt and practiced was indeed also felt and practiced by Whitman. His curiosity reached a culmination in his famous letter to the poet in 1890 asking "in your conception of comradeship, do you contemplate the possible intrusion of those semi-sexual emotions and actions which no doubt occur between men?" (*CWW*, 5: 72). When Whitman resoundingly denied that it was so—though almost all readers now see Whitman's denial as another chapter in a process of self-censorship (prompted perhaps by his awareness that homosexuality had become a topic dangerously much on the public mind)—Symonds determined to find out if the text could provide the answer that the poet would not.

In 1893 Symonds published *Walt Whitman: A Study*, the first full-scale and the most perceptive assessment of Whitman written in England. Finally, Symonds and Ellis's *Sexual Inversion* was published in 1897, four years after Symonds's death. In it his "A Problem in Greek Ethics" (privately printed in only 10 copies in 1883) became the first full-length study of Greek homosexuality to be made available to a larger public.

Whitman's influence can be seen to extend across the entire period, touching writers and texts, embracing and inspiring them. Whitman's writings are among the central discourses of the nineteenth century relative to homosexuality, not only because of what Whitman wrote but because of the way his person and his writings were interpreted by homosexual writers. Thus, as Symonds recognized in his book on Whitman, it is in a sense of no moment what Whitman intended, no matter that in the end Whitman denied what he had all his life advocated. What is of greater importance is what Whitman as a signifier for homosexuality became, and with what kind of interpretive and erotic subtexts this signifier was invested. Whitman stands at a focal center of this study; to know him is to know the subject itself.

Readers who leafed through Rosetti's book might well be alerted to a special content by the titles of some of the *Calamus* poems Rosetti did include. In the 1860 edition Whitman had simply numbered these poems. In the next edition (1866–67) he titled them by their first lines. Rosetti kept some of Whitman's titles, but others he made if anything more pointed, emphasizing their homoerotic content with titles like "To Working Men," "The Friend," "Parting Friends," "The City of Friends," and "Love of Comrades." The selection contained enough of the *Calamus* poems to convince those alerted by the titles that something very special that spoke to a decided homosexual sensibility was contained between the blue covers of the book. Homosexual readers of Rosetti's edition in 1868 would not have encountered the radically sexualized lines of "Song of Myself" unless, like Symonds, they had extended their study by procuring the 1860 edition containing the complete *Leaves of Grass* with the *Calamus* poems. Had they done so they would have been perhaps perplexed—and excited—by Whitman's impressionistic description of an act of homosexual sex in section 26 of "Song of Myself."

One Whitman poem, titled "Appearances" by Rosetti, was in fact *Calamus* 7. In this poem Whitman asserted that the "terrible question of appearances" and indeed of all the uncertainties that life and death offer are answered by "my lovers, my dear friends," but most especially "when he who I love travels with me, or sits a long while / holding me by the hand . . . . then I am charged with untellable wisdom . . . He ahold of my hand has completely satisfied me."

In "The Friend"—Rosetti's title is more homoerotically suggestive than Whitman's "Recorders Ages Hence" (*Calamus* 10), in an age when "friend" had already begun to acquire specific homoerotic implications—Whitman asks history to remember him as "the tenderest lover," one who "often walked lonesome walks thinking of his dear friends, his lovers / Who pensive, away from one he loved, often lay sleepless and dissatisfied at night, / Who knew too well the sick dread lest the one he loved might secretly be indifferent to him, / Whose happiest days were . . . wandering hand in hand . . . / Who oft as he sauntered the streets, curved with his arm the shoulder of his friend—while the arm of his friend rested upon him also." It is likely that Symonds would have responded to the sick dread Whitman described, for in a poem written in 1861 Symonds had described his own sick dread, "with love far off and joy beyond my scope," when he was unable because of his fears about homosexuality to respond when a young man "passed / Before the house with wondering wide blue eye / That said 'I wait: why will you not reply?'"

Also among the poems in Rosetti's selection was one Rosetti called "Meeting Again"—the exquisite lyric "When I heard at Close of Day" (*Calamus* 11)—that concludes, "the one I love lay sleeping by me . . . / his face was inclined toward me, / And his arm lay lightly about my breast—and that night I was happy." In addition to these, the book also offered other detailed scenes of intimate relations between male lovers, as in "Parting Friends"—Whitman's "What Think you I take my Pen in Hand" (*Calamus* 32). In this poem Whitman describes "two simple men . . . parting the parting of dear friends; / The one to remain hung on the other's neck and kissed him, / While the one to depart tightly pressed the one to remain in his arms." Perhaps because of the freedom forecast by such suggestively homoerotic texts as these, just five years later Lord Francis Harvey in a poem called "Song" was able to write about male-male love without equivocation: "His lips touched mine, O Joy, O Bliss! / The wind sang in the tree; I knew his long-drawn rapturous kiss, / I felt his wild, wild, burning kiss:—O joy! he loveth me" (quoted in Reade, 142).

Rosetti's selections also presented the Whitman who saw beyond the intimacies of love and looked more deeply into the mysteries of sex, detailing the insistent demands of homosexual desire as well as the lure of anonymous sex itself. In "Passing Stranger" (*Calamus* 22) Whitman tells the stranger, "you do not know how longingly I look upon you" and confesses "I am to think of you when I sit alone, or wake at night alone, / I am to wait—I do not doubt I am to meet you again, / I am to see to it that I do not lose you." The passing strangers Whitman desired revealed themselves in special ways, by a secret semiotics that must have struck responding chords in an age in which Frederick Faber could write in his poem "Half a Heart," "I warn thee, do not think my fitful love untrue: / I have another, darker self, / Which thou must sometimes view" (quoted in Reade, 67).

Whitman recognized that homosexual men had another and sometimes a darker self concealed behind the necessary facade. He discerns this other self in one seen in a crowd: "I perceive one picking me out by secret and divine signs . . . some are baffled—But that one is not—that one knows me. / A lover perfect and equal! / I meant that you should discover me so, by my faint indirections; and I, when I meet you, mean to discover you by the like in you." This hint that homosexuals reveal themselves to one another in special ways that the other world cannot fathom, that they form a confraternity is a theme that echoes often in the poetry of this period. But Whitman, so even these few selections show, had determined not only to be the poet of sexual difference but also to celebrate as well a social and political difference created by sexual difference. His vision of a worldwide brotherhood of lovers directly attacks the old notion of the solitary and individual sodomite and sinner and celebrates a new sexual politics in which the homosexual stands not for furtive and abhorrent desires but for a new social manifesto proclaiming equality and sexual freedom, at least among men.

Whitman asserts in "Other Lands" (*Calamus* 23, "This Moment Yearning and Thoughtful") that "there are other men in other lands" and that "if I could know these men . . . I know we should be brethren and lovers." He has other even more powerful visions in a poem that Rosetti titled—again more pointedly than Whitman's own title—"The City of Friends" (*Calamus* 34, "I

Dreamed in a Dream"). There Whitman has a vision of a "city invincible to the attacks of the whole rest of the earth; / I dreamed that it was the new City of Friends; / Nothing was greater there than the quality of robust love."

This nation of lovers is further described in *Calamus* 5 that Whitman called "A Song" but that Rosetti titled "Love of Comrades." It is among Whitman's most powerfully visionary political statements. In this homoerotic commonwealth "the love of Comrades," will make the "continent indissoluble." Whitman intends to "make inseparable cities, with their arms about each others necks," and these cities will be created "by the love of comrades" and if there is any doubt as to the gender of these comrades he adds: "By the manly love of comrades." Rosetti also chose to include three other *Calamus* poems in his selection. These are numbers 3, 4, 6, perhaps the most mystical and sexually charged of the group. *Calamus* 3, which Whitman had called "Whoever you are, holding me Now in Hand," Rosetti called "Fit Audience." The poem warns readers of the unique and possibly dangerous consequences of reading Whitman's poems and subscribing to his homoerotic project. "I am not what you supposed" Whitman warns. He cautions that he who would be a "candidate for my affections" must be prepared to travel an "uncertain, perhaps destructive" path; "the whole past theory of your life, and all conformity to lives around you, would have to be abandoned." If, however, they are willing to declare themselves homosexual comrades, then "here to put your lips upon mine I permit you, / with the comrade's long dwelling kiss." Even this sacrament, however, is useless, finally, unless the disciple "guess at that which I hinted"—that is, the primacy and power of homosexual love and the necessity to translate that love into sexual and political action. In *Calamus* 2, "Singing in Spring," Whitman introduces the Calamus image itself, calling the Calamus root "the token of comradeship." This token is sacramental; he commands that his comrade disciples "interchange it, youths, with each other."

If, finally, there could be any doubt as to the intent of these poems and as to the homoeroticism of them, Rosetti included Whitman's statement about the place of "adhesiveness," his special word for homosexual love. This is found in a poem Rosetti calls "Pulse of My Life" and that Whitman called "Not heaving from my Ribbed Breast Only." In this poem Whitman's thesis is that homosexual desire is the foundation of his emotional life. He is afflicted with various kinds of discontent and emotional upheaval—"ill suppressed sighs," the "beating and pounding at my temples," a "hungry wish" and "husky pantings." But of all of these his homosexual feelings, what he calls "adhesiveness," are the strongest. Adhesiveness is not only the central theme of his art but the very pulsing life blood of his existence, and it must, he insists, "show itself" in order to exercise its power in life and in art. Whitman's poetry, of course, is in scope far more extensive than what Rosetti selected, in homoerotic context more complex than was hinted at by the few selections Rosetti provided. But for men like Symonds and

Carpenter, who were themselves trying to define a homosexual identity in their lives and work, these texts proffered a precious gift of revelation and raised a flag to follow into what was to become both a celebration and a battle.

Simeon Solomon's drawing, *Bridegroom and Sad Love*, might well have been an illustration for Alfred Douglas's "Two Loves."

chapter 6

THE NEW CHIVALRY: POETRY AND PORNOGRAPHY, 1850–1895

I am the love that dare not speak its name.
—Lord Alfred Douglas, "Two Loves" (1894)

The December 1894 issue of the little undergraduate magazine *The Chameleon* (the only issue to be published) contained among its suspiciously erotic poems Alfred Douglas's poem "Two Loves," which provided what was to be perhaps the most famous brief description of homosexual love yet written. The response from one of the guardians of respectable culture, Jerome K. Jerome, writing in his own newspaper, *To-Day*, was immediate and damning: "The publication appears to be nothing more nor less than an advocacy for indulgence in the cravings of an unnatural disease. . . . This magazine is an . . . outrage on literature. . . . It can serve no purpose but that of evil. It can please no man or woman with a single grain of self-respect left in their souls."[1]

Such was the public response to a group of texts that began to appear in increasing number midway through the century and that, in one fashion or another, advocate the possibility that one man might kiss the lips of another. Many of those who had produced these texts, however, were no longer willing to nominate their desire as "indulgence in the cravings of an unnatural disease" or to subscribe to the terms or the history inscribed in that phrase. Rather, by the time of Jerome's diatribe the large aim, and in part the achievement, of their work was to erase such terms from the discourses that had begun to define and reflect what these men imagined themselves to be.

Writers determined to create homoerotic texts or to address questions having to do with homosexuality always had with them a prohibitive context that demanded secrecy, counseled evasion, and warned that what they wrote was forbidden and quite possibly dangerous. They published their works in private or limited editions, passed them from hand to hand among friends, or saw them appear in such specialized publications as the Oxford magazine *The Spirit Lamp*, which made a brief appearance as edited by Alfred Douglas, or the more short-lived *Chameleon*, or in *The Artist and Journal of Home Culture*, in which amidst the articles on modern art Charles Kains Jackson occasionally inserted poems and fiction dealing with homoerotic themes. To disguise the intent of the text, writers sometimes—though not always, and increasingly less so toward the end of the century—couched their works in evasive and sometimes coded language in order to allow those who could break the code to feel secure in their participation in a special textual confraternity of knowing readers. Produced, disseminated, and exchanged under a cloud of prohibition and yet responding to the developing discourses that were beginning to redefine sex and sexuality in the widest sense, these texts are one of the most significant bodies of literature concerned with homosexuality published in English or any language up to that time. These texts constitute the source and the site of the literary construction of homosexual identities—a construction that to this day galvanizes and in large part shapes our definitions of homosexuality.

NAMING THE UNNAMEABLE: THE EMERGENCE OF THE "HOMOSEXUAL"

In 1861 England abolished the death penalty for the act of buggery—anal intercourse specifically—but sodomitical offenses were still punishable by 10 years to life imprisonment. In fact, England had the most stringent laws in Europe against sodomy, continuing the prosecution of those apprehended in sodomitical offenses as well as raids on known homosexual gathering places that had been a periodic feature of the control of sodomites since the early part of the eighteenth century. Such legal repression contributed to self-censorship in word and deed by almost anyone whose predilection, as the *Don Leon* poet said, was for males. In 1885 the Labouchere Amendment of the Criminal Law Amendment Act was passed, making illegal "any act of gross indecency" between two males, but so unspecific was that "any" that it also criminalized, in effect, not only homosexual act but homosexual speech.[2] Such criminalization might have cast an anticipatory pall over any utterance concerned with homosexuality in any form. While it is remarkable that such a work as *Don Leon* was written in 1833, it is even more remarkable, given that the situation of men who loved men did not improve but got worse as the century advanced, that there began to appear a literature that powerfully and publicly not only defined but advocated sexual difference.

The 1860s saw the appearance of the word "homosexual" and of Whitman's homoerotic *Calamus* poems. In 1866 a limited edition of the earliest printed survival of *Don Leon* was published by William Dugdale. This decade not only saw the reappearance of *Don Leon* but the composition and in some instances the publication of homoerotic verse by such writers as Algernon Charles Swinburne, John Addington Symonds, Gerard Manley Hopkins, and Frederick Faber. In 1866 Swinburne published *Poems and Ballads* in which two of the poems, "Fragoletta" and "Hermaphroditus" (1863), "created poetic fantasies of male-male genital activity" (Dellamora, 69). The appearance of Swinburne's poems, as Richard Dellamora argues, "moved the discussion of sexual difference" substantially closer to a more general public discourse. (Dellamora, 102).

When, in 1867, Walter Pater published an essay on the German homosexual aesthete and historian of Greek art Johannes Wincklemann, he opened that discourse even more and advocated an ideal of culture founded not on aesthetics alone but on a point of intersection between the sexual and the aesthetic in which this sexualized aesthetic could also be read as decidedly homoerotic (see Dellamora, 102 and passim). When Symonds discovered Whitman in 1865 and was galvanized by his reading into a kind of intellectual and spiritual coming out, and by the time a selection of Whitman's poems appeared in William Michael Rosetti's edition in 1868, several of the key events that can be described as substantially contributing to definitions of homosexual identity and to the formation of a definitive homosexual literature had occurred—in time and seemingly in preparation for Karoly Benkert, a Swiss doctor and homosexual apologist, to coin the word "homosexual" in 1869.

Lord Alfred Douglas asserted in 1894 that homosexuality is the love that dared not speak its name. He was, of course, writing a homosexual version of the legal formula that defined homosexuality as the vice not to be named. By this time discourse attempting to define love between men had become even more active and had adopted "homosexuality" to indicate a species of activity practiced by "homosexuals" (Katz 1976, 148). The medical literature out of which "homosexual" grew was beginning to change the definition of homosexuality, moving it away from religion and the law and into the realm of pathology. Thus, by 1913, for example, E. M. Forster could have the hero of his novel *Maurice*, not yet come to terms with his sexuality, describe himself to a doctor as "an unspeakable of the Oscar Wilde sort."[3] In consulting his doctor and not his priest, Maurice attested that homosexuality had become, according to most medical definitions of the period, a pathology and a "condition," a deviation from the "normal," a manifestation of an unsound mind—indeed, a perversion of sexuality. So urgent had become the need to define what society so furiously abhorred and punished that names for this not-to-be-named condition had began to proliferate. By the time of Douglas's 1894 poem, homosexuality probably had more epithets applied to it than any other minority.

As Symonds wrote in 1891 in "A Problem in Modern Ethics," "The accomplished languages of Europe in the nineteenth century supply no terms for this persistent feature of human psychology, without importing some implication of disgust, disgrace, vituperation."[4] "Sodomite" and "buggerer" were still primary terms; biblical and classical euphemisms enlarged on these in the later seventeenth to early nineteenth centuries, describing homosexuals as "men who lie with men," "monsters in human shape" "catamites" "boy lovers," or as practitioners of "abomination," "unnatural filthiness," "foul sin," or "debauchery." By the early nineteenth century "sodomite" and "pederast" were joined by terms describing those who practiced "degradation," "perversion," and "depravity," while popular slang—some derived from prostitution, both male and female—added other terms of effeminization to the very early "queen" and "molly," among them "Madge-cull," "Marianne," "Mollycoddle," and "Hermaphrodite." Medical studies and homosexual apologia added "invert," "intersexual," "similisexual," "third sex," "androgyne," "Uranian," and of course "homosexual."

The late nineteenth and early twentieth century may have contributed more words of disapprobation than any previous period, adding "counterjumper," "queer," "pervert," "fairy," "fag," "faggot," "pansy," "pouf," "musical," "that way" (from the French *comme ça*), "nelly," and "homo." "Gay"—though deriving from nineteenth century prostitution—did not become fixed (and then primarily in American usage) until the late 1940s. Even as I write, "queer" is undergoing another change, part of the process, it might be theorized, of co-opting the oppressor's terminology for the use of the oppressed, and is being renegotiated by gay and lesbian theorists to valorize not only male-male love but an entire spectrum of identities and sexualities that transgresses against heterosexuality and "middle-class" sexual and social norms.

TOWARD A HOMOEROTIC LITERARY STYLE

If homosexuality had found names in England, it had also begun to create texts and an imaginative literature that defined and defended homosexual life and sensibility. This literature also had begun to construct a literary homoerotic style—one that at once reflected personal style and also created it. The speaker of *Don Leon* is a literate and thoughtful rake, concerned with a social problem and certainly aware of a larger dimension to sodomy than just the sexual, but his tone is nevertheless that of a rake, whose personal style is still largely defined by the desire for and the achievement of sexual conquest. But the speakers in William Cory's lyrics of 1858 and in Mark André Raffalovich's sonnets of 1886, regardless of the surface differences of their style, inscribe themselves within a discourse that links at least one form of nineteenth-century aestheticism with the specifically homosexual, transforming homosexuality into a special kind of aesthetic experience and using a homoeroticized language to describe homosexual desire.

Between 1850 and the early decades of this century many hundreds of volumes of poetry, fiction, and nonfiction dealing with homosexuality were published in England alone. After 1850 it almost seems as if homosexuality became for a time *the* subject for more authors than any other. A bibliography of texts dealing with homosexual subjects written by homosexual and nonhomosexual authors in England and on the Continent would include many of the major literary figures of the time: Byron, Tennyson, Symonds, Joris-Karl Huysmans, Charles Baudelaire, Arthur Rimbaud, Honoré de Balzac, Théophile Gautier, August von Platen, Goethe, Paul Verlaine, Alexander Pushkin, C. P. Cavafy, Hopkins, Pater, Swinburne, Carpenter, Oscar Wilde, A. E. Housman, Forster, and Havelock Ellis. Whitman's hope that "there are other men in other lands, yearning and thoughtful" musing, like him, on lovers, had perhaps spontaneously arisen in the minds of many in Europe, America, and England. Whatever the cause and whatever the origin, by 1895 in both America and Europe, homosexuality had not only found a name but had founded a literature.

Later nineteenth-century homoerotic literature continued what *Don Leon* and Whitman had begun: to write transgressive texts that valorized love between men and insinuated that love into the orthodox moral and social order. But they also began to define a locale of their own, a site protected against homophobia. If socially constructed homophobia had walled them in, some homosexual writers chose not to climb over the walls but to raise them higher by accentuating rather than denying difference. If homosexuals were to be marked off from society and rejected by it, then the discourses constructed by homosexuals almost seemed determined to create a new and private world with a language, myths, manners, and ethics that could be used to define them and them alone. Sodomites, in fear for their lives, had been wary of betraying themselves and risking, literally, their necks, but the new homosexual seemed almost eager to do so, at least in the relative safety of private print.

Homoerotic literature began to construct a safe and isolated world—what Forster would describe in *Maurice* as the "greenwood" and what Bayard Taylor in *Joseph and His Friend* called the "happy valley"—places where homosexual men could escape the restrictive laws of heterosexual society. Nineteenth-century homosexual writers seemed to be animated by the demands of a powerful and not too deeply hidden desirous text, one that insisted that the most effective site for such an affirmation was in a world where the repressive codes of the dominant sexuality held no sway. This active marking of difference is the beginning of a definitively modern homosexual style.

This is not to say that nineteenth-century homoerotic texts rejected the project of law reform advocated by *Don Leon* and of sexual liberation advocated by Whitman. Both *Don Leon* and Whitman had urged that a homosex- ···¹ identity also implied homosexual freedom of action and desire. Though the Arcadian world was one such site for this freedom, both Whitman and *Don Leon* knew well enough that it was only a temporary and finally unsatisfactory site. Both *Don Leon* and Whitman asserted that homosexuality was not a negative but positive influence and hence useful for society. Only by forcing an entry into general society could that construction of the value of homosexuality be disseminated. Hence the active campaign waged, especially by Carpenter near the end of the century, to destroy or at least change repressive laws and to throw open the closet doors and tear down the edifice itself. Whitman had insisted in *Democratic Vistas* (1871) that the "threads of manly friendship" must have the "deepest relation to general politics," while in "Homogenic Love" (1894) Carpenter echoes Whitman by insisting that homosexual love "is a very important factor in society, and that its neglect, or its repression, or its vulgar misapprehension, may be matters of considerable damage to the common-weal" (quoted in Reade, 343).

Homosexual writers in the nineteenth century were influenced by several strong cultural currents, one of which was an aestheticism derived from the eighteenth-century discovery and reevaluation of Renaissance interpretations of classical texts and art, most strongly advanced in the works of Wincklemann and in England championed and fashioned into a homoeroticized discourse by Pater, first in his essay "Wincklemann" (1867) and later in his influential book *Studies in the History of the Renaissance* (1873). Among the classical texts that were becoming available to the university as well as the reading public was a substantial homoerotic literature, to be found not only in the dialogues of Plato, such as the *Phaedrus* and *Symposium*, in which homoerotic love is a basis for the discourse, but also in scattered translations of pieces from the twelfth book of the *Greek Anthology*, a repository of more than 200 homoerotic epigrams written primarily by the poets Meleager and Strato.

The discovery of such texts might be said to have disseminated a homoeroticized climate into the education of young men and even into the culture, since education was becoming available to the middle class. Homoerotic texts of all sorts increasingly deployed an eroticized vocabulary that called on classical texts, not only in the historically specific manner of earlier English literature in which relatively few allusions served as signals (a mention of Ganymede, a reference to Corydon) but in far more complex ways. Any historical, literary, or mythical association with the classical world or with the contexts of classical literature became a signifier for homoerotic content, which was conflated with highly eroticized homoerotic plots and specific verbal coding.

Another social movement that influenced and in a curious way aided the homosexualization of culture and literature was the moral purity movement, which attempted to create (and in large part succeeded) structures for the regulation of sexuality in general and homosexuality in particular. This reform discourse also contributed to a significant change in relations between the sexes that also in part effects this efflorescence of homosexual literature. The family and bourgeois codes that prohibited male-female sex as an object of discussion, creating profound social prohibitions concerning both sexual word and deed, contributed to an atmosphere in which women become increasingly unavailable as actual objects of physical and even verbal desire. Among other things effected by the moral reformers was the segregation of the sexes in education, a practice deemed to be beneficial to the maintenance of chastity.

In England all-male schools were established in addition to those at Oxford, Cambridge, Eton, and Harrow, and thus the incidence of and potential for homosexual contact increased, especially when influenced by an already homoeroticized curriculum. The dissemination of information about vice, no matter how euphemistically presented, was imagined to be an effective deterrent to it. Whether it was retailed in the popular press in the form of lurid reports of homosexual scandals or in the proliferating medical literature that purported to study homosexuality objectively or in the phobia-inducing pseudo-scientific tracts denouncing, but often describing in detail, the horrors of masturbation, prostitution, and all forms of depraved sexuality, especially sodomy, information about sexuality was extensively available. Such a furious sexual discourse set the stage for periodic outbursts of homophobia during the last decades of the century that climaxed in the trial of Oscar Wilde.

The reform movements, of course, grew out of the evangelical religious revivals that were a profound aspect of the social and religious climate at mid-century. A version of religious revival was to be found in England in the rarified though potent ideology of the Anglican Oxford Movement, especially strong at universities, that attracted to it young men who rejected the solid middle-class pieties of evangelicalism that called for the revivification of what was deemed to be lost religious and family values. Instead these young men found attractive the linkage between the sensual and mystical services and symbolism of High Church ritual, the emphasis on celibacy that translated into a kind of pious misogyny, and the vague homoeroticism that permeated the largely all-male precincts of High Anglican style.

Conflated with this religious revival was the revival of medievalism—a Gothic revival in art and architectural style and a reclamation of medieval themes and forms in literature. The world of Gothicism and of the Middle Ages in the interpretation of many young men already emotionally flirting with homosexual attachments stressed knightly comradeship and chivalry and told of a largely all-male world in which women, if they did appear, were distant objects of a static and pallid desire, and in which the real life lay in the close bonding of men in manly valor and honor. Hence in his essay "The New Chivalry" (1894) Charles Kains Jackson could describe his new chivalry as "the exaltation of the youthful masculine ideal" (quoted in Reade, 315). The new chivalry will impose "no irksome or fatuous ties" (of marriage) but will instead create new alignments in which the "ideal partnership" will be between men.

It was generally a small and highly literate group of university-affiliated writers (a privileged and protected class, it must be recognized) who produced texts expressing homoerotic desire during the period. Many of this group were unquestionably in their sexual adventures—and there should be no doubt that there were sexual adventures—cool colonizers, exploiters often of less privileged classes. And certainly many did not seriously consider or were even entirely aware of the brutalizing effects of class discrimination, although some, echoing Whitman's democratic homoeroticism, were advocates of the destruction of class barriers within sexual practice and discourses.

Few writers allocated much text to such barriers, nor is there much evidence that they were concerned with questions of race that even then had begun to enter into the sexual discourse. Their work is unquestionably bound by class, but we cannot judge and dismiss them for this. Even Whitman, who had begun the work of toppling those hierarchies, maintained an allegiance to stereotyped systems of race and gender. Still, Whitman and English homosexual writers produced texts that directly transgressed against and hurled significant challenges at the society into which they were born, and they directly confronted homophobia both as a social prejudice and legal prohibition. To dismiss them for what they did not do in the face of what they did is to dismiss a vital and contributory chapter in the creation of a homosexual identity and in the growth of a movement for homosexual liberation in the very sense that we now use that term.

THE ORIGINS OF A HOMOSEXUAL AESTHETIC SENSIBILITY

Homosexual texts appearing between 1850 and 1895 signaled the disappearance of the rakish and indiscriminate sodomite, concerned only with the gratification of desire and unaware that there might be social, aesthetic, or political implications or consequences bound up with this gratification. He was supplanted by a new man, willing despite prohibition to love men and often eager to identify himself as a member of a special group sharing and even unified by a particular sexual desire and also quite possibly loosely defined by a developing and special aesthetic, social and political position. A bibliography of English texts positively dealing with male-male love that once might have listed only *Don Leon* now could claim as major entries in the 1850s certain portions of Tennyson's *In Memoriam* (1850) and William Johnson's *Ionica* (1858).

In the 1860s a few writers began to produce texts—though perhaps not yet publish them—with titles that hinted, at least to the initiate, through their use of classical allusion, foreign-language title, or sensual phrase what they were about: Swinburne's "Hermaphroditus" (1863), Symonds's *Eudiades* (1868), and Roden Noel's "Ganymede" (1868). Pater's essay "Wincklemann" (1867) proposed that the homosexual German aesthete's "affinity with Hellenism was not merely intellectual" but that the "subtler threads of temperament" interwoven in it were derived from "his romantic, fervid friendships with young men" (quoted in Reade, 83). Pater's essay marks the start of a debate and discourse that would eventually introduce sexual difference as a component and perhaps as a basis—indeed, for Pater and some of these writers perhaps the primary component and only basis—of an "aesthetic" sensibility.

By the 1870s there were book titles like Carpenter's *Narcissus and Other Poems* (1873) and Symonds's *Lyra Viginti Cordarum* (1875), in which classical allusions to Hylas, Ganymede, and "Uranian Love" left little doubt as to what context the poet intended for the youth whose "naked form supine" Symonds described as "very white smooth and fine." Poems like Hopkins's "The Buglers First Communion" (1879) celebrated a "limber liquid youth" breathing "bloom of chastity in mansex fine" (quoted in Reade, 153), which might have alerted certain readers to a subtext that the religious primary text all but concealed. By the 1880s titles like Edward Cracroft Lefroy's "Echoes from Theocritus" (1883) firmly exploited the homoerotic-classical connection, and Raffalovich expressed the anxious emotional crossroads at which guilt and a desire for free expression intersected—an intersection at which many of these writers surely stood—when he anatomized homosexuality in "The World Well Lost XVIII" (1886) as "the passion purest of all out of Heaven, / The love in Hell least easily forgiven" (quoted in Reade, 198).

By the end of the decade and into the early years of the twentieth century, however, even despite the notoriety of the Wilde trial in 1895, numbers of books indicated that homosexuality had fully discovered a voice. Sir Richard Burton's "Terminal Essay" (1885) appended to his translation of *The Arabian Nights* was a history of homosexuality and the first essay on the subject to be published in English. Oscar Wilde's story "The Portrait of Mr. W.H." (1889–95), a speculation on the homoerotic relationship between Shakespeare and the Mr. W.H. of the sonnets, was the "first story in English published for ordinary and unlimited distribution" that involved romantic homoeroticism (Reade, 28). Symonds's essays exploring homosexuality in ancient Greece and modern Europe had been much circulated privately. Carpenter's "Homogenic Love," far from being hidden by private publication, was delivered as a public lecture in Manchester in 1894. So specific now was the voice of a homoerotic discourse that Theodore Wratislaw's poem "To a Sicilian Boy" (1893), in which he rejects the "dull ennui of a woman's kiss" (quoted in Reade, 306) for a moment in the arms of the boy, could now be published openly—albeit to considerable controversy.

Controversial too was Douglas's publication of "Two Loves" and "In Praise of Shame." In "Two Loves," a personification of both heterosexual and homosexual love, homosexual love famously but belatedly responds to the assertion by heterosexual love that his true name is "shame" by replying: "I am the love that dare not speak its name" (quoted in Reade, 362). In "In Praise of Shame" Douglas insisted that "of all sweet passions Shame is loveliest." Indeed, homosexual love almost constantly continued to speak its name. A. E. Housman's *A Shropshire Lad* (1896) becomes more firmly and clearly situated in a homoerotic context when John Gambril Nicholson's *A Garland of Ladslove* (1911), John Barford's *Ladslove Lyrics* (1919), and Edwin Edwinson's anthology *Men and Boys* (1924) is associated with it. Finally, Aleister Crowley's poems published in *White Stains* (1898), including one that concludes "Ah! you come—you kill me! / Christ! God! Bite! Bite! Ah Bite! Love's fountains fill me!" (quoted in Reade, 430), explosively and explicitly brings the century to a close, and Crowley's clearly seminal fountains provide an erotic intertextual clarification of the fountains that Whitman had first released.

Homosexual writers in the nineteenth century turned genres like the short story and the novel to homoerotic purposes in stories like John Francis Bloxam's "The Priest and the Acolyte" (1894) that tells of the doomed love between a priest and his altar boy, or in the pederastic ambience of Frederick Rolfe's "Stories Toto Told Me" (1896). In novels like Howard Overing Sturgis's *Tim* (1891) homoerotic attachments in all-male public schools are depicted, while similar homoerotic relationships taking place in classical times are described in Pater's *Marius the Epicurean* (1885). Even such popular books as Thomas Hughes's *Tom Brown's School Days* (1857) and Dean Farrar's *Eric; or, Little by Little* (1858) and Hall Caine's *The Deemster* (1887) suggest (if they did not always state) that close relationships between boys and sometimes between men and boys, especially between tutors and their students, was a feature of academic and of public life. Pornographic novels like *Teleny* (1893) and *The Sins of the Cities of the Plain* (1881), both anonymously written, provide detailed pictures of homosexual life and sexual practice. Indeed, *Teleny* was the first novel in English to concern itself "with homosexuality at its fullest extent" (Reade, 49). It was embellished by a full quotient of the same intense fantasy that marks much of the verse of the period, while *Cities of the Plain*—the city referred to is Sodom, one of the "cities of the plain" in the Bible—alleges to be a factual presentation of the world of the London male prostitute.

THE LANGUAGE OF HOMOEROTIC TEXTS

Many homoerotic texts—especially in poetry, which is by far the most prominent homoerotic genre of the nineteenth century—written to or about male-male desire share themes common also to male-female desire.

Poems praising the beauty of an object of desire, whether women or men; elegies lamenting the death of beautiful women or men in which the lost lover is also inscribed as an object of desire; lyrics celebrating the joy of a new love affair or lamenting the loss of an old one; and poems expressing jealousy over another lover or detailing the pain of unrequited passion are all common to texts inspired by both kinds of desire and even those few in which, like Swinburne's "Hermaphroditus," there is some recognition of bisexual desire. Still, these texts suggest areas of difference between the "traditional" expression of desire and the existence of structures unique to homoerotic texts. Language is one indicator: locales, characters, and passions are described by its heightened use.

An exotic eroticism is suggested by descriptions of rare colors, gems like sardonyx and chalcedony, or flowers, some of which are themselves associated with homoerotic mythology such as the narcissus or the water lily. Roden Noel, for example, shows in "Ganymede" a picture of "a youth barelimbed the loveliest in the world" with light "falling on his lily side" (quoted in Reade, 131), while Simeon Solomon in "A Vision of Love Revealed in Sleep" describes the handsome and homosexual spirit of love as one whose "lips were parted with desire; his breath was that of blossoms" (quoted in Reade, 133). In Douglas's "Two Loves" homosexual love is described as "full sad and sweet, and his large eyes / Were strange with wondrous brightness staring wide / With gazing . . . his cheeks were wan and white / Like pallid lilies, and his lips were red / Like poppies . . . his head was wreathed with moon-flowers pale as lips of death" (quoted in Reade, 361).

Many books of homoerotic verse were titled with such floral or exotic references so that such a title became a signifier of homoerotic content, such as Edmund John's *The Flute of Sardonyx* (1913), Percy Osborn's *Rose Leaves from Philostratus* (1901), Raffalovich's *Tuberose and Meadowsweet* (1885), Eric Stenbock's *Myrtle, Rue, and Cypress* (1883), and Edward Warren's *The Wild Rose* (1928). Other titles drew on medieval allusion or suggested mysterious or distant lands—a version of Arcadia. Titles that included "south" suggested Mediterranean and hence homoerotic freedom or implied escape to a sexually uninhibited paradise. Medieval phrases conjured manly comradeship while biblical references inevitably invoked David and Jonathan. Hence Edwin Bradford's *Strangers and Pilgrims* (1929), Horatio Brown's *Drift* (1900), Ralph Chubb's *The Secret Country* (1939), Nicholson's *A Chaplet of Southernwood* (1896), Arnold Smith's *The Isle of Mistorak* (1926), John Stuart-Young's *The Seductive Coast* (1909), Symonds's *Tales of Ancient Greece* (1871), and, of course, Bradford's pointed *Passing the Love of Women and Other Poems* (1913).

In the language of Victorian homosexual poetry, evasion and indirection are strategies to encode homoerotic content; absence, in fact, is as revealing as presence. The absence of a gender-defining name or pronoun—"you" rather than "he" or "she"—often indicates that the gender of the poem's subject cannot be revealed, and hence is male. Such absence is often clarified by exotic, sensual, and highly colored language, though this of course is a feature of many texts of the period. For example, in the line "Put on that languor" of Raffalovich's sonnet the "special" context is revealed by "languor," an adjective that falls more comfortably in a passive—and hence for the nineteenth century "unmanly" and effeminate—context, just as Wilde's "Wasted Days" (1877), describing a "fair slim boy not made for this world's pain" (quoted in Reade, 145), sites the youth in the same "unmanly" and thus homoerotic context. This suggestive, exotic, and often gender-imprecise language, of course, is an attempt to define homosexual identity.

The homoerotic suggestiveness of Swinburne's "Hermaphroditus," for example, and the well-established imputation of effeminacy as a characteristic of sodomites and later of homosexuals, reflects the general confusion on behalf of homosexuals and nonhomosexuals concerning the "nature" of homosexuality and the sexual makeup of homosexuals. Nineteenth-century sexual theory offered a wide range of "explanations" for sexual difference, generally oscillating between theories urging that it was congenital and those that it was acquired. Ulrichs posited that homosexuals were a product of the lack of differentiation in the human embryo resulting in what he called "anima muliebris virile corpora inclusa"—that is, a female soul in a male body. This third-sex concept that Carpenter would echo in his essay "The Intermediate Sex" obviously allowed an identity to be posited that included what "normal" society then might well describe as both manly and unmanly characteristics.

The metaphor Ulrichs created does account for an aspect of homosexual style that at one extreme stressed—as can be seen in descriptions of the mollies—identification with an extreme effeminate style. At another remove it associated homosexual style with a behavior pattern that combined languid and effete dandyism of manner and manners with a deliberate attempt to use this "aesthetic" behavioral style as a sign of homosexuality, using it indeed as a defiant gesture made in the face of the homophobic middle class. Thus Victorian homosexual poetry uses terminology to describe men and boys that resonated against the accepted social concept of the homosexual as effeminate—indeed, as a man who wanted to be a woman. If an eighteenth-century molly constructed himself as a woman and dressed like one, a nineteenth-century Uranian by reversing gender roles while imitating them, constructed himself not as a woman but as a male whose effete and effeminate—but not feminine—homosexual style deliberately undermined orthodox gender expectations. Words like "rapturous," "exquisite," "tremulous," "delicate," "yearnings," "sinuous," "heavenly," "adorable," "enchanting," "tenderest," "bliss," and "divinest" used to describe male beauty and love for males comprise a highly charged erotic diction. But rarely in nineteenth-century Uranian poetry is there the presumption that homosexual men are anything but men, no matter how languid may be their manner or tremulous their yearning.

Dark, mysterious, claustrophobic, and often sinister locations mark these poems, with descriptions of "misty," "dreamy," "dark," "dim," or "gloom." An intense and suggestive sexuality often associated with death or sadomasochistic pain is imagined in which lips are "bruised" by "frantic kisses" and a vision of the absolute exotic strangeness of the homoerotic world is conjured up. In Wilde's "Wasted Days" the "fair slim boy not made for this world's pain" (fair and slim equal languid and pale), whose "longing eyes" desire a love that can only bring him pain in this world, has "pale cheeks whereon no kiss hath left its stain." Like Douglas's use of "shame" to denote homosexual love, "stain" is a similar marker since presumably pure heterosexual kisses do not stain in the way that forbidden homosexual kisses must. Indeed, the association of guilt with sexuality, as in Douglas's "In Praise of Shame" where "of all sweet passions Shame is loveliest," causes such kisses to be "furtive," "hidden," or "darker," as in Faber's description of his homosexual nature as a "darker self" and as Tennyson has it when he describes his friend Arthur Henry Hallam as one "loved deeplier, darklier understood."

Symonds uses many of these linguistic markers rather spectacularly, especially in the strange and forbidden world of his "Midnight at Baiae" (1875), a fevered depiction of the discovery by the speaker of a dead young man who has apparently been killed in an orgy of sadomasochistic homosexuality:

> Then was I ware how neath the gleaming rows
> Of cressets a fair ivory couch was spread:
> Rich Tyrian silks and gauzes hyaline
> Were bound with jeweled buckles to the bed:
> Thereon I saw a naked form supine.
> It was a youth from foot to forehead laid
> In slumber. Very white and smooth and fine
> Were all his limbs; and on his breast there played
> The lambent smiles of lamplight. But a pool
> Of blood beneath upon the pavement stayed. . . .
>
> Spell-bound I crept, and closer gazed at him:
> And lo! from side to side his throat was gashed
> With some keen blade; and every goodly limb,
> With marks of crisped fingers marred and lashed,
> told the fierce strain of tyrannous lust that here
> Life's crystal vase of youth divine had dashed.
> It is enough. Those glazed eyes, wide and clear;
> Those lips by frantic kisses bruised; that cheek
> Whereon foul teeth-dints blackened; the tense fear
> Of that white innocent forehead; vain and weak
> Are words, unutterably weak and vain,

To paint how madly eloquent, how meek
Were those mute signs of dire soul-shattering pain.

(quoted in Reade, 144–45)

Late in the century Raffalovich anatomized this combination of effeminacy and effeteness in a sonnet and urged that because "the world has treated us so ill" homosexuals ought deliberately to assume an effete manner and "put on that Languor" in order to intentionally offend "men like that"—that is, the homophobic public. Here he offers a lesson in transgressive homosexual behavior asserting that this pose of effete and effeminate dandyism ought to become a tool of revolutionary social and sexual change:

Put on that Languor which the world frowns on,
That blamed misleading strangeness of attire,
And let them see that see us we have done
With their false worldliness and look up higher.
Because the world has treated us so ill
And brought suspicion near our happiness,
Let men that like to slander as they will;
It shall not be my fault if we love less.
Because we two who never did them harm,
And never dreamt of harm ourselves, find men
So eager to perplex us and alarm
And scare from us our dove-like thoughts, well then
Since 'twixt the world and truth must be our choice,
Let us seem vile, not be so, and rejoice. (quoted in Reade, 226)

Of course, effeminate homoeroticism depicts one side only of the nineteenth-century delineation of homosexual identities and of images of male desire, and so Symonds in *Eudiades* (1868) can describe Melanthias as possessing "wide shoulders, knitted arms, and narrow waist." But when this is preceded by a description in which "the wavy down / That on his smooth white thighs and perfect breast / Lay soft as sleep," then the luxuriance of the description, of a kind generally reserved in poetry for women, as well as the specific attention drawn to his thighs, suggests the operation of a specific kind of erotic desire, just as Hopkins's description of the bugler as one "breathing bloom of a chastity in mansex fine" reveals in the unique use of "mansex" a desire aimed not so much at chastity but at sex.

The manly/unmanly dichotomy is subtly explored in Lefroy's "A Palaestral Study," which appears in *Echoes from Theocritus and Other Sonnets* (1885), the title invoking a classical reference but the poem being an erotic meditation on the desire provoked by the intersection of the passive/effeminate with the active/masculine, a subject that Swinburne had addressed in "Hermaphroditus" and that fascinated writers of the period:

The curves of beauty are not softly wrought;
These quivering limbs by strong muscles held
In attitudes of wonder, and compelled
Through shapes more sinuous than a sculptor's thought,
Tell of dull matter splendidly distraught,
Whisper of mutinies divinely quelled—
Weak indolence of flesh, that long rebelled,
The spirit's domination bravely taught.
And all man's loveliest works are cut with pain.
Beneath the perfect art we know the strain,
Intense, defined, how deep so'er it lies.
From each high master-piece our souls refrain,
Nor tired of gazing, but with stretched eyes
Made hot by radiant flames of sacrifice. (quoted in Reade, 157)

Siting the poem in the palaestra—the Greek gymnasium—clearly indicates that it is male beauty that is the subject. The poem operates ostensibly as a meditation on beauty and draws what are supposed to be aesthetic conclusions about beauty and art. But the beauty under discussion is male beauty, and the language oscillates between images of passive and active sexuality, for under the guise of a reference to wrestling—a primary activity of the palaestra—wherein one set of "quivering limbs" are held by another set of "strong hid muscles," the image of sexual struggle is engaged. This is heightened by the active power of "compelled" and the mutinies that are "quelled." The effeminate/passive pole—invoked by "distraught" and by the "weak indolence of flesh"—is thus set against the powerful sexual implication of "domination," and the conclusion that "man's loveliest works are cut with pain" places the poem squarely within a sexual nexus that connects pain with homosexual love, both physically and emotionally.

The invocation of pain and sexuality is an intense and recurring element in poetry of this period, extending from Symonds's sadomasochistic vision to Crowley's demand, "Bite! Bite! Ah Bite! Love's fountains fill me." Lefroy concludes his poem with an aesthetic observation that great art affects us because we recognize the "strain" that is "intense," a term also used by Symonds in association with sex. Lefroy's point is that this intense strain is created at once by sexual intensity and more deeply by sexual doubt and perhaps even alarm, occasioned by the fact that the scene he has described—a wrestling match between two men—has itself provoked not only an aesthetic response but forbidden homosexual desire, a desire "made hot by radiant flames of sacrifice." Thus, without mentioning a sexual subject, or dealing explicitly with homoeroticism, Lefroy uses language that unites aesthetic reflection with the erotic and creates a powerfully homoerotic text.

GREEK TEXTS AS SIGNIFIERS

Though language is a powerful signifier, the most inclusive signifier of all was Greece. Greek homosexuality had become so recognized as indicative of homoeroticism that mere mention of it in a text, by the end of the century, was enough to make a text suspect as having homoerotic content. Thus in Forster's *Maurice* (1913) Maurice's tutor in Greek commands his students to "omit: a reference to the unspeakable vice of the Greeks" (*Maurice*, 51). In his *Memoirs* Symonds sums up what may well have been a general experience:

> In the Phaedrus and Symposium—in the myth of the soul and the speeches of Pausanias, Agathon, and Diotima—I discovered the true liber amoris at last, the revelation I had been waiting for, the consecration of a long cherished idealism. . . . I had obtained the sanction of the love that had been ruling me from childhood. Here was the poetry, the philosophy of my own enthusiasm for male beauty, expressed with all the magic of unrivalled style. And what was more, I now became aware that the Greek race—the actual historical Greeks of antiquity—treated this love seriously, invested it with moral charm, endowed it with sublimity.
>
> For the first time I saw the possibility of resolving in a practical harmony the discords of my instincts. I perceived that masculine love had its virtue as well as its vice, and stood in this respect upon the same ground as normal sexual appetite. (Symonds, 99)

The Grecian signifier served for many, as it did for Symonds, at once to legitimize and indicate homoerotic content, for an appeal to a revered classical heritage legitimized for some readers what the same appeal signaled to others. Tennyson's memorial tribute to his friend Arthur Henry Hallam, *In Memoriam* (1850), provided relevant "undertones to the condition of certain readers" (Reade, 10). By "condition," of course, is meant homosexuality. In this poem Tennyson explores his feelings resulting from the death of Hallam and creates a relationship in which he describes himself as both bride and widower and hints at the eroticized nature of his affection. But he also places the site of their greatest bliss within the boundary of a Greek, and of an Arcadian, realm. There he recalls wandering with Hallam in a spiritual state in which "not a leaf was dumb; / But all the lavish hills would hum / The murmur of a happy Pan." There the two of them experienced a soul's communion:

> Thought leapt out to wed with Thought
> Ere Thought could wed itself with Speech:
>
> And all we met was fair and good
> And all was good that Time could bring,
> And all the secret of the Spring
> Moved in the chambers of the blood;

And many an old philosophy
On Argive heights divinely sang,
And round us all the thickets rang
To many a flute of Arcady. (quoted in Reade, 157)

Tennyson invokes a Greece where the two of them find themselves "wed" in thought and speech, experiencing this nuptial next to a "spring" that reveals to them secrets of the blood. It is not likely that Tennyson was himself homosexual, though as Richard Dellamora documents, he was certainly aware of the possibility of sex between men (Dellamora, 16ff). The nature of the intimacy and the language used to describe it places the poem firmly within a homosocial and homoerotic context. Indeed, sentimental and eroticized intimacy is perhaps the most remarkable thing about In Memoriam. In Don Leon response to men and boys tends to be far more driven by homosexual desire than by homosocial demands, and what intimacy there is works toward sexual conquest. In Tennyson eroticized intimacy unites a homosexual tradition with what has been called the friendship tradition and marks a tone that will permeate almost all of what will follow. If the friendship tradition presumed a passionate but nonsexual relation between men, Tennyson's poem raises the possibility for the introduction and perhaps consummation of male-male sexual desire in texts.

Tennyson's description of his relationship with Hallam as occurring in a special place that resounds to the language of an "old philosophy" attuned to the emotional "flutes of Arcady" locates his poem in that classical Greek and homoerotic milieu which had been a primary code for writers from Marlowe to Barnfield to Byron. But never before in English literature had the classical been so suggestively and fully conjoined with the erotic and the specifically homosexual as it was between 1850 and 1895. The difference between these texts and, say, Marlowe's use of classical imagery in "The Passionate Shepherd" lies in the Victorians' use of an aesthetic rather than a historical vocabulary in their verse. Marlowe's poem is informed by a Virgilian pastoral tradition, and his mere allusion is sufficient to alert a classically trained reader to the implied reference to Virgil's second Eclogue, in which Corydon laments the loss of his lover Alexis. But in Marlowe there is no overtly expressed sexual desire; indeed, the poem confines the erotic firmly within a philosophical rather than a passionate context, insisting that their love will be founded firmly on the "mind." The eroticism of the proposition to "come live with me and be my love" depends for its eroticism on a recollection of the Virgilian allusion. The Greece of the nineteenth-century homoerotic imagination is not the cool habitation of nonsexual philosophy but a place where the hot flames of the sacrifice create the heat of homosexual passion itself.

As an example of the deployment of both classical settings and the use of coded language consider a scene from Symonds's long poem *Eudiades*. Set in Greece and rich in classical allusion, the poem is in fact an erotic tale in which an older man, Melanthias, falls in love with the young Eudiades. They become lovers and eventually die together, maintaining a "pure"—that is, sex-free—relationship in the best tradition of a reserved and chaste classicism. The subtext of the poem constantly hints at a consummation of the union, however. The sexual event is encased in a legitimizing classical diction and surrounded by classical ambience that transforms the homosexual elements into something that Symonds hoped, perhaps, would seem far less sensational than it actually is:

> Thus by the Love-God's shrine, beneath the trees,
> Fragrant with summer, musical with bees,
> While in the boughs the loud cicada sang
> And through the field glad boyish laughter rang,
> These lovers vowed unspoken vows and blent
> Their throbbing souls in love's accomplishment.
> All was calm, so fair, they scarce could think
> 'Twas but this morn had brought them to the brink
> Of that full stream from which they slaked at will
> The strange sweet thirst that burned and pleased them still.
>
> (quoted in Reade, 119)

At a later point in the poem Eudiades

> Offered the pleasure none may touch and live
> Thenceforth unashamed: "Lo, lover, I will give"
> Said he, "whatever joy is mine. Nay take
> And drink from my soul! from my fountains slake
> Thy thirsty lips! fear not to shed my blood;
> For I will die to do thee any good,
> Or in my body bear thy mark of shame
> To all men visible . . ." (quoted in Reade, 124)

Symonds avers, of course, that their love is "pure" as he later says, but the passionate language leaves no doubt as to what he hopes might be imagined by a reader already devoted to Grecian fantasy. That the love is "strange" already sets it apart from the presumably commonplace world of heterosexual passion. Perhaps only a few readers then would have found Eudiades's willingness to allow Melanthias to slake his "thirsty lips" at Eudiades's fountains a hint at fellatio. Knowing readers, however, might recognize the "mark of shame" that Eudiades is willing to bear as a code for homosexual love. The violence connected with that mark that Eudiades seems willing to suffer in an erotic context seems clearly meant to suggest anal penetration.

Almost immediately after Tennyson published *In Memoriam* numbers of texts that inscribed homosexual desire within a classical setting or implied it by classical allusion began to appear. In 1858 William Johnson, later to take the name of William Cory after his dismissal from his teaching post at Eton in 1872 because of the suspicion of too intimate relations with his pupils, published a small book of poems classically titled *Ionica*. Interspersed among lyrics dealing with such conventional subjects as a tributes to Queen Victoria, to Tennyson, and lyrics extolling poetry, childhood, bravery, and the beauty of young women are poems that deal in one way or another with relationships between the speaker and persons whose names and gender is kept unclear, though the title of the book was enough to signal that the perceived link between classicism and homosexuality might be employed in the text. *Ionica*, in several expanded editions, continued to be published well until the end of the century, and of Johnson's pupils there are several whose own works suggest similar devotion to homoerotic themes, among them, for example, Howard Sturgis, whose novel *Tim* details a homoerotic relationship between two Eton boys. *Ionica* almost immediately began to have an effect, for a copy was given to Symonds, who wrote to Johnson and revealed his own homosexuality. Johnson quickly responded with a letter defending homosexual relationships.

Though chaste, correct, and speaking by implication rather than directly, *Ionica* clearly advocates such relationships. Its first poem, "Desiderato," invokes an unnamed friend who is in fact Charles Wood, one of Johnson's pupils to whom the poems are dedicated. He describes how when they "both were young" that "you leant on him who loved your staff to be," and now he asks Woods to "slouch your lazy length again / On cushions fit for aching brow" and adds parenthetically in a masterful stroke of suggested intimacy: "(For yours always ached, you know)." Johnson was Wood's staff when they were teacher and pupil. Now their friendship has passed because Woods has become a grown man.

Yet Johnson still hopes that Woods will recognize that their friendship was like the sea that "throws toward thee things that pleased of yore, / And though it wash thy feet no more, / Its murmurs mean: 'I yearn for thee.'" Symonds may have been struck by Johnson's use of "yearn," for in his memoirs he remarks on the letter that Cory wrote him: "It was a long epistle on pederastia in modern times, defending it and laying down the principle that affection between people of the same sex is no less natural and rational than the ordinary passionate relations. Underneath Johnson's frank exposition of this unconventional morality there lay a wistful yearning sadness—the note of disappointment and forced abstention. I have never found this note absent in lovers of my sort and Johnson's" (Symonds, 109–10). Symonds's identification of "yearning" as a note in homosexual discourse has an echo in Whitman's use of "pining" in his *Calamus* poems, a term he uses when he too laments the loss of lovers, and Johnson's metaphors of a supporting (and phallic) staff, and the slouching lazy length of his friend, as well as of the implied sexual servility of the foot-washing sea, perhaps innocent in themselves, become in the context heavy with suggestive sexual imagery.

In another poem, "Mimnermus in Church," Johnson seems to advocate the passion of friendship as superior to the more chaste passions of religious faith: "You bid me lift my mean desires / From faltering lips and fitful veins / To sexless souls." The use of "desire" and the qualifying "mean"—that is, base and low—may associate this line specifically with homosexual passion by a reverse use of homophobic language in much the same way that Douglas would use "shame" to equal homosexual desire. Terms like "mean," indicating ungovernable and base lust, more often denoted homosexual desire rather than the presumed purity of heterosexual love. If there is any doubt, Johnson erases it when he says that instead of sexless souls he "with fonder welcome owns / One dear dead friend's remembered tones."

"An Invocation" very nearly proclaims a theory of the connection of classical with British homoeroticism. Johnson hopes that by some trick of time the ancient shepherd Comatas and himself, the modern poet, might be brought together in the present so that they "Beneath this broken sunlight this leisure day might lie; / Where trees from distant forests, whose names were strange to thee, / Should bend their amorous branches within thy reach to be, / And flowers thine Hellas knew not, which art hath made more fair, / Should shed their shining petals upon thy fragrant hair." Like Socrates and Phaedrus who recline and talk of love in the *Phaedrus*, the modern poet lies with Comatas beneath "amourous" branches and admires—employing an equally amorous word—his "fragrant" hair. After exploring the possible benefits of such a transhistorical union, Johnson invokes another element from Platonic homoerotic texts and hopes that "Two minds shall flow together, the English and the Greek." The union of the English and the Greek mind—what nineteenth-century writers imagined to be a kindred devotion to homoerotic texts and practice—is a central theme of these texts. Here this idea underlies Johnson's wish and echoes the assertion of *Don Leon* that in the homoerotic Greece of the imagination lay sexual as well as "mental freedom."

Homoeroticism presides in several others of the poems in which Johnson details the relationship with Wood that began in delight but ended, it seems, unhappily: "One year I lived in high romance . . . in the magic of a smile / I dwelt as in Calypso's isle." We have elsewhere in Johnson's verse seen how the relationship had overtones of a complex but perhaps unrealized sexuality, and in "Deteriora" he confesses that "I would clasp, detain, adore" the "glorious creature" who he loved. But his passion is doomed, for he hears the handsome youth he adores "meditate your gay goodbye." The relationship ends: "We part; you comfort one bereaved, unmanned; / You calmly chide the silence and the grief; You touch me once with light and courteous hand, / And with a sense of something like relief / You turn away from what may seem to be / Too hard a trial for your charity." These formal and elegant lines are as profound and moving an evocation of the loss of love as is Whitman's almost contemporary description of the "sick sick dread lest the one he loved might secretly be indifferent to him."

Many years later Symonds wrote of *Ionica*, "I used to dote on that book when I was a lad at Oxford. But the best things in it (those written at Eton) are morbidly sentimental" (Symonds, 48). He is right in his assessment that the best things in the book are the poems written at Eton, for they are homoerotic. His description of them as "morbidly sentimental" draws on the medical terminology of homosexuality where it is described as a "morbid" condition and also reflects the well-established portrayal of homosexuals as effeminate. Symonds's term also forecasts one defensive and homophobic critical approach to homosexual texts that begins to come very much to the foreground in homophobic texts—legal, social, and literary—of the period. This approach both fears and judges what it could not approve and derives in part from a developing psychology that theorized that homosexuality was an incomplete and stunted form of a sexuality.

The critical presumption that arose from this formula—and that dominated and in some quarters still dominates homophobic social and literary criticism—was that any text with homosexual themes must, like homosexuality itself, also be an incomplete and hence inferior text. What in a "heterosexual" text might be described as an account of high passion or profound emotion was in a homosexual text simply dismissed as "sentimental," even though the textual situation—as here the loss of love—might be very much the same. Of course, Johnson's poems, as "Parting" shows, are quite the reverse of sentimental. Johnson's almost icy text displays a clear-eyed and indeed profound analysis of what was for him unbearable.

Johnson's poems provide, as Symonds did see in his highlighting of Johnson's "yearn," a broader contribution to the homoerotic literature of the nineteenth century, for they continued the specific creation of a homoerotic vocabulary that Tennyson had begun, though for Johnson, unlike Tennyson, there was no doubt about the direction or intention of his desires. Johnson's poems, indirect and often evasive, appealed to an erotic construction of classical texts and to a specifically homoerotic interpretation of these texts and were among the first in English—even before Whitman—to frankly describe the emotional toll taken by unrequited or broken homosexual love affairs in a language that was in the best sense sentimental but also erotically charged.

Tennyson's appeal to Arcady as a site for his love for Hallam and Johnson's inscription of his homoerotic poems within a classical category implied by the tile *Ionica*, including of course his most famous poem, "Heraclitus," made room for poets like Symonds, Swinburne, and Roden

Noel in the 1860s to use titles like *Eudiades*, "Hermaphroditus," and "Ganymede," or in the 1880s and 1890s for Lefroy to write "The Flute of Daphnis" and "A Palaestral Study" and for Charles Jackson and Douglas both to published poems called "Hyacinthus." Other poets published entire volumes with classical titles that signified their content, like Lefroy's *Echoes from Theocritus* (1883) and Edmund Mackie's *Charmides* (1898), or early in and well into the new century Osbron's *Rose Leaves from Philostratus and Other Poems* (1901), Edward Warren's *Itamos* (1903), and Jackson's *Lysis* (1924). Indeed, certain names were such powerful signifiers that many poets used them. Among these Antinous, the lover of the Emperor Hadrian, was enshrined in Symonds's *The Lotos Garden of Antinous* (1871), Montague Summers's *Antinous and Other Poems* (1907), and Fernando Pessoa's "Antinous: A Poem" (1918).

OTHER "TRADITIONS" IN HOMOEROTIC TEXTS

Certain "traditions" have been detected in homoerotic texts, among them an "ironic-aesthetic tradition" in which would fall many of the writers I discuss here, a "democratic tradition" that obviously includes Whitman, an "Anglo-Saxon, Teutonic tradition" that includes writers like Wincklemann and Thomas Mann, a "theoretical" tradition that includes apologies like Wilde's *De Profundis* or Symonds's essays (Rousseau, 138ff). Other schema find that homoerotic texts fall into discourses concerned with types of the male body in which the "pliancy of Narcissus," the "firm but graceful maturity" of Apollo, and the "potency of Hercules" are archetypes, or homosexual roles found in texts have been denominated as "men of war" including sportsmen, cowboys, sailors, soldiers, and comrades, all of whom invoke the eroticized union of sex and violence. Finally, that the union of two men may culminate not in children but in a creative act is seen as a defining theme in homoerotic texts since it firmly advocates the principle that the value of homosexuality lies not in its contribution to enlarging the population but to creatively enriching society.[5]

Other themes specific to homoerotic texts include depictions of utopian worlds where homosexual men can safely express and practice their love, accounts of the search for an "ideal friend," explorations of the relationship between homosexual and heterosexual desire and of the anomalous situation of homosexuals in a hostile heterosexual world, attempts by homosexuals at self-definition and self-discovery (what we call "coming out"), themes that use specific locales and certain specific acts as metaphors for sexual experience and knowledge (such as swimming scenes), and, finally, special depictions of sexual experience itself (Smith, 163–202).

Whitman created an original nineteenth-century site for a homoerotic utopia in his poems celebrating cities of lovers, though the tradition extends as far back as Virgil's second *Eclogue* and enters English literature most obviously in Marlowe's assertion that he will seek a protected place with his lover where they can "all the pleasures prove." Byron's trip to Greece in *Don Leon* also is in search of such a free sexual paradise and specifically homoeroticizes the concept for the first time in English texts. Certainly Symonds's "Love and Death: A Symphony," in which he envisions a world in which comrades are "strewn thick as flowers," echoes Whitman's visionary desire, and it could be suggested that all homoerotic literature of this period was a kind of literary haven in which these sentiments could be safely explored and celebrated.

Bayard Taylor in his 1870 novel *Joseph and His Friend* envisioned a happy valley where Joseph and his friend would "escape" from the stifling laws of men and live happily together. Joseph offers a useful paradigm of the Arcadian ideal as he describes the great valley to his friend. It is place where "it is bliss enough to breathe" and where there is "freedom from the distorted laws of men." Joseph exclaims, "We should be outlaws there, in our freedom!—here we are fettered outlaws." Then they kiss: "each gave way to the impulse of manly love, rarer, alas! but as tender and true as the love of woman."[6] In Forster's *Maurice*, perhaps the culminating and summarizing text of the entire period, Forster sends Maurice and Alec to the "greenwood" that he defines as "big spaces where passion clasped peace, spaces no science could reach, but they existed forever, full of woods some of them, and arched with majestic sky and a friend" (*Maurice*, 191). Maurice and Alec in Forster's Arcadian tale of homosexual love determine to go into the "greenwood" because Maurice, as a homosexual, is "an outlaw in disguise." Perhaps, he muses after he affirms his homosexuality, "among those who took off to the greenwood in old times there had been two men like himself—two. At times he entertained the dream. Two men can defy the world" (*Maurice*, 137).

As Symonds says about a young man of whom he was enamored, "he shared my Arcadian tastes," and Wilde, writing to Douglas, referred to "Sicilian and Arcadian airs" as a euphemism for homosexuality (quoted in Symonds, 117). The invocation of Arcadia—Symonds's reference is direct, since to him "Arcadia" means homosexual—implied the presence of homosexual love and sensibility in a text. In Plato's *Symposium* it is on the shores of the vast sea of beauty, an Arcadian pastoral surely, that "he who, ascending from earthly things under the influence of true love, begins to perceive beauty."[7] Hopkins's "Epithalamion" of 1888 posits this kind of safe haven in the secret pond in which his speaker bathes in communion with a group of young men, and having done so he finds himself transformed.

The central icon of homoerotic texts is this desired object, what Plato's *Symposium* describes as the beloved other half of the divided lovers, who Whitman describes as the "boy I love," a "comrade," a "rough," an "athlete" who is enamored of him. Whether he is an actual lover, such as Wilde's

"Bosie" (Lord Alfred Douglas), a fictional creation such as Corydon's Alexis, or an unspoken metaphoric presence, such as "the sexual invert" who so powerfully occupies the pages of Symonds's "A Problem in Modern Ethics," or a metaphoric representation of desire such as Whitman's fierce wrestler, he dominates the text and commands its intentions. In Bloxam's "The Priest and the Acolyte" the acolyte is the ideal friend that Ronald Heatherington, the priest of the title, has long sought. But finding him, he is now accused by his rector of improper affection for the boy. The rector asks for an explanation, and Heatherington's reply effectively sums up not only the need for an ideal friend but also encapsulates other themes: the process of self-definition and self-discovery, the attraction of the eroticized aesthetic ideal, the need to revolt against homophobic convention, and the radicalizing effect on an individual conscience that confrontation with homophobia can ignite. Bloxam writes,

> I was always different from the other boys. I never cared much for games. . . . My one ambition was to find the ideal for which I longed . . . I always had an indefinite longing for something. . . . I was attracted at once by sin: my whole early life is stained and polluted with the taint of sin. . . . There are vices that are bound to attract almost irresistibly anyone who loves beauty above everything. I have always sought for love: again and again I have been the victim of fits of passionate affection: time after time I have seemed to have found my ideal at last: the whole object of my life has been . . . to gain the love of some particular person.

When the Rector observes that he ought to have married, Heatherington angrily replies with a defence of sexual difference:

> I have never been attracted by a woman in my life. Can you not see that people are different, totally different, from one another? To think that we are all the same is impossible; our natures, our temperaments, are utterly unlike. But this is what people will never see; they found all their opinions on a wrong basis. How can deductions be just if premises are wrong? One law laid down by the majority, who happen to be of one disposition, is only binding on the minority legally, not morally. What right have you, or anyone, to tell me that such a thing is sinful for me. . . . For me, with my nature, to have married would have been sinful: it would have been a crime, a gross immorality, and my conscience would have revolted. . . . Conscience should be that divine instinct which bids us seek after that our natural disposition needs. . . . I have committed no moral offence in this matter; in the sight of God my soul is blameless; but to you and the world I am guilty of an abominable crime—abominable because it is a sin against convention. . . . I met this boy; I loved him as I had never loved anyone . . . he was mine by right; he loved me, even as I loved him. . . . How dare the world presume to judge us? What is convention to us? Nevertheless, although I really knew that such a love was beautiful and blameless, although from the bottom of my heart I despised the narrow judgement of

the world. . . . I tried to resist. I struggled against the fascination he possessed for me. . . . I would have struggled on to the end: but what could I
do? It was he who came to me, and offered the wealth of his love. . . . How
could I tell to such a nature the hideous picture the world would paint? . . .
I knew what I was doing. I have faced the world and set myself against it. I
have openly scoffed at its dictates. . . . In God's eyes we are martyrs, and we
shall not shrink even from death in this struggle against the idolatrous worship of convention. (quoted in Reade, 357–58)

Heatherington's remarkable statement is not only an apologia for same-sex
love and a condemnation of homophobia, but it also recognizes that the irreversible fact of sexual difference has irreversible consequences and that these
consequences are both social and political. To characterize Heatherington's
transformation from a lovesick priest into what sounds like a modern homosexual rights activist may be anachronistic, but there can be no doubt that he
sees his love as having far more than personal significance as he asserts that
what originated as passion has now become a "struggle" against the destructive effects of a blind adherence to homophobic social conventions.

PLATO'S INFLUENCES

When Edwin Bradford published *Passing the Love of Women and
Other Poems* in 1913, he recalled the tradition that valorized men's emotional capacities over women's and by his phrase indicated membership in a special group that proclaimed homosexual love superior in every way to
heterosexual passion. His phrase, of course, derives from the biblical story of
David and Jonathan in 2 Samuel that, in describing their relationship as that
which "passes the love of woman," gave homosexual writers a respectable,
indeed biblical, citation justifying male-male desire. By invoking the David
and Jonathan story—or for that matter the friendship of Christ and John the
Beloved Disciple—and conflating it within the context of contemporary
homoerotic text, as Hall Caine also does in the homosexually evocative section of his novel *The Deemster* (1887), Barford allowed Victorian readers to
accept certain emotions because they were justified by biblical precept
(Reade, 36). Whether even the most obtuse Victorian could accept
Symonds's poem "The Meeting of David and Jonathan" as homoerotically
innocent is a question that the following lines might raise:

Thither with David, fleet of foot, and still,
Lest men should mar his purpose, from the hill
Unto the valley shadows went and ran,
Large in the lucent twilight, Jonathan.
There by an ancient holm-oak huge and tough,
Clasping the firm rock with gnarled roots and rough,
He stayed their steps; and in his arms of strength

Took David, and for sore love found at length
Solace in speech, and pressure, and the breath
Wherewith the mouth of yearning winnoweth
Hearts overcharged for utterance. In that kiss
Should unto soul was knit and bliss to bliss. (quoted in Smith, 181)

But it is to Plato's *Symposium* that so many nineteenth-century writers looked for the valorization of male-male love over heterosexual love. It comes in the speech of Pausanias—the speech that so stunned Symonds—where Pausanias explains that in the affairs of men there are two loves, one the "common Aphrodite" who governs "the love which the baser sort of men feel . . . that is directed toward women quite as much as young men . . . it is physical rather than spiritual . . . its only aim is the satisfaction of desires" (*Symposium*, 45–47). The other love is the "heavenly Aphrodite" who in fact is "the elder and is the daughter of Uranus." Those who are inspired by this love "are attracted toward the male sex and value it as being naturally stronger and more intelligent." They "do not fall in love with mere boys but wait until they reach the age at which they begin to show some intelligence." By choosing this age "their intention is to form a lasting attachment and a partnership for life" (*Symposium*, 90–91).

Heterosexual love that is equated here only with an illicit and merely physical passion can hardly stand against the high passion that values comradely dedication and looks for a combination of deep feeling and intellect. Pausanias continues that if the lover and the beloved act in accordance with the noble principle that insists that the purpose of love is to seek excellence in one and instill it in the other, then in that case "it is honorable for a boy to yield to his lover." In the later speech of Diotima, she avers that "those whose creative instinct is physical have recourse to women . . . but there are some whose creative desire is of the soul, and who long to beget spiritually not physically" and produce "progeny which it is the nature of the soul to create," such as art and poetry. Such men as these are like the man who finds "beauty embodied in his friend" and who "keeping him always before his mind" succeeds in "bringing to birth the children he has long desired to have, and once they are born he shares their upbringing with his friend; the partnership between them will be far closer and the bond of affection far stronger than between ordinary parents, because the children that they share surpass human children by being immortal as well as more beautiful" (Plato, 45–46, 90–91).

Whether Plato intended it or not, homosexual writers appropriated this as a defining text for arguing the superiority of homosexual passion and homoerotic love over heterosexual. Thus in his essay "The New Chivalry" Charles Kains Jackson asserts that under this new chivalric dispensation where a boy and a girl are of "equal outward grace the spiritual ideal will prevail over the animal and the desire of influencing the higher mind, the boy's, will prevail" (quoted in Reade, 316). Or as Edwin Bradford notes in his group of poems also called *The New Chivalry*, "boys need love, but not the love of woman, / Romantic friendship, passionate but pure, / Should be their first love" (quoted in Smith, 177). Not only in the capabilities of friendship and in intellect was it presumed that men excelled, but in sex itself, as Theodore Wratislaw in his notorious "To a Sicilian Boy" pointedly insists: "Between thine arms I find my only bliss; / Ah let me in thy bosom still enjoy / Oblivion of the past, divinest boy, / And the dull ennui of a woman's kiss!" The Sicilian boy's mere kiss will obliviate all women's kisses. Symonds also speculates on the question, "What is the charm of barren joy? / The well-knit body of a boy / Slender and slim, / Why is it then more wonderful / than Venus with her white breasts / And sweet eyes dim?" (quoted in Smith, 73).

For Symonds there is a political and moral as well as a sexual dimension to male-male attraction. He answers his own question in the language of a sexual politics when, in his memoirs, he describes how potently revelatory was his consummated sexual encounter in a "male brothel" with "a strapping young soldier":

> For the first time in my life I shared a bed with one so different from myself, so ardently desired by me, so supremely beautiful in my eyes, so attractive to my senses. . . . This experience exercised a powerful effect upon my life. I learned from it . . . that the physical appetite of one male for another may be made the foundation of a solid friendship. . . . I also seemed to perceive that, within the sphere of a male brothel . . . permanent human relations, affections, reciprocal toleration, decencies of conduct, asking and yielding, concession and abstention,—find their natural sphere: perhaps more than in sexual relations consecrated by middle-class matrimony. (Symonds, 254)

Though heedless, it seems of the commodity he has made of the young soldier by engaging in prohibited homosexual sex Symonds has effectively erased the negative interpretation of the act that had heretofore prevented him from seeking what he desired. By embracing what he had been taught to believe was vice he has discovered in it all those virtues that he had once believed were associated only with "middle class matrimony" and never with homosexuality.

PHYSICAL PROWESS AND HOMOSEXUAL DESIRE

The association of athletic activity with homoeroticism in texts—voyeuristic depictions of young men bathing, wrestling, or engaging in sport—derived from the Greek appreciation of athletic prowess is enshrined in so many of the texts of this period that it becomes a genre unto itself. Descriptions of men engaged in athletic events provided excuses for erotic descriptions as Reginald Brett, Viscount Esher, shows in a poem describing a player: "He moves Titanic 'mid the strife of games, / So fleet of foot, so sure of eye, so glorious, / With stately youth, and beauty which enflames / Desire for him" (quoted in Smith, 91). Lefroy's picture of a young man playing football is equally desirous: "If I could paint you friend, as you stand there, / Guard of the goal, defensive, open-eyed, / Watching the tortured bladder slide and glide / Under twinkling feet, arms bare, head bare / the breeze a-tremble through crow-tufts of hair." The young man sees the opposite team member about to make a pass and "you leap and fling / Your weight against his passage, like a wall, / Clutch him, and collar him, and rudely cling / For one brief moment till he falls—you fall" (quoted in Smith, 72–73).

Lefroy's picture of the handsome athlete gives him a chance also to describe the two engaged in a kind of wrestling embrace, itself a textual site for homoeroticism, as Lefroy's "A Palaestral Study" demonstrates. The wrestling scene and the eroticism of wrestling is powerfully fixed as a homoerotic site by Whitman, both in the person of the fierce wrestler in "Song of Myself" and in the "two boys clinging together" of the *Calamus* poems. So too Walter Pater, writing in "The Age of Athletic Prizemen" (1895) about the Greek sculptor Myron's statues, becomes lyrical about the youths who were Myron's subjects: "when he came to his main business with the quoit-player, the wrestler, the runner, he did not for a moment forget that they too were animals, young animals, delighting in natural motion, in free course through the yielding air" (quoted in Reade, 309). Pater's prose might well be a poem to a football boy or a handsome wrestler, and the essay's title "The Age of Athletic Prizemen" provides a term—"athletic"—that was to become another coded reference for homosexuality. Forster knew this, for in *Maurice* he observes about Clive's attempt to emotionally hurt Maurice, who is in love with him, that "his knowledge was incomplete, or he would have known the impossibility of vexing athletic love" (*Maurice*, 111).

The primary athletic image that Victorian homoerotic poetry liked to employ was that of the naked youth ready to plunge into the sea. This trope is engaged in *Don Leon*, it may be recalled, when Byron describes swimming with Giraud, an event that he transforms into a pedagogical and sensual experience: "How oft, when summer saw me fearless brave / With manly breast the blue transparent wave, / Another Daedalus I taught him how / With spreading arms the liquid waste to plough. / Then brought him gently to the sunny beach, / And wiped the moisture from his breech." Hopkins wrote perhaps the best example of the genre in "Epithalamion" (1888). In this poem a "listless stranger" comes on some boys, "a bevy of them" with "dare and downdolphinry and bellbright bodies." He watches them from a distance as they swim and then "he hies to a pool neighboring" and strips. This pool is the "sweetest, freshest, shadowist; / Fairyland" (quoted in Reade, 223–25). In short, it is Arcadia, Whitman's *Calamus* pondside. The boys swim in their pool and he in his, but the real though separate communion transforms him, and "we leave him, froliclavish, while he looks about, laughs, swims," his listlessness gone forever. What the listlessness is Hopkins soon discloses, for this text is "sacred matter" and the site and the twin pools symbolize "Wedlock" and the water and the swimming "Spousal love." The stranger has now been joined to the young men by this ritual act, a special kind of homoerotic baptism that has washed away listlessness, the fear of homosexual encounter. By the time that Frederick Rolfe wrote "Ballade of Boys Bathing" in 1890 to memorialize "the boys who bathe in St. Andrews bay" who are "ruddy tanned and bare" (quoted in Reade, 226–27), it was but a short step to Alan Stanley's "August Blue" (1894), which conflates sex and swimming:

> Stripped for the sea your tender form
> Seems all of ivory white,
> Through which the blue veins wander warm
> O'er throat and bosom slight,
> And as you stand, so slim upright
> The glad waves grow and yearn
> To clasp you circling in their might,
> To kiss with lips that burn. (quoted in Reade, 347)

TEXTUAL APPROACHES TO "COMING OUT"

When Symonds wrote to Whitman in 1891 asking directly whether his poems could be construed to be advocating homosexual affections and the physical realization of such affections, Whitman's response, at once explosive and cautious, suggests his own fear that his texts will cast a dangerous shadow on his life and his own awareness of the power of social demands for sexual conformity. Such a fear is explored by Symonds in the poem "What Cannot Be" (1861), which describes how the speaker in a fit of self-incrimination and dissatisfaction with life "nursed rebellious scorn" against "high heaven." What he rebels against is not only the sexual conventions of society represented by "high heaven" but the "doom" he feels that is inevitable for himself as a homosexual in a homophobic world. A young man passes the speaker's house and with a glance seems to invite him to a life of erotic bliss, a life of love and "the brotherhood of strength" that seems to be "of all convention free." But the speaker is too fearful of the consequences of flouting convention and ends the poem alone, wracked by "sharp self-disdain" and fearful that the apples of love might hide "dust within" (quoted in Reade, 60). The text reflects Symonds's uncomfortable situation as a homosexual in society before he experienced the revelation of Plato, Whitman, and sex itself. But even these epiphanies did not entirely erase his sense of alienation as Symonds's own case history, anonymously presented in Ellis and Symonds's *Sexual Inversion*, so eloquently testifies: "He has suffered extremely throughout life owing to his sense of the difference between himself and normal human beings. No pleasure he has enjoyed . . . can equal a thousandth part of the pain caused by the internal consciousness of Pariahdom."[8]

Raffalovich also recognizes the problem of being homosexual in a heterosexual world. In "The World Well Lost IV" (1886) he indicates the difficulty that attends on daily confrontation with that homophobic society that he so telling nominates as "They":

> Because our world has music, and we dance;
> Because our world has colour, and They gaze
> Because our speech is tuned, and schooled our glance,
> And we have roseleaf nights and roseleaf days,
> And we have leisure, work to do, and rest;
> Because They see us laughing when we meet,
> And hear our words and voices, see us dressed
> With skill, and pass us and our flowers smell sweet:—
> They think that we know friendship, passion, love!
> Our peacock Pride! And Art our nightingale!
> And Pleasure's hand upon our dogskin glove!
> And if they see our faces burn or pale,
> It is the sunlight, think They, or the gas,
> —Our lives are wired like our gardenias. (quoted in Reade, 198)

Raffalovich's brilliant poem not only anatomizes the price of difference in a world where sexual conformity is prized but also details a particular kind of homosexual identity as well. Here the homosexual is the precise opposite of the Whitmanesque comrade. He will become the grand queen and old auntie of the 1950s, a sexual dandy whose close early relation is the effeminate molly and who will dominate discourses that define homosexual identity well into the twentieth century, finally giving way to (though not disappearing) the macho men of the 1960s.

Raffalovich's text highlights the need for a constant masquerade that conceals the real beneath an invented identity so that his life, like the gardenia that he wears in his buttonhole, is a careful contrivance supported against collapse by a hidden wire. The damaging effects of homophobia inflict the same wounding self-disdain that Symonds mentions, so that the speaker doubts that there can be the possibility of "friendship, passion, love." But even though the text paints a grim picture of an outsider world predicated on sexual difference—"our" world as opposed to the one "They" inhabit—the title of the sonnet nevertheless suggests that the world of sexual conformity is one well worth losing.

When the discomfort of masking their homosexuality becomes too much to bear, the reaction of many is to cast caution aside and reveal themselves, to "come out"—and this is precisely what Raffalovich advocates in "Put on that Languor" where he insists that despite the fact that "men like that slander as they will," yet in fact the homosexual "never did them harm." Therefore he insists it is the duty of homosexual men to confront sexual conformity, for between "the world and truth must be our choice, / Let us seem vile, not be so, and rejoice." The coming out story, often conflated with the ideal friend plot and with texts describing erotic men or sexual fantasies, may be the primary textual event of homoerotic literature. The coming out story deals with the recognition of homosexual orientation but links that recognition with an awareness that homosexuality has public, that is, social and political, consequences also.

Thus Whitman's first *Calamus* poem, in which he determines that the "secret of his nights and days" must be told "for all who are or have been young men," pivots on the "for" that makes his confession a political act. In this sense it can be said that any homoerotic text is a coming-out story. But some coming-out stories are more spectacular than others, and some have more powerful political resonance. *Don Leon* certainly possesses such resonance, as does Forster's *Maurice*, and the texts of Symonds, Hopkins, or Johnson make public, no matter how evasively, what had been concealed. And so when an obscure poet like Herbert P. Horne trumpets his desire in a poem called "Non Delebo Propter Decem," he unequivocally places homosexuality in a religious context and both declares himself and places his desire in the transgressive social context that the coming-out story requires:

> Ye priests of men, ye priests ordained
> By the pure hands of God alone,
> Live on! for we, through you, have gained
> Our stablishment, that else were gone.
> Awake, ye silent priests, and move
> With power throughout the approaching years!
> Ye sinews of all human love,
> Ye just of Sodom. Wrath appears!
> Awake, awake, and gain for men
> Time yet, to lust and sin again! (quoted in Reade, 246)

Horne's poem implies that priests may themselves be involved in the very homosexual practice they are bound to condemn. His primary assertion, however, is that religion has in effect established homosexuality by condemnation of it and therefore has made it possible for homosexual men to continue to seek the forbidden delight of what otherwise might never have been considered either lust or sin if the church had not proscribed it.

The coming-out story effectively appears whenever a homosexual writer is willing to allow homoerotic desire to enter the discourse. That the nineteenth century did not create such specific examples of the genre as have appeared in the twentieth is not so much a testimony to a failure of nerve or a lack of awareness but to the power of homophobia. *Don Leon,* of course is anonymous; Symonds's *Memoirs,* though amazingly frank and written in 1892, were kept from publication for nearly a century. But the point about a coming out story may not so much be the author as the story itself.

The silence imposed by homophobia and the need to declare the nature of desire intersect in Nicholson's poem "I Love Him Wisely" (1892) and produce a small but telling masterpiece:

> I love him wisely if I love him well
> And so I let him keep his innocence;
> I veil my adoration with pretence
> Since he knows nothing of Love's mystic spell;
> I dare not for his sake my passion tell
> Though strong desire upbraid my diffidence;-
> To buy my happiness at his expense
> Were folly blind and loss unspeakable.
> Suspicious of my simplest acts I grow;
> I doubt my passing words, however brief;
> I catch his glances feeling like a thief.
> Perchance he wonders why I shun him so,—
> It would be strange indeed if he should know
> I love him, love him, love him past belief! (quoted in Reade, 307)

The prudent distance that the speaker keeps between himself and the man he loves is a gulf across which the strong current of sexual desire arcs like an electric charge. Though many texts of this period obscured the fact that males were the subject and the object of desire, and some insisted that friendship of a pure and high Platonic sort was their only message, sex is the (sometimes) invisible term of their various erotic equations, for sexuality is, as Foucault suggests, what the nineteenth century had discovered, and sex is what its obsessive discourses so constantly and furiously debate and define, castigate or celebrate.

PORNOGRAPHIC TEXTS

When William Dugdale published *Don Leon* in 1866 he was not offering the work as a radical text meant to encourage homosexuals to break the shackles of homophobia. Nor is it likely that he saw it as an apologia for an oppressed minority. Rather, he saw a chance to capitalize on the notoriety of Byron's name and the public's fascination with sodomites. Dugdale was the leading pornographic publisher of his time and in that text he surely saw a chance to make some money from a select audience of connoisseurs of sexual curiosa by providing it with another tasty bit of pornography that wittily praised anal intercourse and had the added *frisson* of also dealing with the sweet forbidden fruit of sodomy. Dugdale was, in fact, only adding one more title to an already prodigious literature of explicit sexuality that was primarily directed toward male-female sexual tastes but did have a homosexual content also. In an age that had tried to transform "Victorian" into a synonym for sexual prudery and emotional repression, the pornography industry saw perhaps its most effulgent flowering. It is against this background that the development of homoerotic literature must also be placed. Homosexual pornography, whether pictorial or verbal, has always been a feature of sexual discourses, and De Sade's work testifies to this. In England, the Earl of Rochester's *Sodom* provided a place for buggery in a literary pornographic text, and John Cleland's *Memoirs of a Woman of Pleasure*, known as *Fanny Hill*, contains some homosexual scenes, though pejoratively treated. And even in *Don Leon* the defended act of anal intercourse—by which homosexuals were most usually defined—is presented as heterosexual copulation, with the homosexual act implied not stated.

In 1881, however, there appeared what purported to be the confessions of a homosexual male prostitute called *The Sins of the Cities of the Plain; or, The Confessions of a Mary-Anne*, written allegedly by a one Jack Saul, homosexual male and the "Mary-Anne" of the title. The book is of some interest because it alleges to present a true relation of the subculture, and it does so minimally, registering some information about male prostitution and the London locales in which it was practiced, introducing material on the "clubs" that catered to homosexual men and to latter-day mollies and providing a vocabulary of sexual terms. Its descriptions of sex acts are repetitive and without much originality, and information about the subculture is provided only to present an opportunity to describe yet another massive organ, splendid endowment, athletic encounter, or "triune" sexual tangle, though the specificity with which these events are described leaves no doubt that at least in the fantasy world of pornography no avenue and no combination of partners that might lead to orgasm was ignored.

Still, the person who is described by Jack Saul in the opening pages does look back to Captain Whiffle and ahead to the boys in the band and registers at least a sartorial and perhaps a cultural connection:

> My attention was particularly taken by an effeminate fellow. He was walking in front of me, and looking into shop-windows from time to time, and now and then looking 'round as if to attract my attention.

Dressed in tight-fitting clothes, which set off his Adonis-like figure to the best advantage, especially about what snobs would call the fork of his trousers. Evidently he was favored by nature by a very extraordinary development of the male appendage. . . .

He had small and elegant feet, set off by pretty patent leather boots, a fresh beardless face, and almost feminine features. He wore auburn hair, and sparkling blue eyes, which spoke as plainly as possible to my senses, and told me he must be one of the "Mary-Annes" of London who I had heard were often to be seen sauntering in the neighborhood of Regent Street, or the Haymarket, on fine afternoons or evenings.[9]

The world of *Cities of the Plain* appears also in what is perhaps the most remarkable work of English homoerotic pornography of the nineteenth century, and a text that can tell much about those other homoerotic texts that in a promiscuous intertextuality may depend on it to explicitly say what they only were able to imply. This is *Teleny; or, The Reverse of the Medal*, anonymously produced and published in 1893, attributed to, though probably not written by, Oscar Wilde.[10] Though written in English and in England, *Teleny* is the story of a young Frenchman who finds himself caught up in the homosexual subculture of Paris and there discovers and acts on his homosexuality. Paris, of course, is the foreign and exotic local of the perverse, and the book provides substantial opportunity for its narrator to explore the seamy as well as the glittering locales of this subculture. This is the very milieu Raffalovich describes in "The World Well Lost IV," where the world is fragrant with gardenias; in *Teleny* the signature flower is the effete and exotic heliotrope. Unlike Jack Saul, Camille Des Grieux—whose name recalls not only the exotic bohemian world but its most scandalous text, *Camille*, and is also a happy elision of the masculine Des Grieux with the lady of the camelias herself—is of the privileged class to which men like Symonds and Raffalovich also belonged.

The sexually innocent Des Grieux is aware of being attracted to men but has not dared to act on this attraction. His story begins in a temple of high aesthetic culture at a concert, where he hears the playing of and is transfixed by the handsome young pianist, René Teleny. Teleny's playing invokes in Des Grieux extravagant visions and sexual response: "As I listened to the playing I was spellbound. . . . I longed to feel that love that maddens one to crime, to feel the blasting lust of men who live beneath the scorching sun." The music invokes Egypt, "where Adrian stood wailing, forlorn, disconsolate, for he had lost forever the lad he loved so well."

If the elision of love and crime is not enough and the invocation of Hadrian and his beloved Antinous not sufficient, then when the music conjures up "the gorgeous towns of Sodom and Gomorrah," there can be little doubt what sexual subtexts haunt the mind of Des Grieux. In the midst of the sensuous performance Teleny looks into the audience and, as if attracted by the intensity of Des Grieux's fantasy, "cast one long lingering, slumberous look at me, and our glances met" (6–7). They exchange that pointed and riveting look that is a sign of sexual fraternity and desire, a sign so common in the traffic of homosexual life that it recalls Whitman's "Do you know what it is as you pass to be loved by strangers? / Do you know the talk of the turning eyeballs?" Teleny's look sends Camille into further homoerotic and masturbatory raptures that also serve the intention of the text to arouse its readers:

> That thrilling longing I had felt grew more and more intense, the craving so insatiable that it was changed to pain; the burning fire had now been fanned into a mighty flame, and my whole body was convulsed and wracked with mad desire. My lips were parched, I grasped for breath; my points were stiff, my veins were swollen, yet I sat still, like all the crowd around me. But suddenly a heavy hand seemed to be laid upon my lap, something was bent and clasped and grasped, which made me faint with lust. The hand moved up and down, slowly at first, then faster and faster it went in rhythm with the song. My brain began to reel as throughout every vein a burning lava coursed, and then some drops even gushed out—I panted— (7–8)

After the concert he seeks out Teleny and finds him in a group of young men. One of them, Briancourt, is dressed in "white flannel . . . a very open Byron-like collar, and a red Lavalliere cravat tied in a huge bow." The Byronic collar, open neck, and red tie tell a tale and give a sign, the least of which is the mention of the notorious Byron's name. The red cravat signals inversion as is attested to by Ellis, who wrote that "it is notable that of recent years there has been a fashion for a red tie to be adopted by inverts as their badge." The American "invert" who told Ellis this writes, "It is red that has become almost a synonym for sexual inversion" (quoted in Katz 1976, 52). In *Sexual Inversion* Ellis comments further on sartorial signs, noting the keeping the neck uncovered "may certainly be observed among a considerable proportion of inverts, especially the more artistic among them. The cause does not appear to be precisely vanity so much as that physical consciousness . . . induces the more feminine to. . . cultivate feminine grace of form, and the more masculine to emphasize athletic habit" (Ellis, 177).

But Briancourt does not attract; it is at Teleny that Des Grieux can only look. Teleny has very nearly stepped out of a poem by Symonds: his face is pale, his hair ashy and curled, and his eyes deep blue but with "a scared and wistful look as if he were gazing at some dreadful dim and distant vision." An aura of "deepest sorrow" and "painful glamour" mark him as one set apart. If that is not enough, he will soon reveal to Des Grieux that he is marked by what he refers to as "my fate, that horrible, horrible fate of mine." Thus his beauty is conflated with his difference—one that combines the exotic with the vaguely sinister, glamour with a hint of something fearful and unknown.

Teleny, like the serpent, transfixes Des Grieux. He is the sexual tempter whose allure, in the myths of homophobia, cannot be resisted even by the innocent man: "I felt a strange flutter within me, and the fascination of his looks was so powerful that I was hardly able to move. . . . I was quivering from head to foot. He seemed to be slowly drawing me to him, and I must confess the feeling was such a pleasant one that I yielded entirely to it."

Until now their congress has only been at a distance, but they shake hands. Teleny's grip is a "magnetic hand, which seems to have a secret affinity for Des Grieux's." The choice of "affinity" inscribes Teleny's grasp within that circle of "sympathy" that so surrounds homoerotic texts, so much so that "sympathy" had come to have a "special" meaning. Signs are everywhere here, for signs are everything to the homosexual, who must find in the seemingly most innocent gestures a world of secret meanings. Teleny's touch thrills and enthralls Des Grieux—who is in a sense rapidly being transmuted into Camille—and he reads the touch like a text: "It set me on fire; and, strange to say, it soothed me at the same time. How much sweeter, softer, it was, than any woman's kiss. I felt his grasp steal slowly over all my body, caressing my lips, my throat, my breast; my nerves quivered from head to foot with delight, then it sank downwards into my veins, and Priapus, reawakened, lifted up his head. I actually felt I was being taken possession of, and I was happy to belong to him" (12). Like David and Jonathan's love, Teleny's grip passes the love of woman, but in pornographic texts it must erase it entirely, and so as Teleny's grasp steals over his entire body Des Grieux becomes a penis, caressed nearly into orgasm and certainly into surrender by Teleny's erotic hand.

The affinity that Des Grieux felt is now ratified by the invocation of "sympathy." Teleny tells the group of men that he is moved to play his best when he knows that he is heard by a "sympathetic listener," one "with whom a current seems to establish itself; someone who feels exactly as I do while I am playing, who sees perhaps the same visions I do." The "current" he describes is that electric sympathy that so hypnotized Des Grieux, and it is soon clear that Des Grieux's visions are precisely those that visit Teleny as he plays. That they share similar visions serves to confirm the larger text to which this scene alludes—the Platonic myth of the divided lovers who seek one another in order to be reunited in perfect love. But the text also implies that there is a psychological bond that implicates both of them and perhaps all homosexuals in a homosexual sensibility. Real or not, this sensibility is, as a concept, one of the important contributions of nineteenth-century homoerotic texts.

After the concert a romantic promenade, hand in hand, produces further excitement for Des Grieux, and now in no unspecific terms: "All the blood vessels of my member were strongly extended and the nerves stiff. . . . I felt a dull pain spread over and near all the organs of generation, whilst the remainder of my body was in a state of prostration, and still—notwithstanding the pain and languor—it was a most pleasurable sensation to walk quietly on with our hands clasped, his head almost leaning on my shoulders" (22). It is a brilliant passage, for the romantic hand-holding and the head on the shoulder can be replicated in any number of heterosexual idyls that especially stress the innocence of just such a scene. But here are two men, and beneath the placid even too sweetly romantic surface and the elegant attire passion impatiently waits to spend itself. The mark of their desire is "pain and languor," that same charged word used by Raffalovich when he urged his lovers to "put on that languor which the world frowns on" as a gestural (and verbal) sign of homosexual desire. They conclude their first encounter by recourse to that erotic and scientific metaphor Whitman used when he sings "the body electric" and describes the erotic shock of recognition that passes between lovers. For Teleny and Des Grieux "there was a current between us, like a spark of electricity running along a wire" (23).

A nightmare resulting from his encounter with Teleny leaves Des Grieux so overwrought that it requires his mother to calm him. She put "her fresh hand upon my hot forehead" and "the soothing touch of her soft hand cooled the burning fire within my brain and allayed the fever raging in my blood." This is the fire and fever of homosexual desire, of course, and it is a telling detail that only his mother can cool it. She comforts him further with a glass of "sugared water flavored with essence of orange flowers." It takes no profound reading in popular psychology to recognize in the soothing hands and intimate bedside scene the cloying and overaffectionate mother. The orange water marks her intimate encouragement of his already somewhat effete manner—a manner underscored when he tells us that his hobby is collecting "old majolica, old fans, and old lace."

His mother is beautiful, intelligent, charming, and can deny Des Grieux nothing, ordering champagne for him in the morning when he petulantly demands it. What is more she is a widow, and she fears that her son has inherited her husband's mysterious "sensual disposition." Thus Des Grieux is inscribed precisely within a psychiatric model that would be imagined to produce the invert—a strong, sexually attractive mother with whom he has developed an "unnaturally" close relationship, and an absent father. To this is added the potential curse of some congenital disorder, an affliction that especially touches Des Grieux, since homosexuality was by then theorized to be a symptom of a congenitally "morbid" nature. Like Goethe's Werther, he is beset with emotional conflict, but again in search of signs and interpretations he ceaselessly analyzes his feelings: "I was conscious of . . . a vague feeling of unease and unrest. There was an emptiness in me, still I could not understand if the void was in my heart or in my head. I had lost nothing yet I felt lonely, forlorn, almost bereaved. I tried to fathom my morbid state."

His morbid state is not helped by a conversation with his mother who suggests that Teleny may be advanced in his career by some wealthy woman. Des Grieux is appalled by this suggestion and his reaction, prompted both by jealousy and misogyny, is that if this is the case "it is a disgusting world." So inflamed and irrational does he become at his mother's offhand suggestion that behind every great man one must always "*cherchez la femme*" that he asserts that "I loathed the whole of womankind, the curse of the world." The source of his loathing is detailed, along with specific sexual adventures that exacerbated it, in the chapters that follow. Des Grieux has always had little doubt, as *Don Leon* put it, that his "predilection is for males." Indeed, he says, "I was predisposed to love men and not women, and without knowing it I had always struggled against the inclinations of my nature." He defines his sexuality as a predisposition and an inclination and so sites himself within the new medical discourses that explained homosexuality as congenital and within the homoerotically positive discourses that attempted justification by erasure of the stigma of the unnatural. His struggle against his inclinations—that is, his guilt—has led him to experiment with heterosexuality, and it is the outcome of these experiments, some conducted before his meeting with Teleny, that prompt his outburst against women.

His determined attempt to fall in love with a young girl—"I had done my best to persuade myself that I was deeply smitten"—is twice thwarted, each time scatologically, first when he happens on his "English damsel perched upon a closet seat" and again when he discovers her out of doors in the act of urination and defecation. The association is so horrible to his sensitive nature that "the only love I ever had for a woman thus came to an end." Indeed, subsequent experiences that involve women and sex are attended by horrendous and extravagant consequences. His first visit to a brothel as a youth is no schoolboy orgy resplendent with the wonder of sexual discovery but a nightmare in which he confronts prostitutes of appalling monstrosity: "It was the first time I had seen a naked woman, and this one was positively loathsome . . . her belly a huge heap of blighted wheat . . . her legs two massive columns . . . her whole body one mass of quivering fat." He flees the brothel, "cured forever of the temptation of again visiting such a house of nightly entertainment." Although these grossly depicted scenes contain sexual description to forward the purpose of the text as pornography, they provide an ironic homosexual countertext to the medical prescription that urged young men "afflicted" with homosexual desires to seek out female companionship or to undertake marriage as a "cure."

Des Grieux's love for Teleny is now so passionate that it is very nearly out of control, yet he is not yet able to escape from the homophobic prejudice he imagines to be the voice of morality: "I was young and inexperienced, therefore moral; for what is morality but prejudice? . . . I had been inculcated with all kinds of wrong ideas, so when I understood what my natural feelings for

Teleny were, I was staggered, horrified; and filled with dismay, I resolved to stifle them." Suffering like Byron in *Don Leon* under the whiplash of conventional morality, he turns to history, religion, and science for an explanation and justification of his desire:

> I read all I could find about the love of one man for another, that loathsome crime against nature taught to us not only by the very gods themselves, but by all the greatest men of olden times, for even Minos himself seemed to have sodomized Theseus. I, of course, looked upon it as a monstrosity, a sin . . . yet I had to admit that the world—even after the cities of the plain had been destroyed—throve well enough notwithstanding this aberration. . . . It was but time for Christianity to come to sweep away all the monstrous vices of the world. . . . The popes had their catamites. . . . I also read in modern medical books, how the penis of a sodomite becomes thin and pointed. . . . [I]t is true since then that experience has taught me quite another lesson . . . as for my penis . . . its bulky head . . . (63–65)

Like Byron and Maurice, he grows disgusted with conventional moral codes, longs to answer the calling of his desires, and feels that if he can escape to Arcadia he will be safe from the unjust laws of men: "There were moments, however, when, nature being stronger than prejudice, I should right willingly have given up my soul to perdition—nay, yielded my body to suffer in eternal hellfire—If I could have fled somewhere on the confines of this earth, on some lonely island, where in perfect nakedness I could have lived for some years in deadly sin with him, feasting upon his fascinating beauty" (65–66).

The strength of homophobia has impelled him to stifle his desire for Teleny and to avoid him. His desire will not allow him to do so, however, and he goes to a concert where Teleny is playing. He is shocked to discover that Teleny too has been suffering and appears "careworn and dejected" and his playing has become lackluster. But when Teleny sights Des Grieux in the crowd, a transformation takes place, and the old fire is rekindled in both of them. But still paralyzed by fear—a victim of his own internalized homophobia—he can do nothing but be rude to Teleny when he attempts to speak to him. Still enthralled by desire, he also can do nothing else but follow Teleny when he leaves arm in arm with Briancourt, the young man of the red tie and Byronic open collar, into the streets of Paris and into the homosexual underworld. Here the text provides what may be an exaggerated or accurate but still valuable picture of the homosexual marketplace of 1893.

As he shadows Teleny he is aware that he is being shadowed himself by a man, who "tried to keep pace with me but also to catch my attention, for he hummed and whistled snatches of songs, coughed, cleared his throat, and scraped his feet." His companion is "slightly dressed. He wore a short black velvet jacket and a pair of light grey, close fitting trousers marking the shape of his thighs and buttocks like tights. . . . Then always looking at me with an inviting leer, he directed his steps toward a neighboring Vespasienne." More men appear: one also signals interest in Des Grieux, for he "either unbuttoned or buttoned up his trousers." This man also follows him and when "he was close to me, I smelled a strong scent . . . his eyes were painted with kohl, his cheeks were dabbed with rouge, for a minute I doubted whether he was a man or woman." Yet another "came with mincing steps, shaking his buttocks, from behind one of the pissoirs. He was old . . . wiry, simpering . . . and he wore a wig with long flaxen locks. . . . His looks were not only very demure, but there was about him an almost maidenly coyness . . . that gave him the appearance of a virgin pimp."

There now appears quite another type, "a workman, a strong and sturdy fellow." He is accosted by the old man but ignores him and instead comes to Des Grieux. He is "a brawny man, with massive features," precisely the type Des Grieux prefers. The workman makes a sexually explicit gesture of invitation to Des Grieux, but so overwhelmed is he that he does not respond, yet "notwithstanding the creepy feeling these men gave me, the scene was so entirely new that I must say it rather interested me." But his interest turns to horror when he sees Teleny and Briancourt in conversation with a young soldier. He hurries on, sure that Teleny has recognized him and "sick at heart" and "hating myself" he muses "whether I was any better than all these worshippers of Priapus who were inured to vice. I was pining for the love of one man who did not care more for me than for any of these sodomites." Horror-stricken, he attempts suicide by trying to leap into the Seine.

Des Grieux has been catapulted into homosexual life, for his terrible passage through the unacceptable world of heterosexual desire has convinced him that there is no place there for him. His penetration into the underworld of homosexuality makes him feel equally an outcast, however; even the glimmer of interest that it arouses does not convince him that he can live in such a milieu. The repressed passions and torment that drive Des Grieux to his suicide attempt will now be liberated and assuaged by Teleny, who appears and saves him from self-destruction. Safe in Teleny's arms, he can struggle no more and when Teleny says, "I love you madly! I cannot live without you." He can do nothing but respond, "Nor can I. . . . I have struggled against my passion in vain, and now I yield to it, not tamely, but eagerly, gladly. I am yours, Teleny! Happy to be yours, yours forever and yours alone!"

They return to Teleny's house, an exotic site like a scene out of Huysmans's A Rebours or Symonds's "Midnight at Baiae." The room is "redolent with the strong, overpowering smell of white heliotrope," and the walls were covered with "white, soft, quilted stuff, studded all over with silver buttons; the floor was covered with the curly white fleece of young lambs; in the middle of the apartment stood a capacious couch, on which was thrown the skin of a huge polar bear. Over this single piece of furniture, an old silver lamp—evidently from some Byzantine church or some eastern synagogue—shed a pale glimmering light, sufficient to light up the dazzling whiteness of this temple of Priapus" (136). This temple recalls a visit made to Eric Stenbock, a minor nineteenth-century homosexual poet, by the painter Simeon Solomon, who described Stenbock in his exotic quarters: "he had on a magnificent blood red silk robe embroidered in gold and silver. He was swinging a censer before an altar covered with lilies, myrtles, lighted candles and a sanctuary lamp burning with scented oil. The air was so heavy with incense . . . that I felt quite faint" (quoted in Reade, 37).

Devotees of Priapus as they are, they soon make sacrifice: "I was in a state of ecstatic joy. . . . I squeezed the whole rod with all the strength of my muscles, and a most violent jet, like a hot geyser, escaped from him, and coursed within me. . . . it set my blood on fire" (148). What is described graphically here is also pictured in an 1899 poem by Crowley in which he describes how, in a sexual encounter with a "boy of red lips," the "fond ruby rapier glides and slips / Twixt the white hills thou spreadest for me there" (quoted in Smith, 98). Teleny and Des Grieux experiment with every kind of sexual possibility, and the description of their lovemaking provides a catalog of the possibilities of homosexual desire. When they have reached the last of many orgasms, Des Grieux discovers that in sexual release he has also been released from the homophobia that had paralyzed him: "the world that had hitherto seemed to me so bleak, so cold, so desolate, was now a perfect paradise" (153). Like Byron in *Don Leon* and like Symonds after he has slept with the strapping soldier, Des Grieux rejoices in the freedom that he has gained by embracing homosexual love: "far from being ashamed of my crime, I felt that I should like to proclaim it to the world" (153).

He discovers not only personal freedom but recognizes the falsehood of the proscription of homosexual love as a crime against nature: "Had I committed a crime against nature when my own nature found peace and happiness thereby? If I was thus surely it was the fault of my blood, not myself." Of course, he speaks in terms that suggest that his understanding of homosexuality is still colored by the social condemnation of homosexuality as a "fault"—though now not a moral but a physiological one—and as "lust" and an overwhelming passion: "When I had tried to bridle my lust, was it my fault if the scale of reason was far too light to balance that of sensuality." Yet he determines to struggle against his desires no longer: "Fate . . . had clearly shown me that if I would damn myself, I could do so in a more delicate way than drowning. I yielded to my destiny and encompassed my joy" (154).

The story concludes with a homosexual masquerade ball that becomes an orgy of promiscuous embraces, allowing the author to create a tour de force of homoerotic sexual description. The ball ends with a sexual experiment gone wrong involving a handsome Arab soldier. The soldier, though mortally injured, refuses to seek medical help: "What go to a hospital and expose myself to the sneers of the nurses and doctors—never!" He leaves the party and once at home "he locked the door and took a revolver and shot himself." Suicide rather than discovery is the soldier's choice just as suicide rather than acceptance of his desire was Des Grieux's choice until Teleny saves him. And in the end Teleny too takes his own life after Des Grieux discovers Teleny in a sexual encounter with his own mother, brought about because Teleny has had to submit to her sexual blackmail as the price for her payment of his substantial debts and, it is hinted, to lure Teleny away from her son.

Des Grieux finds Teleny dying, they are reconciled, but it is of course too late for happiness. The book ends, as indeed it must, in tragedy, like the scores of homosexual novels that would be written after it. It ends in death because, like Bloxam's "The Priest and the Acolyte," there seems to be no better choice, life being what it is, for "an unspeakable of the Oscar Wilde sort." The conflation of homosexual passion and death, indeed, is one of the master elements of these texts that describe the desire that is allowed no place or any name. At Teleny's funeral the text of the sermon reads, "His remembrance shall perish from the earth, and he shall have no name in the street. He shall be driven from the light into darkness, and chased out of the world" (242).

Teleny is a pornographic text, full of explicit, imaginative, and often eloquent depictions of all sorts of sexual connections. But it is more than that. It is also a serious representation of the destructive—indeed, mortal—effect of homophobia on a positively presented emotional and sexual relation between two men. In some ways *Teleny* is a more accurate mirror than many of the texts I have discussed of the crisis point at which homoerotic texts had arrived as the dark clouds of the Wilde trial began to obscure what light these texts had begun to generate.

Though *Teleny* ends by affirming what could hardly be denied—as George V, when the subject of homosexual men was broached, replied, "I thought they shot themselves"—it also affirms the newly developing sense of homosexual identity and the value of that identity. It sites this affirmation within the traditional environment of homosexuality presented as a sexual perversion only. It juxtaposes a sexual text that reflects stereotypes about the perversion and promiscuity of sodomites against a tale of fidelity and high romantic love between two men. By valorizing sex as a function of high romance and fidelity instead of as a sign of depravity, *Teleny* strikes powerfully against the received opinion that homosexuals were monsters of perversion. It not only offers a full-scale, sentimental, and triumphantly homosexual love affair but daringly and wittily uses the prime convention of the sentimental heterosexual love plot—salvation by love—as its metaphor. *Teleny* does what Raffalovich urged his lovers to do: "Since 'twixt the world and truth must be our choice, / Let us seem vile, not be so, and rejoice."

Though the power of love, even as in the best heterosexual fables, does triumph, though only for a time, over adversity, Des Grieux's greatest triumph is over himself and over the homophobic social sanctions to which he had subscribed. In choosing to follow his desire he joins with *Don Leon*'s Byron and Bloxam's Ronald Heatherington, with Raffalovich and Symonds, and with numbers of other writers of the period whose texts, in effect, make the body a political battleground.

John Addington Symonds

chapter 7

A PASSION EVERYWHERE PRESENT: J. A. SYMONDS
AND HOMOTEXTUALITY, 1873–1891

There is a passion . . . present everywhere and in all periods of history. . . . Yet
no one dares speak of it, or if they do they bate their breath, and preface their
remarks with maledictions.
    —John Addington Symonds, "A Problem in Modern Ethics" (1891)

    In an 1889 letter to Henry Dakyns, John Addington Symonds
described himself as "a character somewhat strangely constituted in moral
and aesthetic qualities."[1] In another letter written toward the end of his life
to his daughter Madge, he enlarges on this idea: "I love beauty above virtue
and think that nowhere is beauty more eminent than in young men. This
love is what people call aesthetic in me. It has to do with my perceptions
through the senses . . . there is nothing I was born to love more. . . . [W]ith
my heart and soul I love physical perfection" (quoted in Grosskurth, 271).
Symonds's perception of the erotic as the driving force of the aesthetic is the
dominant metaphor of his writing, as his speculations turn from belletristic
literary criticism to the concerns of what gender studies now calls "theory."
    To elaborate his theory Symonds wrote two essays that are landmarks in
the identification of homosexuality and in the advocacy of the legal and
social rights of homosexuals. In his *Memoirs* (written in 1889 but not published until 1984) he characteristically laments that "it was my destiny to
make continual renunciation of my truest self, because I was born out of sympathy with the men around me" (Symonds, 218). His "truest self" is his
homosexuality—what he called the "problem"—which tormented him
throughout his life, although this torment did not prevent him from acting

on his sexual desires. Nor did it prevent him—indeed, it impelled him—to write voluminously and illuminatingly about the "problem." His sense that this renunciation in some way affected his literary work is a characteristic but ultimately incorrect assessment. His poetry is almost entirely a mirror of his "truest self" and a site for the exploration of a galaxy of homoerotic concerns, as well as being some of the most interesting and among the best written by homosexual Victorian poets.

When his poetry ceased to provide a sufficient stage for his speculations, Symonds turned to the weaving of a carefully considered argument for the rights of homosexuals and to an equally ambitious project to reclaim for homosexuals a history and to create for them an aesthetic that would serve the demands both of criticism and morality. Eminent Victorian to the end, he tried to reconcile in his life and work his passionate homosexual desire and his conviction that his body was his to use as he saw fit. Observing that the extent of homosexual literature was unknown to most readers, he sought in his critical texts sometimes only to suggest this literature's presence, sometimes to make it clearly known. He indicated his concern by his choice of subjects: ancient Greek poets, Italian and English Renaissance literature, and the writers Cellini, Michelangelo, Sir Phillip Sidney, and Walt Whitman.

Symonds surely must have read Walter Pater's famous, even notorious, "Conclusion" to *Studies in the History of the Renaissance*, written in 1868, in which Pater brought desire and art together in a potent evocation: "While all melts beneath our feet, we may well catch at any exquisite passion, or any contribution to knowledge that seems, by a lifted horizon, to set the spirit free for a moment, or any stirring of the senses, strange dyes, strange flowers, and curious odors, or work of the artist's hands, or the face of one's friend" (quoted in Reade, 20). All of Symonds's writing is motivated by a longing for the face of a real or imagined friend as he attempts to capture on the erotic page homosexual desire and define its sensibility—a project painfully highlighted against what he saw as the spiritual and erotic poverty of his own bleak times.

Symonds spent much time trying to find and define texts to which he felt clung an "aura" of difference, a trace however faint or an echo however distant of the erotic flutes of Arcadia. When he wrote about the Greek poets or Italian literature, about Sidney or Shelley, Michelangelo or Whitman, all artists who in some way were concerned with the beauty that resides in the physical perfection of young men, he tried to perceive the linkage of that physical beauty with an eroticized aesthetic theory. His keen ear, ever alert for homoerotic nuance, did not fail to hear the subtext, just as he must have noted it when Pater explained that his "Conclusion" might "possibly mislead some of those young men into whose hands it might fall." Symonds determined that leading, not misleading, young men out of the paths of Victorian heterosexual orthodoxy—especially if those young men had already heard but had not yet dared to respond to the call of homosexual desire—was a worthy mission.

His reading of Plato and Whitman prompted him to his tasks, the first of which was *Studies of the Greek Poets*, which he began writing between 1865 and 1868 and published in 1873. His conclusion to the work was almost, he feared, as incendiary as Pater's, and it was in fact more outspoken. (In fact he believed that it had caused him to lose his professorship of poetry at Oxford; however, it is likely that the conclusion's not so veiled attack on Christianity more than its veiled praise of homosexuality was responsible for that loss.) In the conclusion he characterized the "genius" of Greek literature in a typically erotic metaphor as "a young man newly come from the wrestling ground, anointed, chapleted and very calm. . . . The pride and strength of adolescence are his—audacity and endurance, swift passions and exquisite sensibilities, the alternation of sublime repose and boyish noise, grace, pliancy, stubbornness and power, love of all fair things."[2] The passage conflates history and desire, signaling its interests by its central metaphor of the naked young man and by its subsidiary descriptions of him as a passionate possessor of "exquisite sensibilities." He is linked to Plato and the *Symposium* by the assertion of his love of beauty and all things fair.

Symonds opens his argument when he observes that Greek morality was "aesthetic and not theocratic," thus attacking the theocratic and unaesthetic morality of his own times. For the Greeks, "the sensual impulses, like the intellectual and the moral, were then held void of crime and harmless" (568). By comparison, his own time had produced a "separation of flesh and spirit wrought by Christianity." The unhappy result of this rupture is "the abhorrence of beauty as a snare and the sense that carnal affections were tainted with sin, the unwilling toleration of sexual love as a necessity, the idealisation of celibacy and solitude" (568). Of course it is just these elements that apologists for Judeo-Christian doctrine proclaim as central virtues, and so Symonds's assertions were not only dangerous in their muted advocacy of an officially illegal homosexual love but could well seem heretical to doctrinaire readers.

Though Symonds's text pledges an uneasy allegiance to Christian doctrine, the focus of his desire is clearly elsewhere. He hopes that there may be a reclamation of the Greek ideal, but he fears that there are those "to whom Greece is a lost fatherland." He is clearly one of those, and though he does not say it there can be no doubt that "those" are men like himself who loved men and that in Greece he finds the pure and exemplary repository of that love. Perhaps, he wonders and hopes, in "modern men" there may still be a place for such "natural" exercise of what he subtextually deems to be a "natural" desire. If such a thing can be then it will strike at what he tellingly and daringly targets as "conventionalities and prejudices." We must "imitate the

Greeks . . . by reproducing their free and fearless attitude of mind" and acknowledge "the value of each human impulse" and aim "after virtues that depend on self-regulation rather than on total abstinence and mortification. To do this in the midst of our conventionalities and prejudices . . . is no doubt hard. Yet if we fail of this, we lose the best the Greeks can teach us" (554–55, 570–7).

His terminology leaves no doubt that he intends to construct a radical advocacy for reform of attitudes toward homosexuality. Setting Greek "free and fearless" attitudes of mind—the same terms used in *Don Leon* and the very virtues Byron went to Greece to find—against the sex negativity of Christianity makes even sharper that pointed "each" that modifies "human impulse." Even the homosexual must now be included. If mortification and abstention are banished as tools of a repressive morality, then religious demands that homosexuals refrain from practicing their "sin" can no longer be met and medical strictures that prescribe abstention as a "cure" or self-denial as a medicine can no longer be observed. If convention and prejudice no longer govern the lives of those for whom Greece is indeed a lost father-land and a metaphor for their desire, then their very human impulses will be valued the same as any other. Symonds implies that laws, morality, religions, and social attitudes must be changed, for if "the best of the Greeks" was lost so would civilization itself be lost.

"A PROBLEM IN GREEK ETHICS"

Out of Symonds's research for *Studies of the Greek Poets* came the essay "A Problem in Greek Ethics," which was not published until 1883, and then in only 10 privately printed and circulated copies. Describing in his *Memoirs* his reaction to the conception and writing of the essay, he wrote, "My object is to explain the feelings of the Greeks about passion, to show how pederastia was connected with their sense of beauty, and how it affected their institutions. . . . I dare not attempt the labour. My brain will not stand it; I lose my sleep; my stomach refuses to act; and obscure aching pressure . . . grinds me down" (Symonds 1892, 172).

Symonds articulates the central argument of "A Problem in Greek Ethics" when he includes the study of Greece as a part of an implied greater study of homosexuality: "For the student of sexual inversion ancient Greece offers . . . alone in history . . . the example of a great and highly developed race not only tolerating homosexual passions, but deeming them of spiritual value."[3] It is of course spiritual value that Christianity specifically denies to homosexuality. This may be the first time in English, incidentally, where the word "homosexual" is used since the term first appeared in German in 1869.

The remainder of his task is spent in supporting the argument for toler-ance and spiritual value. Homosexual passions for the Greeks, he says, are those denominated by the Greek word *pederastia*, the love of older men for youths that he finds everywhere and "very early," though he demurs at assigning it to Homer, defining the love of Achilles and Patroclus as "heroic friendship." He is able to document its appearance in the earliest myths of Greece, citing the myths of Ganymede and Zeus and of Laius and Chryssipus as founding myths of Greek pederasty.

Symonds was well aware that Greek homosexual texts had long been hidden, either by bowdlerized translations, as was the case for example with Sydenham's eighteenth-century translation of Plato's *Symposium* that deleted references to same-sex love, or else by a kind of willful refusal to see what was there, as was the case with Benjamin Jowett, the nineteenth-century translator of Plato, who maintained that Plato's discourse about same-sex love was a "figure of speech" and only a "matter of metaphor" rather than the description of real emotion between males (quoted in Grosskurth, 268). Symonds supports no illusion that the Greeks were sexual idealists, subscribers to the pure and sexless interpretations of Platonic affection that allowed his own age to read Greek texts as Jowett had done. He documents "two forms of separate masculine passion clearly marked in early Hellas—a noble and a base, a spiritual and sensual" (6). What he says is no doubt reasonably accurate, but it is of use not so much in analyzing Greek sexual economy as it is in illuminating that of Symonds's own times.

The central emotional crisis of Symonds's life, and in the lives of so many homosexual writers of the nineteenth century, was the contradiction they perceived between the spirituality of homosexual desire and the sensuality of homosexual sex. This resulted in an attempt by some to sublimate desire to the spiritual, by others to valorize the union of the two, and in a few to reject the spiritual for the carnal. Symonds's mention of this here and his creation of a dichotomy within the Greek homoerotic discourse speaks as much to his anxieties and those of his times as it does to a true relation of the sexual organization of Greece.

Defining homosexuality as a "unique product of their civilization," Symonds firmly conflates sex and civilization in the face of Christian teaching that sex is inimical to man's civilized and spiritual aspirations. Greek love was "a passionate and enthusiastic attachment subsisting between man and youth, recognized by society and protected by opinion, which though it was not free from sensuality, did not degenerate into mere licentiousness" (8). This definition marks homosexual desire as everything that it was not in the nineteenth century and indicates that what was allowed to the Greeks—passion, enthusiasms, sensuality—are precisely what was now forbidden.

Symonds finds evidence of pederasty in ancient Greek tales of the loves of the gods for mortal youths and in legends of devoted masculine friendship like those of Orestes and Pylades, Hercules and Hylas, or Harmodios and Aristogeiton. In the history of the Dorian Greeks he finds the "earliest and most marked encouragement to Greek Love" and pauses for a moment at one of his favorite themes, the difference between effeminacy and "manly love." The former he sees as a characteristic of "savage tribes," the latter of civilized man. The Dorian Greeks only, according to his thesis, practiced "the distinctive features" of comradeship, "tolerating no sort of softness," while the homosexual organization of "barbarians"—among whom he Eurocentrically includes "the North American Bardashes, the Tescats of Madagascar, the Cordaches of the Canadian Indians" and the "primitive peoples of Mexico, Perus and Yucatan"—valorized "effeminate males who renounce their sex, assume female clothes, and live either in promiscuous concubinage with the men of the tribe or else in marriage with chosen persons" (30). Such effeminacies, he says, were considered "pathological by Heroditus," and he presumably considered them so as well.

Symonds is at his most culture-bound here, betraying a blindness to racial, class, and cultural difference even while advocating sexual difference. His imprisoning self-inscription within middle-class notions of the proprieties and boundaries of gender roles is painfully obvious in his dismissal of "effeminacy" as an organizing factor in sexual subjects. But in his valorization of "masculine" comradeship and "manliness" Symonds is attempting to extricate that concept from the middle-class sex and class nexus of exclusively "heterosexual" discourse, which was even then claiming "manliness" as its exclusive preserve. From his excursion across cultural boundaries into the comparative study of modern, Greek, and "barbarian" cultures he recognizes that what his own age had constructed as an "essential" characteristic of the sodomite, the molly, and even of the new homosexual—effeminacy—was in fact a social construction. His research proves, he believes, the "universality of unisexual indulgence in all parts of the world." The Greeks were able to "moralise and adapt to social use a practice which has elsewhere been excluded in the course of civil growth." Instead of abandoning it as "a remnant of more primitive conditions"—a criticism of theories that saw homosexuality as an early psychological or cultural phase that civilizations and people "grew out" of—he asserts that the Greeks "chose to elaborate it into the region of romance and ideality" (20).

As evidence of this he embarks on a study of Greek poetry and drama, touching on the expected sites of homoeroticism in the texts of Theognis, Anacreon, and Pindar and mentioning the lost pederastic plays of Aeschuylus and Sophocles, the former's *Myrmidons* and the latter's *Loves of Achilles*. In a long discussion he examines homoeroticism in Plato's *Symposium* and in the *Symposium* of Xenophon. He does not fail to address Plato's seeming disapproval in the *Laws* of the very pederasty he had so warmly endorsed in the *Symposium*. He correctly argues that much modern condemnation of homosexuality has been based on this position, and from it has been derived the only definition of Platonic love that modern times has found acceptable—pure love free from carnal desire. Symonds slyly, though always maintaining the tone of the investigator, suggests that Plato's seeming change of mind in fact was a change of heart based on the cooling of desire and the advent of old age when passion had been replaced by the necessity of sexless contemplation.

In his youth Plato felt "sympathy for love so long as it was paiderastic and not spent on women; he even condoned a lapse through warmth of feeling into self-indulgence. As an old man, he denounced carnal pleasures of all kinds, and sought to limit the amative instincts to the one sole end of pro-creation" (52). Citation of these texts here constitutes the creation of a scholarly "set-piece" comparable to the deployment of a "list of great homo-sexuals" that had already become a feature of apologias for same-sex love. Here it marks one of the points to which gay literary studies can refer in the search for homosexuality's origins.

Symonds concludes that in Athens homosexuality was "closely associat-ed" with "liberty, manly sports, severe studies, enthusiasm, self sacrifice, self control, and deeds of daring" (62). He then asks a question that could only be asked within the context of a developing theory of homosexual identity: Was there "not something special both in the Greek consciousness itself and also in the conditions under which it reached maturity, which justified the Socratic attempt to idealize paiderastia?" He answers it as follows:

> what the Greeks worshipped in their ritual, what they represented in their sculpture was always personality—the spirit and the flesh in amity and mutual correspondence; the spirit burning through the flesh and moulding it to individual forms; the flesh providing a fit dwelling for the spirit. . . . [I]t followed as a necessity that their highest emotional aspirations, their purest personal service, should be devoted to clear and radiant incarnations of the spirit in a living person. (53)

For the Greeks, that "living person" was male, for "the female form aroused desire. . . . [I]t also suggested maternity and the obligations of the household" while "the male form was the most perfect image of the deity, subject to no necessities of impregnation, determined in its actions only by the laws of its own reason and its own volition." To stress that male volition involved male-male sex Symonds points out that the Greeks "had never been taught to regard the body with a sense of shame . . . and to accept its needs and instincts with natural acquiescence" (53–54).

When Symonds arrives at the conclusion of his essay, he gives in to the promptings of desire and returns in effect to poetry, forgetting scholarship to assert that "the Greeks admitted, as true artists are obliged to do, that the male body displays harmonies of proportion and melodies of outline more comprehensive, more indicative of strength expressed in terms of grace than that of woman. I guard myself against saying—more seductive to the senses, more soft, more delicate, more undulating" (68). Having abandoned his pretense, he continues with an extravagant celebration of the pleasures of the male body:

> The Greek lover, if I am right in the idea I have formed of him, sought less to stimulate desire by the contemplation of sensual charms than to attune his spirit with the spectacle of strength at rest in suavity. He admired the chastened lines, the figure slight but sinewy, the limbs well-knit and flexible, the small head set upon broad shoulders, the keen eyes, the austere reins, the elastic movement of youth made vigourous by exercise. Physical perfection suggested to his fancy all that he loved best in moral qualities. Hardihood, self-discipline, alertness of intelligence, health, temperance, indomitable spirit, energy, the joy of active life, plain living and high thinking—these qualities the Greeks idealised, and of these "the lightning vision of the darling" was the living incarnation. (69)

Shedding the lover's and donning again the scholar's mantle he adds, "there is plenty in their literature to show that paiderastia obtained sanction from the belief that a soul of this sort would be found within the body of a young man rather than a woman."

The obvious misogyny of this passage vitiates any claim that might be made that Symonds felt much rapport with the nascent feminist stirrings of his own time. But that is not his subject. Symonds is interested in constructing a "moral" economy—he calls it "moral qualities"—within the political and sexual use of the body, not outside of it. This economy he defined as "manly" and it valorized homosexual desire as opposed to nineteenth-century social and moral organizations that excluded homosexual desire from any definition of "manliness."

He also goes to great pains to erase the reading of "Platonic Love" that Jowett supported as nothing more than metaphor. The Greeks were not innocent, and their sensuality was no Platonic celibacy, no abstention from the prompting of "needs and instincts." Symonds insists that the Greeks were instead healthy in comparison to the moral and spiritual sickness of modern times: "to the Greeks there was nothing criminal in paiderastia. To forbid it as a hateful and unclean thing did not occur to them. Finding it within their hearts, they chose to regulate it rather than root it out" (92). In Arcadia, utopia could be found as well.

But now, Symonds sadly suggests, the moral dispensations of the modern world have changed all that, and it may well be that the fatherland is lost forever. What stands between him and that lost fatherland is Christianity and its deployment of sexual asceticism as the hallmark of virtue. Christianity has, in the cult of Mary the Virgin, "proclaimed that woman is the mediating and ennobling element of human life." If one had not read Symonds's description of beauty as the exclusive province of the male, this comment might pass as a piety designed to conclude an essay that might have seemed to dwell dangerously long on a subject that the Virgin's cult abhorred. But Symonds has no such intention when he observes that Christianity coupled with medieval romantic and chivalric ideals sanctioned a "cult of woman" to which "we owe the spiritual basis of our domestic and civil life." His text is double-edged, for it is modern domestic and civil life that condemns homosexuality. He engages again that constant subtext that affirms that intolerance of sexual difference is the spiritual and moral sickness of modern times. His rejection of the Christian ethic and middle-class morality is summed up in his dismissive word "domestic."

Through scholarship Symonds mounts a sustained attack on civil and domestic homophobia and unveils the first published defense of homosexual desire. That it came from the heart there can be no doubt; that he feared the consequences of even its limited publication is indicated by his warning to the friends to whom he sent copies to "be discreet about it." But valor had overcome discretion, for the subject of his text was also the subject of his life. As he wrote to Edmond Gosse in 1890, "You will not doubt I am sure, that what you call the 'central Gospel' of that essay on the Greeks has been the light and leading of my life" (quoted in Grosskurth, 271).

"THE DANTESQUE AND PLATONIC IDEALS OF LOVE"

The work Symonds began in "A Problem in Greek Ethics" he continued in "The Dantesque and Platonic Ideals of Love," published in 1890. This time he publicly offered in the pages of *The Artist* an essay that, like the earlier text, was couched in the terms of legitimate scholarship but was an even more direct advocacy of homosexual love. His stated objective in this essay is to examine the point where the attitudes toward love as defined in Plato and in Dante intersect, using each as signs for a wider social-sexual organization. He argues that both are chivalric loves, by which he means that each idealizes a type of desire to a point so intense that the Greeks called the love "mania" and chivalric codes defined it as "jouissance," an untranslatable word but one that implies rapturous joy. Both definitions called love an enthusiasm and both deified and exalted the object of desire. Both sited desire outside of the bounds of marriage and both saw it as leading to a higher state of spiritual perfection, and both allowed sensual gratification—the Greek in homosexual attachments, the Dantesque in heterosexual adultery. Both were marked as "abnormal" in nineteenth-century terms because both violated Christian ethics. Symonds allows the obvious objection to the "abnormal" definition to constantly hang fire as a logical absurdity of the text—that is, reading Greek practice as a violation of Christian ethics has meaning only to those who are Christians and could hardly have been meaningful to the Greeks.

Symonds begins by pointing out that while Dante's text claims to be based on a foundation of Platonic love, that foundation suffers from a false definition, for that love "in the true sense of the phrase was the affection of man for man," an affection that had the intention of "promoting a martial spirit in the population, securing a manly education for the young, and binding the male members of the nation together by bonds of mutual affection."[4] Furthermore, "however repugnant to modern tastes" was Greek love, it "existed and flourished in the highest-gifted of all races" yet it was neither an "effeminate depravity nor a sensual vice." This affection, he hurries to add, "rigidly and expressly excluded" the love of women from its scheme, and its intention was to find in such love the route to philosophical standards for a just and moral conduct of life. For Dante, however, the love of women was inscribed as the philosophical and emotional center of his texts, and because that love was "anti-nuptial and anti-matrimonial," it represented, Symonds suggests, an outlaw passion outside of the bounds of Christian moral teaching on the proper relation of the sexes.

Both forms of desire resulted in socially condemned actions—adultery in the one, homosexuality in the other. But Symonds argues that "whether termed 'mania' or 'joy' the passion is precisely the same in quality; and whether "the object which stirred it was a young man as in Greece, or a married woman as in medieval Europe, signified nothing" (77). Of course to the Victorian mind Symonds was addressing it signified everything, and Symonds knew it. His unspoken text says that convention is willing to accept transgression as long as it is heterosexual. His ironic text further argues that even though "Greek love was tainted with a vice obnoxious to modern notions, and that medieval love was involved with adultery" yet these "amorous enthusiasms of an abnormal type presented themselves to natures of the noblest stamp as indispensable conditions of the progress of the soul upon the pathway toward perfection" (81). The unspoken question is: If the one, why not the other?

Symonds argues that since Platonic love in medieval European texts was founded on a philosophy of "manly courtesy" centered on "devotion to the female sex" that "raised the crudest of male appetites to a higher value," the net result was a gender-bound transaction within a sex-centered economy that in deifying women objectified rather than liberated them. Greek practice offered far more to women, he insists, as "in those states where the love of comrades became an institution, women received more public honor and enjoyed fuller civil liberty and power over property" (64). Thus, what Symonds does not say but what he hopes to be deduced is that where pederastic affections are present and approved, the status of women will be improved. Greek "love of comrades"—his term of course is Whitman's and is solidly anchored in the nineteenth century—places homosexual love within a much more complex and valuable emotional, political, and spiritual context than the similar Platonic passion he discerns in the Renaissance, for in Greece the love of comrades was capable of "binding friends together, spurring them on to heroic actions and to intellectual pursuits in common," whereas chivalric medieval love, he argues, had little "to do with those connections profitable to the State and useful to society" (76).

In seeking to compare Renaissance and Greek manifestations of Platonism in erotic texts and in society Symonds has shown that a desire that was at the center of his life and that he saw all around him ought to be reassessed by a society that valorized the "illicit" heterosexual passion of Dante but rejected the same romantic passion between men. Renaissance texts, unlike those produced by the "frank Greek nature," veiled what they meant: "Saying one thing when you mean another, clothing simple thoughts and natural instincts with the veil of symbolism, drawing an iridescent mirage of fancy over the surface of fact by half-voluntary self-sophistications" (83).

"A PROBLEM IN MODERN ETHICS"

Symonds wrote "A Problem in Modern Ethics" in 1891, while he was composing his remarkable *Memoirs*. For his work he looked into those texts (none English) that had addressed what he always thought of as "the problem." He began an inquiry into contemporary homosexuality in order to correct the "vulgar errors" of nineteenth-century texts that presented descriptive or "scientific" inquiries into the causes and nature of homosexuality; he sought to comment on what he felt were inaccurate or intolerant aspects of certain studies and highlight positive aspects of others, and in the process disseminate his own theories.

As early as 1852 some medical theorists proposed a distinction between "innate" and "acquired" sexual characteristics that, as Jeffrey Weeks has pointed out, "were to be the poles of debate for generations" (Weeks, 26ff). This distinction raised the question of whether "sexual inverts" could be held responsible for their acts. In 1868 Karl Heinrich Ulrichs, himself homosexual and writing in Germany under the name of Numa Numantius, began to publish a series of pamphlets advocating homosexual rights and classifying what he believed to be a separate sexual entity, a third sex. In 1870 was published what Foucault identifies as the first appearance of the homosexual "species"—Karl Westphal's "Contrary Sexual Feeling," wherein Westphal argued that homosexuality was a kind of moral insanity resulting from a congenital reversal of sexual feeling.[5]

For Paul Moreau in his *Des aberrations du sens génétique* (1887), pederasts and sodomites were a class of people whose emotional constitution wavered between sanity and insanity and whose "malady" was hereditary. Benjamin Tarnovsky, a Russian researcher, insisted that homosexuality was "incurable" and that homosexuals could not help being what they were since the condition grew from parental genes damaged by epilepsy, alcoholism, or a number of other psychological or physiological traumas. Cesare Lombroso in Italy categorically placed homosexuals in a kind of moral and psychological criminal class, concluding that they were insane and should be committed to asylums. In 1889 Dr. Richard von Kraft-Ebing published *Psychopathia Sexualis*, containing the "autobiographies" of more than 200 "inverts," as he called them. Almost all of these studies asserted their "objective" approach to the issue. We can get some sense of the bias on which this "objectivity" was founded in Paolo Mantegazza's conclusion in "I Pervertimenti dell'amore," in which he argues that homosexuality can be cured if "studied with the pitying and indulgent eye of the physician."

Symonds was not interested in pity and realized that most of these essays had in fact contributed only to a different kind of classification, transferring homosexuality from sin to sickness. Of them all, only Ulrichs's pamphlets seemed to attempt to positively identify and explain the issue. Symonds realized that Ulrichs's contributions, available only in German, might be a potent weapon to level against intolerance and a useful platform from which to educate and advocate.

If "A Problem in Greek Ethics" offered a historicized agenda advocating homosexuality as both an identity and as a style of life, "Modern Ethics" offered a historicized argument for decriminalization and for the adjustment of social attitudes toward homosexuality. It also attempts to rescue the study of homosexuality and homosexuals from the historians of sin and crime and from the investigators of pathology and disease—from the priests, the state, and the doctors—and to return it to those to whom Symonds argues it rightfully belongs, homosexuals themselves. To do this he calls for a new kind of scholarship that will accomplish a change in law and attitude by providing access to the "complete history of inverted sexuality" ("Modern Ethics," 75).

It is no longer possible, Symonds argues, to dismiss the study of homosexuality and homosexuals with the reason that "to investigate the depraved instincts of humanity is unprofitable and disgusting" ("Modern Ethics," 15). He argues that it is not the object of the investigation but the attitude of the investigator that has uncritically attached the label of depravity. Because "no one has yet attempted a complete history of inverted sexuality in all ages and in all races," science has not brought to the study its presumedly objective and amoral scrutiny. And because homosexuality has been subject to historical erasure in texts he urges the need for systematic study of homosexuality not as a pathology, crime, or disease but as the record of people who share a sensibility. He had already documented this sensibility in Greek texts and reminds his readers of the absurdity of claiming on the one hand to be heirs of Greece and on the other of condemning what he insists is central to the heritage: "It [is] impossible to maintain that this passion was either a degraded vice or a form of inherited neuropathy in a race to whom we owe so much of our intellectual heritage" (76).

A systematic study of "inverted sexuality" would be "well worth doing. Materials, though not extremely plentiful, lie to hand in religious books and codes of ancient nations, in mythology and poetry and literature, in narratives of travel, and the reports of observant explorers" (75). His categories are deliberately inclusive of many genres. His point is that if homosexuality is found everywhere in history and in texts, then it cannot be presumed to be marginal. His observations foreshadow modern gay theorists who attempt to place difference at the center, not the periphery, of the investigation of social and cultural arrangements.

The tone of "A Problem in Modern Ethics," which is divided into eight parts, is perhaps less detached and scholarly than Symonds's previous essays. Here he engages an occasionally withering irony that barely masks an angry sense of the injustice of the position of homosexuals in society. This is the homosexual advocate's radical voice raised against oppression. Although Symonds was no activist, his was the first call in English prose urging homosexuals not to hide but to resist.

In "Modern Ethics" Symonds asks why "Christian nations" (i.e., modern Europe) have "introduced a new and stringent morality into their opinions on this topic and enforced their ethical views by legal prohibitions of a very formidable kind." He observes that this morality is "now almost universally regarded as a great advance upon the ethics of a pagan world" (5). The population demarcated by that pointed "almost," with its intimations of otherness, is the primary audience for his remarks, while the rest of those whose universal regard has condemned homosexuality Symonds intends to educate.

The lesson commences with an assertion that the intellectual foundations of moral disapproval are derived from faulty science, for the early Christianity from whence the prohibition derives possessed no "delicate distinctions, no anthropological investigations, no psychological analysis." To this list of scientific disciplines he adds a more disturbing absence that confronts Christianity on its own ground: Christians had "no spirit of toleration." His homosexual audience would no doubt have agreed that the nineteenth century that prided itself on the virtual invention of delicate scientific distinctions and anthropological and psychological analysis was similar at least to those earlier times in having no spirit of toleration.

Toleration is the presumed message of religion, and when called "objectivity" it is the foundation of science. Symonds argues from this that no phenomenon—whether it is the laws of physics, the psychology of primitive peoples, or the sexual habits of a minority—can be studied in an atmosphere in which preconceived notions have prejudged the results of investigation, and no investigation of the social and political ramifications of sexuality can be studied without historicizing this study and siting it within the framework of material culture. In this spirit, and in the spirit of delicate distinction, he lists a number of what he calls "vulgar errors" about homosexuality. He attacks stereotypes and confronts some heretofore unexamined clichés that categorize and stigmatize homosexuals.

One error he cites is the belief that homosexuals "originally loved women" but are in effect heterosexuals gone wrong who from "a monstrous debauchery and superfluity of naughtiness, tiring of normal pleasures" have sought out other avenues of desire. He counters this old sodomitical definition by promising to "prove" by reference to "medical jurists and physicians" that homosexual desires are "inborn and . . . incontrovertible" (11). Using the prestige of modern science, he argues what is logically correlative to their position: if homosexuality is inborn it cannot be acquired, and no amount of debauchery can produce it.

The second "error" is that homosexuals are commonly believed to be "despicable, depraved, vicious, and incapable of humane or generous sentiments" (11). Most people—here he quotes Gibbon—"touch with reluctance and dispatch with impatience" the study of homosexuality and "expect to discover the objects of their outraged animosity in the scum of humanity" (12). If "Greek history did not contradict this supposition, a little patient enquiry into contemporary manners would suffice to remove it. But people will not take this trouble," nor will they read Greek history or examine contemporary manners except to subject them to what Symonds implies is a mandatory erasure of homosexuality from history.

The erasure of homosexuality from texts or its presence in discourse only as an absent or pejorative term prevents the serious construction of a positive discourse about homosexuality. The only available discourse is one that traffics in signs. This semiotics of appearance, gesture, and style, Symonds's suggests, are socially constructed and serve homophobia since it is the "common belief that all subjects from inverted instincts carry their lust written in their faces; that they are pale, languid, scented, effeminate, painted, timid, oblique in expression" (14–15). That these signs are not "essential" Symonds deduces as obvious, since "the majority" of homosexuals "differ in no outward detail . . . from normal men" and are therefore invisible. "Were it not so, society would long ago have had its eyes opened to the amount of perverted sexuality it harbours" (15).

The other significant "error" he addresses is that homosexuality "produces spinal disease, epilepsy, consumption, dropsy and the like." He ironically suggests that if this were so, then "Sophocles, Pindar . . . all the Spartan kings and generals" would be "one nation of rickety, phthisical, dropsical paralytics" (13). Casting irony aside, he locates the true disease of homosexuality in homophobia: "Under the present laws and hostilities of modern society the inverted passion has to be indulged furtively, spasmodically, hysterically; the repression of it through fear and shame frequently . . . convert it from a healthy outlet of the sexual nature into a morbid monomania" (13).

Symonds spends the remainder of the essay summarizing contemporary legal, medical, historical, and anthropological texts and responding to those he considers false and homophobic. He concludes that sexual inversion ought to be approached from the point of view of embryology rather than physical pathology. Aside from anticipating the American Psychiatric Association's removal of homosexuality from the list of "disorders" nearly a century later, his comments foreshadow recent research that suggests possible physiological attributes of homosexuals. His recommendation about embryology stems from his study of Ulrichs, who theorized that homosexuals were a third sex, a female in a male body.

While this advocacy of a third-sex theory may seem simplistic and raise more political questions than solve sexual ones, Symonds is seeking to liberate homosexuality from the figurative straitjacket of a medical model based in almost all cases on some variation of a theory of congenital disorder. He concludes that "there is good reason for us to feel uneasy as to the present condition of our laws" and argues that "it seems clear that sexual inversion is no subject for legislation" (130). His comments even now seem to resonate powerfully against the present and proposed state of our laws.

Summarizing Ulrichs, Symonds argues that "the present state of law . . . is flagrantly unjust to a classs of innocent persons . . . who are guilty of nothing that deserves . . . punishment," that "no social evil ensues in those countries" that have placed homosexuality "upon the same footing as normal," and that "toleration of inverted passion threatens no danger to the well-being of nations" (105). Though he claims to speak in Ulrichs's translated voice, this is Symonds himself speaking. He eloquently concludes in the voice of the political and sexual radical: "If I have taken any vow at all, it is to fight for the rights of an innocent, harmless, downtrodden group of outraged personalities. The cross of a crusade is sewn upon the sleeve of my right arm. . . . We maintain that we have the right to exist after the fashion that nature made us. And if we cannot alter your laws, we shall go on breaking them" (114).

When Symonds began to write there were no studies in English and a few in other languages that dealt in any scientific or historicized manner with homosexuality. What few there were mostly concentrated on condemning, defining, or explaining homosexual behavior within the parameters of sin, crime, or sickness. Symonds's project not only delineated homophobia (though he had no word for it) but it also attempted to chart homophobia's intersection with the political, cultural, emotional, spiritual, and social organization of homosexuals. His attack on the unexamined stereotyping of homosexuals included an urgent rejection of effeminacy as a necessary sign of homosexuality. This may well reflect personal anxiety produced by pressures evident in the 1880s that demanded from the "normal middle class male" a masculinity that certainly contributes to what Adrienne Rich would later categorize as "compulsory heterosexuality," but it also reflects an attempt to rewrite homophobic constructions of homosexual identity in such a way as to radically destabilize what had heretofore been the private possession of the normal middle-class male—"masculinity." By insisting not only on a historically documented sexual component to classical "Platonic" relations but on the presence of it in Victorian notions of male-male Platonic relations, he mounted a frontal attack on that other, very nearly sacred and certainly romantic, aspect of the normal middle-class male experience—the presumed "purity" of passionate friendships between men.

E. F. Benson, repressed homosexual and author of a score of books in which that repression serves as a tantalizing subtext, writes of such friendships: "To suppose that this ardency was sensual, is to miss the point of it and lose the value of it altogether. That the base of the attraction was largely physical is no doubt true, for it was founded primarily on appearance, but there is a vast difference between the breezy open-air quality of these friendships and the dingy sensualism which is sometimes wrongly attributed to them."[6] Symonds would agree in part with this. Although he sought to rescue homosexual desire from the common definition of "dingy sensualism," he also knew that a comment like Benson's was the chief weapon of homophobia and a capitulation to the deliberate blindness that insisted that sex in texts must only be read as metaphor. Symonds understood that words could maim and silence kill, and he surely knew as well that the animosity that sought to erase sex and homosexual desire from texts could as destructively touch men's lives, as the example made of Oscar Wilde would soon terribly demonstrate.

When he wrote his *Memoirs* in 1889, speaking in the third person about himself, he added an eloquent testimony to the power of realized desire to create transformed and transforming texts:

> At length, when he has reached the age of twenty-nine, he yields to the attraction of the male. And this is the strange point about the man, that now for the first time he attains mastery and self control. Contemporary with his indulged passion he begins to write books, and rapidly becomes an author of distinction. The indecision of the previous years is replaced with a consciousness of volition and power. . . . Altogether he is more of a man than when he repressed and pent within his soul those fatal and abnormal inclinations. Yet he belongs to a class abhorred by society and is, by English law, a criminal. What is the meaning, the lesson, the conclusion to be drawn from this biography? (Symonds, 283)

This passage is immediately followed by a tortured disquisition on the position of the nineteenth-century homosexual as a person torn between the "spontaneous" and "natural action of his appetite" and the proscriptions of an "acquired respect for social law," one who is daily forced to see his desire "not in the glass of truth to his own nature, but in the mirror of convention." This answers his question about the meaning, the unhappy lesson to be learned from the effects of institutionalized homophobia.

Edward Carpenter

chapter 8

HOMOGENIC LOVE: EDWARD CARPENTER, 1894

The Homogenic passion is capable of splendid developments. . . . [I]t is well
worthy of respectful and thoughtful consideration.
                                        —Edward Carpenter, "Homogenic Love" (1894)

        Edward Carpenter enlarged on J. A. Symonds's project, adding
to it by markedly insisting that homosexuals, like women and the working
class, were involved in a struggle for individual rights. Carpenter argued that
homosexuals' rights would be granted and themselves accepted if society was
educated about homosexuality; in doing so he codified and even invented
some of the valorizing myths that were to be read as definitions of a homosexual identity in the twentieth century.
        Since his discovery of Whitman, Carpenter began in earnest to address as
a public problem the homosexuality with which he had been so long personally familiar; it was from this moment that his awareness of even wider social
issues also dated. He began to express some of his views in a long prose poem,
Towards Democracy, modeled on Whitman; the first version appeared in
1883, and he eventually published the poem in four parts over the next few
years. *Towards Democracy* is an extended versification—in a style that
Havelock Ellis described as "Whitman and water"—of Carpenter's advanced
views on the need for working-class egalitarianism, the sexual and political
rights of women, and the special place of homosexuals in society. But it was
soon clear that poetry was not enough, and that a powerful polemic was
needed to address all of these topics and especially the one that was closest
to him, what he perceived as the oppressed condition of homosexuals and
oppressive social attitudes toward sexual love generally. For him, the rela-

tions between society and those who he called the "intermediate sex" had become a subject that "has great actuality and is pressing upon us from all sides."[1]

To this end Carpenter published the essay "Homogenic Love" in 1894 and expanded on much of what Symonds proposed in his earlier pamphlets in essays written over the next 10 years, collected in *The Intermediate Sex* (1908). Though the Wilde trial in 1895 nearly drowned Carpenter's objective advocacy of homosexual rights beneath the nearly hysterical outcry of the press and public for the blood of Wilde and for the virtual extirpation of homosexuals, Carpenter was not deterred, though he too was attacked in the press, and he continued his work by publishing *Iolaus: An Anthology of Friendship*, the first anthology in English of homosexual texts—texts that Carpenter hoped were representative and positive approaches to homosexual love in literature through time. This anthology did much to contribute to a construction of homosexuality as transhistorical and essential—a message that had also been an occasional subtext of Symonds's historical studies and the hope that stood behind Whitman's question as to whether there were "men in other lands yearning and thoughtful" who felt as he did. Carpenter continued to write about homosexuality well into the early years of the twentieth century, producing *Intermediate Types among Primitive Folk* (1914); several essays on Whitman, including *Days with Walt Whitman* (1906); and "Some Friends of Walt Whitman: A Study in Sex Psychology" (1924).

"Homogenic Love" took up the work that had been suspended when Symonds died in 1893. Like Symonds, Carpenter discusses homosexuality in Greece, details modern medical discussions of it, advocates legal reform, and invokes Whitman as the source of the new erotic law and its major prophet. In "Homogenic Love" Carpenter also asserts the universality of homosexual passion: "the passionate attachment between two persons of the same sex is . . . a phenomenon widespread through the human race, and enduring in history, has always been more or less recognized; and once at least in history—in the Greek age—the passion rose into direct consciousness and justified, or even it might be said glorified, itself; but in later times—especially during the last century or two of European life—it has been treated by the accredited thinkers and writers as a thing to be passed over in silence, as associated with mere grossness and mental aberration, or as unworthy of serious attention."[2] Symonds had made a similar declaration in his privately printed and distributed pamphlets, but this is the first time a commercially published (and to some degree extensively circulated) English-language pamphlet condoned homosexuality.

"Homogenic Love" argues that "it may be doubted whether the higher heroic and spiritual life of a nation is ever quite possible without the sanction of this attachment in its institutions; and it is not unlikely that the markedly materialistic and commercial character of the last age of European civilized life is largely to be connected with the fact that the only form of love and love-union that it has recognized has been founded on the quite necessary but comparatively materialistic basis of matrimonial sex-intercourse and child bearing" (quoted in Reade, 344).

This sweeping claim—indebted, as Carpenter willingly admits, to Whitman's assertion in *Democratic Vistas* (1870) that "fervid comradeship" will "counterbalance and offset" that which is "materialistic and vulgar" in American democracy—is a broadside attack on gender and sex roles as prescribed by what Carpenter, were he writing now, might call the Judeo-Christian middle-class patriarchy. Carpenter also makes very clear his recognition that power and desire, as Foucault would later put it, are very much inscribed within the intimate, often brutal, discourses produced by interconnected commercial and sexual economies—economies that Carpenter is dedicated to changing if not overturning.

In *The Intermediate Sex* Carpenter laid the groundwork for advances in what we now call "theory." His title is indebted to Ulrichs's "third sex" theory, and in the volume he speculates that the subject of homosexuality is of "growing importance" owing either to "the increase in the number of men and women of intermediate or mixed temperament" or because "more than usual attention happens to be accorded to them." Carpenter here introduces into the English homosexual discourse a significant new term: women. Not that women had been ignored in the continental medical literature concerned with homosexuality, though their "cases" are neither as numerous nor as carefully studied as those of men. But lesbians had been largely invisible in texts—both homophobic and homophilic—addressing homosexuality. Carpenter's strategy is to demonstrate, as did Symonds, that far from being the monsters of particular depravity identified by homophobic discourses, homosexuals were in fact representative of all kinds of moral natures: "the great probability is that, as in any other class of human beings, there will be among these [homosexuals] too, good and bad, high and low, worthy and unworthy—some perhaps exhibiting through their double temperament a rare and beautiful flower of humanity, others a perverse and tangled ruin" (Carpenter, 186).

Carpenter's text undermines the negative theories assigning difference to homosexuals based on a supposed congenital or physiological inadequacy or "abnormality." His argument moves a step further than that advanced by Symonds, who was perhaps more fascinated by difference than by similarities between sexualities. Whereas Symonds tended to suspect or at least wanted to believe that homosexual men are *essentially* different from nonhomosexuals, Carpenter at first tries to fit homosexuals within a spectrum of sexuality that is constructed from "inner psychical affections and affinities" that "shade off and graduate in a vast number of instances most subtly from male to female, and not always in correspondence with the outer bodily sex" (190).

But if he theorizes essentiality he also forecasts social construction and glancingly suggests dubiety about fixed modern presumptions about gender and sex roles. Here he also implies his argument's reliance on a theory of androgyny. Allowed this speculation that homosexuals fall outside of social expectations concerning sex and gender, he feels free to suggest the possibility that such sex roles and gender expectations may not in fact be immutable facts of nature but may be what we now would describe as socially constructed. He hints at this in the opening pages when he urges that concerning "facts of Nature" we have to "preserve a certain humility and reverence and not rush in with our preconceived and obstinate assumptions" because the seeming sudden appearance of homosexuals in life and in discourse may be an indicator of "some important change," some "new form," some "new types of human kind . . . emerging, which will have an important part to play in the societies of the future" (Carpenter, 186).

If he is reluctant or unable to fully imagine the social construction of sexualities at this juncture, he embraces the concept at the end of the essay when he speculates "how society would shape itself if free" in matters concerning love and marriage "if the present restrictions and sanctions were removed." Here he asserts that "the law, the Church, and the strong pressure of public opinion interfere, compelling the observance of certain forms; and it becomes difficult to say how much of the existing order is due to the spontaneous instinct and common sense of human nature, and how much to compulsion and outside interference: how far, for instance, Monogamy is natural or artificial" (Carpenter, 242).

His striking willingness to attack the artificiality of sex roles and gender characteristics contrasts with the metaphysical, even transcendental, plane to which he now ascends as he attempts to discover what social utility there may be in this newly emerging species. His argument that homosexuals have special roles to play in society—roles they fulfill better than nonhomosexuals—now forces him, however, into constructing what amounts to a theory that at least suggests an "essential" nature for homosexuals.

Their primary and noblest work will be in the "domain of love," since homosexuals have "an immense capacity" for attachment that will allow them to become "reconcilers and interpreters of the two sexes" and "teachers of future society." Marking homosexuals as teachers and mediators foreshadows an elaboration of the socially useful roles he believes homosexuals play that appears in *Intermediate Types among Primitive Folk*. There he argues that homosexuals in "primitive" societies engage in certain vitally useful social functions and are especially suited to the prosecution of these functions, among which he includes the prophet, priest, magician, and inventor. His point, like Symonds's exercise in comparative anthropology with the Greeks, is to locate homosexuality in all cultures, not just the European, and by finding allegedly similar roles played by men who share presumably similar desires in cultures different from the European, to essentialize homosexuality across culture and across time.

The categories of prophet, magician, priest, and inventor are derived from the thesis he presents in the second section of *The Intermediate Sex*. Here he seems to focus more sharply on the difference he had attempted to underplay in the opening pages. Invoking the "New Woman"—the product of a nascent feminist consciousness that was developing as a result of the growing intervention of women in politics and social policy—he describes her as "a little more masculine in some ways than her predecessor." He suggests that the "New Man," therefore, though "by no means effeminate," is "a little more sensitive in temperament and artistic feeling than the original John Bull." (John Bull, the true-blue, sodomite-hating Englishman—an example can be seen in the sailor in *Roderick Random* who so horrifies Captain Whiffle—is the embodiment of the middle-class normal masculine English male, the enemy of both Symonds and Carpenter.)

Though effeminacy is not posited as a characteristic of the New Man, it is perceptions of effeminacy that Carpenter is addressing. He is laying the groundwork to translate "effeminacy" from a pejorative context that says "weak" and "unmanly" and also devalues women to a valorizing context that marks it as "sensitive," "artistic," and "intuitive." Of course Carpenter is to a degree trapped in preconceived gender-bound concepts here as much as are the discourses he attacks. For him, such qualities as the intuitive, the artistic, and the sensitive are aspects of "the feminine sensibility." The homosexual is "a remarkable and . . . indispensable type of character in whom there is such a union or balance of the feminine and masculine qualities that these people become to a great extent the interpreters of men and women for each other" (Carpenter, 190). In his suggestion that homosexuals interpret nonhomosexuals to each other—that is, make sense of the emotional and cultural materials of nonhomosexual lives—can be found the argument that homosexuals are bearers and originators of culture. This thesis resonates against the lists of great gay artists, writers, and musicians that will be constructed by later apologists to justify homosexual cultural importance.

It is evident to Carpenter that there are certain salient facts about homosexuals that directly contradict popular conceptions: they exist in considerable numbers, rather than being a rare accident of nature; there is "nothing abnormal or morbid" in their constitutions, and they are not necessarily emotionally or medically damaged; their temperament, far from being accidental and assumed, is inborn and cannot be changed by simply embracing "normal" sexuality. But because of popular prejudice and misunderstanding owing to inadequate education about homosexuals, homosexuals do "suffer a great deal from their own temperament" but not because of what they inherently are but because of the way society has defined them and also marginalized them: "how hard it is . . . that a veil of complete silence should be drawn over the subject, leading to the most painful misunderstandings, and perversions, and confusions of mind; and that there should be no hint of guidance;

nor any recognition of the solitary and really serious inner struggles they may have to face!" (Carpenter, 194).

Symonds, it may be recalled, tried to resexualize the desexualized metaphors of Platonic love that his age read into Greek texts. Carpenter argues that homosexual attachments are "often purely emotional in their character, and to confuse the Uranian with libertines having no law but curiosity in self-indulgence is to do them great wrong." This might seem to be a retreat from Symonds's position and to cater to those repressive discourses that accept male friendship only if it exists outside of the contexts of desire and sensuality. Yet his position hinges on the assertion that such friendships are not "necessarily sexual, or connected with sexual acts." Emphasizing "necessarily" allows him to attack the same "vulgar error" that Symonds enumerates—namely, that homosexuals are motivated solely by lust and are devoid of the "normal" human passions of love and kindness. His divorce of homosexuality from the narrow compass of sexual libertinage allows him to place homosexuality within a much larger framework, as one point in a spectrum of sexual difference. As he says, there is "an immense diversity of human temperament and character in matters relating to sex and love," a diversity that is not satisfactorily explained by the fixed poles of sex or by antipodes of gender, or by the creation of narrow dichotomies of sexual appetite. Homosexuality, he says later in the essay, "adds new range and scope to the possibilities of love" (Carpenter, 217).

Carpenter again may seem to be treading ideologically dangerous ground when he attempts to describe the "general characteristics" of homosexuals, of which he posits two types—the extreme and the "normal type." The extreme type is the cliché of the effeminate homosexual that homophobic texts have made familiar. This type is

> not particularly attractive, sometimes quite the reverse. In the male of this kind we have a distinctly effeminate type, sentimental, lackadaisical, mincing in gait and manners, something of a chatterbox, skilful at the needle and women's work, sometimes taking pleasure in dressing in women's clothes; his figure not infrequently betraying a tendency towards the feminine, large at the hips, supple, not muscular, the face wanting in hair, the voice inclining to be high-pitched . . . while his dwelling-room is orderly in the extreme, even natty, and the choice of decoration and perfume. His affection, too, is often feminine in character, clinging, dependent and jealous, as of one desiring to be loved almost more than to love. (Carpenter, 196)

If Symonds tried to rescue homosexuals from effeminate stereotypes by insisting on their "healthy masculinity," Carpenter rather backhandedly acknowledges that popular perceptions of effeminate homosexuals may well be founded in homosexual styles—that is, some homosexuals are indeed effeminate. This is the homosexual that everyone imagines, everyone derides, and everyone fears. Carpenter's citation of a stereotype of the effeminate homosexual seems almost as homophobic as the homophobic descriptions he challenges. Indeed, it is clear that he shares some of the dislike and fear.

Carpenter's comments, however, diverge from homophobia when he insists that "these extreme developments are rare," whereas the popular homophobic perception insists that this is the only type of homosexual. Carpenter decenters effeminacy from its traditional site as the prime characteristic of all homosexuals to a marginalized position as a characteristic only of a few. Indeed, the "normal type" of homosexual is "embodied in men and women of quite normal and unsensational exterior":

> Such men, as said, are often muscular and well-built, and not distinguishable in exterior structure . . . from others of their own sex; but emotionally they are extremely complex, tender, sensitive, pitiful and loving. . . . [T]he logical faculty may not be well-developed, but intuition is always strong. . . . [A]t bottom lies the artist-nature . . . such a one is often a dreamer, of brooding reserved habits, often a musician, a man of culture . . . with a peculiar inborn refinement. (Carpenter, 197)

Carpenter is myth-making here, asserting positive stereotypes of the creative and sensitive homosexual in order to displace negative images. To a certain extent he seems to be attempting to normalize homosexual subjectivities by inscribing them as versions of "normal" sexuality, but in fact he has a rather different agenda. Not only does he move homosexuals out of the shadows of monstrosity and away from the presumed weaknesses of effeminacy, but he carries them into the realm of a supermale, whose affections, talents, abilities, and intuitions are more refined, more profound, and more complex than those of "normal" men and women.

Whereas Symonds had implied a doctrine of homosexual superiority when he associated homosexuality with the highest standard of Greek civilization, Carpenter no longer implies but asserts that the materials that create civilizations are the special possession of homosexuals who are, in his formulation, very nearly a race apart: "The instinctive artistic nature of the male of this class, his sensitive spirit, his . . . hardihood of intellect and body . . . may be said to give" because of his "double nature . . . command of life in all its phases, and a certain freemasonry of the secrets of the two sexes." It is remarkable that "some of the world's great leaders and artists have been dowered . . . with the Uranian temperament" (Carpenter, 200).

Carpenter has radically shifted homosexuality's philosophical terrain from that which attributed abnormality to sexual difference to one that attributes spiritual, intellectual, moral, and intuitive superiority to a sexually different "temperament." If homosexuals are privileged possessors of special attributes denied to "normal" men and women, then far from being disruptive, dangerous, and destructive of the social fabric, homosexuality instead is "a very important factor in society," and its "neglect, or repression, or its vulgar misapprehension, may be matters of considerable danger or damage to the common-weal" (216).

Indeed, Carpenter argues, a new form of social organization is necessary. Homosexuals may be the instruments toward that reorganization: "marriage is of indispensable importance to the State as providing a workshop as it were for breeding and rearing of children, another form of union is almost equally indispensable to supply the basis for social activities of other kinds," among which he numbers the maintenance of democracy by drawing "members of different classes together" and the creation of the artifacts of culture. Homosexuality forms "an advance guard of that great movement that will one day transform the common life by substituting the bond of personal affection and compassion for the monetary, legal and other external ties which now control and confine society" (219).

Carpenter here recognizes what Foucault would later describe as the domination over desire by power. He also recognizes that sex must be separated from procreation if there is to be a nonjudgmental discourse about it: "popular opinion has probably been largely influenced by the arbitrary notion that the function of love is limited to child-breeding; and that any love not concerned with propagation of the race must necessarily be of dubious character. . . . But nowadays . . . it is not unreasonable to suppose that a . . . revolution will take place in people's views of the place and purpose of the non-child-bearing love." If sex is divorced from the public and social need for reproduction then no sexual activity can be condemned since removal from the public sphere of social necessity and the laws and customs that support that necessity sites sexual behavior only within the personal and not the public realm where, Carpenter implies, neither custom nor law ought intervene. Homosexuality must also be recognized as having a relation to contemporary discussions concerning class, women, gender, and education. The "lasting compulsion that may draw members of the different classes together" will also have a profound effect on the relation of sexuality with politics. Just as women who "are working out the great cause of their sex's liberation" will be emancipated because of the recognition of the necessary link between sexuality to politics, so homosexuals will benefit from that same process.

Carpenter is clear that homophobia is the obstacle that stands between homosexuals and their liberation from the narrow confines and control of society. The most effective way to remove that barrier is to recognize "the panic terror which prevails in England with regard to the expression of affection" between members of the same sex. This is the homosexual panic later to be identified as a primary component of homophobia. Carpenter would ameliorate it through education: "The much needed teaching and the true morality on the subject must be given—as it can only be given—by the spread of proper education and ideas, and not by the clumsy bludgeon of the statute book. . . . [M]odern people should recognise" homosexuality "in their institutions, and endeavor at least in their public opinion and systems of education to understand this factor and give it its proper place" (Carpenter, 220).

Advocating education as the positive power that will destroy homophobia, Carpenter argues that homosexuality has a history to be reclaimed, an identity to be defined, and a useful social role to be deployed. His writings attempt to define that identity, establishing a valorized image of the homosexual as a special and superior species, a possessor of special talents and abilities—indeed, the standard bearer of a new age. Whatever we may feel about the significance or even the reality of Carpenter's myths, it remains that his advocacy of a liberationist position concerning sexual difference forecasts and pointedly defines current attempts to institute rainbow curricula in schools, establish gay studies in universities, and pass civil rights legislation lifting restrictions against homosexuals in all areas of public life.

Bacchus (1868), by Simeon Solomon. A homosexual, Solomon painted portraits that appealed to the homoerotic sensibilities of the mid-nine-teenth century.

chapter 9

INVERTS AND HOMOSEXUALS: HAVELOCK ELLIS, 1897

"Homosexual" is a barbarously hybrid word, and I claim no responsibility for it.
It is, however, convenient, and now widely used.
 —Havelock Ellis, *Sexual Inversion* (1897)

When J. A. Symonds sent "A Problem in Modern Ethics" to 50 friends, many responded with biographical reminiscences of their homosexual lives, some of which were published in Havelock Ellis and Symonds's *Sexual Inversion* (1897), the eventual first volume of Ellis's *Studies in the Psychology of Sex* (1901). These accounts offer fascinating voices in that eager confessional that Foucault has identified as so informative a part of the nineteenth-century sexual discourse. What they tell, of course, was no doubt subject to their perception of what Ellis or Symonds hoped to hear as well as to perceptions about what "being homosexual"—a very new word and a very new concept—was supposed to imply. Foucault suggests also that there may have been a certain degree of pleasure derived from the revelation of sexual secrets. The generosity of their accounts certainly supports Foucault's contention that "modern societies . . . dedicated themselves to speaking of [sex] *ad infinitum* while exploiting it as the secret" (Foucault, 1: 35).

The cumulative effect of these texts is to construct categories, customs, myths, and fantasies that suggest that nineteenth-century homosexuals conceived of themselves as a part of a group and possessors of an identity controlled by their desire. Some respondents were English, some American. Their ages vary as do their professions and situations in life. The youngest is 20, the oldest in his seventies. Most were in the middle years when the book was published in 1897. Sometimes an identifying profession is supplied—

"physician," "engaged in business," "now at university," "artist," "government official," "employed in a workshop," "an actor," "without profession," "of independent means," "a brain worker," a "clerk." The texts are given in their subjects' own words or are paraphrased by Ellis or Symonds. The subjects describe themselves in youth, tell when they first discovered an attraction to their own sex (usually very early), describe their relationship with masturbation and with other boys and men, and reveal the time, place, details, and often the partner of their first homosexual experience. They disclose their fantasies and erotic dreams, paint pictures of ideal friends and describe real ones. They admit their sexual prejudices and preferences, reveal their attitude toward women, and theorize about the morality and the nature of homosexuality. They construct ideological connections between homosexuality and art, music, or literature and speculate about the possibility of long-term homosexual relationships.

The oldest respondent discovered his homosexual desire in the 1820s and claims that when he was between six and eight "the sight of the naked body of young men in a rowing match on the river caused great commotion" (Case 27). The youngest rather proudly lets us know that by the time he was 19 he had "had relationships with about 100 boys." A man in his thirties relates desire and identity: "at the age of twenty-four I began to understand the relationship of the physical phenomena of sex to its intellectual and imaginative manifestation. . . . [I]t was the study of Walt Whitman's *Leaves of Grass* that first brought me light upon this question" (Case 13). That "question" of course is the homosexual question. In his own case study Symonds reveals that this was the same question that began to torment him in his earliest years and that became clear to him in an intellectual revelation at 18 when he read Plato to discover that "his own nature had been revealed." As we have seen, in reading Whitman he also found the sexual signifier that allowed him to conclude "that his sexual dealings with men have been thoroughly wholesome to himself, largely increasing his physical, moral, and intellectual energy, and not injurious to others" (Case 25).

Symonds died in 1893, and his literary executor insisted that the first edition bearing Symonds's name be suppressed and his name deleted from later editions. In the cases that Symonds collected and that Ellis finally included in his book in 1897 it is evident that homosexual attachments and attraction is neither a late nor an artificial occurrence; indeed, most respondents felt it early and believed it congenital. One man's homosexual desires "began at puberty" (Case 4); another notes that "at the age of 8 or 9 . . . I felt a friendly attraction toward my own sex and this developed after the age of puberty into a passionate sense of love" (Case 7). One young man recalled that "at the age of five I recollect having a sexual dream connected with a railway porter. It afforded me great pleasure to recall this dream, and about that time I discovered a method of self-gratification (there is not much teaching required in these matters!)" (Case 8). A university student explains that "when I was 10 . . . I first began to form attachments with other boys of my own age, in which I always had great regard to physical beauty" (Case 11). The young man who had relations with 100 boys by the time he was 19 said that "at the age of 4 I first became conscious of an attraction for older males" (Case 12).

Symonds himself is quite specific: at about the age of 8 "he became subject to curious half-waking dreams. In these he imagined himself the servant of several adult naked sailors: he crouched between their thighs and called himself their dirty pig, and by their orders he performed services for their genitals and buttocks which he contemplated with relish" (Case 25).

For many, loneliness, solitude, and a sense of temperamental difference from others were conditions of youth. One man describes himself as having a "strongly nervous temperament . . . and sensitive." An "American, of French descent, aged 31," reports that "I was a dreamy indolent boy. . . . I was passionately fond of flowers, loved to be in the woods and alone" (Case 9). An Englishman was "a delicate, effeminate boy," while another was "always delicate and averse to rough games." Symonds was "a weakly and highly nervous child, subject to night terrors and somnambulism, excessive shyness and religious disquietude" (Case 25). An Englishman in his seventies says that at school he was "shy and reserved, and had no particular intimacy with anyone, though he desired it" (Case 27). Case 10 says that "as a child . . . I lived too much alone and spent most of my time in reading. I was very sensitive to ridicule . . . so that I shrank from the other boys, while at the same time I longed for their friendship. I withdrew into myself and indulged my imagination."

These fragments support some clichés of homosexual boyhood: loneliness and sensitivity coupled with wishful idolizing and vague eroticizing of older heroes and an obsession with the seemingly unobtainable ideal friend. The American, who loved to be in the "woods and alone," was "constantly falling in love with handsome boys whom I never knew; nor did I try to mix in their company, for I was abashed before them . . . sometimes I played with girls . . . but I cared for them little or not at all" (Case 9).

In nearly every case there is one common thread: at the strongest repugnance toward and at the least disinterest in women. While most of these men often seem appalled by sexual relations with women, many like women as social or intellectual companions. Many express sentiments similar to those of Case 5: "He is very good friends with women, but has strong repulsion from sexual relations with them, or any approach to it." Case 4 is similar: "While very friendly and intimate with women of all ages, he is instantly repelled by any display of sexual affection on their side." An Englishman, who describes himself as "high bred, refined, and sensitive," says that "I am capable of a great regard and liking for women when I deem them worthy of it; otherwise I have a strong repulsion to them, and have never touched a woman" (Case 15). Another Englishman "intellectually likes women very much," though sexually they "do not attract him" (Case 18). The Paris-born Englishman feels "absolute indifference" to women. "He admires them in the same way as one admires beautiful scenery" (Case 23).

Edward Carpenter reports that "my feeling toward the female sex was one of indifference and later . . . one of absolute repulsion" (Case 7). One man has had dreams about women, though "the latter have usually partaken somewhat of the nature of nightmares" (Case 8), while Symonds, though he dreamed of naked sailors, and as we shall see later on, of beautiful young men, "never dreamed of women, never sought their society, never felt the slightest sexual excitement in their presence, never idealized them" (Case 25).

For many of these men homoerotic dreams were confusing, though not confused, indicators of desire. But once desire was clear, physical gratification was not far to seek, nor, was much teaching needed to learn its methods. Thus, masturbation plays an important part in these accounts. Masturbation, according to medical and moral opinion, was immoral, sinful, and injurious to health and sanity. The father of a 34-year-old artist tells him that "if you do this, you will never be able to use your penis with a woman." The young man's doctor solemnly assured him that "masturbation is death. A number of young men come to me with the same story. I tell them they are killing themselves, and you will kill yourself too" (Case 13). Yet despite the prohibitions of priests and parents, these men did it not only alone but as a shared activity between strangers, friends, and lovers and as a communal delight in groups.

While it is clear from these studies that all the other forms of sexual activity in which men can engage were engaged in, masturbation seems to have been the most common and the most widely preferred; it inspired neither the occasional repugnance connected to what they all call "paedicatio" or the rarer unwillingness to engage in fellatio. Indeed, it was the one thing few of these men could resist, and all the testimonies suggest doubt as to its unnatural origins. "In early youth," one man "masturbated to excess, sometimes three times daily" (Case 3). Some were more careful, practicing "onanism to a limited extent" (Case 4). Others embraced it eagerly. The American declared, "Once while bathing I found that a pleasant feeling came with touching the sexual organs. It was not long before I was confirmed in the habit. At first I practiced it seldom, but afterward much more frequently" (Case 9). The university student may have been influenced by a father's stern advice, for "at 12 [I] learned masturbation, apparently by instinct, and I regret to say, practiced it to excess for the next seven years, always secretly and with shame. . . . [M]asturbation was often practiced daily" (Case 11).

A Scot who loved a shepherd boy "practiced masturbation many years before puberty and attaches importance to this as a factor in the evolution of his homosexual life" (Case 17). Perhaps while the Scot dreamed of his shepherd, an Englishman of about the same age masturbated "in a sort of dreamy state between sleeping and waking"; his masturbation was "accompanied by lascivious thoughts and dreams of men" (Case 28). An Irishman is not reticent about his practice: "At about the age of 14 he practiced masturbation with other boys of the same age and also had much pleasure in bed with an uncle with whom the same thing was practiced. Later he practiced masturbation with every boy or man with whom he was on terms of intimacy; to have been in bed with anyone without anything of the sort taking place would have been impossible" (Case 19). One man writes, "Inverts are, I think, naturally more liable to indulge in self-gratification than normal people, partly because of the perpetual suppression and disappointment of their desires, and also because of the fact that they actually possess in themselves the desired form of the male" (Ellis, 162).

These pages are a repository for descriptions of that "dreamy state between sleeping and waking" in which thoughts and dreams of men were so lasciviously entertained. A man who discovered masturbation while "having a sexual dream about a railway porter" is joined by another, also responding to a costume, who has fantasies about circus performers: "I longed to see them naked, without their tights, and used to lie awake at night thinking of them and longing to be loved and embraced by them. A certain bareback rider, a sort of jockey, used especially to please me on account of his handsome legs, which were clothed in fleshlings to his waist, leaving his beautiful loins uncovered by a breech clout" (Case 9). He "used to take great pleasure in watching men and boys in swimming." An Englishman in his fifties who is a government official "finds that uniform or livery (soldiers, sailors, grooms and footmen) are a temptation" in dreams as well as life (Case 16). Symonds "enjoyed visions of beautiful young men," more specifically of "the large erect naked organs of grooms or peasants" (Case 25).

Case 26 seems to have spent his life in an erotic dreamland. He desired in his dreams to "nestle between the thighs or have my face pressed against the hinder parts of my object of [male] worship." One of his earliest dreams was to "imagine myself in a tank with three lovers floating in the water above me. From this position I visited their limbs in turn; the attraction rested in thighs and buttocks only." One vividly imagined circumstance was the notion "of a serried rank of congregated thighs across which I lay and was dragged. . . . I was able in my imagination to lie in the thick and stress of conglomerated deliciousness of thighs struggling to hold me; I was able to imagine at least six bodies encircling me with passionate contact."

The twilight world of erotic fantasy provided a fertile ground out of which could grow other ideals. In these histories men describe their ideal friends and what attracts them to other men: "The chief characteristic of my tendency is an overpowering admiration for male beauty. . . . I have absolutely no words to tell you how powerfully such beauty affects me. Moral and intellectual worth is, I know, of greater value, but physical beauty I see more clearly and it appears to me to be the most vivid (if not the most perfect) manifestation of the divine" (Case 9). Athletes are fixed stars in the cosmos of homosexual desire. For one man, "his male ideal has . . . for some years tended toward a healthy, well-developed, athletic or out of door working type, intelligent and sympathetic, but not especially intellectual" (Case 4). Carpenter says that "now, at the age of 37—my ideal love is a powerful strongly built man of my own age or rather younger, preferably of the working class. Though having solid sense and character, he need not be specially intellectual. . . . Anything effeminate in a man, or anything of the cheap intellectual style repels me very decisively" (Case 7).

Case 18 is attracted to "youths from 18 to 24, slightly built, and pretty rather than handsome. Big muscular men have little attraction for him." For the Irishman youths between the ages of 18 and 25 must have "an intelligent eye, a voluptuous mouth" (Case 19). An English actor is "attracted to individuals who are slightly effeminate, especially boys between the ages of 14 and 18" (Case 20), and a 27-year-old Scot prefers "boys about 17 to 20 years of age. . . . I like the smooth hairless face and body of a boy: a slight feminine trait adds to the attraction, but it must not be too developed" (Case 22). The Paris-born Englishman prefers boys who are "fair, smooth-skinned, gentle, rather girlish and effeminate with the effeminacy of the ingenue not the cocotte. His favorite must be submissive and womanly; he likes to be the man and the master" (Case 23). Symonds, who consorted in later life with the strikingly handsome gondolier, Angelo Fusato, "has always loved men younger than himself . . . he is not attracted by uniforms but seeks some uncontaminated child of Nature" (Case 25).

These ideal friends are the creations of desire, and communion with the ideal is most often achieved. Masturbation and the imagined ideal friend go hand in hand. But on gaining a sexual majority, few of these men were content to languish in the dream world. They sought real life instead, sometimes obsessively choosing paths untrodden, hoping that their dreams would become real. Most of them seem to be, as Case 3 elegantly puts it, "tormented by the great wish." This vague formula precisely points to sex. To be embraced by a friend was the great wish of Case 3, more explicitly, to have sex with a man. His preferred activity was limited to mutual masturbation. When he was 20, he and another young man "went through a portion of those ceremonies which, unlike fellatio or paedicatio, are not repellant to my more esthetic nature. Neither is mutual masturbation (with the right person) at all disagreeable to me." A 33-year-old "manual worker" used his hands only for work and resisted putting himself in anyone else's. Though his "homosexual feeling is clear and defined" he seems to avoid actual sex. He has a relationship with a man, but "so far as the physical act is concerned this relationship is definitely not sexual, but it is of the most intimately possible kind, and the absence of the physical act is probably due largely to circumstances. There is no conscious desire for the physical act for its own sake, and the existing harmony and satisfaction is described as very complete.

There is, however, no repulsion to the physical side, and he regards the whole relationship as quite natural" (Case 1).

The vital information in this description of a nonsexual homosexual relationship is the observation that the subject's homosexuality is founded in identity, not in a physical act. This young man, who is "mentally bright, though not highly educated, a keen sportsman, and in general a good example of an all-round healthy Englishman," stands at one end of a homoerotic spectrum that extends from his contented abstinence to examples of others' obsessive pursuits of the pleasures of the great wish. Carpenter has "never had to do with actual pederasty, so called," by which I presume he means anal intercourse. He continues, "My chief desire in love is bodily nearness or contact, as to sleep naked with a naked friend; the specially sexual, though urgent enough, seems a secondary matter. Pederasty, either active or passive, might seem in place to me with one I loved very devotedly and who also loved me to that degree, but I think not otherwise . . . and I think that the actual sex gratifications (whatever they may be) probably hold a less important place in this love than in the other [heterosexual love]" (Case 7).

Indeed, many of the men seem to be uninterested in those acts by which homosexuality is usually defined: "We never attempted, nor had any inclination to attempt to penetrate the anus, from this practice I used to invariably find that we shrank as unnatural and beastly" (Case 14). Another Englishman does not "practice paedicatio and very rarely fellatio. I like embracements, spooning, and real kissing, followed by mutual masturbation" (Case 15). Another, having a young officer get into bed with him and have "him inter-femora several times . . . always desired that done to him with some violence, or to take himself the active part. . . . [H]e abhors paedicatio" (Case 16). An Englishman, age 35, "finds that mere contact of body to body is sufficient to produce the physical effects and pleasure of coition. Paedicatio disgusts him, unless he is passionately devoted to a person who insists upon it, and even then he feels it to be debasing and bestial. Fellatio excites him intensely" (Case 18).

Fellatio enters into the experience of several men. One man has "been an active participant in paedicatio and has tried the passive role out of curiosity, but prefers fellatio" (Case 27). A 70-year-old Englishman "is exclusively passive; also likes mutual fellatio." A 34-year-old Englishman "likes paedicatio to be practiced on him, but he does not care to practice it." Fellatio, however, he likes either actively or passively, and he is also able to satisfy himself by intercrural connection" (Case 29). For the Paris-born Englishman, as for many of these respondents, "paedicatio is the satisfaction he prefers, provided he takes the active part, never the passive role" (Case 23). A 34-year-old Englishman says, "I like [men] to practice paedicatio on me and I prefer it done roughly, and I rather prefer men who are carried away by their lust and bite my flesh at the supreme moment and I rather like the pain inflicted by their teeth and elsewhere" (Case 29).

For Symonds, "The methods of satisfaction have varied with the phases of his passion. At first they were romantic and Platonic, when a hand touch, a rare kiss or mere presence sufficed. In the second period sleeping side by side, inspection of the naked body of the loved man, embracements, and occasional emissions after prolonged contact. In the third period the gratification became more frankly sensual. It took every shape: mutual masturbation, intercrural coitus, fellatio, irrumatio, occasionally paedicatio . . . . he himself always plays the masculine active part" (Case 25).

Case 26 seems to have an obsessive desire to precisely enumerate the landmarks in his sexual journeys: "I developed a liking for imagining myself between two lovers. . . . it was my habit to analyze as minutely as possible those who attracted me. I studied with attention their hands, the wrists. . . . I estimated the comparative size of the generative organs, the formation of the thighs and buttocks, and thus constructed a presentiment of the whole man." He describes himself as lost, though he did not wander alone, in a "perfect maze of promiscuity."

Before departing from these fascinating men who revealed their homosexual feelings and sexual experiences, it is worth asking what they felt about homosexuality itself. From what sources, outside of their own private needs and sexual experiments, in history, literature, or life, did they derive explanation of and justification for their desire? What convictions support the fact that few of these men reject or desist from their hopeful pursuit of the great wish, from their attempt to answer their own homosexual question? Many had discovered homoerotica in literature and art that raised their consciousness, that gave a history to and justified their overwhelming desire. We recall that Case 13's "study of Walt Whitman's Leaves of Grass first brought me light upon this question." We know that Symonds too found Whitman a revelation. A 31-year-old American does not mention Whitman, but in "some writings of Mr. John Addington Symonds" he discovered "certain allusions" that, coupled with "recent experiences . . . stirred me to a full consciousness of my inverted nature." Certain paintings and sculptures affected him— "some Praxitilean demi-god, or Flandrin's naked brooding boy." For him the "old Platonic mania" was as powerful as the great wish (Case 9).

The university student finds confirmation in art and literature too: "Male Greek statuary, and the Phaedrus of Plato have a great, though only confirmatory influence on my feelings. My ideal is that of Theocritus XIII, wherein Hercules was bringing Hylas to the perfect measure of a man" (Case 11). An Englishman added an aesthetic dimension to his sexual emancipation when he "became familiar with pictures, admired male figures of Italian martyrs, and the full rich forms of Antinous" (Case 27). This Englishman also read with avidity "the Arabian Nights and other Oriental tales, translations from the classics, Suetonius, Petronius," finding in them other sites of homoerotic desire. A literary man engaged in sadomasochistic fantasies not only while masturbating but while reading: "I was so possessed by masculine attraction that I became a lover of all the heroes I read of in books. Some became as vivid to me as those with whom I was living in daily contact. For a time I became an ardent lover of . . . Edward I, and of Julius Caesar" (Case 26).

The concealed and substantial life of homosexuality was hedged by fascination. To be homosexual was at once tantalizing and impossible, the need of comrades and the need for concealment creating a painful tension. As one respondent offhandedly says, "It seems to me in this country to be forbidden that one man should care very much about another. In fact I have heard people say that they can't understand how one man may feel any affection for another." Troubled by the fact that he did, the respondent went to the doctors. On hearing his confession, one doctor "walked out without a word. He would not see me again." The second doctor "would hardly listen. He at once said that such inclinations were unnatural, and evidently made up his mind that I was insane." "It is really a matter of psychology, not of medicine, and poets know more about such matters than doctors" (Case 10).

Though English schoolboys were often presumed to be perpetually engaged in steamy homosexual adventures, it is probably just as true, as the university student says, that "at school the idea was held in abhorrence by an enormous majority, and public opinion is a strong factor" (Case 11). Case 13 agrees: "All these things were treated by masters and boys alike as more or less unholy . . . a kiss was as unclean as fellatio." Case 14 sensibly insists that "it is better to spread abroad the spirit of open comradeship which is natural to men and boys," but "against this stands the law, which is a relic of the ages gone by. It is a farce, where every public school boy knows, and in most cases practices, homosexual habits, to attach a penalty to this practice."

Despite social prohibition, however, these men affirm themselves as Symonds had done. C.M., "although he has suffered so much from unsatisfied homosexual desires . . . says that he would not be prevented from being an invert by any consideration." This firm assertion is as powerful as Carpenter's: "I cannot regard my sexual feelings as unnatural or abnormal, since they have disclosed themselves so perfectly naturally and spontaneously within me" (Case 7). R.S., the young American stirred to consciousness by reading Symonds, is not sure of the origins but is without doubt as to the validity of his homosexuality: "I suspect that the sexual emotions and even the inverted ones have a more subtle significance than is generally attributed to them; but modern moralists fight shy of transcendental interpretations or see none, and I am ignorant and unable to solve the mystery which these feelings seem to imply" (Case 9). Not so ignorant at all is this appealing and introspective young man, for it is precisely the transcendental nature of these feelings, their implications and not their facts, that serves as the subject of both Symonds and Carpenter and as the subtext of so many of the homoerotic texts of the nineteenth century.

"To me," W.W. (Case 10) concludes, "what other people call unnatural is the most natural of all conditions." This theme is repeated: "I am an absolute believer in the naturalness of my inclinations" (Case 15); "He sees no harm in homosexual passions" (Case 17); "He does not consider he is doing anything wrong and considers his acts quite natural" (Case 19). An English actor insists, "This love is right, and capable of being made noble, far more so than the love of woman, and to call it unnatural is grossly unjust and untrue" (Case 21). The Paris-born Englishman, inventing social construction with a verbal Gallic shrug, disdains judgment: "He has no moral feelings on these matters; he regards them as outside ethics; mere matters of temperament and social feeling" (Case 23). Another says, "I believe that affection between persons of the same sex, even when it includes the sexual passion and its indulgence, may lead to results as splendid as human nature can ever attain to" (Case 4).

The eloquent Case 26 celebrates his own spendid result: "I believed I was a rebel from the law, natural and divine, of which no instinct had been implanted in me. . . . I was 30 however, before I found a companion to love me in the way my nature required. Under sexual freedom I have become stronger." Stronger too became the young man who discovered his homosexuality in Whitman's pages, for he found a comrade, "a young man some years younger than himself and of lower social class, whose development he was able to assist . . . his love lighted up the gold of affection that was within me and consumed the dross. It was from this that I first learned that there was no hard and fast line between the physical and spiritual in friendship . . . everything in life began to sing with joy, and what little of real creative work I have done I attribute largely to the power that was born in me during those years" (Case 13).

These men seem to feel that homosexuality is unique to themselves, and they declare it the central question of their lives, feeling also a profound alienation from their own sex. As Carpenter says, "My own sexual nature was a mystery to me. I found myself cut off from the understanding of others, felt myself an outcast. . . . I was . . . on the brink of despair and madness with repressed passion and torment" (Case 7). Another respondent "felt much perplexed and depressed by my views on sexual desire and was convinced they were peculiar to myself" (Case 8). For yet another, so solitary were these cognitions of vice that "I had an idea at that time that the whole thing was so much an original invention of his and mine that there was no likelihood of it being practiced by anyone else in the world" (Case 26). The great wish is fulfilled in these texts when it is discovered that these passions are not unique: "Later on . . . though slowly, I came to find that there were others like myself" (Case 7). Or as another learns: "My next discovery was that my case, so far from being peculiar, was a common one, and I was quickly initiated into the mysteries of inversion, with its freemasonry and argot" (Case 8). Indeed, manly love was everywhere, as one correspondent observed: "Of its extraordinary prevalence I am assured, for I have found it everywhere—I have travelled much—and in all stations of life."

The men who share their homosexual lives construct in composite "the homosexual" whom Foucault describes as a species; together they produce a homoerotic and a homosexual text. Attracted to men early in life, they engaged generally with eagerness in masturbation, which was often an obsession, and—sometimes willing, sometimes reluctantly, sometimes not at all—in the other possibilities of homosexual play. Many of them confessed to being dreamy or indolent in youth, and these dreams became rich fantasy lives inhabited by handsome, available, and muscular young men—roughs, shepherds, workingmen, soldiers, and sailors—or by more passive and effeminate youths. In life as well as fantasy, they ardently pursued friendship, love, and sex, some of them sharing quite incredibly active and adventurous sexual experiences. All of them, without exception, looked for the ideal friend. They responded to women as social, but rarely as sexual, beings, expressing often a positive abhorrence of the notion of heterosexual union and an equally positive conviction that homosexual love was nobler, more passionate, and more profound than heterosexual love.

Almost none of them expressed any desire to be anything other than what they were, even though many of them keenly felt that they were outcasts in a world that condemned what to them seemed natural and imperative emotions. They celebrated homosexuality and considered it natural, elevating, and the source of creative power. Many of them suspected that they were a discreet and physiologically unique species. The language of their texts is heavily freighted with the common imagery of homoerotic literary and imaginative conventions. Nearly all of them express a deep sense of isolation and alienation from the common expectations of male sexual conduct, generally represented to them by stern fathers, teachers, doctors, or priests. These writers recognized that the "sex" from which they were alienated was that which habitually conformed to received and published sexual standards concerning the nature of gender roles and their conflation with "masculine" or "feminine" style. Their project is to claim for themselves a place where a more transgressive sexuality could reject the old business of sexual barter and politics and to recast the definition of masculinity, inscribing within it the possibilities of same-sex desire and the physical consummation of that desire. Together they shared in the production of a defining discourse about sexuality—about what Ellis finally decided to call homosexuality.

E. M. Forster in 1938, 24 years after he finished *Maurice* and 33 years before the novel was finally published.

Chapter 10

INTO THE GREENWOOD: E. M. FORSTER, 1913

Two men can defy the world.
                —E. M. Forster, *Maurice* (1913)

E. M. Forster's novel *Maurice* is the British herald of the homo-erotic texts of the twentieth century. Though it was written in 1913, it was not published until 1970 and thus the dates of its writing and its publication enclose the social and literary ferment in England that saw advocacy of homosexuality translated from the obsessed concern of a coterie of largely minor writers and activists to become a central anxiety in modern social life and a major theme in modern literature—the subject, direct or implied, of books by some of the most important English writers of the twentieth century. Forster's book was written against a background that included the still-fresh wounds of the Oscar Wilde trial and a desire by homosexuals—not entirely quelled though considerably weakened by that trial—to pursue what many now considered to be the imperative cause of homosexual liberation.

The sentencing of Wilde in 1895 cast a long shadow on most of those who might have wanted to reveal their homosexuality or write about it. The major works resisting homophobic law and public opinion—those of Carpenter and Ellis—were subjected to suppression and censorship. Ellis's *Sexual Inversion* was effectively banned from publication, and Carpenter's *Love's Coming of Age*, containing his essay on "The Intermediate Sex" was refused publication by his publisher (though it was later published as a book by the more radical Labour Press). In 1911 when Carpenter looked for the book-length version of *The Intermediate Sex* in the British Museum Catalogue, he was told that it had been banned from the catalogue because of its subject matter. It was not to be entered into the catalogue until 1913.

When Forster wrote *Maurice* in 1913, the literary energy released by the Uranian poets of the 1880s and 1890s was still to be found in some works published after 1900 by writers like A. E. Housman, E. E. Bradford, John Leslie Barford, and Ralph Chubb, the last and in some ways the most interesting of the Uranians, whose poems were published up until his death in 1960. In 1913, however, homosexual acts, whether in public or in private between adults, were still criminal. There were no organizations in England advocating homosexual reform, and homosexuality was rarely spoken of in public or in the press. George V was of the opinion that homosexuals shot themselves, and "decent" society—when it was willing to talk about the subject at all— was largely of the opinion of Forster's character Clive, that "the sole excuse for any relationship between men is that it remain purely platonic."

Despite this homophobia, however, the criminologist George Cecil Ives founded the first reform society in Britain dedicated to alleviating the persecution of homosexuals. Ives described his project as a mission "to set all loves free" (quoted in Weeks, 119). His greatest service to what he called the "war of Liberation" was his founding of the Order of Chaeronea sometime in the mid-1890s. Though he saw the project as a cause, he was very much aware that the social climate demanded secrecy in pursuit of the goals of the cause; thus the society was a secret one, with strict vows of confidentiality. Named after the Theban Sacred Band of lovers, the order described itself as "A Religion, A Theory of Life, and Ideal of Duty"; it sought to "demand justice for all manner of people who are wronged and oppressed by individuals or multitudes or laws" (quoted in Weeks, 123).

Among the order's members may have been the scholar and poet Montague Summers; Laurence Housman, a minor poet; Housman's far more famous and talented brother, A. E. Housman, whose poems in *The Shropshire Lad* managed at once to be immensely popular and to encode a subtle homoeroticism. Other possible members were the Uranian poets John Gambril Nicholson; Charles Kains Jackson, whose 1894 essay "The New Chivalry" had in effect advocated marriage between homosexual men; the socialist C. R. Ashbee, who advocated manly love as an antidote to the evils of the capitalist work place; and Samuel Cottam, another poet and bibliophile of Uranian materials. Ives's diaries suggest that there were also members in America, Germany, France, and Italy.

The history of this group remains to be written and a measure of its influence taken. Just how long it lasted is unknown.[1] Ives, however, was very clear about what needed to be accomplished. His belief, he said, "refuses all compromise with religious parties, all compromise with existing sexual morality, all compromise with the class system in any shape" (quoted in Weeks, 126).

At about the time Forster was planning *Maurice*, Ives, together with Edward Carpenter and some of the aforementioned men, were planning a reform society that would not, like Chaeronea, be secret but that would present itself in public as a society for the study of sexual matters generally, including a project to educate the public about homosexuality. Since many of the founders of what would finally be called the British Society for the Study of Sex Psychology were themselves homosexual, it is not surprising that, as Jeffrey Weeks says, "the discussion of homosexuality was inevitably at the heart of the society's work" (Weeks, 134). Responding to the work of Magnus Hirschfeld in Germany, whose Scientific Humanitarian Committee, founded in 1897, was the first homosexual reform organization in the world, and whose book *Homosexuality in Men and Women* (1914) was tremendously influential, and to the writing of Adolf Brand, whose German magazine *Der Eigene* was seen as a call to new and active awareness of the rights of homosexuals, Ives and members of Chaeronea formally organized the British Society in July 1914, and Edward Carpenter was elected its first president. Forster finished *Maurice* at the same time.

Forster was perhaps aware of some the activity on behalf of homosexuals. He claims, however, in the 1960 "Terminal Note" to the novel, that *Maurice* was directly inspired by a visit to Edward Carpenter and Carpenter's lover George Merrill. Carpenter was, Forster recalls, "a rebel appropriate to his age." He was not only a socialist and a poet but "a believer in the Love of Comrades whom he sometimes called Uranians. It was this last aspect of him that attracted me in my loneliness. For a short time he seemed to hold the key to every trouble. I approached him . . . as one approaches a saviour." After his visit, during which, Forster also recalls, Merrill "touched my backside," thereby uniting Carpenter's idealistic homoerotic theory with direct homosexual sensation, Forster "immediately began to write *Maurice*."

Maurice was a book unlike any ever written in England, a story in which a respected member of the upper middle-class establishment becomes a rebel against birth and class: he not only enters into a love affair with a social inferior—a gamekeeper—but his love affair ends not in disaster or in death but in idyllic happiness. If it were not for the fact that D. H. Lawrence had not yet written *Lady Chatterly's Lover*, this book might in outline be mistaken for that. But it did what Lawrence had not intended, though some suspect he might have wanted to do: the lovers are men, and rather than mere social indiscretion, their love is revolution. As Forster puts it, "A happy ending was imperative. I shouldn't have bothered to write otherwise. I determined that in fiction anyway two men should fall in love and remain in it for the forever and ever that fiction allows" ("Terminal Note," 250).

Maurice is in every way the solid representative of English probity. But into his psychology Forster "dropped an ingredient that puzzles him, and wakes him up, and torments him, and finally saves him." This ingredient is Maurice's love of comrades and sexual desire for men. Because of his torment, Maurice becomes exasperated by the "very normality" of his life and his respectability. His comfortable job, his comfortable home, "gradually turn out to be Hell." Maurice realizes, in what his age had come to firmly believe was the crucial and central arena of sexuality, that he is a rebel. There is no alternative for him, Forster argues, but to rebel against society itself and against the "comfortable" symbols of sexual and class repression, and "he must either smash them or be smashed."

Forster's is the first novel of a major British author to confront crucial questions raised by sexual difference and same-sex desire and to resolve them, as he puts it, without recourse to "a lad dangling from a noose or with a suicide pact." It is also the first homoerotic novel to inscribe in fiction Whitman's and Carpenter's awareness that a portrayal of same-sex desire must recognize that the inequities of class must be defined in sexual as well as social terms, and to propose that sex between men can erase class inequality. Finally, Forster's book may well be the first homoerotic text that directly advocates a kind of revolutionary action against what Christopher Isherwood would eventually call the "heterosexual dictatorship" in order to eradicate sexual and social oppression. This revolutionary advocacy is embodied not only in Maurice's love for Alec the gamekeeper but in Maurice's confrontation with Clive, once his Platonic lover at Cambridge, who in order to take his place "in society" represses his homosexual desire and sacrifices his love for Maurice. At the end of the novel Maurice tells the complacent Clive, now married to a woman who is equally a symbol of middle-class sexual repression, that he has shared everything with Alec, including his body, and that their first nearly sacramental consummation took place in the bedroom of Clive's family home, a bastion of the very society that Forster urges Maurice to smash.

To bring Maurice to the moment when he can answer Alec's call to love and rebellion and strike his blow at society in the person of Clive, Forster creates for Maurice a story that is not, like *Teleny*, Raffalovich's sonnets, or Wilde's life, filled with actual or suggested scenes of the perverse or with the hot-house sensibility or amoral transgressions that those texts display. Maurice encounters no *louche* or *outré* sexuality—indeed, until Alec appears there is no sex at all. Maurice moves in the privileged realm of Cambridge and in the wider realm of the English upper-class, largely male, establishment (although he represents, as Forster says, "suburbia," the middle, not the upper class). He is neither effete nor effeminate; nor is he especially precocious or possessed of that alleged "sympathy" or the "sensibility" that nineteenth-century myth ascribed to homosexuals. Forster goes to some pains to make him ordinary and even a bit dull; at one point he describes him as mediocre.

The unconscious world of this very English lad is, however, populated by dreams in which a half-understood image, the ideal friend, constantly reappears: "he could die for such a friend . . . they would make any sacrifice for each other" (22). Maurice is also tormented by the discovery of sexual desire, but he is as unclear about what his desire means as he is about the meaning of his dreams: "he longed for smut, but heard little and contributed less, and his chief indecencies were solitary." His sexual discovery "took place in a trance." But when he discovers, he thinks, a friend in his classmate Clive

Durham, "his heart had lit never to be quenched again, and one thing in him at last was real" (40) Out of the mass of half-formed prejudices, uncontested moral dicta, and unconvincingly held proprieties of his heterosexualized upbringing, Maurice at last confronts in a moment of homosexual desire something that seems to him true, something that invokes the felt thrill of reality.

The idyll Forster creates between Maurice and Clive derives from the wishful texts of nineteenth-century homoerotic poetry, from Pater's Epicurean Marius and his friend, from the passionate realities of schoolboy romance known to any English public schoolman, from Tennyson, from Whitman, from Carpenter, and not a little from the informing classical myth of selfless male love as much imagined in as derived from the Greeks that dominated English school life and literature. In Clive's company Maurice reads Plato, encounters the *Symposium*, and encounters homophobia when a Greek master "observed in a flat toneless voice" during translation class: "Omit: a reference to the unspeakable vice of the Greeks." The love whose name is forbidden turns out, he discovers, to be on everyone's tongue. "He hadn't known it could be mentioned, and when Durham did so in the middle of a sunlight court a breath of liberty touched him" (51).

It is not long, and it does not take too many innocent embraces from Clive (apparently they never have sex), for Maurice to realize that "he would not deceive himself so much. He would not—and this was the test— pretend to care about women when the only sex that attracted him was his own. He loved men and always had loved them. He longed to embrace them and mingle his being with theirs" (62). The middle-class Maurice and the upper-class Clive continue their affair. Forster describes it as a new cre- ation, as a construction built in spite of moral disapprobation. They write their passion—as Whitman had done—in a new and invented tongue: "their love scene drew out, having the inestimable gain of a new language. No tradition overawed the boys. No convention settled what was poetic, what absurd. They were concerned with a passion that few English minds have admitted, and so created untrammeled" (93). But when the Arcadian idyll of their academic life ends, and when they enter the professions—per- haps the first characters in English homoerotic texts actually to work—their love is confronted by the threat of society: "So they proceeded outwardly like other men. Society received them, as she receives thousands like them. Behind society slumbered the Law. They had their last year at Cambridge together. They traveled in Italy. Then the prison house closed, but on both of them. Clive was working for the bar, Maurice harnessed to an office. They were together still" (99).

They are not destined to stay together. Clive takes a trip to Greece and returns out of love with Maurice, changed from one "who loved men" to one who will "henceforward love women." Forster has allowed Clive to con- front the spiritual home of his presumed homosexuality, and there, perhaps

Forster implies, Clive discovers that what he felt was not passion but a construction from books, and that his love for Maurice was a blend of lust never realized—and which Clive feared to realize—and the condescension of an upper-class man for the middle-class youth he sought not to love but to change: "He had found in Maurice a nature that was not indeed fine, but charmingly willing. . . . He educated Maurice, or rather his spirit educated Maurice's spirit, for they themselves became equal" (98). It is Clive's presumption of their inequality inscribed in that telling "became" that foretells the end of their relationship.

When it does end Maurice is left alone and is transformed once again. He recognizes that his position in society is untenable. He is living a lie. In one of their last conversations he says to Clive, "'You and I are outlaws. All this'—he pointed to the middle-class comfort of the room—'would be taken away from us if people knew.'" When Clive is gone Maurice dreams his outlaw status: "He grew more bitter, he wished that he had shouted while he had the strength and smashed down this front of lies. . . . He was an outlaw in disguise. Perhaps among those who took to the greenwood in old time there had been two men like himself—two. At times he entertained the dream. Two men can defy the world" (135).

Maurice turns to social action to assuage his grief. He teaches arithmetic to working-class youths and gives up golf to play football with them at a settlement house in South London. But his dreams are still about men, and he discovers himself admiring the youths he teaches and very nearly attempts the seduction of a handsome boy staying at his parents' house. He is so horrified by his desire that he resorts to answers drawn from class-bound and moralistic attitudes. He attributes his admiration for the handsome youths solely to "lust" and reminds himself that "the feeling that can impel a gentleman towards a person of lower class stands self condemned." His solution—abstinence and hard work—is equally middle class: "he had only to keep away from boys and young men to ensure success" (151). When success does not come he consults a doctor, who refuses to believe his assertion that he is "an unspeakable of the Oscar Wilde sort" and refuses even to discuss it. He assures Maurice that when "you get the right girl, there'll be no more trouble then" (161).

The remainder of the novel focuses on Maurice's meeting with Alec who works as a gamekeeper at Penge, Clive's estate. An uneasy reconciliation with Clive, now married, brings Maurice there, but a different and more dangerous Maurice than Clive suspects. Clive, now taken his place in society as squire and politician, is the very picture of upper-class heterosexual respectability. As for Maurice, he has become a wary inhabitant of a world that he now sees as dangerous to men like himself: "there was now a complete break between his public and his private actions" (170).

What remains is for the relationship of Maurice and Alec to weave itself into a rich tapestry. It begins with glances between them, and comes to fruition when, one night at Penge, in the midst of a dream about "big spaces where passion clasped peace, spaces no science could reach, but existed for ever, full of woods some of them, and arched with a majestic sky and a friend," Maurice suddenly awakens and with a sure sense of destiny about to be fulfilled, opens the window and cries "Come!" In response, the "head and shoulders of a man rose up" at the window, and Alec, the young god come to lead Maurice at last to sexual revelation, appears. What remains is for their desire to turn to love, and for them to depart for the greenwood, both out-laws. As Maurice says to Alec, "All the world's against us. We've got to pull ourselves together and make plans while we can" (229). Many pages later—after arguments between them, after Alec determines to leave England but then remains for Maurice's sake, after Maurice recognizes that the class gulf between them has been bridged and eradicated by love—they meet at last in the abandoned boathouse at Penge, and Alec answers him: "And now we shan't be parted no more, and that's finished."

All that is left is for them to enter into their greenwood, their Arcadia. But before that Maurice has one more task to perform. In a final interview Clive—blind and determined to ignore what had passed between them and what it signified—imagines that "the core of blackness" he discerns in Maurice comes from an unhappy relationship with a woman. He urges Maurice to consult his wife, since "where a woman is in question I would always consult another woman." Maurice confronts the entire edifice of het-erosexist prejudice when he answers: "It's miles worse for you than that; I'm in love with your gamekeeper." Clive reacts with horror not only because of Maurice's admission that he is after all not "normal" and has returned, as Clive says, "to the land through the looking glass" but because "intimacy with any social inferior was unthinkable to him." But the horror turns to fear and disgust when Maurice strikes the final death blow to Clive's heterosexual complacency: "'I have shared with Alec,' he said after deep thought. 'Shared what?' 'All I have. Which includes my body.' Clive sprang up with a whim-per of disgust. He wanted to smite the monster and flee, but he was civi-lized." He resorts to the only cliché he knows: "But surely, the only excuse for any relationship between men is that it remain purely platonic" (242–43). But there is no answer, for Maurice has disappeared into the night, returning to Alec who waits for him near the path to the greenwood. Forster leaves Clive alone in the darkness with nothing but the "petals of the evening primrose"—that quintessentially Uranian flower—that Maurice had earlier plucked, fallen in a little pile at his feet.

Forster's *Maurice* is the first modern homosexual novel, heir to those who tried to make society think about homosexuality. *Maurice* marks the end of what Whitman, Pater, and Symonds had begun. *Maurice* can rightly claim to be the first and best modern homosexual novel because it predicts in every way what the best homoerotic novels of the twentieth century written before Stonewall would ultimately achieve: confrontation, with the intention of changing, society; the construction of a positive identity for homosexual readers; a rewriting of social myths of sickness, insanity, perversion, and universal effeminacy, without sacrificing the essentiality of difference.

In the "Terminal Note" Forster assures us that "Maurice and Alec still roam the greenwood" in that forever world that fiction ensures. For the rest of us Forster fears that the only difference in social attitude toward homosexuality has been a change "from ignorance and terror to familiarity and contempt." What the "public really loathes about homosexuality is not the thing itself but having to think about it." Written at the beginning of modern gay times, it compelled those who read it when it was finally published in 1970 to think again. For readers today, Forster's novel ought to be no museum piece, no dated performance of an antique sensibility, no "artistic failure"; it is not, as some critics insist, a "study in repression and guilt."[2] Guilt and repression are indeed components of the novel, but it is about a victorious confrontation with those socially created and homophobic responses.

The novel creates in Maurice a character who resonates against and elaborates and confirms in fiction the sketches recorded in Ellis's pages and forecasts modern experiences to be described in twentieth-century novels and twentieth-century lives. Failure to recognize Alec as a major creation in modern or any fiction is a failure of critical perception. There is nothing like Alec in homoerotic fiction prior to this. No homosexual of his class has so authentically spoken or been allowed to speak. No member of his class has been so effectively the catalyst for personal sexual revolution in British homoerotic texts. Though Maurice determines to "fight," finally both light and leading in matters of sexual liberation comes from Alec; it is he who forces open the closet door. The novel's confrontation with homophobia can only remind us that the ignorance, terror, familiarity, and contempt that Forster defines as the components of homophobia are as powerfully present now as when Alec and Maurice struck their blow against them, defying the world.

When *Maurice* appeared in England a year after Stonewall, many readers might have seen the exclusive greenwood into which Maurice and Alec vanish as the goal—what Forster calls a "happier year" in his dedication—toward which they would willingly march. Writing 10 years before Stonewall, Forster believed that his book "marked the last moment of the greenwood." There is now, he writes, "no forest or fell to escape to today." Perhaps he was right. Dubious as he may have been about the continued existence of the greenwood, and despite the pessimism that was always with him as he surveyed mankind's botched attempts merely to connect, perhaps, were he living today, he might feel that the greenwood must be established here and now in the midst of, not separate from, society.

When he wrote *Maurice*, however, Forster feared that the greenwood was the only place in which men who loved men, and the books written by and about them, could find a safe haven. He specified in his will that *Maurice* was not to be published until after his death. When *Maurice* was finally published, homosexual activity between adult males in private had been decriminalized, though not legalized, in England. A gay rights movement had begun, and in the Gay Liberation Front England saw its first radical and activist homosexual liberation group modeled on a group first founded in America. Still, the radical reevaluation of gay life that Stonewall both symbolized and in part initiated in America had no such result in England. Nor were the achievements of the gay movement so immediately spectacular there as in the United States. By that time, however, England could claim that among the major contributors to modern world literature many of the greatest were English, and many of those were homosexual.[3] Some of these writers not only did not hesitate to reveal their homosexuality but made homosexuality an informing aspect of their work.

Dust jacket depicting the protagonist of Blair Niles's *Strange Brother* (~~1920~~)—as handsome as he is doomed.

1931

chapter 11

INTOLERABLE LIVES: AMERICAN HOMOPHOBIA, 1880–1914

These inverts are not fit to live with the rest of mankind. . . . Their lives ought to be made so intolerable as to drive them to abandon their vices.
—Dr. T. Griswold Comstock (1895)

When both English and American writers after 1860 responded to Whitman's call to write manly love into literature in deliberate resistance to its absence, what they produced made a contribution to a literary construction of homosexual identities, created the possibilities of defining homosexual experience as a landscape among cultural sites, and enrolled it as one among several discourses that recognized that difference as much as similarity contributed to cultural definition. These writers responded to medical texts that were creating what was coming to be called "sexuality." These texts posited two very separate and quite different kinds of sexuality: one assumed to be healthy and "normal," the other "perverted" or "abnormal." A person's "sexuality" was now defined not only by one's sex and gender but by the sex of one's object of desire. Statements about sexuality came to imply a set of moral and social judgments about the subject's mental "health" that depended on a social and sexual mythology that traded in terms such as chastity, love, perversion, and lust.

Definitions of sexuality inevitably relied on the presumption that certain fixed characteristics of "masculinity" or "femininity" were an irreducible component of every sexual subject. Sexuality was, in some late nineteenth-century definitions, the dominating and defining principle of all human actions. As Dr. William Howard explained it in 1904, "Every physician should understand the sexual side of life, for it is sexual activity that governs

life, permits the continuation of the species and promotes crime and its causes. It is the basis of all society" (quoted in Katz 1983, 312). Dr. Howard's definition stresses two primary aspects of sex and sexuality that the end of the
century saw as inextricably associated: that sex functioned as the guarantor
of procreation and, conversely, it was the abyss from which crime—seen here
as an activity caused by uncontrolled sexual urges—so threateningly
appeared.

Walt Whitman had forecast Dr. Howard's universalizing definition 30
years earlier, using the new word "sexuality": "It has become . . . imperative
to achieve a shifted attitude . . . towards the thought and fact of sexuality, as
an element of character, personality, the emotions, and a theme in literature.
I am not going to argue the question by itself; it does not stand by itself"
(*PW*, 2: 728). Whitman had offered the same argument about erotic attraction to men—what he called "the need of comrades"—when he described it
in the first of the *Calamus* poems as "the life that does not exhibit itself yet
contains all the rest." Whitman's early position in *Calamus* concerning
manly love looks ahead to Dr. Howard's more general observation that sexuality "governs life" and is "the basis of society." But Whitman resists—at
least for manly love—its association with crime and instead insists in
Democratic Vistas that "loving comradeship" is the "spiritualizing" "counterbalance and offset of our materialistic and vulgar American democracy . . .
without which it would be incomplete, in vain, and incapable of perpetuating itself" (*PW*, 2: 414–15). By the end of the century writers who advocated
manly love and its sexual expression and who believed that manly love had
social as well as sexual implications increasingly resisted the demonization by
psychologists and the law of what they were coming to describe—the term
was first used in an American medical text in 1892—as "homosexuality"
(Katz 1983, 231–32).

When J. A. Symonds wrote to Whitman in 1890 to ask directly if the
Calamus poems suggested physical intimacy between men, Whitman in his
reply professed horror that they could be construed to suggest such "morbid
inferences." His use of "morbid"—a term associated in medical texts with
perversion—shows that Whitman too was aware that since 1860 the love of
comrades had been redefined as a sickness, not a sin, and that society was no
longer content to see in it mere friendship. In an 1870 letter approving of
the American writer Charles Warren Stoddard's "adhesive nature & outlet
thereof"—though whether the outlet for adhesive desire was to be found in
homosexual consummation or in homoerotic texts he cannily refrains from
saying—Whitman had warned Stoddard about the "hard, pungent, gritty,
worldly experiences & qualities of American practical life" that repulse
"extravagant sentimentalism." By this he meant, in the context of adhesive
sentiments, too blatant an expression of romantic homoeroticism in texts.
Whitman warned Stoddard that "American practical life" was suspicious of
the kind of "extravagant sentimentalism" that might be read as an expression

of homoerotic sentiment. Whitman himself was very aware of the destructive power of homophobia, as is evidence by the gradual disappearance from his post-*Calamus* texts of any sentiment that might be construed as homoerotic, by his deletions from later editions of some of his poems with similar sentiments, and by his response to Symonds's letter. There was reason for Whitman's caution.

Though by 1892 most states had removed the death penalty for acts of sodomy, it was still criminal and punishable by prison. Homosexuals were increasingly marked by science as diseased members of the healthy social body that ought to be removed. What science talked about within the boundaries of its own discourses was also becoming part of popular discourse as well. Science became part of popular knowledge and sexuality became an open rather than a hidden topic. Public knowledge of perversion grew as did public fascination with it.

The popular press published sensational accounts of sex crimes, and popular literature offered material for any taste, including that for the perverse. As David S. Reynolds points out, "Sex scandals were often featured in penny papers, reform literature, and trial pamphlets, and in time a frankly erotic popular literature emerged." After the 1830s Reynolds discerns "a new kind of dark literature featuring perverse sexuality" and documents novels of the 1840s and 1850s—among them, George Thompson's *City Crimes*—that "deal openly with homosexuality" and that detail lurid homosexual encounters (Reynolds, 211ff). This is not to say that the word "homosexual" was on every tongue or that the front pages of newspapers detailed stories of pederasty. But by 1890 the public had become more convinced that homosexuals were a distinct and possibly dangerous class—one on which they did not look benignly.

The high romance, healthy passion, and democratic desire that Whitman associated with manly love was by 1890 defined instead as sexual abnormality, physical degeneracy, effeminacy, and even insanity—the very infirmities Whitman had long claimed to be alien to himself and to his art. Thus by 1890 he could insist that there was no homosexual or homoerotic content intended in his works, asserting that "such morbid inferences" seemed "damnable" and were "disavow'd" by him. Whatever construction may have been put on this remark by later critics, what it does show is Whitman's keen awareness that the gritty reality of American life—at least as that reality was defined by those who shaped its scientific, legal, and moral discourses at the turn of the century—was no more tolerant of the love of comrades than it had been in 1855 when Thomas Higginson could find no words save in Latin to describe the horror of what he had read in Whitman's poetry.

In 1924 Edward Carpenter speculated on what he thought Whitman must have felt: "He, Whitman, could hardly with truthfulness deny any knowledge or contemplation of such inferences; but on the other hand he took what we might call the reasonable line, and said that, while not advocating abnormal relations in any way, he of course made allowances for possibilities in that direction and the occasional development of such relations, why, he knew that the moment he said such a thing he would have the whole American Press at his heels, snarling and slandering, and distorting his words in every possible way. Things are pretty bad here in this country, but in the States (in such matters) they are ten times worse" (quoted in Katz 1976, 364).

Whitman was not denying his homosexuality; he was responding to the fact that after about 1880 American medical texts seemed to be increasingly obsessed with the topic of sexual inversion, and the press had begun to be attentive to this obsession. Conceptions of homosexuality as a medical "problem" found their way from the circumspect pages of professional journals to the press and thus to popular perceptions. Thus in a 1902 review of a performance of Oscar Wilde's *The Importance of Being Earnest* the *New York Times* had difficulty in separating the play from the scandal connected with its author. It found the play to be "inextricably associated with the saddest and most revolting scandal"—a scandal that caused the "clouds of social retribution" to close about Wilde who "crept away to a by-street in the Latin Quarter to die like a rat." Anyone who sees the play, the *Times* moralized, wishes to "dissociate the man Oscar Wilde from the playwright" and "rejoice in the excellence of his quality, while not forgetting its defect." The "defect"—a term freighted with "medical" implications—is the homosexuality of its author for "the simper of Bunthorne leers from the pages" and even though the play is the "best thing of its kind in the language" yet the paradoxes created by the brilliant play and Wilde's fate "somehow spell the awful name of truth" as "the inversions of common sense rebound upon the author" (quoted in Katz 1983, 307). The 1902 *Times* review is a later example of the kind of criticism leveled against Whitman in 1855 and is testimony to the increasingly homophobic commentary that read difference as disease.

In 1892 the word "homosexual" appeared in America, imported from Europe, and it may have been first used by Dr. James Kiernan in an American medical journal when he defined the "pure homosexual" as one whose "general mental state is that of the opposite sex" and defined a "heterosexual" more confusingly as one who had "inclinations to both sexes" but who in addition practiced "abnormal methods of gratification" (quoted in Katz 1983, 232). Kiernan's "heterosexual" is a category very much in transition, but his "homosexual" is the familiar unmanly and effeminate male who imitates a woman. Whitman had long inveighed against texts that were "without manhood or power" and in which "men might easily pass for women." At a time when male-male eroticism was being conflated with effeminacy and "morbid" psychological dysfunction, it may not be surprising that he might take offence at a suggestion that his texts might morbidly inscribe such a "mental" state, and suggest some of the presumed weaknesses of the opposite sex that "inverts" were supposed to display.

Whitman very much prided himself upon reflecting, representing, and expressing what America thought and felt and though he may not have used it or even heard it, "homosexual" and what it implied was very much in the air. What it implied is detailed in a talk given by Dr. C. H. Hughes in 1893, wherein he classifies all homosexual acts as "eroto-pathia or erotomania." These are "perversions of the proper and natural human passions." Proper human passions are "the ardent affections of the heart" that are "chaste and honorable" and that lead to reproduction. Abnormal passions are "strange morbid perversions" that can "destroy both body and mind" (quoted in Katz 1983, 245).

Dr. George J. Monroe in 1899 deemed the sexual habits of "perverts" to be "so abominable, so disgusting, so filthy, and worse than beastly" that they were too terrible even for doctors to write about (quoted in Katz 1983, 301). Not only were homosexuals seen as people who willingly and defiantly practiced forms of sexual activity radically different from the norm, but it was imagined that they had created a social organization in which these practices flourished and even a literature in which these practices were advocated. If individual homosexuals were disturbing, they were at least ultimately trivialized by being declared objects of pity or contempt; in groups, however, they were deemed a threat to morality and the family.

To define what was "normal" the primary task of the medical study of sexuality was to construct a paradigm of the "abnormal" and place abnormality within a scientific rather than a legal/theological discourse. By the 1880s in both England and America, Victorian medical theorists and social commentators had participated with social custom and belief in creating an increasingly rigid division between the social and sexual activities of men and women, assigning to each very different roles. The "true woman" was to be submissive socially and sexually, the manager of domestic life, pious as well as morally "pure." Men were socially and sexually assertive, benign rulers of the patriarchal family, and active providers of material goods. Victorian theorists argued that these roles were dictated by nature and biology and that their qualities were "naturally" associated with the biological female or male. Thus the biologically sexed woman was presumed to be naturally "feminine," the biologically sexed male naturally "masculine," and gender was defined as having fixed and immutable "natural" characteristics.

Enfolding these roles was an insistence that "love" was the proper— indeed, the only—channel through which determined roles might be emotionally expressed and played out. "Love" as outlined in marriage manuals and social purity tracts was seen to be only truly possible in a male-female, masculine-feminine context. Thus love between men expressed in literature was deemed not only suspect but impossible. As Thomas Higginson wrote of Whitman in the Nation in an 1892 review, "There is the . . . curious deficiency shown in him . . . of anything like personal and romantic love. Whenever we come upon anything that suggests a glimpse of it, the object always turns out to be a man and not a woman." When Higginson describes the lack of "romantic love" as a "deficiency," he writes in the same vocabulary of texts that describe the presumed "mental deficiencies" of homosexuals. He points the finger of perversion directly at Whitman by equating Whitman with his texts. Finding Whitman himself deficient, he can then assert that if there is anything that "suggests" romantic love it cannot possibly be romantic love since the object is inappropriate, even impossible.

When confronted with social or literary examples of male-male sex or any affection in which the biological term "woman" was eliminated and the characteristics of the "feminine" consequently absent, readers like Higginson deemed it impossible for "love" to exist. In the absence of the "normal" polarity in a text, all that was left to formulate was the "abnormal," a formulation that by the 1880s was well under way, creating that other familiar description of homosexual passion: "l'amour de l'impossible." Once the concept of the "abnormal" in social relations was invented, it was not difficult to apply it to sexual relations. Once appropriate social, sexual, and emotional roles were established for male and female "sexualities" it became necessary to create the sexual pervert in order to define normal sexuality and explain and control those who deviated from it.

Victorian sexual theory presumed that males and females "naturally" engaged in sex as active and passive partners. The binary opposition of active and passive seemed, so they believed, almost to be written into the structure of sex itself. But a problem arose when sex was imagined between two men. Popular perception, supported by some documented sexual practice but mostly by unexamined preconception, assumed that deviant sexual acts were of one kind only—anal penetration. A man who wished to penetrate another male presented a problem for Victorian sexual theory. What he wanted to do was presumed to be active, aggressive, and hence masculine. But because his desires were not directed toward their "natural" object, a woman, his activity was abnormal, his actions perverse, and the definition of masculinity was compromised. It should be recalled that the early constructions of the (male) sodomite saw him originally as debauched, then as a "masculine" penetrator of boys, and only later as an indiscriminate and effeminized participant in homosexual practice.

By the 1880s some sexual theorists seemed almost to want to erase such "active" sexual consumers from consideration in order to establish the effeminate homosexual as the essential type. Men who were inserters were therefore increasingly denominated as examples of acquired and hence "vicious" perversion whose sexuality was informed by the deliberate and lustful pursuit of abnormal vice as opposed to the "real" homosexual whose desires were congenital and hence involuntary, whose feelings and mannerisms were effeminate, and whose primary sexual pleasure was derived from being penetrated. A man who liked to be penetrated was presumed to be sexually passive and had thus rejected "masculinity" and adopted "femininity." Thus he was appropriately described as "effeminate" and his physical mannerisms were presumed to be the mirror of a sexual and psychological deficiency. If a man wished to be penetrated then his emotional makeup must be female (see Katz 1983, 145).

Concepts of the normal only developed because the idea of the abnormal had historically preceded them. In a sense, sodomites had first to be demonized before nonsodomites could be valorized, just as the term "straight" could only exist after "gay" was invented. Whereas the word "homosexual" appeared in American texts in 1892, "heterosexual" was not coined until the beginning of the twentieth century. Creation of separate categories of the homosexual and the heterosexual allowed greater and more precise social control over those believed to be socially and sexually undesirable. As one doctor asserted, "Society, organized into government . . . is specially concerned with the maintenance of chastity and morals" and argues for the "perpetual sequestration" of "sexual perverts from society" (quoted in Katz 1983, 247).

Fueled by such commentaries and by interpretations and misinterpretations of scientific theory—even by the work of relatively "liberal" commentators like Havelock Ellis—the image of the homosexual by the end of the century was that of an effeminate weakling who was morbid, morose, melancholy by nature, abnormally sexed, and physically deficient. Tragically, homosexuals themselves often accepted rather than questioned the definitions society and medicine imposed on them. Medical definition, according to Katz, "served to induce the invert to accept an anti-invert morality"; homosexuals responded to what he calls the "social production . . . of shame and guilt" (Katz 1983, 156).

The transfer of social control of sexual perversion from the church to a hegemony created by an alliance between the law and science is perhaps the most important element in the construction of the kind of homophobia discernible in texts in late nineteenth-century America. Describing this transfer of social power over perversion, Dr. George Shrady writing in 1884 in "The New York Medical Record" on the subject of the "Perverted Sexual Instinct" suggests that the passions exhibited by such "debased men" do in fact deserve "the considerate attention of the physician," since these persons "have an irrepressible desire to act the part of the opposite sex." Thus "conditions once considered criminal are really pathological and come within the province of the physician." Such men "have a mincing gait" and are "of the artistic, poetical, and imaginative temperament, often exhibiting a tendency to rather weak philosophizing" though "sometimes they are of a vigourous understanding." In most cases there is a great mental distress felt through a consciousness of their unnatural instincts that can lead them to "melancholia" or "insanity and suicide" (quoted in Katz 1983, 197–98).

In Shrady's analysis the homophobic clichés of effeminacy are combined with the newer medical models that assert mental instability and pathology.

A few years later Dr. G. Frank Lydston, in a lecture on sexual perversion published in the *Medical and Surgical Reporter* in 1889, theorized that "sexual perversion" had "until a recent date" been "studied solely from the standpoint of the moralist." But now this "unfortunate class of individuals . . . characterized by perverted sexuality" must no longer be viewed only in "the light of their moral responsibility" but instead as "victims of a physical and . . . mental defect" (quoted in Katz 1983, 213–14).

By 1899 the medical assessment of homosexual acts had become in some quarters very nearly rabid in its condemnation. Dr. Monroe defined sodomy as unnatural intercourse between man and man and pederasty as anal intercourse between man and woman. These acts are so abominable he insists that the "medical profession . . . are loath to write about them." Write about them he did, however, and he assures the anxious reader that most of these vices are "practiced to a greater extent among the low and degraded than . . . among the better class" (quoted in Katz 1983, 301–302). Dr. Monroe's introduction of class as a distinction marking perversions tallies with the racism also found in various accounts of homosexual practice in which the presumption is that the "better class" of white men would not engage in such activities and that "colored men" habitually do so. As Dr. F. E. Daniel wrote in 1893, sexual perversion and "illicit intercourse" was especially prevalent among "the lower classes, particularly negroes" (quoted in Katz 1983, 241–42).

Case histories and learned dissertations provide verbal pictures of the "typical pervert" who was almost always described as an "unfortunate creature." Shrady's assertions of effeminacy are echoed in 1889 by Dr. Lydston, who warned that colonies of "male sexual perverts" exist in every community, that "they are often characterized by effeminacy of voice, dress, and manner," and that because of "a defective physical makeup" their "physique is apt to be inferior" (quoted in Katz 1983, 213).

By 1892 Dr. T. Griswold Comstock assured readers that "perverts" are "natural objects of disgust to normal men and women," and because their sexual relations are "practiced in an unnatural manner" "Nature will surely avenge herself upon the offender. Mental disturbance and insanity will often follow" (quoted in Katz 1983, 226). In 1906 Dr. Howard argued that the "whole psychic life" of the invert is "feminine," and that since "sexual inverts live a life apart from the rest of mankind" they "become morbid, introspective, and suspicious" (quoted in Katz 1983, 319).

No doubt some homosexuals were effeminate, some cross-dressed, and some were morbid and suspicious, perhaps understandably so in such a social climate. Medical discourse confirmed the kind of marginal definition Dr. Allen Hamilton formulated when he described homosexuals as being a "class by themselves," while Dr. Comstock argues that they possess a "mysterious bond of psychological sympathy." Comstock socially and sexually isolates homosexuals from normative morality when he avers that "instances have been authenticated to me where such perverts meeting another of the same sex have at once recognized each other, and mutually become acquainted and have left in company with each other to practice their unnatural vices" (Katz 1983, 227).

Medical descriptions of such groups—operating ostensibly as attempts at classification and speaking presumably as dispassionate science rather than as partisan religious or moral discourses—nevertheless contributed to the creation of a climate of sexual anxiety very similar to that created by the moral purity tracts of the late eighteenth and early nineteenth centuries. An 1889 lecture by Dr. Lydston raises the specter of numerous and well-organized colonies of homosexuals. "There is," he says, "in every community of any size a colony of male sexual perverts; they are usually known to each other, and are likely to congregate together" (quoted in Katz 1983, 213). Like vampires and criminals they are engaged in a conspiracy to subvert and even destroy society, but their practice is neither irrational nor haphazard, for in the age of science their lust uses the chilling efficiency of science itself as they look not for victims but for "subjects" on which to practice what Lydston very nearly implies are sexual experiments.

Lydston contributes to the formation of a myth of a "homosexual conspiracy" that midway through the twentieth century would have disastrous and even tragic consequences for many gay people. His lecture also shifts the focus of certain medical texts that defined homosexuals as weak and "unfortunate creatures" to one that demonizes them as sexual monsters whose activities, not indeed unlike those of vampires and criminals, should be a legitimate object of fear and suppression. Lydston also asserts that homosexuals have constructed a well-organized underworld also dedicated to social disruption, since there are "establishments whose principle business is to cater to the perverted tastes of a numerous class of patrons (quoted in Katz 1976, 214).

In 1890 Dr. Charles Nesbitt discusses one such establishment, a New York City bar called The Slide, where "a great number of these queer creatures assembled each night" dressed in both male and female costume. Another club in the Bowery was a "place where fancy gentleman go" to meet male prostitutes and where "fairies or male degenerates" gather (quoted in Katz 1983, 219–20). In an article in the *American Journal of Psychology* in 1896, Colin Scott described "peculiar societies of inverts . . . where the members dress themselves with aprons, knit, gossip and crochet." Scott warns that the "'Fairies of New York' are said to be a . . . secret organization" (quoted in Katz 1983, 44). Dr. Francis Anthony confirms in 1898 the dreadful potential attached to such secret organizations and their universal prevalence: "I have been told that there is" in "nearly every centre of importance—a band of urnings, men of perverted tendencies, men known to each other as such, bound by ties of secrecy and fear and held by mutual attraction" whose purpose is to "draw boys and young men, over whom they have the same jealous bickerings and heart burnings that attend the triumphs of a local belle" (quoted in Katz 1983, 294). The network was extensive, as a sympathetic commentator, Xavier Mayne, suggests when he quotes a "distinguished European singer" who attests to the widespread nature of the American homosexual underworld: "He has never been in any country where the Uranian element was so widely distributed and averaged such high-class moral and intellectual types as in North America" (quoted in Katz 1983, 330).

Opinions about just who participated in this subculture differed radically. The European singer—himself apparently homosexual—attested to the intellectual and moral tone, while Dr. Monroe insisted that these vices were "practiced to a greater extent among the low and degraded than . . . among the better class." Dr. Anthony reports, however, that homosexuals embrace "not as you might think, the low and vile outcasts of the slums, but men of education and refinement, men gifted in music, in art and in literature, men of professional life and men of business and affairs" (quoted in Katz 1983, 294). These varying opinions, of course, served only to fan homophobic flames. It was one thing if homosexuals were to be found only among the "outcasts of the slums," but if they populated the ranks of "men of business and affairs" then indeed the catalog of fears might be justified.

Multiple definitions of homosexuals were conflated with an even more anxiety-ridden concept—that homosexuality, once engaged in, was irresistibly attractive. As Dr. Monroe observes, "There must be something extremely fascinating and satisfactory about this habit; for once begun it is seldom ever given up" (quoted in Katz 1983, 302). Thus the myth that homosexuality is so "fascinating" that the innocent—"boys and young men"—are powerless against it; homosexual pleasures are so intense that against them "normal" sexual experience seems pale. Homosexual practice is conflated with drugs and with disease: once tried, like opium, the "habit" cannot be extirpated; once infected by the disease of homosexuality the "victim" is incurable. The homosexual was being constructed into a creature not unlike that other sexually implicated monster of the late nineteenth century, the vampire, whose victim, once tainted, was beyond salvation.

By 1898 Dr. Anthony saw the control of sexual perverts as a kind of crusade to be undertaken by doctors, not unlike the crusade mounted against the vampire by Dr. van Helsing in Bram Stoker's *Dracula*. Indeed, against van Helsing's obsessed urging to plunge the stake without mercy into the vampire's heart, Anthony's text can be played: "It may fall to the lot of one of you to be the active means of destroying such a school of vice and perversion. Nay, more than that, it may be your son or the son of your intimate friend whom you are called upon to rescue. If it comes in the line of duty to take a hand in the overthrow of such a circle, I beg of you to let no dread of notoriety, no consideration of position, . . . come between you and the fulfillment of such a duty. Exercise all due charity, have the suspected and accused submitted to a most thorough examination to determine his responsibility, and then have him removed from the community to his proper place, be it asylum or be it prison" (Katz 1983, 294). Anthony chillingly forecasts the attitude toward homosexuals that would dominate social constructions of and social reactions to homosexuality by nonhomosexual power for the next 50 years.

By the beginning of the twentieth century medical science had legitimated homophobia by inscribing it within the presumed "objective rationality" of its proscriptive and prescriptive discourses. For those who doubted the truths of religion and could find no way to punish homosexuality by invoking the law of God, or for whom the laws of man did not go far enough to effectively suppress homosexual acts, it could now be stigmatized far more effectively by declaring it to be behavior that was not only immoral and illegal but sexually unnatural, emotionally abnormal, mentally diseased, and hence dangerous to the familial foundations of society.

A homosexual author who submitted a book to Dr. Comstock, whose business as head of the Society for the Suppression of Vice was "hunting down inverts and haling them off to prison," was told that his book ought to be destroyed." Dr. Comstock's opinions, expressed in 1900, are not tempered with the pretense to reasoned discourse that medical texts assumed and so what he says may suggest what the popular voice was beginning to say: "These inverts are not fit to live with the rest of mankind. They ought to have branded in their foreheads the word 'Unclean.' . . . [I]nstead of the law making twenty years imprisonment the penalty for their crime, it ought to be imprisonment for life. . . . They are willfully bad, and glory and gloat in their perversion." [1]

Frontispiece illustration of Fay Etrange from Robert Scully's *A Scarlet Pansy* (1933).

chapter 12

CONFRONTING THE RIDDLE: AMERICAN HOMOEROTIC TEXTS, 1897–1933

The history of homoerotic literature in the late nineteenth and early twentieth century is one of unanticipated resistance to rampant homophobia. One voice raised in resistance was that of the pseudonymous Professor X who spoke in a letter that had appeared in the first edition of Havelock Ellis and J. A. Symonds's *Sexual Inversion* (1897). Ellis and Symonds described him as "an American of eminence who holds a scientific professorship in one of the first universities of the world." His letter, they observe, is "the furthest extent to which the defense of sexual inversion has gone, or, indeed, could go, unless anyone were bold enough to assert that homosexuality is the only normal impulse, and heterosexual love a perversion" (Ellis 1897, 275).

While Symonds's might have wanted to make such an assertion, Ellis was unable ever to bring himself to define homosexuality other than as "sexual inversion" and as an "aberration from the usual course of nature," insisting that "we"—meaning medical science and the state—"are bound to protect the helpless members of society against the invert." Though Ellis was among the most sympathetic of the scientific commentators on homosexuality, his sympathy is still informed by older concepts of sin and filled with tentative qualifications: "If we go further, and seek to destroy the invert himself before he has sinned against society, we exceed the warrant of reason, and in so doing we may, perhaps, destroy also those children of the spirit which possess sometimes a greater worth than the children of the flesh" (Ellis, 1897, 158).

Professor X, who may have been James Mills Peirce, has no such compunctions.[1] He confronts the question of morality and of individual and social health and states that "no breach of morality is involved in homosexual love." After arguing that the many homosexual persons he has known are "particularly high-minded, upright and refined" he reverses his discourse and argues that heterosexuality "as it actually exists in the world" makes men and women "sensual, low-minded, false, every way unprincipled and grossly self-ish." It is "a travesty of morality" to invest heterosexuality "with divine attributes and denounce the other as infamous and unnatural." He then attacks the argument that passion is "naturally" directed by male desire for the female. "Passion itself is a blind thing. It is a furious pushing out, not with calculation or comprehension of its object but to anything which strikes the imagination as fitted to its need. It is not characterized or differentiated by the nature of its object, but by its own nature."

He thus modernly posits a theory of sexual orientation rather than sexual preference, shifting desire from the object to the subject. He points out that it is not so much procreation as pleasure and desire that ought to be the "moving influence in the matter" of sexuality. For him, homosexuality is not an aberration nor "a lamentable mark of inferior development." It is not "inverted or abnormal" or "an unhappy fault, a 'masculine body with a feminine soul,'" but instead a "natural and pure and sound passion." Professor X argues that either homosexuality should be recognized as a normal sexual response or that the very notion of the norm itself should be abandoned.

Though Professor X might like to erase Whitman's separatist "men like me" formulation, his text is the logical extension of Whitman's argument of 1870 that "fervid comradeship" is the necessarily transgressive and effectively spiritual cure for the ills of a "materialistic and vulgar American democracy"—a democracy made ill by its ascription of sexual normality solely to relations between men and women. Whitman argued that the "spiritualization" of American democracy and of "general politics" would be achieved when "threads of manly friendship" ran through "the worldly interests" of America. Professor X—perhaps the first to use the word "homosexual" in an American defense—adds to the spiritual and political a significant reference to the question of social "health." He addresses not only the moral but the medical discourse when he argues that homosexual desire "tends when duly understood and controlled by spiritual feeling, to the physical and moral health of the individual and the race" (quoted in Katz 1976, 374–76).

Professor X's letter can be read as the slight beginning of a movement both literary and political that would urge that homosexuality is not a deviation from "normal heterosexuality" but a part of a larger spectrum of desire and that would advocate the decriminalization of homosexuality, seek to shift social attitudes toward it, and hint at the formation of a distinctively modern and American social and political identity among homosexuals.

By the time Peirce's letter appeared in the first American edition of Ellis's *Sexual Inversion*, America could still claim only a small number of texts other than those of Whitman—primarily the guarded hints in Thoreau, the intimation of same-sex desire in Meville's novels and poems, several poems of

Bayard Taylor, and the sexual dubiety in Theodore Winthrop's novels *John Brent* and *Cecil Dreeme* from the 1860s. In 1870 some readers might discern the allusively homoerotic subtext of Taylor's novel *Joseph and His Friend* and a similar aura in the island exoticism and largely all-male eroticism of Charles Warren Stoddard's *South-Seas Idyls* and *The Island of Tranquil Delights*.

In 1889 appeared *A Marriage below Zero* by "Alan Dale" in which a young woman must contend with another man for the love of her husband. She loses her handsome though slightly effeminate husband, who has never consummated the marriage, to the villainous Captain Jack. When she discovers her husband and the Captain alone in a room she imagines, correctly, the worst. In one last attempt to save her marriage she follows them to Paris where she too late finds her husband a suicide, discovering his body in a room in which two portraits, one of her husband the other of the Captain, look down on the melodramatic scene. The book is resolutely homophobic and introduces the homosexual villain into American fiction. What is remarkable about this book, though, is that it stands nearly alone among nineteenth-century American fiction that dealt with homosexual desire in presenting a homophobic and negative picture of same-sex love.

Much homoerotic fiction and poetry after 1900 chose immediate and modern life in which to situate characters and conduct the business of their texts. Rather than imagining separate cities of lovers they put their characters, often flamboyantly, on the streets of New York, Boston, and Chicago. Novelists were no longer willing to lament that their love could not speak its name; instead they spoke it openly and confronted homophobia where they saw it, advocating active resistance to what they saw as social, medical, and political oppression. What many of these post-1900 texts have in common is the sense that homosexual identities can no longer be founded on ancient models and that justification can no longer be derived exclusively from the past.

The principle argument of many of these texts was that homosexuals— certainly different, very much outcasts, and perhaps even a separate species—should confront rather than retire from society, achieving power by this confrontation. There is evidence that in the writings of German homosexual activists like Benedict Friedlander, Adolf Brand, and Magnus Hirschfeld American homosexuals found hope for new attitudes toward homosexuality in the same way that Symonds found it in the works of Ulrichs three decades earlier. In 1897 Hirschfeld founded the Scientific Humanitarian Committee, whose official journal, *Jahrbuch für Sexuelle Zwischenstufen*, published articles dealing with historical, social, psychological, and autobiographical information about homosexuality. It is fair to say that at the beginning of the century most American homosexuals were still largely cut off from what was happening in Europe, but an anonymous letter sent from Boston in 1907 to the German *Monthly Reports of the Scientific*

Humanitarian Committee indicates the situation of American homosexuals at the time:

> I'm always delighted to hear about even the smallest success you have in vanquishing the deep-rooted prejudices. And here in the United States we really need this kind of activity. In the face of Anglo-American hypocrisy, however, there is at present no chance that any man of science would have enough wisdom and courage to remove the veil which covers homosexuality in this country. And how many homosexuals I've come to know! Boston, this good old Puritan city, has them by the hundreds. . . . [H]omosexuality extends through all classes. . . . There is an astonishing ignorance among the Uranians I've come to know about their own true nature. This is probably the result of absolute silence and intolerance, which have never advanced real morality at any time or place. But with the growth of the population and the increase of intellectuals, the time is coming when America will finally be forced to confront the riddle of homosexuality. (quoted in Katz 1976, 382–83)

Some texts did confront the riddle, though it may well be that they remained as unknown to the Uranian friends of the anonymous Bostonian as their "true natures," since almost all of them were privately printed in small numbers. In 1906 Edward I. Prime-Stevenson, writing as Xavier Mayne, published privately and in Italy the first openly homosexual American novel, *Imre.* Two years later, also in Italy, he published a monumental study, *The Intersexes,* the first survey by an American on the subject of homosexuality. Other texts produced between 1900 and the end of World War I that also addressed the "riddle" of homosexuality were Stoddard's novel *For the Pleasure of His Company* (1903), set in San Francisco, in which the hero, as in Stoddard's other books, eventually seeks happiness in the South Seas. *Autobiography of an Androgyne,* which details an incredibly well-observed homosexual underworld, was written around 1895 by the pseudonymous Earl Lind (who signed himself "Jennie June") and published in 1918; Lind followed this in 1922 with an autobiographical sequel, *The Female Impersonators.* At the end of Henry Blake Fuller's novel *Bertram Cope's Year* (1919) a thoroughly modern young American man goes off with his boyfriend.

Sherwood Anderson's "Hands" (1919) details what the anonymous Boston writer had described as the "deep-rooted prejudice" of "Anglo-American hypocrisy"; it is a story that institutes as a genre dramas of remorse, ultimate tragedy, and homophobic moralizing. In 1933 appeared *A Scarlet Pansy,* written by the possibly pseudonymous Robert Scully, a novel that is an outrageous and unknown masterpiece of American homoerotic writing. It is our first great contribution to the serious transgressions that gay novels would later achieve and the original example of what is the central and most significant contribution that homoerotic texts have made to

American literature: the deployment of fantasy, spectacle, and resistance, captured in a style and manner informed by that ironic sublime that drives the mechanisms of satire, parody, imitation, mocking self-denigration, and social confrontation both offensive and defensive, produced within the self-referential yet never static aesthetic that this novel first called "camp." In these works it was assumed that homosexuality was a subject that could be—indeed, ought to be—written into American literature.

XAVIER MAYNE

It may well have been this assumption that impelled Edward Irenaeus Prime-Stevenson, an author and music critic who adopted the pseudonym "Xavier Mayne," to write *The Intersexes* and *Imre*. There is no biography of Prime-Stevenson. The primary sources are the autobiographical sketch he wrote for *Who's Who*, a brief biographical essay written by the equally pseudonymous Noel I. Garde, and an entry in the *New American Dictionary of National Literary Biography* compiled by "CDW." Prime-Stevenson was an aesthete and a professional writer, a considerable traveler, and a man of voracious curiosity. He was born in 1868 and died in Switzerland in 1942. Nothing he wrote remains as anything save a footnote. Though he trained for the law, his writer's avocation became a vocation and he published his first book in 1887 under his own name, a boys' book called *The White Cockade*. Astute readers of homoerotic texts will find hints of Prime-Stevenson's interests there, and a later book, *Left to Themselves, Being the Ordeal of Philip and Gerald*, further substantiates what *The White Cockade* implied.

Writing as Mayne in *The Intersexes*, Prime-Stevenson coyly comes out when he describes *The White Cockade* as "a little tale of the flight of the Young Pretender by E. I. Stevenson issued in Edinburgh some years ago. Passionate devotion from a rustic youth toward the prince and its recognition are half-hinted as homosexual in essence. The sentiment of Uranian adolescence is more distinguishable in another book for lads, Philip and Gerald by the same hand, a romantic story in which a youth in his latter teens is irresistibly attracted to a much younger lad, and becomes, *con amore* responsible for the latter's personal safety, in a series of events that throw them together—for life."[2] Prime-Stevenson also allowed CDW in his biographical sketch to say that "under a pseudonym" he is the author of "several volumes in a seriously important field of psychiatric research." This revelation enhances the *Who's Who* entry, where he is noted to be the author of "several works privately printed in Europe under a pseudonym."

Pseudonyms and private printings were enough indication as was needed to let readers know that sex was the topic discussed in privately offered pages and that homosexuality might well be hidden behind the pseudonym. These privately printed pseudonymous works were *The Intersexes* and *Imre*. While the Edward Prime-Stevenson who wrote another handful of books—*The Creditors, Janus*, a book of short stories, *Her Enemy, Some Friends*, a book of music criticism called *Long-Haired Iopas*, and *The Square of Sevens*, a book on cartomancy—may not command even a footnote in American letters, Xavier Mayne, equally obscure, deserves considerably more.

The Intersexes

In 1908 Prime-Stevenson/Xavier Mayne published a monumental study, *The Intersexes: A History of Similisexualism as a Problem in Social Life*, the first survey in English to attempt a full-scale study of homosexuality. Unlike Symonds's and Carpenter's far shorter works that addressed primarily classical or specific nineteenth-century texts, Mayne surveys the history of homosexual texts from ancient to modern times, attempting to catalog and critique them and to document the lives of homosexual men and women, observing them not simply as homosexual but as members of society whose contributions he associates with their homosexuality.

Mayne dedicates *The Intersexes* to Richard von Kraft-Ebing, whose *Psychopathia Sexualis* of 1886 was one of the first exhaustive studies of the medical "problem" of what was called sexual inversion. Mayne says that his work would not have been undertaken "without his suggestion and aid." Mayne is not, though, primarily interested in explaining homosexuality from a medical standpoint. He insists that it is not the homosexual but the non-homosexual who must change to accommodate what he insists is a natural manifestation of human affection. Unlike European studies of sexuality, which were most often written by nonhomosexuals in the legal or medical professions and were essentially informed by homophobia, Mayne reveals his homosexuality subtly and repeatedly points up the homophobia inherent in these earlier studies.

The Intersexes situates homosexuals—the "intersexes"—at a midpoint in a sexual spectrum. He sites homosexuality—"similisexuality"—in "social" rather than moral or even medical life. Mayne's is the first American text to attempt to theorize homosexuality in a historical rather than in a moralistic or medical context, and Mayne is therefore, as Noel I. Garde dubbed him in 1958, the "father of American homophilic literature." *The Intersexes* is the first work of nonfiction by an American to be written from a positive homosexual viewpoint by an avowed homosexual. Mayne's text therefore becomes the first American essay in what we now call lesbian and gay studies.

Widely read in many literatures, especially the German and French writing of his own time, Mayne does not dive deep, but he casts a wide net, and if a canon of homoerotic texts were desired, he provides the materials to create one. This is not to say that he has not thought hard and probably long about his subject: his thought and research results in a text of more than 600 pages. His theory defining homosexuality is simple; it is part of a graduated and natural system of sexual differentiation:

> Nature has always maintained in the human species a series of graduated and necessary Intersexes between the two great sexes that we recognize as distinctly "man" and "woman," i.e. as the extreme masculine and feminine type. These sexes are not physically obvious. . . . The average eye and mind have never learned even how to look for them, though they are around us daily in their positive attributes. . . . Their subtle separation . . . begins at a deeper plane . . . the psychological, not physical. . . . Their existence is as irrefutable as it is immemorial. For centuries the world has narrowed man down into two sexes. There are at least two more than our traditional anthropological spectrum has perceived and recognized, each of primary importance. (Mayne, 16)

He argues that sex is not determined by physical structure, that biology is not destiny: "Sex is determined by the sexual instinct: by desire physical and psychical of one human being for another, no matter what his or her bodily aspects." It follows then that if the intersexes—homosexuals—fall between the extremes of masculine and feminine then the Uranian is the one "partaking most of the outwardly masculine, yet not fully a man, the other [the Uraniad, the woman] leaning toward the typic feminine, yet not fully a woman." They are therefore "each indisputably a blend of the two extreme sexes." Mayne's theory derives of course from Ulrichs's third-sex theory though differs from it in that he does not advance Ulrichs's formula that the homosexual male is a woman trapped in a male body. Nor does he accept any formula that stigmatizes homosexuals as mentally or physiologically aberrant. Instead, homosexuals combine attributes of both sexes and form separate but biologically equal sexual structures equidistant on a scale of sexuality.

These two separate sexes are "indisputably entitled to recognition as to its individual rights"; Mayne argues that each sex "exists now as ever in a most important proportion to the rest of mankind." His achievement is not so much to construct a theory of homosexual etiology as to construct an argument against oppression: "We find them victims of sexual repression, seekers after a sexual expression they cannot obtain without disgraces, dangers, crimes." Difference, he insists, is a prime cause of homosexual oppression: "It is true that they present . . . many traits, claims, theories, impulses, practices, deviations from the more or less normally human. . . . They have sex idioms that repel and terrify us." Here he recognizes the existence of a homosexual style and theorizes its categories as far broader than mere sexual acts.

Mayne defines homophobia as a negative reaction to homosexual style inspired by fear. He also recognizes the effect homophobia can have on society: "a great proportion of Intersexual lives are led . . . under a sexual, social, and moral ban that blots our human civilization" (Mayne, 18–20)—a blot his book tries to erase. He recognizes that the basis for any discussion of homosexual texts has to be founded in a language. Literary tradition and language, he argues, allows the term "love" an exclusively heterosexual context. If "love" is allowed into a same-sex discourse it has to be recast as "friendship" and erotic content is erased or denied: "the whole theory of so-called Platonic friendship is ill-sustained by the realities in human-nature and social history," for "love must contain sexual desire, the wish for physical possession of beauty." The instant, he says, "that we even vaguely want to possess, and even vaguely feel that we would be willing to surrender ourselves . . . then no matter how impossible, how terrifying, how bewildering such an impulse be to us, we love, we love sexually" (Mayne, 21–24). In effect he argues that Platonic friendship is a social and literary construction that serves a homophobic agenda: it denies the reality of desire and attempts to erase the possibility of passion from same-sex relations.

After initial chapters theorizing homosexuality, Mayne attempts to survey it historically "in the brute world." He points out the existence of homosexual acts among animals, asserting that this natural animal instinct therefore erases the definition of homosexuality as an act against nature. He points up its existence in what he calls "primitive" cultures, citing both Greek historians and modern "explorers" who discovered it "in the wilds of the savage world" (Mayne, 41). Not only among so-called savages, but among the ancient Egyptians, Scythians, Assyrians, and Babylonians has it been "taken for granted as natural."

He confronts the proscriptions against homosexuality in the "Mosaic Code" and wonders why "Mosaic laws set severe penalties against masculine similisexualism." His discussion of the Bible's Sodom story is especially provocative. He argues that

> the entire episode of Lot and the wicked men of Sodom does not afford any grounds for arguing that Sodom was destroyed on account of similisexual tastes and practices, or that Sodom was really given to such. Further, we have no proof that homosexual intercourse was ever special to Sodom, ever was or is an offense to God, even to a Jehovistic concept of God; nor that what the world's statute-books, and pulpit parlance especially have so long termed "sodomy" should ever have such a meaning. (Mayne, 43–44)

He asserts that the story of Sodom is in fact a story about "violated hospitality" rather than an injunction against sodomy—a reading that predicts the work of such later scholars as Derrick Bailey, who 70 years later concluded that "nowhere does [the Sodom text] identify that sin explicitly with the practice of homosexuality."[3]

Mayne surveys the history of homosexuality—in Greece and Rome, in the early Christian era, in the Middle Eastern and Oriental cultures, in medieval and Renaissance Europe, and in Europe and in England from the seventeenth century to his own time. His study defines some of the parameters of the historicized study of homosexuality and proposes that such a study ought to be the site of a disciplined academic project rather than an arena for moralistic judgment and social condemnation. He recognizes that it is just such judgment that is the chief enemy of homosexuals and of the study of homosexual history. Anatomizing the critical as well as the general attitude throughout history he finds that the "law knows no philosophic questioning attitude toward homosexuality. . . . Social England is horrified at the very existence of homosexual passion. The Englishman affects not to understand how classic and aesthetic Greece and Rome gave place to such feelings. Often he really refuses to believe that the reference to it, which he reads in his school days or in his study, refer to concrete similisexual emotion, physically gratified. He construes the verses of . . . the Greek poets, the sonnets of Michelangelo, or Shakespeare as mere idealism or allegory. He declares the homosexual man to be a monstrosity, a freak of Nature" (Mayne, 62).

Mayne insists that homosexuals, no matter what their position in society, necessarily become resistant adversaries to social orthodoxies: "Each day proves how powerless are legal provisions to lessen the similisexual impulse in humanity the world over: how vain are ethical or religious positions to pit it out of the heart and the life impulses of mankind in each class. Similisexual love flourishes today in every phase of finer or deteriorated character and expression, from binding the master-bond of high souls to being the living of the sordid male prostitutes of a boulevard. It defies clandestinely all penalties, and all social intolerances" (Mayne, 71).

For Mayne the homosexual "instinct is inborn" and to be found everywhere. To demonstrate this he writes chapters devoted to identifying homosexuals in every area of society: "Military and Naval careers, Athletic Professions and in Royal, Political, or other Aristocratic Life," as well as in "Distinctively Ethical, Religious, and Intellectual life and in the Distinctively Aesthetic and Professional Environments." Listing famous homosexuals as a justification for homosexuality is a familiar strategy and can be found as a feature of most homosexual polemics. Mayne's chapters may well be the longest as well as the most encyclopedic example of the practice. His purpose in identifying homosexuals in military history is to undermine "the notion that the man-loving man is always effeminate in body and temper," a misconception countered "by the fact that in scarcely any other profession—in no other walk of practical life—has the full sexualism of romantic passion been more general than in the ranks of soldiers and sailors." From literature his examples range from the biblical story of David and Jonathan to the memoirs of the American General Morris Schaff, in whose *The Spirit of Old West Point* Mayne finds "delicate suggestions of the Uranian emotions in young and soldierly comrades."

Mayne's discussions of homosexuality in literary texts demonstrate the multicultural and historical extent of homoerotic literature. He argues that "the most expressive outlet for the Uranian temperament is that of belles-lettres. His capacity for feeling, for romance, find vivid expression in literature. Often his pen and paper have been his only confidants and sometimes in fiction or in verse of genius he has taken the world into his secret." Homosexual literature, he argues, is "a very largely serious, deeply emotional literature." It is serious because "the Uranian's temperament and problematic social life have checked his mirth. His gaiety tends toward irony or is of that artificial good humor often characteristic of him" (Mayne, 279). When he insists that homoerotic texts are "serious" he confronts what is the most universal charge brought against them—that they are trivial, sentimental, and inferior as literature.

Mayne's thesis that irony and artifice are special hallmarks of homoerotic textuality derives from Wilde but also predicts not only later discussions of "camp" as a special kind of homosexual discourse but recent attempts to identify the special elements that define gay linguistic and semiotic style. Mayne defines the obstacles that homoerotic texts must surmount: "Not only does prejudice in society and religion obstruct [the Uranian] press. Exasperating are the comments of critics, editors, translators . . . to conceal or to ignore altogether the personal homosexuality of such and such a writer and of his literary intentions. The conventional modern biographer avoids recognizing the homosexual nature in his subject" (Mayne, 279–80).

The sexuality of writers like Whitman and Hart Crane, for example, has until recent reevaluation been ignored in their lives and denied in their texts, often being proclaimed as irrelevant to both the life and the text. Mayne's confrontation of critical homophobia not only defines the issue but mounts a counter-attack. It is impossible to do justice to all that Mayne discusses, all the unknown texts he lists and translates, many for the first and only time, or to his intriguing speculations on homoerotic textuality. If canons are sought, Mayne provides a foundation for them.

Mayne mentions Whitman, of course, as one of the classics, and he alludes to Emerson's "neo-Grecian attitude to friendship," though he is not sure it can properly be called "Uranian." He alludes to Stoddard's *South-Seas Idyls* and names a few very minor and now unknown writers. He discloses that in the tales of one H. C. Bunner "something of the Uranian strain occasionally echoes." An elegy on the death of a young man by George Woodberry, a professor at Columbia, is "hellenically passionate," while the verses of W. E. Davenport imitate Whitman. Mayne's speculation that homosexuality lies at the heart of American letters—a "racial Uranianism"—predicts a late twentieth-century critical reading of American literature that now has laid claim with considerable authority not only to Whitman and Crane but to Melville, Thoreau, Dickinson, and Henry James in the nineteenth century and that reads homosexuality and difference as a primary theme of twentieth-century American texts.

Imre

Imre is the first homosexual novel written by an American in which there is no dissembling, no coded discourse, no pretense that friendship is Platonic or that desire is allegorical. It is an elegantly written, romantic, even florid text, breathless in its passionate account of a male homosexual love affair and equally passionate in its defense of homosexual life and love. The story—not set in America but in exotic Hungary—is about a man who falls in love with a handsome Hungarian officer and, after some agony, reveals his secret to him and happily finds that the officer reciprocates. The novel details the history of its narrator, Oswald, as a homosexual man; it relates his coming out before such a phrase was available and reminds us of the small autobiographies in Ellis, who described Imre as a "notable narrative of homosexual development" that was "probably more or less real." If Oswald is the spokesman for Mayne/Stevenson, even in a fictional re-creation, then we have here a document that reveals if not the factual than the emotional and psychological biography of the mysterious Stevenson.

The growth of Oswald's identity as a homosexual is described at length. Oswald tells us that "I felt myself unlike other boys in one element of my nature. That one matter was my special sense, my passion, for the beauty, the dignity, the charm . . . what shall I say . . . the lovableness of my own sex."[4] His narrative is the story of search, of loss, of exile. He searches for an ideal friend, for he knows that "at the root and fibre of myself, there was the throb and glow, the ebb and surge, the seeking as in a vain dream to realize . . . that passion of friendship . . . the Over-Friendship, the Love-Friendship of Hellas—which meant that between man and man could exist—the sexual-psychic love." He "recognized what such emotions meant to most people today—from the disgust, scorn and laughter of my fellow men when such an emotion was hinted at. I understood perfectly that a man must wear the Mask." He is perplexed by his emotions, yet in books he comes "face to face with the fact that though tens of thousands of men, in all epochs, of the noblest natures, of most brilliant minds . . . had been such as myself" yet others "of this same race, the Race Homosexual, had been also . . . trivial, loathsome . . . the very weaklings and rubbish of humanity."

Oswald is apparently horrified by what homophobic writers were then describing as effeminate monsters. He reveals his own kind of homophobia when he rejects "effeminate artists, the sugary and fibreless musicians, the lady nancyish, rich young men . . . the second rate poets and neurasthenic precieux poetasters . . . the cynical debauchers of little boys, the pederastic perverters of clean-minded lads in their teens; the white haired satyrs of clubs and latrines" (Mayne, 111–17). One is staggered by the vehemence of his catalog, enlisting as it does every homophobic cliché. Yet it echoes the same accusations against effeminacy that Whitman advanced in 1855 and recalls also passages from Symonds and Carpenter. Beneath the overheated protest, of course, Mayne has enlisted himself in the campaign to erase imputations of perversion and effeminacy from definitions of homosexuality. His real point is that social conceptions of homosexuals read them only as effeminate perverts. By asserting a supervirile masculinity, Mayne writes very much in the tradition of Benedict Friedlander, writing in 1902, who saw male-male relationships as the most perfect and highest form of masculine expression and argued that homosexuality was the highest form of gender development.

The ideal homosexual Mayne defines is no effeminate but a quite different, even rather frightening, figure, one who conceals behind the exaggerated images of Victorian masculinity his own homosexual nature: "such human creatures as I am have not in body, in mind, nor in all the sum of our virility, in all the detail of our outward selves, any openly womanish trait! Not one! . . . In every feature and line and sinew and muscle, in every moment and accent and capability we walk the world's ways as men. We hew our ways through it as men, with vigour, with success, honour . . . one master-instinct unsuspected by society for, it may be, our lives long! We plough the world's roughest seas as men, we rule its states . . . direct its finances and commerce . . . we forge its steel . . . we fill its gravest professions . . . fight in the bravest ranks of its armies as men. . . . So super-male, so utterly unreceptive to what is not manly, so aloof from feminine essences, that we cannot tolerate women at all as a sexual factor" (Mayne, 113–14).

Protesting too much perhaps, Oswald takes care to deny that gesture, gait, and speech are signs that identify all homosexuals. He argues that imputations of weakness, effeminacy, and ineffectuality recognize only a small segment of the homosexual population, most of whom in fact are largely undistinguishable from others, the same as heterosexuals in all respects save the "master-instinct" that ultimately differentiates them. He asserts both difference and assimilation, and his text balances on the uneasy awareness that assimilation—his "super-male" image—is, after all, still a mask that conceals the difference born of that "master-instinct."

But no matter what problems he has with exterior identities and roles, Oswald has no doubt about sex. He is "the man-loving man, whose whole heart can be given only to another man, and who when his spirit is passing into his beloved friend's keeping would demand, would surrender his body with it." He seeks the "eternal, mysteriously-disturbing, cruel Type, which so vibrates sexually against my hidden self" (Mayne, 121). Mayne's desire conflates with Whitman's rough and rowdy comrades and with that creation of the late nineteenth century, the congenitally constituted homosexual supermale whose sexual passions were deemed to be his dominating instinct.

This figure—whose archetype Whitman most powerfully created in his fierce wrestler—has a special place in American homoerotic texts.

If Mayne engages homoerotic mythology here, suggesting, as I argue, an especially American form of homoerotic myth, he also calls on other homoerotic mythologies to inform his text. He invokes Arcadian gardens in which it is safe to reveal his sexual secret when he and Imre go into a park where "the public is not admitted" in the midst of which is a statue to two soldiers who died in battle for one another. In this safe garden dedicated to male-male love, Oswald declares himself to Imre and tells the story of his discovery of his own homosexuality, his doomed love for a nonhomosexual male and of his self-imposed exile from America, of his coming to terms with the nature of his desires, and of his search for an ideal friend. Finally he tells Imre, "My search ended when thou and I met. . . . I love thee as can love only the Uranian . . . once more helpless, and therewith hopeless, but this time no longer silent, before the Friendship which is Love, the Love which is Friendship" (Mayne, 150).

Oswald has exiled himself from America not only for reasons of the heart. He is a sexual exile from his native land, for America represents for him a place where there is "so dense a blending of popular ignorances, of century-old and century-blind religious and ethical misconceptions, of unscientific professional conservatism in psychiatric circles, and juristic barbarisms; all of course accompanied with the full measure of British and Yankee hypocrisy toward the daily actualities of homosexualism" that it is impossible for him to live there.

Having revealed his secret to Imre, it remains only for Imre to respond. At first he does not, swearing Oswald never to mention the subject again until he, Imre, breaks the silence. Of course the silence is broken, and Imre confesses that he is homosexual and that his life has also been masked and hidden: "He wore his mask each and every instant; resolving to make it his natural face before himself! . . . He bound his warm heart in a chain, he vowed indifference to the whole world, he assisted no advances of warm, particular regard from any comrade." But the appearance of Oswald convinces him that he had "found the one friend in the world out of a million-million men not for me." Then Imre reveals his deepest secret and explains why he was not originally honest with Oswald. It is because there is within him "the psychic trace of the woman. . . . I am not as you, the Uranian who is too much man! I am more feminine in impulse."

Imre begs Oswald to help "make myself over." Oswald rehearses a catalog of "womanly" virtues: gentleness, nobility, serenity, patience, virtue, and the subject is abruptly dropped and the text returns to its high romantic and homoerotic tone as the two of then vow eternal love and fidelity. If Oswald is the supermale and Imre the male who has at last and at least verbally externalized the woman within, a persona that does not detract from his male sexuality but only adds other dimensions to it, then they enact other erotic mythologies here as well. They reflect at the same time as they resist middle-class heterosexual inscriptions of "natural" relationships, perhaps predicting for their future relationship "active and passive" and even "masculine" and "feminine" domestic transactions.

Mayne either does not notice or does not care to discuss the disjunction between Oswald's desire to surrender his body to a cruel type like the dashing cavalier he must have imagined Imre to be and Imre's implication of his "feminine impulse" (Mayne, 197–200). Perhaps Mayne believes as Imre does when he asks Oswald to help him deal with the impulse and "make it less," that the love of a good man can exorcise the woman within. The anti-feminist inscriptions of this text of course resonate against general misogynistic attitudes of the time, but they also suggest specific themes to be detected in later homoerotic American texts in which women are predatory monsters who attempt to lure good young gay men into a life of enforced heterosexuality, smothering mothers who emasculate their sons, or girls-next-door who reverse Imre's prescription and are convinced that homosexuality is just a phase that can be cured by the love of a good woman.

Mayne's ideal friend is the masculine-identified homosexual who, like Whitman, rejects the aesthete for the rough, rejects the revealing pose of a Wilde or the put-on languor that Raffalovich urges. This too marks a theme in American homoerotic texts, perhaps best pictured in J. C. Leyandecker's illustrations of the Arrow Shirt Man. The pederastic yearnings discovered in nineteenth-century English texts and the man-boy flavor so prominent in them, or the aesthetic flamboyance that markedly displays homoeroticism in other English texts of the same period, is not a primary feature of American homoerotic books. This is not to say that the effete and the effeminate will not also be inscribed in and describe American homosexuality, either in its style or in its texts. Texts of the 1920s and 1930s display a spectacular "camp" sensibility, that special American renegotiation of aestheticism. American homoerotic fiction, poetry, and drama will design complex emotional fantasy or stage giddy masquerades of the sexes in order to mount exotic challenges to "normal" sexuality. It will create flamboyant texts that in plot, language, and character resist and mock similar expectations about gender—and this resistance will become perhaps the greatest theme and achievement of American homoerotic texts. *Imre* stands very much in the tradition of nineteenth-century American homoerotic idealism that combines romance with masculine desire and desire for the masculine. *Imre* is an Arcadian text like *Calamus*, and it initiates in fiction in the twentieth century what in gay books will become that special American urge to deify, desire, and surrender to an exaggeratedly masculine homoeroticism.

Imre is not, I suppose, a very "good" book—that is, it is improbable, sometimes ridiculous. Yet as Ellis suggested, it may well be the truth. It certainly represents a pivotal moment and a defining one when American homoerotic fiction, as it were, comes out. It gathers together many of the myths and

inventions of the nineteenth century concerning homosexuality—homophobic or homophilic—and weaves them into a story that appropriates for itself
the special ending that heretofore had been thought appropriate only to heterosexual romance: "and they lived happily ever after."

In *Imre* Oswald describes how "I changed my life . . . to avoid
gossip. . . . A few months later I started on a long travel-route to the continent. . . . But now I knew that I was to be a refugee, an exile! For so began
those interminable and restless pilgrimages. . . . [M]y unexplained and perpetual exile from all that earlier meant home, sphere, career, life" (Mayne,
142). Prime-Stevenson had also quit America. The 1901 *Who's Who* entry
notes that he spent much time abroad. By 1906 he resided in Europe "for
professional and personal reasons." In 1908 he "has retired to reside perma-
nently in Europe." In Europe he became a vagabond man of letters, sending
articles back home on European doings, writing music revues that appeared
in *Harper's*. These ceased by 1911. *Imre* had been published, as had *The
Intersexes*.

The *Who's Who* of 1912 gives one more additional clue to the nature of
Prime-Stevenson's pseudonymous books. They are now described as important studies in the psychiatry of sex. That "sex" has now been added to the
description is telling and hints again at his desire to make himself known, to
come out, as does the fact that in 1913 he published under his own name the
stories in *Her Enemy, Some Friends* and includes a quote on the title page
from *Imre*.

If Prime-Stevenson revealed his life—or a life that he invented—in the
novel he wrote as Mayne, it was precisely what most homosexual writers
were doing. Whitman claimed that his entire body of work was an autobiographical construction, and homoerotic desire informs and impels that text,
sometimes tallying with the facts of his life, more often with the more urgent
dramas of the desiring imagination. Both Symonds's and Carpenter's scholarly explorations were impelled into existence when their own homosexuality
was clarified by their discovery of it in the text of Whitman. In America
Whitman, Melville, Taylor, Stoddard, and Mayne himself rely on both actual, spiritual, and eroticized autobiography to create both fiction and identities, to site homosexual men and homoerotic desire within the broad
constructions ordering sexuality—power, knowledge, nonhomosexual desire,
and homophobia—constructions that these writers increasingly claim that
society has produced and, as they all insist, arrayed against them.

It is problematic, and it may not matter, how accurate their recollections
or how precise their use of them, or how psychologically telling or personally
revealing these turn out to be when tallied against facts collected in the texts
of literal scholarship. Yet in a sense autobiography is the prime homotextual
genre; in every text we invent and reinvent ourselves. Our earliest texts participated, however, not so much in the process of defining what homosexual-

ity "is" as they engaged in a constant creation of it, doing what Foucault has suggested is our own most important task and the task that recent gay texts indeed undertake—entering into the risky and exhilarating business not of being gay but of constantly becoming gay.

EARL LIND

Earl Lind, unlike Mayne, did not go into exile. He stayed in America, and in 1919 and again in 1922 he published his reminiscences of a life spent in the homosexual underworld of New York. *Autobiography of an Androgyne* surveys his homosexual life, especially that portion of it as an active "androgyne" in New York between 1895 and about 1905. *The Female Impersonators* details more of that life; it offers Lind's speculations on the history and causes of homosexuality, some cases histories of fellow androgynes, some excerpts from news accounts of crimes committed against them, and a sampling of medical opinion about them. Lind wrote under the pseudonym of Ralph Werther and cruised the New York streets using the name Jennie June, dressing appropriately to lend verisimilitude to this pseudonym. That these were pseudonyms to disguise the writer Earl Lind does not entirely decide the question as to whether Earl Lind is not also a pseudonym as well.

In two volumes, with photos of himself so posed as to obscure identity but little else, Lind describes his life as a member of an American sexual underworld. He participated in, observed, and recorded a world to which Mayne only briefly alludes. Lind was precisely the sort of person Oswald in *Imre* despised and might have described as "womanish beings" or else as "Lady Nancyish, rich young men of higher or lower society, twaddling aesthetic sophistries; stinking with perfume like coquettes." Lind was not rich, but there is some small irony in the fact that he is a somewhat better writer than Mayne and dared to do what Mayne only fantasized, and write about what Mayne was unwilling to reveal or accept.

Though written under so many pseudonymous layers, *Autobiography of an Androgyne* purports to be a true relation of a promiscuous homosexual life and the autobiography of what even then were called "fairies," what Lind calls androgynes, and what we would call drag queens. The book is also a first-rate erotic fantasy—it is full of sex—and as Jennie June he becomes a character as fabulous as any in fiction, a true fairy godmother to those later activist androgynes who threw the first stones at Stonewall.

Lind was an incredibly active seeker of homosexual experience. He also thought constantly, sometimes profoundly, about what he saw to be his anomalous position, for he believed himself to be a woman trapped in the body of a man. Thus his choice of "androgyne" to describe himself, and to our eyes his rather one-sided vision of homosexuals as imprisoned feminine spirits. His formula recalls the theories of Ulrichs and reflects popular prejudice as well as then-current medical speculation about the "nature" of the homosexual. Lind's vision of himself reflects the instability of homosexual identity constructed by homosexuals and nonhomosexuals alike. His understanding of homosexuality was as much a product of his reading as of self-perception. That he became what theorists said he ought to be is the subtextual lesson, though perhaps not necessarily the tragedy, as his critics might have said, of this book.

Autobiography of an Androgyne specifically relates Lind's discovery of the direction of his sexual desire, his subsequent adventures in fulfillment of that desire, his doubts and anxieties about what he "is" and what he did, and his transformation into Jennie June, both brother and sister to Maggie, girl of the streets. He discloses a richly textured picture of homosexual life and provides detailed pictures of homosexual places, practices, and self-conceptions. This book and *The Female Impersonators* reveal a rich sensual life, an autobiography of sex and sensibility. Lind's mind is an overdecorated room, filled with specific and graphic scenes of sexual experiment, usually rendered in part in Latin and embellished with some of the furniture of nineteenth-century morality, religiosity, and sentimentality. Yet the primary motif is curiously modern: liberation, freedom, sexual emancipation, tolerance for sexual difference.

Though Lind's life has been forgotten and his books ignored, his contribution needs to be reclaimed as one of the early voices creating the discourse of gay American history. His books are examples of that special American genre, the fictionalized autobiography, or at least the autobiography that escapes the constricting claim of mere fact to make a case for the truth of the imagined self. Thoreau wrote one of these, so did Whitman. If Lind's Jennie June is a creature of fact, he is truly fabulous, and Lind owns a master hand in the retailing of biographical detail. His life—he would prefer "her" life—has a baroque splendor that would be the envy of Beckford or Huysmans; it certainly foretells the same fabulous technique in John Rechy's *City of Night* (1963), which is, after all, our own version, masculinized, of Jennie June's books.

Lind is also a master of the art of the erotic confessional tale as well as of the art of what might be called high operatic pornography: suspenseful, titillating, even, indeed, arousing if one knows a little Latin, though not much Latin is required to guess just what is being done, with what, how, and to whom. *Autobiography of an Androgyne* is told in a breathless, confidential style that lures the reader into a sexual adventure as Jennie June in one or another of her various disguises disappears into rooms or back alleys with handsome young men who throw themselves at her feet or, in more violent moments, throw her at theirs. We read of American sex, back-street orgies, and Bowery love enshrined in this dead tongue for the sake of "scientific" propriety: "whenever I have encountered *virum* who appeared to me as exceptionally beautiful, a strong desire has immediately arisen *membrum virile in ore recipere*." We follow with interest his transformation from a "low-class fairie" cruising Stuyvesant Park to a high-class drag queen looking for men on the "gay Rialto," 14th Street. We watch with incredulity Lind's—now June's—seduction of a squad of U.S. Army men and watch with fascination his deeply felt masquerade as the coquettish Baby June.

But there is another side to this text. Lind confronts with incredible bravery society's cruel and often violent response to him. He hides nothing and makes it clear that the men he entertains are as eager for sexual sensation as he. Few men reject him, though many attempt to kill him after using him, and many make the first advances. Lind has no erotic interest in his sexual confreres; he does not seek out liaisons with other homosexuals, though they thickly populate his book. With a very modern pride and in very eloquent voice he argues for (indeed, demands) that society recognize not only the sexual but social and political rights of those "fairies" and "androgynes" who, even then, may have been called gay people, for as early as 1868 Will Hayes, a female impersonator, sung a song about the "Gay Young Clerk in the Dry Goods Store" that recalled the popular ascription of effeminacy to "counter-jumpers," the dry goods salesmen who were mocked as "weak and effeminate" in an 1860s parody of Whitman's "Song of Myself" (Katz 1983, 315).

Born in New York in 1874, the fourth of 11 children, Lind comes from a family he describes as "enormously respectable religious people," none of whom "ever distinguished themselves." Lind asserts that there are no "bad strains" in his blood to account for his sexuality, yet then yields to current medical theory and calls insane relatives and overaffectionate uncles to account: "A maternal second . . . cousin was mildly insane" an uncle "half-witted" and "a paternal and also a maternal uncle, besides being extreme dipsomaniacs, lacked the energy to earn their own livings, and also never married. The fact that the maternal uncle used to fondle me excessively. . . . I had innumerable relations *cum pueris*. The earliest I can remember occurred when I was three and a half years old. A boy of nine had myself, a brother of five, and another of fifteen months *sugere penum erectum*." This, we know, happened in 1877. "For several years," he continues, "he sought me occasionally for the same purpose. My two brothers complied only a few times, while I eagerly grasped every opportunity" (Lind, 30).

These opportunities, he attests, were daily occurrences, for "while engaged in games with boys, sometimes fellatio would occur every few minutes." By the time he was seven—in 1882—he recalls that "I doubtless had more than one thousand such experiences." Indeed, his conception of himself was nurtured in the fertile ground of a charged erotic imagination: "My thoughts were entirely of boys and of myself as a girl. I imagined all sorts of flirtations and amours with every good-looking boy with whom I went to school. . . . I would imagine myself breaking into their houses after they had gone to bed, and attaining my desire. I would imagine a dozen of them standing behind a long screen, with *erectis* sticking through the apertures, and myself going from one to another. . . . I would imagine myself walking on a lonely road and meeting a handsome youth who would force me to fellatio. . . . I would imagine myself a beautiful girl skating in the rink, and having a bevy of boys frolicking with me—I falling down and having several of them pile on top of me" (Lind, 40).

How striking is his reiterated "I would imagine" as he invents himself, not sure whether he is to become an eroticized criminal breaking into houses to rape sleeping boys, a sexual athlete performing sequential stunts in anonymous phallic games, a passive youth forced to perform what no force was necessary to achieve, or, most transgressively, the innocent though alluring female object of a gang-rape by those youths whose "frolicking" makes them sound so curiously innocent. Imagining himself to be a girl would become his primary idée fixe, but imagining himself to be one pales next to his final settled conviction that in fact he was one. Yet he is not entirely happy in this role, and he plots the most extreme measures in order to shed all vestiges of masculinity: "I have been doomed to be a girl who must pass her earthly existence in a male body" (Lind, 41).

At first his conviction seems founded not so much on some instinctive awareness of "the feminine" in his makeup as, he might say, it is on the fact that engaging in fellatio is his fondest and most obsessive sexual pleasure. True men, of course, do not "commit" such an act, and therefore his logic (and that of his times) leads him to conclude that if he does desire what he imagines to be a passive act, then he can only be a woman. Like his times, he inscribes identity within sexuality and polarizes sexual activity within strict gender-bound terms.

In 1891 Lind entered a New York City university where, in keeping with his religious upbringing, he took up the study of theology and became even more devout. But New York then as now exerted its known temptations. Faith provided no defense against the desire to soothe his unbidden cravings for sex and men: "While walking the street, my gaze would be riveted on stalwart adolescents, and I would halt to look back at the handsomest that passed. . . . Even in the midst of continuous prayer my delirious imagination brought obscene images before me. . . . I would go raving about the room like an insane person . . . and if it had not been for the lateness of the hour. . . . I would have gone in search of fellatio which alone would pacify me. . . . Finally on an evening in June, I arose from my studies and prepared for my first nocturnal ramble" (Lind, 59).

For Lind, this ramble would mark the beginning of his erotic life in the streets. The sexual pilgrim seeking his special holy grail on the streets of New York is no longer Earl Lind, a somewhat pudgy "model student" with a "child-like and bland smile," but one who wanted to be "looked upon as a member of the gentler sex." The reader "now beholds me for the first time transformed into a sort of secondary personality inhabiting the same corpus as my proper self, to which personality I soon gave the name Jennie June." Jennie June is not yet ready, however, to "adopt feminine attire . . . as some other ordinarily respectable androgynes are in the habit of doing when going out on similar promenades," since "the mere wearing of it in the street by an adult male would render him liable to imprisonment." For his first adventure he donned a "cast-off suit" and "placed some coins in my pocket and several bills in a shoe, stuffed a few matches in one pocket and in another a wet sponge . . . and carefully went through my clothing . . . to make sure that I had not left by oversight some clue to my identity" (Lind, 60–62).

Jennie June soon encounters an example of the stalwart adolescent who people her dreams, a youth "about my own age seated alone on a beer keg in front of a bar room," and speaks aloud for the first time, providing the first recorded scene of homosexual seduction in American letters:

> June: What big, big strong hands you have! I bet you are a good fighter.
> Stalwart Adolescent: There's a few as kin lick me but not many.
> June: I love fighters. If you and I had a fight, who do you think would win?
> Stalwart Adolescent: I could lick half a dozen like yer together.
> June: I knew you could. I am only a baby.
> Stalwart Adolescent: Hah. Hah. Only a baby!
> June: Say, you have a handsome face.
> Stalwart Adolescent: Me hansome! Stop yer kiddin.
> June: Really you are handsome. I am going to tell you a secret. I am a woman hater. I am really a girl in a fellow's clothes. I would like to get some fellow to marry me. You look beautiful to me. Would you be willing to?
> Stalwart Adolescent: How much does it cost yer to git married? Give me V [$5] and I'll be yourn, or else git out of here.

Whether June's euphemism of "married" recalls the same formula used by the mollies of London when they retired to have sex, the young man clearly knows what is meant. But all is not to end with wedding bells, for "my statement that I had not that amount with me brought the threat of pummeling." Just as the incorruptible American boy is about to put on corruption for less than a fiver, his pals come along and righteousness leads him to call out, "I've got a fairie here," and the boy and his pals rob Lind/June and beat him/her up and chase him through the streets. He escapes and slumps on a doorstep and draws strength from the biblical text "the way of the transgressor is hard." But so much a transgressor is he destined to be that before the night is over he approaches one boy after another. In the deserted streets he approaches "one or two young dockrats who were still abroad, but they simply ransacked my pockets, gave me a parting blow, and went on their way" (Lind, 63–66).

His first ramble fills him with shame and guilt, but he warns the reader not to "begin to set his own virtue against the apparent depravity of such as I. If he has not fallen so low as I, it is not necessarily because he is morally good, and I morally bad, but because in him there has been no overpowering impulse to do what mankind regards as unspeakably low." Lind's mature assessment of his "overpowering impulse" reflects the medical judgment of his time that "depraved" sexual impulses were so irresistible that those "afflicted" by them were in some sense not responsible for them. Lind seems torn between acceptance of a theory that stigmatizes him and a wish to deny the moral stigma that inevitably accompanied it.

Shame and guilt lead him to try to find a "cure." He goes to a faith healer, but without success. He throws himself into his work, but study confuses him further. Having encountered homophobic violence in the streets he discovers its more passive though no less virulent form in academia when his professor assures him that Socrates' "Phaedo had been a slave devoted to unmentionable uses." He leaves New York for the summer fearing that he "might become insane." Abstinence enforced by life in a small town, together with much prayer, leads him to believe that he is cured, but "gradually I had to admit the truth, that no change had taken place" (Lind, 69–71).

On returning to New York for the new term the call of the streets is hard to resist, and neither study nor philosophy offers consolation. But finally in what now has become a habitual search he finds what he seeks: "He addresses a tall, muscular, splendid specimen (subsequently a member of the New York police force) who continues in conversation with him. . . . The spirits of the little one are visibly heightened. If we watched closely . . . we would have seen the little one throw his arms around the neck of his companion, and kiss him passionately. Finally they pass out of sight down one of the dark covered alleys. . . . When after an interval the pair emerges again, the smaller is clinging tightly to his companion, as if afraid he might escape."

It is hard to say whether Lind's months in the country, his reading of Plato, or his considerable energy spent on being a practicing homosexual have contributed to what now seems to be a fairly accomplished seductive technique. Some readers might ask if his reckless approaches to ruffians, resulting as they often do in violence, do not bespeak an obsession that defies simple good sense and self-preservation. Yet he does succeed in finding affection. Lind may have had a transgressive or at least a wry purpose in mind when he lets us see the "little one" take one of New York's prospective finest into an alley for love. There is also a kind of throw-away bravery in Lind's open pursuit of his desire, and there is considerable skill in Lind's creation of June. At any rate, what is soon to become virtually a second career is begun in earnest, and Lind saves his companion for history and testifies also to the easy morality of the streets in 1892 when he allows the future policeman to say at parting: "You kin find me round this block any time. Just ask any one fur Red Mike" (Lind, 71–72).

The midnight triumphs of Jennie June in no way change the daylight tortures of Earl Lind as he strives to conquer his desire "in order if possible to be cured of my abnormality." He goes to doctors who advise him to marry or, as a practical alternative, accept castration under the assumption that the addition of a "good" woman to his life or the subtraction of a "defective" organ from his body will accomplish much the same "cure." Another doctor tries hypnotism, another "drugs and stimulation of the brain," for which read shock therapy. He undergoes the entire repertory of medical tortures devised by twentieth-century science to cure homosexuality with the result that after several months "I was rendered almost a physical and nervous wreck by the powerful drugs administered, but my amorous desires showed no change."

So little changed is he that at a convention for missionaries he attempts to seduce his pious roommate, "a rather athletic student from another college." His roommate apparently yields in the dark of night but the next day, harkening to the charitable precepts of the faith and the stern exhortations of the Bible, exposes Lind and humiliates him publicly so that he is forced to flee the convention. Lind concludes that his "abnormality bars me from the ministry" (Lind, 74). Life becomes even more tortured, psychiatric visits continue, the streets still call him to nightly rambles. He finally discontinues his treatment, and, as if in reward for rejecting medical punishment, Red Mike appears again, like an angel, this time in the company of several chums.

June—it is no longer Lind who speaks—joins them and the beer pail is passed around as they lounge in the door of an abandoned warehouse. "I reclined in the arms of one after the other, covering face, neck, hands, arms, and clothing with kisses, while they caressed me and called me pet names. I was supremely happy. . . . At the end of the hour, we adjourned down an alley, where the drinking and love making continued even more intensely." Lind tells them the story of his life and "sang with them in the mock soprano or falsetto that fairies employ, trying to imitate the voice of a woman." Music does not soothe the sexual beast, however, and Red Mike and his friends turn on him and Lind is robbed and raped by the gang: "With my face in the dust, and half-suffocated by one ruffian's tight grip on my throat I moaned and struggled with all my might because of the excruciating pain. But in their single thought for animal pleasure, they did not heed my moans and broken entreaties to spare me the suffering they were inflicting."

He escapes into the brightly lighted Mulberry Street; "two of my assailants had followed me," but amazingly "they expressed their regret . . . and assured me of their friendly feelings. 'You are only a baby,' they said, and 'so we will fight for you and protect you.'" June is overwhelmed by their "gallantry" and goes back where "the gang received me kindly, petted and soothed me . . . and sobbing with happiness. . . . I rested my head against their bodies. To lie in the bosom of these sturdy young manual laborers, all of whom were good looking and approximately my own age, was the highest earthly happiness I had yet tasted."

This is the first adventure of its kind for Lind, and it is the model for many that will follow. In his diary he writes, "What a strange thing is life! Mephistopheles last night carried me through one of the experiences through which he carried Faust. My carnal pleasure was aroused as never before. . . . My present psychical state is most strange. I cannot yet repent of my conduct Friday night, yet on a Sunday morning following I had one of the happiest experiences of nearness to God that I ever had. . . . I have in my heart the intense desire to save from their lives of sin those in whose company I was Friday night" (Lind, 77–80). This mawkish sentimentality is not enough to conceal, however, that his true vocation is to be a missionary not of Christ but of Eros.

The book's remaining 200 pages and much of the second volume record just such adventures as this, though often in more explicit detail. This vignette is a model: a search for love and sex, the discovery of it followed all too often by terrible punishment, and a dogged return for more. Though he consorts with other male homosexuals—the "fairies of New York" who he calls his "brother and sister courtesans"—his desire is directed at roughs. Yet throughout the book his altruism surfaces again and again as he goes out of his way to help some appealing young man who inevitably turns against him.

Improbable as Lind's missionary zeal may seem, this mixture of sex and sentimental spirituality is a dominant theme in the book. While it may not be the muscular Christianity that Dr. Arnold urged on young men, it does suggest that instead of hell the souls of homosexuals can be destined for heaven too. Though barred by his "abnormality" from saving souls for Christ, he will try to convince his readers that instead of being monsters homosexuals are men whose lives carry a deeper and more profound stamp than merely that impressed by sexual desire. Indeed, he determines to "follow Nature's behest" and live "according to the dictates of my peculiar instincts." When he does this "I was happier than I ever had been before. . . . I had arrived at the conviction that while the voice of the world would cry 'Shame' I was acting according to the dictates of reason and conscience" (Lind, 81–83). This revelation leads him to become a sexual suffragette, marching for the rights of those who he clearly sees as his people.

In *The Female Impersonators* Lind records the language of the streets, of the inhabitants of the Bowery or, as he says, of the more "high class" purlieus of 14th Street. He reveals the complex choreography of demimonde homosexual life: names, gathering places, cruising sites, sexual practices, even fragments of camp conversation. We meet Frank-Eunice, Angelo-Phyllis, Prince Pansy, Manon Lescaut, early sisters no doubt to our own Ru Paul, Lady Bunny, Afro-Ditee, Lypsinka, and Flotilla de Barge. We know that Lind joined the Cercle Hermaphroditos, a club formed to "unite for defense against the world's bitter persecution" of homosexuals. For entertainment they frequented Paresis Hall, the Hotel Comfort, and The Pugilist's Haven, all apparently gay bars. They met in Stuyvesant Square and cruised 14th Street, which Lind describes as being "as gay as any European bright light district I was fated to explore." (Is this an early use of "gay"?)

Lind's description of life on this gay Rialto is fascinating: homosexual men wore red ties to distinguish themselves so that if they were not in drag they would be known to the apparently vast numbers of nonhomosexual men who were looking for androgyne love. Men carried their female impersonating lovers to sumptuous drag fetes with names like the Philhedonic Ball. And homosexual men lived together in unobtrusive relationships that were envied by the likes of Jennie June and her confidant, a member of the Cercle Hermaphroditos, who called himself Roland Reeves.

Even during the most intense years of Lind's nocturnal rambles he pursued his studies, became master of several languages, was demonstrably aware of the materials of what we now call gay studies, and was a talented writer able to spin out a tale and capture those details that turn mere texts into art. Though his masquerade obviously did not represent the lives of all homosexuals at the turn of the century, the social mask was a fact for every one of them, and June's confrontations with homophobic violence represents only one aspect of the homophobia that touched them all.

Lind opines at one point in *The Female Impersonators* that "the emergence of androgyny is a sign of national health" (Lind, 48). That opinion alone strikes at the heart of centuries of homophobia and qualifies Lind to be a founding member of that academy that is even now constructing theory out of homosexual life. At the end of the book he lets us know why he is to be valued: "My own is a Herculean task: to be an intellectual iconoclast. To break the last remnant of cultured man's savage, criminal instincts and mores." "Surely," he continues, "we androgynes who for two thousand years have been despised, hunted down, and crushed under the heel of normal men . . . have no reason to be ashamed of our heritage" (Lind, 39).

Mayne's novel and Lind's texts articulate two of the great themes that will inform twentieth-century homoerotic texts: Mayne's that two "real men" can find love in the context of the radicalizing idea that homosexuals need not be the monstrous creatures or the "imitation women" homophobia constructs them to be; June's that the invert's most potent weapon is difference and that the enactment of transgressive sexual identity can not only flourish in the face of American homophobia but perhaps even eliminate it.

HENRY BLAKE FULLER

Henry Blake Fuller's *Bertram Cope's Year* can claim to be the first truly modern gay novel in American literature. No New York firm wanted to publish it, and so Fuller convinced a friend to do so as a personal favor. No one bought it or reviewed it, however, and finally Fuller collected the unbound sheets from the press and destroyed them. Perhaps this was because "the accent of . . . psychic Uranianism" for which Mayne so intently listened, and for which readers were also increasingly alert, can be heard subtly in its pages. Though as unread now as it was when it was published in 1919, the novel is nevertheless a skillfully written realistic comedy of manners that recounts a year in the life of Bertram Cope, a handsome and exceedingly eligible young bachelor, described at various times as lithe, muscular, manly and, even once, as "glittering."

Cope takes a position as an English instructor in a small midwestern college town while completing his thesis and there becomes the object of the attentions of both men and women. He drifts into the circle of and becomes the object of the manipulative wiles of Medora Phillips, the grande dame and social leader of the town. She is a woman who arranges lives. Her pretensions are supported by money and by a showy devotion to culture and art that she uses as a weapon to maintain her social status. Phillips presides over what she likes to think of as a salon in which the cultural and social life of the town is centered, in a house that is furnished, Fuller broadly hints, in a taste that verges on the ostentatious. Boarding in her house are three young women, Carolyn, Hortense, and Amy, each of whom, as Fuller also lets us know, is a rather mediocre dilettante, devoted to the kind of middle-brow culture that Medora Phillips dispenses. Each of the three is ripe for marriage, and Phillips plots to provide each of them with a suitable husband. When Cope appears, Phillips sees him as a perfect opportunity and attempts to match him with one after another of the women. But Cope resists. His resistance is polite but tinged with panic as it appears that he may be seduced against his will into a union—the very idea of which, as is soon revealed, he clearly abhors.

Running as an obbligato plot to this conventional comedy of marital manners is a more unorthodox narrative that details Cope's relations with two men, Basil Randolph and Cope's boyhood "chum," Arthur Lemoyne. Randolph is a middle-aged bachelor of independent means, impeccable taste, genteel manners, and excellent social and professional "connections" who lives a cultivated life surrounded by his collections of china and exotic objects. He tends to "cultivate" young men. Indeed, he feels "prompted to 'collect' them" very much as he collects curios. He invites them to elegant little dinners, puts in a good word for them in their professional lives, and helps them navigate through the tricky waters of small town social life. He is however constantly disappointed by his "youths," for, as he says, "you give them an evening among your books, with discreet things to drink, to smoke, to play at, or you offer them a good dinner at some good hotel; and you never saw them after."

Randolph is what his kindlier times euphemistically described as a perennial bachelor and what a less tender age would soon call an old queen. Of course Randolph does have designs on Cope, though nowhere does he openly express more than an avuncular interest in the welfare of the young man and a desire for his Platonic companionship. But in the world of his fantasies there is quite a different intention. His infatuation with Cope leads him to go so far as to find a larger apartment and in it prepare a guest room so that he can on occasion, as he says, "put a man up." The man he has in mind is Cope, and the bedroom Randolph fantasizes is a bower of bliss: "There would be a convenient little spare room wherein a young knight, escaped from some 'Belle Dame Sans Merci,' might lean his sword against the wardrobe, prop his greaves along the baseboard, lay his steel gauntlets neatly on the top of the dresser, fold his hands over the turned down sheet of a neat three-quarter-width brass bedstead, and with a satisfied sigh of utter well being pass into sleep."[5]

Though Randolph arranges things for Cope and imagines the possibility of a relationship between them, Cope resists, though not so strenuously as he resists Medora Phillips's promptings of matrimony. He is not, however, unwilling to accept Randolph's largesse or the fruits of his influence. Cope is also willing to be often a guest at Phillips's opulent dinners and at her beach house. Intervening between the plotting of Basil Randolph and Medora Phillips, and casting a long shadow over everyone's plans, is Arthur Lemoyne, Cope's boyhood friend, with whom Cope has lived before, and who reappears midway through the book to come and live with him again. Lemoyne—dark, somewhat effeminate, cool to women—is also an actor and his most accomplished roles seem to be those that involve cross-dressing. Randolph and Phillips both dislike Lemoyne—Randolph because it is clear to him that Cope and Lemoyne have a special relationship that will prevent any possibility of his having one with Cope, Phillips not only because she sees Lemoyne as an obstacle between Cope and marriage with one of her charges, but also because his manner suggests unorthodox sexuality and gender ambiguity by which she is clearly appalled.

Fuller adds to the usual concerns of the social comedy the problematic ingredient of homosexuality in general and in particular suggests that there may be more versions of homosexual identity than those identified by the clichés society accepts. It is not hard for Medora Phillips and her circle to recognize what Arthur Lemoyne "is." He is described as "a young man of twenty-seven . . . with dark limpid eyes, a good deal of dark wavy hair, and limbs almost too plumply turned. His hands displayed certain graceful slightly effected movements of the kind which may cause a person to be credited—or taxed—with possessing the artistic temperament. . . . He was a type which one may admire—or not" (Fuller, 202). Fuller's masterful dash in "—or taxed—with" and "admire—or not" conveys all the horrific prospects that homophobia can threaten. The suspicion of difference is quite subtly though damagingly suggested.

When Lemoyne takes a female role in the college play, Medora Phillips raises a verbal eyebrow to Cope. "He is an artist," Cope replies, to which she archly responds, "Not too much of one I trust; I confess I like boys in such parts when they frankly and honestly seem to be boys. That's half the fun—and nine-tenths the taste." "Taste?" Cope asks. "Yes, taste. Short for good taste. There's a great deal of room for bad. A thing may be done too thoroughly. Once or twice I've seen it done that way by—artists" (Fuller, 280). There can be no doubt that Phillips is fully convinced that Lemoyne's art is a disguise for what he really is—an effeminate homosexual. She associates "bad taste" with Lemoyne's cross-dressing and then quickly translates that, without saying it, into gender confusion, sexual perversion, and homosexuality.

Her assumption is that only heterosexuality is in good taste and that anyone who is a cross-dressing "artist" must also be homosexual, that anyone who is seemingly "manly" is heterosexual. She assumes this about the manly, tasteful, and seemingly normal Cope, and about that impeccable paragon of good taste, Basil Randolph. By casting homosexuality and therefore homophobia within a discourse that predicates judgment about them as a question of taste, Fuller allows his book to reverse Phillips's judgment—and here is its most potent thrust. For the tasteful Cope and the tasteful Randolph are, of course, both homosexual, and thus homosexuality equals "good taste" while Medora Phillips and her young women possess no real "taste" at all.

Although Fuller as satirist leaves no character unscathed—Cope is vague, somewhat petulant; Randolph somewhat fussy and even pitiful, yet his sympathies clearly lie with the men and his sharpest darts are directed at the conventional pretensions of middle-class society. Fuller juxtaposes the rather gaudy and "elaborate" taste of Medora Phillips who moves through rooms overdecorated with "objet" and fussy "lambrequins" against the quiet perfection of Basil Randolph's apartment, where "everything was rich and handsome," or compares the civilized cultivation of Randolph's style to the ostentation of Medora Phillips's life, or contrasts Amy's or Carolyn's fevered desire for matrimony with Cope's measured, reasoned, polite avoidance of it, or compares Cope's scholarly doctoral thesis with the mediocre poetry or sentimental painting of the young women. Fuller uses the weapons of style and aesthetics to comment about sexual difference. Without ever really dealing with direct questions about sexuality or sexual difference or transgression, Fuller nevertheless creates a contest between what he sees as a homosexual as opposed to a heterosexual style.

Wandering off toward the beach during one of Medora Phillips's house parties, Randolph and Cope on impulse take a swim together. After their dip as they sit together on the sand Randolph summons his courage to make one small gesture: after Cope rolls in the sand to dry himself, covering his body with a fine coat of sand, Randolph tentatively reaches out to apply more sand to an unprotected "bare shoulder blade." There is no more than that, but the gesture defines the nature of Randolph's desire and the cautious limits he sets to them. But it is enough for Cope who keeps asking Randolph how much time they have before they must return to the party. Nothing of course transpires.

Cope, though, soon reveals himself in the most circumspect way when he asks who will be at the party. Randolph explains that at parties like this there are always numbers of women. Cope hopes that "there'll be enough fellows to look after the stove and the pump—and them [the women]. I'm not much good at that last." Randolph quickly pursues the opening and observes that he has never "enlisted any woman's best endeavors" to induce him to marry. Cope quickly responds, "I hope I shall have the same good luck," after which they dwell on the strategies women employ to trap men. As Randolph points out, "You're maneuvered into a position where you're made to feel you 'must.'" Cope answers, "Don't dwell on it! You fill me with apprehensions" (Fuller, 88). The scene is familiar enough in those social comedies where bantering men good-naturedly complain about women's wiles, even as they prepare willingly to marry them. But Cope's dismissive comments about marriage and Randolph's supporting assertions show that here are two men whose attention is never fixed on women. The scene presents only barely realized homoeroticism, yet bathing men is a central motif in homoerotic literature, and is enough to suggest what Fuller wants to convey.

Cope is no more attracted to Randolph than he is to any of the women, even though he has allowed himself to become very nearly engaged to one of them. But by ignoring her he causes a rift and she breaks off the engagement. Arthur has also now appeared, and the two of them take an apartment, taking time out from their delight only for minor disagreements over décor. When Cope finally receives the letter breaking his engagement to one of Phillips's charges, Lemoyne and Cope return to their apartment after a midnight walk, both immensely relieved. As they are about to step across the threshold "Lemoyne impulsively threw an arm across his [Cope's] shoulder. 'Everything is all right now,' he said in a tone of high gratification; and Urania, through the whole width of her starry firmament, looked down kindly upon a happier household" (Fuller, 232). It is Urania, of course, as Fuller very well knew, who, in Plato's *Symposium*, watches over and protects homosexual lovers.

Fuller here makes clear what may hitherto have been suspected, for this is a book of coded and indirect clues. At the end, however, there can be no doubt, at least about Lemoyne. In a moment of "camp" high comedy, Arthur, acting a drag role in a play, is—as Phillips predicted—too good at his art. He elicits instead of the plaudits the suspicions and even the scorn of most of the town. In an excess of identification with his role, Arthur makes a pass at a heterosexual actor: "In his general state of ebulliency he endeavored to bestow a measure of upwelling femininity upon a performer who was in the dress of his own sex." He is asked to leave the play, the college, and the town. Cope stays on to get his degree but leaves as soon as he has it, without a good-bye to Medora Phillips or to Basil Randolph.

Phillips ultimately cannot associate Cope's involvement with Lemoyne with the perversion that to her is written so clearly in the signs of Lemoyne's effeminacy and his cross-dressing. Indeed, she presumes that Cope will return, this time to pursue his wooing of the last of the women, despite the fact that he has sent her a curt and dismissive letter that can only mean farewell. When Randolph suggests that Cope has gone off with Lemoyne, Phillips will not accept it. Fuller's text is a battleground for the possession of a young man by two kinds of desire—desires that both the text and its characters presume, as society presumes, to be necessarily and irreconcilably opposite.

Though the homosexuality of the characters is only implied, Fuller realistically anatomizes the toll that the self-imposed role-playing of closeted homosexuals exacts on those who, like Randolph, prefer to keep their desires secret and repressed. Randolph realizes his fantasy about a new apartment and creates the spare room for "a guest," by which he means Cope, and imbues that room with a futile mythology, though he will be ultimately thwarted in his wish to have Cope as a lover. The text also anatomizes the reaction of heterosexuals to two kinds of homosexual identity—homosexuals like Basil Randolph, who "pass" as straight and therefore do not threaten the social arrangement but participate in it, and those like Cope, whose seeming normality precludes heterosexual society from seeing him as a monster like Lemoyne.

Randolph also reacts badly to Lemoyne, and while much of his reaction can be laid to jealousy, much also can be categorized as internalized homophobia. While Lemoyne threatens consolidated conceptions of gender and implies perversions, Cope is able to pass unscathed, his obvious dislike of women ignored by the very women he rejects, his "masculinity" remaining undamaged even when Arthur, in *louche* flamboyance, very publicly drapes his hands across Cope's shoulder and often touches his hand, also in public, too long and longingly. Cope and Arthur's public affection and their public living arrangements mark them, in a sense not to be realized for half a century, as "out" and as the first modern "gay couple" in American fiction.

In the tradition of Wharton and Henry James, Fuller employs a distanced and ironic tone to describe the contest for Cope's affections and with an equally ironic eye discerns and draws the telling gesture that will anatomize and reveal the often pretentious and generally rather shallow motivations of the small-town midwestern life of his generally not too likable characters. His ostensible subject, like Wharton and James, is the effect that marriage in middle-class American life has on relationships between men and women. Like Wharton and James also, he explores the effect of rigid social structures on the lives of those who are committed to maintaining the tight web of those structures and who are too enmeshed in them to escape, and like James and Wharton, he focuses on those who are willing to break free of the strictures or at least transgress against them. Again like James and Wharton, he pits youth against age, experience against innocence, knowledge against naïveté.

The determined though ironic innocence of Fuller's tone supports the real purpose of the text—to portray, without moral or social condemnation, the homosexual triangle of Lemoyne, Randolph, and Cope. Fuller also allows Cope to go off with his friend at the end without hint of social retribution—indeed, with the stronger hint that they may live happily ever after. Near the end of the book Basil Randolph observes that "language was made to conceal thought." Fuller weaves his web of homoerotically suggestive language around a thought too horrendous to utter directly—or at least too horrendous for heterosexual society as represented by Medora Phillips to entertain: that some young men do not want to be married and that they may indeed find their lives more fulfilled by other young men.

Bertram Cope and Arthur Lemoyne as a couple contribute to the construction of identities, even clichés, about gay couples that would be depicted in American fiction. Both handsome and talented, Arthur is given to drag, pretense, and interior design; he is bitchy, effeminate, with a sharp tongue and sharper wit. Bertram is literate and literary, something of a stud, but also with an edge of bitchy knowingness that grows as the book progresses. He is flirtatious and self-absorbed. Neither of them are averse to using the affections of an older man for advancement. Still, they resist the very institutions in which they have for a while found a home when those institutions threaten to forcibly enroll them as members—Cope by rejecting marriage, Lemoyne, more transgressively, by rejecting the very images and roles of masculinity and gender conformity valued by those institutions, and both of them, most transgressively of all, by choosing each other and deserting the institutionalized, heterosexual world. They declare the failure of heterosexist institutions, the poverty and hypocrisy of Randolph's choice to remain closeted within the confining walls of heterosexual society, and by leaving together and presumably living together they proclaim the genuineness and meaningfulness of their desire as well as of the lives they intend to lead.

SHERWOOD ANDERSON, CARL VAN VECHTEN, AND ROBERT McALMON

In 1919 there appeared a short story that would be the precursor of a certain kind of homosexual fiction, Sherwood Anderson's "Hands."[6] If Fuller's novel is a homosexual comedy of manners, "Hands" is a tragic allegory of the homosexual as outsider, intellectually and morally superior to a world that condemns him and willfully misunderstands him. Wing Biddlebaum lives in Anderson's Winesburg, Ohio, a man "forever frightened." His "slender and expressive" hands are always attempting to express what he is unable to put into words. He is only able to fully express himself in the company of young George Willard, in whose presence he "lost some of his timidity, and his shadowy personality, submerged in a sea of doubts, came forth to look at the world." With Willard, Biddlebaum was able to express his dreams, foremost among which was his vision of a world in which "men lived in a kind of pastoral golden age" where "clean limbed young men" gathered "about the feet of an old man who sat beneath a tree." This

Arcadian and Hellenic vision so inspires Biddlebaum that while retailing it to young Willard he reaches out and puts his hands on the boy's shoulders. As he "raised the hands to caress the boy" a "look of horror swept over his face," and he abruptly hurried away, leaving Willard "perplexed and frightened upon the grassy slope."

The secret of Biddlebaum's hands and the source of his fear lies in his past. Biddlebaum had once been a schoolteacher, and his real name was Adolph Myers. His intimacy with the boys of the school had led him to "talk until dusk upon the schoolhouse steps, lost in a kind of dream. Here and there went his hands, caressing the shoulders of boys, playing about the tousled heads. As he talked his voice became soft and musical. There was a caress in that also. In a way the voice and the hands, the stroking of the shoulders and the touching of the hair was part of the schoolmaster's effort to carry a dream into young minds." But when he caresses a "half witted boy" who had "become enamored of the young master" tragedy follows and the boy accuses him of "unspeakable things." "Hideous accusations fell from his lips." Soon "through the Pennsylvania town went a shiver. Hidden shadowy doubts that had been in men's minds concerning Adolph Myers were galvanized into beliefs."

Myers is confronted and beaten by one of the parents and at midnight is run out of town by a gang of a dozen men: "As he ran away into the darkness . . . they ran after him, swearing and throwing sticks and great balls of mud at the figure who screamed and ran faster and faster into the darkness." His enforced exile recalls and may be based on that of Horatio Alger, another fabricator of American dreams, who was also run out of town for "unnatural familiarity with boys." Anderson's anatomy of irrational bigotry is a powerful depiction of American homophobia and of the destructive effects that preconceptions about sexuality can have on the individual.

The ineffectual even effeminate Biddlebaum is in every way the outcast, and at the end of the story, when he has been deprived of the company of Willard, his fate is made more terrible when it is made clear that even Biddlebaum himself does not understand the source or nature of his impulses and desires. His homoerotic dream of a golden age populated by clean-limbed young men—a vision of a city of lovers that Whitman made germane to American homoerotic fiction—can never be explained or made acceptable to a world that reads that innocent dream as a nightmare of perversion and interprets his expressive caresses not as a medium for illumination but as the touch of a monster. For Biddlebaum's neighbors, the transgression represented by his touch is even more horrible than that represented by his dream. They do not comprehend or are even aware of the dream, but the touch invokes their worst fears. Biddlebaum is forced to "keep his hands to himself," and in doing so as he confines his gestures he also symbolically and emotionally imprisons himself, forced not only to change his name but to deny and erase his desire and his identity.

Though Biddlebaum may have been unable to name the desire that ultimately impelled him, he is aware of the outward sign—the desirous searching of his hands for the bodies of young men. Though Anderson's portrait of Biddlebaum may be intended to be sympathetic, Anderson seems to see Biddlebaum's fate as the only possible fate for an outcast homosexual, whereas Mayne and Fuller allow their characters to triumph over bigotry and the identities assigned to them by society. Fuller and Mayne deny that tragedy and isolation are necessary elements in homosexual lives, and as their characters step through the open closet door they become the first in American fiction to "come out" and carry the discovery of their identity into a world that lies, for good or ill, all before them.

Coming out is portrayed not so much as a sexual but as a social incursion in several books written after the war. Sex is far more prevalent in life—as Jennie June attests—than in texts. A handful of novels and stories, while implying sex as a constant subtext, mark difference as the major text by the display of outrageous personal, verbal, and visual—what was even then called "camp"—style. In texts written after the war, including *Bertram Cope's Year*, coming out is not so much a private discovery of the interior nature and direction of desire but a public display of difference that implicates (though does not necessarily deploy) sex and suggests sexuality. Writers like Carl van Vechten implied though did not state sexual difference in their novels. Van Vechten relied on witty, bitchy, and precious dialogue to mark the difference of his characters, placing them in a bohemian and irresponsible atmosphere where the chief desire of most of them was to be amused.

No characters in van Vechten's novels are directly presented as being homosexual, and in fact in *The Blind Bow-Boy* (1923) they are all almost deliberately implied to be the opposite. But implication is everything and has a double edge. Nothing can be proved, but we have this description of Paul: "A young man in white flannels, a young man with curly golden hair and blue eyes and a profile that resembled somewhat Sherril Schell's photograph of Rupert Brooke, a young man with slender, graceful hands which he was inclined to wave rather excessively in punctuation of his verbal effects, reclined on a divan upholstered in green taffeta, smoking a cigarette in a jade holder of a green so dark and so nearly translucent that it paraphrased emerald."[7] Van Vechten paraphrases homosexuality here as the signs surround this young man like smoke from his cigarette, but nowhere in the text do we ever know what we already know about him. Paul has vague vices that are surrounded, intimated, and protected but never revealed by language, by signs of difference.

At a later point in the book van Vechten deals firmly with the genre of dark and punitive homosexual fiction when he has his superbly named heroine, Campaspe Lorillard, wittily confront Waldo Frank's only vaguely and suggestively homosexual though ultimately homophobic novel, *The Dark Mother* (1920), in which the male villain is hinted to have an erotic interest in the innocent hero. A review of the book in 1920 confirmed what suspicions readers might have. *The Dark Mother* offers the "valuable reminder that there are vast areas of life that our literature has not yet known how to include" (Austen, 37). Van Vechten, speaking as Campaspe Lorillard, also reviews Frank's book in his book and has no doubt how such vast areas ought to be included in texts: "Nevertheless she opened the book and read a sentence or two. Then with some impatience, she tossed the volume aside. Why, she wondered did authors write in this uncivilized and unsophisticated manner? How was it possible to read an author who never laughed? For it was only behind laughter that true tragedy could lie concealed, and only the ironic author who could awaken the deeper emotions. The true tragedies of life were either ridiculous or sordid. The only way to get the sense of this absurd, contradictory, and perverse existence into a book was to withdraw entirely from reality. The artist who feels the most poignantly the bitterness of life wears a persistent and sardonic smile" (van Vechten, 160).

As thick here as around Paul are the signs of difference—special signs of those times vis-à-vis definitions of homosexuality—that read homosexuality as absurd, sordid, unreal, perverse, contradictory, yet nevertheless something best interpreted through irony and a constant pose of sardonic detachment: in short, by the central mechanisms of camp, the application not of the transcendent or of the profound but of the surface sublime, to make real life unreal and hence bearable and understandable. What van Vechten describes here is his own method. He said at one point, "My formula at present consists of treating extremely serious themes as frivolously as possible" and thus it may be that Ronald Firbank—another master of the deconstruction of reality—wrote to him approvingly to say how happy he was "to have attracted another butterfly like myself" (quoted in Austen, 39–40). Van Vechten's method is not his invention—we have seen Raffalovich advocate it and Wilde perfect it—but it is a method that would come to have a specifically American turn in the hands of homosexual writers. In these books identity is not predicated so much on the consummation of desire as on the manifestation of desire through a language that purveys heightened, fantastic, and often distorting verbal, personal, and visual articulations of the erotic self while confronting on every side the conventions of society in the midst of which these books bravely, irritatingly, and urgently site themselves.

Set in Europe—Paris and Berlin—but populated by Americans is a book by Robert McAlmon, one of the best writers of the period and one of the first to present openly homosexual characters, whose group of stories *Distinguished Air* (he subtitled the group "Grim Fairy Tales") was published in a limited edition by McAlmon's own Contact Editions Press in Paris in 1925. It includes the title story and "Miss Knight," a full-length and even sympathetic portrait of a drag queen from Illinois who confesses, "Whoops, dearie! What us bitches will do when we draw the veil. Just lift up our skirts and scream."[8] Miss Knight—a near relative of Jenny June, though without June's real intelligence, "refined" and "elegant" pretensions, or social perspicuity—represents the outlandish and exotic picture of homosexuals that the few novels of the 1920s that bothered to present them had begun to draw. The story "Distinguished Air" is set in Berlin and introduces the "fairy" Foster Graham. "Miss Knight" is set in Paris, the bad Old World where homosexuals are more likely to be found than in the purer American landscape.

Whereas the homosexuals portrayed by Mayne were serious and supervirile, gay novels of the 1920s seemed to emphasize the homosexual identities that Fuller had hinted at in *Bertram Cope's Year*. McAlmon's Foster Graham walks into the narrative wearing trousers "drawn in at the waist" and a "coat padded at the shoulders, so that the descending line to the waist gave his figure a too obvious hour glass appearance" (McAlmon, 10). Graham "was camping, hands on hips, with a quick eye to notice every man who passed by." Graham's sartorial signs look back to Smollett's Captain Whiffle and ahead to some of the boys in the band. He is also, incidentally, the first real American "fairy"—a term current in Lind's books and certainly dating to the nineteenth century—as opposed to a real American "drag," to be identified as such in fiction written by an American.

McAlmon's use of "camp" in the mid-1920s suggests its likely availability even earlier, thus allowing its use as a marker of homosexual style to characterize the verbally facile characters of van Vechten, whose witty, bitchy repartee established for homosexual identities in American fiction what Ronald Firbank had created in England—a tradition of arch and self-conscious linguistic pyrotechnics that defines the male homosexual as much by the way he speaks as by the way he acts or dresses and places him in a scene where the amusing repartee mirrors an equally amusing and irresponsible life. While gay life and identity as depicted in novels of the 1920s may not have been what all gay life was really about, these novels do construct one reality as well as a fictional mythology. Roger Austen observes in *Playing the Game: The Homosexual Novel in America* (still the best though not the most exhaustive discussion of the gay novel in America), "For a more accurate glimpse of what it was like to be gay in this country during the twenties" we must rely on sources like Hart Crane's letters in which "there is more truth about what it meant to be gay . . . than can be found in all the fiction published during the decade" (Austen, 49).

What Austen refers to is Crane's descriptions of his sexual exploits with various young men—often sailors, and his seeming rejection of anything effeminate. Miss Knight also has her share of the military, however, and she does seem to have pinpointed one vital identity constructed by homosexual and nonhomosexual alike. Homosexuals were now "queers" whose behavior, when not blatantly crossing gender roles, was seen to be almost constantly suggestive of difference. Miss Knight constantly seeks out what she calls "rough trade," thus locating another bit of homosexual argot firmly at an early point in the century. Indeed, the use of "cruising" and "queer," the repeated use of "Mary" and "drag" and even "gay" in a vaguely sexual context, suggest these words' currency at this early date. Miss Knight, recalling the street exploits of Jennie June, picks up soldiers, sailors, and assorted other uniformed professionals, wittily gloating as she sits with her hand in their pocket, "My god, Mary, I've got my hand on a real piece of meat at last, oh Mary" (McAlmon, 59).

That some of the guidelines for the sexually permissible were very much in flux, and that Miss Knight is no invention, is suggested by George Chauncey, Jr., in his study of sexual activity among sailors in the 1920s in Newport, Rhode Island. Sailors who had sex with known "queers" or "fairies" were nevertheless themselves not stigmatized by the association. As Chauncey explains, "The sailors believed that their physical sexual contact with queers remained acceptable so long as they avoided effeminate behavior and developed no emotional ties with their partners."[9] Chauncey's study is useful for an understanding of the 1920s novel in that it shows how effeminacy rather than sexual activity was a mark of homosexuality. When novels of the 1920s portrayed homosexuals they were still constrained from reporting specific homosexual activity, but they could imagine effeminacy. They rejected, for better or worse, the masculinized homoeroticism earlier celebrated by Melville, Whitman, Bayard Taylor, and Stoddard and still imagined by Mayne.

The queer was imaged in the fictional extremes of the cross-dressing Miss Knight or the effeminate and exotic characters created by van Vechten. By the 1920s homosexual literature was beginning to make a small mark on the American literary landscape, but that mark seemed to almost unanimously construct homosexual men as effeminate, as perverts, and as queers, but with the exception that in literature at least "fairies" and "queers" were often not the dangerous monsters they had been in earlier conceptions but were instead amusing, sometimes endearing, and almost always trivial pleasure seekers. Miss Knight disappears at the end of the story to New York, not to the usual death that awaited her brothers and sisters in novels to come. From New York she writes a friend—signing her name "Charlie Knight"—and decently repays a loan she owed. The friend comments, "Didn't I tell you the bitches could look out for themselves? . . . That one! If she was run over by a truck or a steam roller she'd turn up, about to appear in Paris, or London, or Madrid, or Singapore. She's just that international" (McAlmon, 69).

International, too, is Foster Graham, who appears after a night of debauchery, looking "even more exquisite than he had yesterday." The narrator wonders "how he could continue to look so nonchalantly poised and contained" (McAlmon, 44). In Hemingway's The Sun Also Rises Jake Barnes wonders much the same thing but translates it into the homophobia that was never far from hand when he observes about homosexuals, "I was very angry. Somehow they always made me angry. I know they are supposed to be amusing, and you should be tolerant, but I wanted to swing on one, any one, anything to shatter that superior simpering composure." Barnes's expression of homosexual panic blinds him perhaps to the double possibilities to be read into his image of swinging on a homosexual. But the anger provoked by their simpering, their effeminacy, and their superior airs—the irritatingly distinguished air that McAlmon also sees in Foster Graham, who is constantly "nonchalantly poised and contained"—gives a clear hint as to the nature of mid-1920s homophobia.

Barnes does not care about sin or crime, he may not even be very interested in theories about sickness or insanity. What enrages him is style and the erasure of his notions of what a real man ought to be by the overwhelming efficiency and effeminacy of homosexual style. Not only do homosexuals carry off their own masquerade with seamless effectiveness, they seem to him, in the sheer bravado displayed in their manner, to "do" life itself better than he does. Barnes's irritation at gay superiority stems from the nagging suspicion—McAlmon's amazement over Graham's nonchalance—that what is supposed to be "natural" in him is, in comparison to the high theatricality of homosexual style, tarnished, inadequate, unreal. Whatever homosexuals were supposed to "be" according to "normal" definitions—lonely, loveless, sexually inadequate, and unfulfilled—is given the lie by a polished and proficient surface. The highly mirrored accomplishment of homosexual style reflects against Barnes's own life—one that seems in reflection to be drab and, indeed, lacking in any style at all. In the presence of homosexuality, heterosexuality becomes invisible, and gay people know it and let it be known that they know it.

McAlmon's book can claim to be a text that, if it does not originate, at least represents a significant moment in homosexual literary history. Just as *Imre* is the first full and positive portrayal of homosexuality in American fiction and *Bertram Cope's Year* the first to site homosexual relationships in modern American life and suggest that the protagonists may live happily ever after, McAlmon's stories are the first to reproduce in fiction the world that Jennie June has described in fact. My list of "firsts" is intended only to indicate certain early sites in which forms of homosexual identity can be found. The unapologetic completeness of McAlmon's picture shows how Miss Knight has invested identity and desire in her masquerade. Miss Knight is so far "out" that she creates new kinds of masquerades, the woman within worn flamboyantly on the body of the man without.

A SCARLET PANSY

McAlmon set the stories of *Distinguished Air* in decadent Europe because it was no doubt out of keeping with the he-man virility of America. He-men Americans like Jake Barnes and McAlmon's narrator tried "to be tolerant" but only barely repressed their homophobia. McAlmon had published Hemingway as well as his own work from his Contact Editions Press in

Paris, and though his narrator shares some of Barnes's prejudices and tone, the anger that makes Barnes want to "swing on" a homosexual is converted in McAlmon's book into a weary—and wary—tolerance. It may well be, however, that the grim author of these grim fairy tales may have allowed himself a pseudonymous lark, for some believe and there is slight evidence to suggest that one of the unacknowledged and funniest masterpieces of gay fiction, A Scarlet Pansy (1933),[10] may have been written by McAlmon under the name Robert Scully.

From the tone and scenes of the book it seems, as Austen has pointed out, "as if Scully had found a copy of The Autobiography of an Androgyne and yielded to a temptation to parody the adventures of Jennie June" (Austen, 63). Austen facetiously makes a useful point. Not only is the book set between 1900 and 1914, but the language and style suggest an earlier date. In fact, the narrator indicates that the story is being told shortly after the war, 15 years before the acknowledged publication date of 1933. Of course an author can set his book whenever he wants, but a book as transgressive as this may have had to wait more than a decade for publication. The absence of McAlmon's terse Hemingwayesque prose and the florid tone may be enough useful proof that the book is not by McAlmon at all. Like Miss Knight, however, who habitually shouts "Whoops, dearie!," Fay Etrange, the scarlet pansy of the title, also frequently uses that locution as well, and both Fay and Miss Knight delight in "lifting the veil" to shock the bourgeoisie. Also, each has a brother who is disgusted by her/his difference, and certain episodes in A Scarlet Pansy appear also in "Miss Knight."

Whether the book is by a pseudonymous Scully or a real McAlmon is mostly of interest to bibliophiles; what is of interest is the possibility that the story that McAlmon told in 1925 was recorded earlier in A Scarlet Pansy. If this is so, then A Scarlet Pansy is the earliest fiction to portray an American homosexual whose drag serves an even more radical and original purpose than that of Jennie June's daring masquerade and who is even more flamboyant than Miss Knight. Indeed, A Scarlet Pansy does seem almost to translate Jennie June's facts into fiction, save that A Scarlet Pansy transmutes Jennie's sometimes morose seriousness into wicked high camp. June, that self-created character, does have much in common with Fay Etrange. The world June inhabits and her descriptions of sexual customs often seem mirrored in A Scarlet Pansy, and June and Fay both are on the lookout for rough trade. Both are determined to confront rather than succumb to homophobia.

Fay Etrange (in whimsical French "strange fairy") inhabits a dubious world in which sex is the text's constant secret and in which gender is the constantly deconstructed and destabilized concept. The narrator never allows the truth about sex to be told. Instead, a play on gender conceals and verbal play denies access to whether Fay is—in the book's terms—male or female, a gendered "real man," a cross-gendered "fairie" or "pansy," or that most fabulous of all creatures, an (un)real woman. Though always referred to as "she," Fay plows fields with her brother and works harder than most men in a coal yard. Rather than plow the fields she "would have preferred to be with her mother doing womanly tasks, sewing, cooking, beautifying the home, but her father resented any such attempts"—to do what? Make a woman out of her? If she is "she" then where lies the resentment? "Thus the instincts that were normal to Fay were somewhat thwarted in her home life"—but what instincts are these? Only the "appropriate" ones for a woman, surely. "She" is frequently taunted by her brother Bill for "her manner of speech or her graceful movements—the antithesis of his boyish ideal" (Scully, 14–16).

Yet she must reproduce that boyish ideal when she plows the fields. How double edged this is, this hint at lisping speech and effeminate movements, surely not a boyish ideal. Yet why should she not be graceful, why should she not desire to do womanly things if she is indeed a woman? And her father's desire to prevent her from it—so as to do what? Make a man out of her? Reinforce "her" manliness by denying her womanly instincts? It is also clear that Fay is neither a baby June nor a mannish woman, as medical texts of the time were wont to call lesbians. By the time we reach this dizzying point all gender stereotypes have been parodied, and it is clear that this book is no mere lark but instead one that has a target fixed in its sights. The tongue of the narrator firmly in cheek needs little decoding to understand that stereotypes are being broken on every side and that sex, sexuality, and gender roles are the target. Doubly intending nearly every description and event, the narrator carries Fay through a series of eroticized adventures in which gender becomes a thing to be deconstructed and language is a vehicle to deceive.

After the first few chapters the narrator engages Fay in a more transgressive role. At one point Fay finds herself in New York. There "she lived a life of actualities and a dream life. In this dream life she was successful, financially at ease, the centre of a deferential admiring circle of people. Curiously she never pictured any real women in this circle. The avenue seemed full of gay people those days, persons as happy as she." The "real women" absent from her dreams of course define the truth of her reality, and that delicious misdirection—"persons as happy as she"—allows "gay people" quite possibly to enter the language of American fiction here for the first time if the book was written after the war. If we still wonder, the narrator adds to the conflation of "no real women" with "gay people" a third term that eroticizes the text: "At intervals were stationed the mounted policemen. Their splendid figures . . . the thigh outlined by the pressure against the horse's side all combined to make a picture which she found irresistibly appealing" (Scully, 104). These are "real men," and they will be the object of her search throughout the book. If the passage were to be emptied of all its content then the linear reading provides this linkage: no real women / gay people / real men. "Gay people" mediates and provides a bridge between no real women (who are men) and real men themselves.

This crucial passage constructs the equation that (un)real women = men = gay men. In terms of the seductions Fay undertakes, another equation can well read (un)real women (gay men) + real men = gay men. The equation can be carried one step further if it is presumed that desire is governed by some kind of principle of exchange, however unequal: that is, unreal women = gay men = real men = unreal women. Just as in Fay's dreams, there are no women in this book, and if she has her way, ultimately no nongay men either. Scully is proposing Fay-as-spectacle in a phantasmic deconstruction of the unexamined assumptions of heterosexist formulas for gender and sexual difference.

Fay's interest throughout the book as she moves from a small town in Pennsylvania and from there to Baltimore, Chicago, New York, Washington, San Francisco, and eventually Paris and Berlin is to find real men. To find them she frequents the streets as we have seen, goes to "fairy bars," dresses in "drag," and "cruises." In the process she encounters "pansies," "fairies," and "queens." She "camps" and "dishes" with her "sisters," comments on those who are "too obvious" and those who have just been "brought out." She loves to "drop her veil" in front of firemen, policemen, and soldiers, shouts "Whoops, dearie!" a great deal, in speech pretends to "lisp," and makes puns on "browning" and "going down." She goes to parties not only with fairies and queens but with "dikes" and "bulldikers," "butches" and "bitches." She is wryly aware that "this year's trade is next years competition" and cruises nationally, in places like Lafayette Park across from the White House; she picks up sailors on Riverside Drive in New York, meets men in the American West and in San Francisco, and internationally in Paris and Berlin, where she picks up sailors who admiringly say, "You are a real queen." She describes her friends as "Miss Kitty" or "Miss Ella" and makes visits with them to "tearooms" in New York. Like Whitman and Jennie June, she finds firemen, Irish cops, and street car conductors especially accommodating.

A Scarlet Pansy is a rich indicator of the availability of gay terms, a fictional mirror of gay life that reciprocally enlarges on scenes from both Lind and Mayne. It is also, quite simply, a very funny book. Bertram Cope's Year can be set against it, but the sheer inventive lunacy of A Scarlet Pansy makes it the first sustained site of high camp and homosexual satire in American fiction. Unlike the Jennie June texts and "Miss Knight," where homosexuality, drag/cross-dressing, and gender dubiety serve as confessional revelations or "serious" fictional portrayal, A Scarlet Pansy is far more radical, for it breaks gender boundaries but does not reinforce gender stereotypes. It does not insist that Fay is a woman trapped in the body of a man who succumbs passively to male conquest or victimization. Fay has no imprisoning restraints. Her behavior is a gender-breaking weapon she cheerfully uses in a deliberate attack on social conventions. Every policeman is ready for a fling with her, every soldier succumbs, and every sailor begs for her company.

Unlike Jennie June, however, who allowed herself to be victimized by them, Fay makes these real men her passive toys and in a sense erases their stereotyped masculinity by conquering it, bringing them to their knees before her triumphant otherness. Jennie June believes herself to be a woman. Fay knows precisely what she is and does not hesitate to use her remarkable intelligence and the spectacle of her consummate masquerade to seduce "real men" into situations so eroticized and emptied of sexual restraint and moral content that "real men" no longer care that she too is as much a "real" man as they. They are all powerless against her and indeed seem eager to give up their "masculine" roles. She seduces doctors, lawyers, bankers, and even ministers. When she conquers an American cowboy, masculine symbol of the American dream, it is clear that Fay's dreams have become synonymous with the nation's.

Fay is no good-hearted and charmingly illiterate Miss Knight, no mincing homosexual or pouting baby June. Not only can she can shovel coal and plow fields, but she is a financial and intellectual genius who creates a fortune for herself; earns several advanced degrees, including a medical degree; becomes a doctor; masters several languages; and independently travels all over the world, advocating freedom for her sex (whichever it may be), very much like the "New Woman" who was even then striking fear into the conservative hearts of real men. She ends up very rich in Paris on the eve of World War I. There she becomes a war hero(ine), a transgressive Florence Nightingale. She has met an American soldier—an incredibly handsome, football-playing, decent All-American boy, impeccably and extensively successful with women—who in the frenzy of wartime has become her lover. Patriotically unable to remain in Paris while American boys are fighting at the front, and while her own boy is there, she joins him, and in a hysterically poignant moment of high-camp melodrama, having taken the bullet meant for him, she dies in the arms of her Lieutenant Frank. Like all great American heroes, she dies for love and country.

Whenever A Scarlet Pansy was written, whether after the war or in the 1930s, it predicts resistance to a host of novels of the 1930s, 1940s, and 1950s that constructed homosexuals as perverted, passive, invariably sensitive, and weakly effeminate men who "walk in shadows" and inhabit "twilight worlds." What were described as "problem novels" of the 1930s anatomized homosexuality as an illness and generally condemned homosexuals to death or celibate isolation. Common to most of them was a somber, serious, and generally humorless presentation. A Scarlet Pansy, however, not only predicts but overturns every cliché. Fay is an active sexual subject, not a passive sexual object. Her questions go beyond "What or who am I?" to the more crucial and profound "What or who am I not?" She looks for the essential difference that marks and helps to define the boundaries of homosexual identity.

Fay breaches the barriers against homosexuality with sheer erotic bravado and sexual spectacle. Unlike the many homosexual men in later novels who are believed, like their real-life counterparts, to suffer from "gender confusion," Fay has no doubt about her identity: it is both "not real man" and "not real woman." For Fay, gay people, "all of them as happy as she," are all also as dangerous as she. In every sense Fay merges the world of real men into her own world, making it up as she goes along and sending it up even in the face of her policeman and the heterosexuals he guards. Dangerous Fay is ready to take him—take them all—on.

J. C. Leyandecker used his lover as the model for his "Arrow Shirt Man" illustrations of the 1940s.

chapter 13

SINISTER DECADENCE: HOMOPHOBIA, PATRIOTISM, AND AMERICAN MANHOOD, 1933–1950

There are ten million male and female "queers" in this country. . . . There is something terribly sinister in this decadence—in this repulsive suggestion of senility and impotence. It is so out of keeping with the lusty traditions, the he-man virility of our country.

—Dr. James Segall, "Inversions and Perversions" (1934)

In 1933 an advertisement for a book by Dr. La Forrest Potter called *Strange Loves: A Study in Sexual Abnormalities* luridly warned, "Do you know what really goes on among the men and women of the Shadow World? Do you know that their number is constantly increasing? The strange power they wield over normal people is almost unbelievable" (quoted in Austen, 58). At one point in the book Dr. Potter looked back on the impeccable sexual climate of prewar America and nostalgically recalled, "Before the war we used to consider homosexuality as a more or less foreign importation. We regarded ourselves as the true exponents of the sane and uncompromising traditions of our pioneer ancestors. . . . All those foreigners who were fortunate to have been permitted entrance to our shores, so we thought, were leavened by our practical matter-of-factness. The dross of abnormal desire—assuming that they may have been thus infested when they landed in this country—was burned away in the melting pot of our staunch masculine or commendably feminine characteristics."[1]

Dr. Potter's clichés resonate against the common currency of homophobic texts of the period and centuries before. He deploys the familiar accusations and links homosexuality not only with the destruction of what he suggests are virtually nationally encoded gender roles but clearly implies that homosexuality and homosexuals are effectively un-American. Because of the "infestation" of homosexuality, however, the pioneer and heterosexual American virtues have been weakened and now the danger is clear and increasingly present: "Today there are homosexual 'joints,' 'queer' clubs, pervert 'drags' or homosexual plays in practically every considerable American city." Not only general society but American youth has been tainted by homosexuals, for "today there is scarcely a schoolboy who doesn't know what a 'pansy' is" (Potter, 4–5)

If his readers were in doubt about what every schoolboy apparently could easily recognize, Dr. Potter gives a sketch to help define the "born homosexual" whose differences should be obvious "to his family, and to all informed persons with whom he may come in contact. These characteristics, or differences, may be noticed from an early age and ought to be the subject of surveillance and possibly alteration. "The 'girlishness' of the male homosexual, or the 'boyishness' of the female invert" are symptoms, Dr. Potter warns, that if still manifest after age 14 "will bear watching." If a boy is "deeply interested in cutting out paper dolls or embroidering his initials on his pocket handkerchiefs" then steps may be taken—"the proper kind of suggestion, gland stimuli, endocrine treatment and direction"—to make "men of their boys and women of their daughters" (Potter, 93–96).

Dr. Potter's concern that homosexuality has undermined American virtue predicts an intense and anxious reading of homosexuality as un-American in the years between 1933 and Stonewall, a reading that will be most spectacularly translated into the political arena in the 1950s in the destructive attacks that link communism and homosexuality mounted by Senator Joseph McCarthy and his aide Roy Cohn, our most notoriously homophobic homosexual, and in the smaller though equally combative theater of American literary criticism where homophobia will masquerade as judgment in the hands of a number of American critics, who will argue that homosexuality can have no place in the American literary tradition. It would be comforting to be able to say that it is some indication of how far we have come since Stonewall that sentiments like Dr. Potter's ought now to be laughable. With little change, however, they represent opinions accepted and espoused still by many who are neither powerless nor sympathetic. What Dr. Potter said in 1933 only indicates how little the homophobic discourse changes, and the chilling familiarity of it tells us how far we have yet to go.

Mayne observed in 1908 that despite the "enormous diffusion of Uranianism and of similisexual intercourse in the United States," Americans knew little about homosexuality: "as to popular literature in the vernacular to aid the American Uranian to understand his own case or to understand the conditions of similisexualism in other countries, this is still eminently lacking. The topic of similisexualism is tabu in the United States and in Canada, except through observations by and for medical students and physicians" (Mayne 1908, 638). What American's nonhomosexual public knew about homosexuality in 1908 was a compound formed from popular mythology, usually anti-homosexual medical texts, and (perhaps) the visible presence of cross-dressing homosexuals like Jennie June in some large cities.

A report by a Chicago commission appointed to study sexual perversion in 1911 perhaps accurately reported what it discovered but also anatomized what was generally believed about homosexuals:

> It appears that in this community there is a large number of men . . . who mostly affect the carriage, mannerisms, and speech of women; who are fond of many articles ordinarily dear to the feminine heart; who are often people of a good deal of talent; who lean to the fantastic in dress and other modes of expression, and who have a definite cult with regard to sexual life. They preach the value of non-association with women from various standpoints and yet have practices which are nauseous and repulsive. Many of them speak of themselves or each other with the adoption of feminine terms, and go by girls' names or fantastic application of women's titles. They have a particular vocabulary and signs of recognition of their own, which serve as introduction to their own society. The cult has produced some literature, much of which is incomprehensible to one who cannot read between the lines, and there is considerable distribution among them of pernicious photographs. (quoted in Katz 1983, 335)

The report notes that the commission was "unable to gain entrance into the circles of the well-to-do which are engaged in these practices, nor did they concern themselves with the lowest stratum of society which is the class most observable in our courts" (quoted in Katz 1983, 335). Police infiltration into the kinds of circles in which Jennie June and Fay Etrange moved, together with their highlighting of "well-to-do" and criminal classes suggests that the police concluded that homosexuality was prevalent in all classes. Lind/June's report of the membership of the Cercle Hermaphroditos hints that many of them, like Lind/June, were members of professional and educated groups that the Chicago police might well have described as the "respectable classes."

Mayne points out that the circulation between classes was perhaps not as difficult for homosexuals as it was for the police: "the thousand and one homosexual ties in social life—of all grades—between high-natured, respectable and moral types of American young men, or between types lower in the intellectual and ethical scale, are to be traced everywhere." Perhaps Mayne is simply documenting what Whitman had discovered, that in "the midnight orgies of young men" desire storms the barricades of class.

Texts intended to warn the public against the dangers of the newly identified homosexual were increasingly available to many more than just physicians and medical students. In his book of sexual advice *Confidential Chats with Boys* (1911), Dr. William Howard warns,

> Never trust yourself in bed with a boy or a man. No matter if you are so situated that there is only one bed to be had. Sleep on the floor. . . . There are

things in trousers called men, so vile that they wait in hiding for the innocent boy. These things are generally well-dressed, well mannered—too well
mannered in fact—and pass as gentlemen. . . . Look out for these vermin,
be suspicious of any man in trousers who avoids real men, who never takes
interest in manly sports, who tries to see you alone and prefers to go
bathing with boys instead of men. They are only waiting to teach boys to
help them in self-abuse or something far nastier. . . . If you should be so situated that you find yourself in bed with a man, keep awake with your eyes
on something you can hit him with. At the slightest word or act out of the
way, HIT him. (quoted in Katz 1983, 337—38)

The insinuation of that "too well mannered" helps to construct the twentieth-century effeminate homosexual predator whose forte is the molestation
of boys and who is an appropriate subject for homophobic violence, a national sport to the prevalence of which Jennie June has attested and which is
here justified by Dr. Howard's exhortation to gay-bashing—"HIT him"—in
defense of manliness and virtue.

The self-abuse that such men are ever ready to help boys master is only
exceeded in horror by the "something far nastier" that Dr. Howard intimates
that they might propose. What that something is Dr. Francis Shockley suggests in a 1913 essay about the relationship he saw between homosexuality
and paranoia. He outlines the specific result of sleeping with men as told by
one of his patients, a man called X, who, because of a large number of guests
at his house, had one night to share a bed with "a clergyman of considerable
prominence." During the night the clergyman "attempted to hold perverted
relations" with X. Before this X had displayed "paranoid" symptoms, including the conviction that his wife and friends were "acting peculiarly toward
him." After his homosexual experience "X gave himself up to many relations
with males. His interest in life returned, and the depression rapidly gave way
to contentment, which enabled him to progress rapidly with his work." That
X discovers that having homosexual relations cures depression may seem all
to the good.

Dr. Shockley is constrained to warn, however, that even though
"absolutely no deterioration of intellect" could be discerned in this "quiet,
well-dressed man of rather youthful and masculine appearance" who no "one
would have considered . . . in any way effeminate"—a type that Dr. Howard
may not have counted on—yet he did find "sexual gratification in the feminine role of fellatio." Dr. Shockley finally seems less interested in whatever
beneficial effects homosexual sex had for X and concentrates instead on the
horror he associates with performing in a "feminine role." Penetration may
suggest effeminization of the male to Dr. Shockley. Katz speculates also that
"this act was evidently considered feminine because it was judged to be
demeaning—thus the role of the female" (Katz 1983, 343).

Before he gave himself up to relations with men, Dr. Shockley's patient
might have agreed in principle with Dr. William Robinson who, in 1914,
argued that homosexuality is a "sad, deplorable, pathological phenomenon,"

and that homosexuals "showed a distinct inferiority to the normal man."
Because X was demonstrably better off after "perverted" sex than before it,
however, he might have debated Dr. Robinson's point that "homosexuals are
not satisfied with their condition and would give a good deal to get rid of it,"
since they "considered their condition a very great punishment, though some
were resigned to it." We cannot be sure if X's contentment shook Dr.
Shockley's conviction that nothing was so appalling as taking the feminine
role in anything, but we can infer what Drs. Shockley and Robinson might
conclude from Mayne's history of an American who, worried about homosexuality, confided in a European friend who "was perfectly satisfied with his
own psychic organization. He told [him] that he was 'foolish to worry,' that
'thousands of men were so,' and that it was only a question of concealment
and custom" (Mayne, 92–93).

The worried American could not accept so cosmopolitan an answer, and
Mayne details a tragic story of depression, loneliness, attempted suicide, nervous collapse, and concealment, furnished Mayne says from the journal of an
American physician. The story Mayne repeats could well serve as the plot for
a homosexual novel like *Strange Brother* or *Twilight Men* or one of Drs.
Shockley or Robinson's case histories. That the life of Mayne's unhappy subject may well be also a consequential construction influenced by the kind of
texts and homophobic attitudes represented by the writings of Drs. Howard
and Shockley is open to question but a real possibility.

World War I internationalized homosexuality. When Alfred Adler's essay
"The Homosexual Problem" appeared in English translation in 1917, it carried with it the weight of new science and suggested that since the war
homosexuality was not simply more obvious but was actually increasing.
Adler, with Jung and Freud an expositor of psychoanalytic theory, asserted
that "the barriers of society against the toleration of perversion remain
unshaken by every theory" that attempted to explain or advocate homosexuality, for these barriers are built on "the safeguards and disinclinations of normal feelings." Homosexuals, Adler asserted, show "an active hostility to
society" and are ready to take "hostile measures" against the "requirements of
social life" as represented by the "normal sexual act." The homosexual feels
"inferior to women" and indeed homosexuality itself is a "flight from
women." The homosexual attempts to justify his perversion by establishing
"the irresponsibility of his conduct"; his "low self-esteem," lack of "constraint," and "cowardice" brand him as a social misfit. Adler observed a "sinister often well concealed obstinacy" that revealed the homosexual's
unwillingness to be "cured." The only "concession" society ought to make to
the homosexual is "concealment and noninterference" (quoted in Katz 1983,
374–77).

Adler's diatribe is an egregious example of homophobia masquerading as
science, and it is also nearly a checklist—inferiority, cowardice, hostility,
lack of constraint, fear of women—of the characteristics that will be ascribed
to the homosexual and featured as "scientific truth" in novels written after

World War I. The dangerous increase in homosexuality defined not as a problem for the doctor in his study but for decent folk on the streets is as inherent in Adler's remarks as it is obvious in Dr. E. S. Shepherd's observation that "our streets and beaches are overrun by male prostitutes (fairies)." He argues that many "intermediates" should not be judged by their "lowest manifestations" and assumes that among their number there may be "a number of valuable citizens." These are few, he implies, but science may yet discover a way to "put us in a position to salvage many who are socially worthless" (quoted in Katz 1983, 379–80).

Dr. Shepherd's article is actually intended to be a rebuttal of one by Dr. Robinson, who had apparently suggested that society might be better off if homosexuals were eliminated. Dr. Shepherd allowed that "one is frequently tempted to agree" with the elimination save that "such wholesale elimination" might remove "a number of valuable citizens." Though Dr. Shepherd was seemingly sympathetic to homosexuals, underlying his sympathy is the presumption that most homosexuals are socially worthless.

The social worth of inverts was of special interest to—and generated considerable anxiety within—the military after World War I. In the 1918 article "Homosexuality—a Military Menace," written to help the U.S. Army recognize homosexuals, Dr. Albert Abrams reported that a raid on a San Francisco "vice club" and the "gruesome revelations pertaining to this club of homosexualists invited the attention of the military authorities, who saw the corruption that must necessarily ensue among the soldiery if it were not summarily suppressed." It is obvious to Dr. Abrams that "in recruiting the elements which make up our invincible army we cannot ignore what is obvious and which will militate against the combative prowess of our forces." This prowess will be adversely affected, he argues, because "from a military point of view the homosexualist is not only dangerous but ineffective as a fighter." If Dr. Abrams's logic is spun out, the homosexual's weakness will prevent him from conquering the enemy, but his sexual power will allow him an easy triumph over the American fighting man. Dr. Abrams's anxiety reflects and establishes the terms of the battle the army would continue to wage against its own. As recent history shows, this war rages still.

In 1919 the U.S. Navy investigated conditions at the Naval Training Station at Newport, Rhode Island, where rumors circulated of homosexual conduct at the base and between civilians and sailors. A later commission investigated the investigators and discovered that "the investigators, while acting as decoys to trap perverts, had several times engaged in sodomy." It was alleged that the investigators had "used highly improper and revolting methods in getting evidence"—namely, seduction and entrapment of known civilian "queers" and known homosexual sailors. The decoys were asked by their superiors to "use their own discretion and judgement whether they should or should not actually permit to be performed upon them immoral acts" (Chauncey, 294). In addition, a respected member of the Newport clergy was accused of facilitating homosexual contacts. The minister was prose-cuted but acquitted.

The navy did not prosecute the decoys or any sailors known to have been "serviced" by "queers," even though they may have initiated the sex, and only attempted to prosecute in conjunction with the civil court known homosexuals whether sailors or civilians. The distinction made between get-ting and giving was one that may not have been lost on the charitable phi-losophy of the man of God, and it remains a marker in popular myth to distinguish the "real" and "practicing" homosexual from the innocent male who was usually "too drunk last night" to know that practice can lead to per-fection. The navy's entrapment of homosexuals in 1919 forecasts a military policy constant until this writing and forecasts also the public witch hunts staged by the U.S. government against civilians in the 1950s, against which a small group of homosexuals would mount not only literary but organized political and social resistance.

In 1926 Dr. Joseph Collins published *The Doctor Looks at Love and Life*, a book much reviewed and one of the earliest popular books to look at homo-sexuality in a somewhat less punitive fashion than previous texts. Dr. Collins was willing to admit that homosexuality "has been in existence as long as man has" and quite perceptively notes that "it will probably be difficult to convince the generation succeeding ours that . . . it was improper to utter the word homosexuality, prurient to admit its existence and pornographic to dis-cuss the subject. It was proper to read novels in which it was treated more or less openly if the setting was European; decadent people in decadent coun-tries. Here, if it existed at all, it could not flourish, our soil is unfavorable, our climate prejudicial, our people too primitive, too pure" (quoted in Katz 1983, 429).

Dr. Collins's assessment for succeeding generations sharply defined his own, though his attitude toward homosexuality seems at first somewhat unusual for his time. He admits that "the majority of homosexuals are not degenerates" and claims "to have known many well-balanced homosexuals of both sexes." But when he confronts homosexual claims to "superior intellec-tuality and affectivity" or when he sees them "point with pride at their mem-bership list" of famous homosexuals, Dr. Collins fulminates that "their claim has no justification." Though he hopes to "convince the majority of my read-ers that Urnings are not monsters in human form" he does so by arguing that "they are to be the most pitied of all nature's misfits."

Dr. Collins claims to have known homosexuals who are "husky, articu-late, self-opinionated and even domineering." Lest his readers worry about the possibility of too many domineering and undetectable homosexuals loose in the streets, Dr. Collins assures them that homosexuals "are not nature's elect, but deviates who will one day disappear from the world when we shall have guessed the last riddle of the sympathetic nervous system and the duct-less glands" (quoted in Katz 1983, 429). Despite its disclaimers of "understanding" and appeals for "toleration," Dr. Collins's book is a common homophobic text. Like Drs. Robinson and Shepherd, he concludes that the eventual elimination of homosexuals will be all for the good of society.

As the work of Freud and psychoanalysis gained ground after the war, homosexuals increasingly were made subject to the disorders that psychoanalysis was inventing in order to construct paradigms of the normal and the abnormal: paranoia, neurosis, and arrested sexual development. Late nineteenth-century theories that saw homosexuality as congenital and perhaps physiological were giving way to the idea that homosexuality was an abnormal condition potentially curable. The presumed polarity between "homosexual" and "heterosexual" began to be firmly established in popular discourse by the late 1920s, with "homosexuality" first being used in the *New York Times* in 1925 and "heterosexual" not appearing there until 1930, when a reviewer of André Gide's *Immoralist* referred to Michael as proceeding from a "heterosexual liaison to a homosexual one." By the late 1920s public perception that homosexuality was somehow the diametric opposite of heterosexuality was being shaped by such comments as those by Dr. Robinson, who in 1925 affirmed what perhaps everyone wanted to believe: "Homosexuals are mentally, morally, and physically different from normally sexed men and women" (quoted in Katz 1983, 425).

The psychoanalyst Dr. Clarence Oberndorf announced that the "male homosexual may be annoyed by the social hazards of his perversion and seek some means for escaping from the ostracism and legal jeopardy, but rarely wishes to be cured when he appreciates that the cure involves relinquishing the inversion" (quoted Katz 1983, 458–59). Thus the abnormal homosexual was set against the normal heterosexual, an exemplary creature that the homosexual could, should he wish to, become. Because of their willful refusal to embrace what was becoming compulsory heterosexuality, then, as Dr. John Meagher warned in 1929, "if the pervert homosexual insists on not following advice, he knows society's attitude and must bear the responsibility for his conduct" (quoted in Katz 1983, 458).

The threat implicit in Dr. Meagher's comment predicts the appearance of officially sanctioned homophobia and increased violence against homosexuals. Such violence seemed to have become the norm, as illustrated in an April 1929 raid on a New York City bath house by the city's police. This description of the raid may be the first eyewitness report—by a German visitor—of official violence against homosexuals and of blatant and homophobic police brutality:

> All at once there's a whistle, someone yells Hallo, and everyone has to go out in the front room. The baths is locked shut. Various people were struck down, kicked, in short the brutality of these officials was simply indescribable. A Swede standing next to me . . . got hit so that two of his ribs were broken. . . . Ten more policemen arrived. . . . Everyone . . . was put in the paddy wagon . . . taken to the station and jailed. By noon on Sunday we

appeared before the magistrate's court . . . and were charged with things we hadn't done. All the fifty-five people there were fined ten dollars or two days in the workhouse, except for four who were sentenced to six months, three weeks, two weeks, and one month. . . . It's probably fair to say that there's more freedom in every European country, especially German and France, than in the famous and infamous U.S.A. (quoted in Katz 1983, 453)

In 1933 Magnus Hirschfeld's Institute for Sexual Sciences in Berlin, from which Hirschfeld had conducted his crusade for homosexual emancipation, was raided by Nazi youth and much of his archival material destroyed or dispersed, marking the beginning of the Nazi offensive against homosexuality. The U.S. Army, however, had been by this time routinely investigating homosexuals for more than a decade. By 1937 the FBI had begun to collect its private files on known or suspected homosexuals in public life—among them some that implied that the master collector, J. Edgar Hoover himself, was homosexual.

In 1936 a small incident reported in the *New York Times* suggested that Nazi brownshirts might have adopted a new uniform in the United States. They called themselves the White Legion. As the *Times* reported,

A shouting jeering mob, about 100 men and women, severely beat William Haines, former motion picture star, and Jimmie Shields, a companion, near Manhattan Beach, and drove them and nineteen friends out of town. . . . At his antique and interior decorating shop in Hollywood. . . . Mr. Haines declared he did not know the reason for the mob's acts. "It was a lynch mob alright," he said. "Some wild or untrue rumor must have stirred them up. It might have been some sort of clan or secret organization." Several men in the Manhattan Beach area said today they were members of an organization known as the White Legion and that they aided in the demonstration. Others openly boasted on the streets of participating in the disturbance. (quoted in Katz 1983, 523)

Whereas the "wild or untrue rumor" goes unreported in the *Times*, the seeming objectivity of the identification of Haines as an "antique and interior decorating shop" proprietor with a "companion" might give some readers a clue if not to the nature of the rumor than to the nature of the men. The subtle marking of Haines as homosexual by associating him with clichés about homosexuals hints at the real cause of the attack. The rumor about Haines produced for him much the same result that a similar rumor did for Wing Biddlebaum in Anderson's "Hands" or for Horatio Alger, who was also run out of town on suspicion of having "unnatural relations" with boys.

By the time of Haines's attack in 1936, homosexuality was becoming more than just a subject spoken about indirectly. In the 1938 movie *Bringing up Baby* Cary Grant, dressed in a woman's housecoat, explained his choice of clothes "because I just went gay all of a sudden," and both homosexuality and "gay" became the possession of the general public. Going gay may have not been all that sudden, but it was still too sudden for the *Times* reviewer, who objected that the script was filled with objectionable and suspicious clichés "like the one about the man wearing a woman's negligee" (quoted in Katz 1983, 537). Newspapers had by then been reviewing with some regularity though often negatively books, plays, and a few movies with homosexual themes. Between 1938 and 1941 the *Times* reviewed nearly a dozen books dealing with male and female homosexuality. In 1941 F. A. McHenry called for American journalists to be less circumspect in their reportage of homosexuality, especially of crimes against homosexuals, and urged that because the homosexual "suffers intensely from social ostracism" homosexuality should not be presented in the press as "an overt offense against the community." By 1948 "the homosexual" for good or ill had become newsworthy to the press, though the coverage still usually involved unspecific reports of the murders of homosexuals, speculations that homosexuals were involved in espionage against the United States, or negative reviews of books about homosexuals.

When the Alfred Kinsey's *Sexual Behavior in the Human Male* (the "Kinsey Report") appeared in 1948, however, homosexuality entered spectacularly into mainstream consciousness, so much so that *Parents' Magazine* felt called upon to respond to the report's finding that 37 percent of the male population had some homosexual experience between adolescence and old age and that 4 percent to 10 percent of American men were exclusively homosexual. *Parents' Magazine* insisted that "homosexuals are not born—they are made." "Homosexuality," the magazine reported, "is not a reflection on sex but only a sign that it has been diverted into the wrong channels, according to our social and cultural standards." These standards "are the monogamous ones of marriage and the establishment of a family." Homosexuality runs counter to these standards and homosexuals often "find themselves in dark alleys and dead end streets seeking expression for their instinctual drives in socially unacceptable ways."

Ignoring the logic that finds homosexuality at once constructed—made, not born—and instinctual, this commentary now sites homosexuality in a new and modern realm. No longer the product of congenital inversion, no longer the irresponsible plaything of a mysterious biological destiny—unless of course they are not, as might say Gore Vidal, who was then publishing his homosexual novel *The City and the Pillar* that speculated on just these questions—the homosexual was instead a product of the American home and hearth. If homosexuals were made in America, it was now the responsibility of heterosexual parents to keep a watchful eye out for tell-tale signs, forgetting or ignoring the implicit indictment that was brought against them and what they stood for if their daughter or son did suddenly go gay.

Perhaps sensitive to the feelings of parents who might have to face this possibility, *Parents' Magazine* called for pity, not punishment, as homosexuals "through no fault of their own have been unable to fall in love with a person of the opposite sex" even though they "would like to if they could."

Homosexuality "is not wicked or unfortunate since it is often sterile instead of creative." That homosexuals are presumably unable to have "meaningful" adult heterosexual relationships is seen to be a symptom of their emotional sterility. The exclusive linkage of heterosexual desire and fecundity with creativity is one of the most significant though muddled theses to be found in American homophobic texts. It is also an idea that resonates against the primary objection to homoerotic literature raised by critics in the 1950s and 1960s—that homosexual texts are in some sense lesser art. If homosexuals cannot find heterosexual love, then it follows that they must be emotionally sterile, and if emotionally sterile, then aesthetically uncreative. It is an easy jump to the presumption that gay literature must also suffer from the same sterile and uncreative disability that afflicts its authors.

Parents' Magazine promoted an image of homosexuals as sterile and uncreative members of society and fostered the idea that they were more to be pitied than feared. Other magazines soon took arms against Kinsey's implication that homosexuality was perhaps not a foreign import at all but part of the very fabric of the republic. *Time* magazine—soon to be known for its virulently homophobic position—published the opinions of Dr. Lawrence Kubie, a psychiatrist, who argued that Kinsey's "implication that because homosexuality is prevalent we must accept it as 'normal' or as a happy and healthy way of life, is wholly unwarranted" (quoted in Katz 1983, 630–33).

Before Kinsey attempted to dispel myths and prejudices against homosexuality, a 1941 book called *Sex Variants* by Dr. George Henry repeated for the twentieth century what Ellis and Symonds had done for the nineteenth and presented detailed "case studies" of nearly 100 homosexual women and men. Like Kinsey, Dr. Henry was concerned not only to objectively report his observations but also to confront what he described as "rigid standards of human conduct to which we profess to adhere" that "hamper us in approaching" the study of sex in general and of homosexuality in particular. Dr. Henry not only confronted rigid standards—by which he meant prejudice—but also tried to undermine stereotypes. As he says, "There are strong indications . . . that there are no two homosexuals alike and that homosexuality is associated with an almost endless variety and complexity of human problems."[2] While he still cites homosexuality as a "problem," he sees that it may be a problem created not by the homosexual but by society, and he is among the first to recognize what the "Kinsey Report" of 1978—subtitled "Diversity among Men and Women"—would assert.

Dr. Henry is determined to counter "the prejudice and misinformation [that] have been for centuries associated with what has been commonly termed sexual perversion" (Henry, ix). Because of this prejudice "little progress has been made in understanding and dealing with the problem." Dr. Henry's general assessment of attempts is probably accurate, though his well-intended generalization does not take into account the work done by homosexuals themselves, which has been the subject of this study. In 1948 Dr. Henry warned that what advance had been made in the study of homosexuality and what change had been accomplished in the "attitudes of prominent citizens and leaders in public life" with regard to "a better understanding of the sex variant" has not been equalled by a change in the attitudes of general society. He supports this assertion with a detailed account of the persecution of some 30 homosexuals as the result of a crusade against vice that took place "in a large residential community."

Dr. Henry urges that the persecution, which involved surveillance, entrapment, and arrest, often on spurious information, was the result of "justice tempered with ignorance and prejudice." It was, he says, the response "of persons . . . whose righteous indignation over the discovery of a sex variant in their midst [led] to action which is reminiscent of witch hunting" (Henry, xv). Dr. Henry may have perhaps been too sanguine both about the greater tolerance he detected among prominent people and leaders and in his assumption that the righteous indignation and its dreadful consequences— the ruin of the reputations and the suicide of some of the accused—represented only "the behavior of a minority of persons in some communities."

Dr. Henry published a single-volume edition of the book in 1948 intended for a wider and more popular audience. The next year *Newsweek* perhaps spoke for the majority of Americans whose opinions it professed to represent as well as shape. In an essay entitled "Queer People" *Newsweek* pointed out that "the sex pervert, whether a homosexual, an exhibitionist, or even a dangerous sadist, is too often regarded merely as a 'queer' person who never hurts anyone but himself. Then the mangled form of some victim focuses public attention on the degenerate's work." *Newsweek* makes a bow to medicine and "compassion" when it urges that the degenerate—a term under which it has conflated all homosexuals—may be "brought to the realization of the error of his ways" by psychiatric rehabilitation. But the damage has been done. Morality and homophobia can now walk hand in hand, for "a sterner attitude is required if the degenerate is to be properly treated and cured . . . the sex pervert [ought to] be treated not as a coddled patient, but as a particularly virulent type of criminal" (quoted in Katz 1983, 652).

All these writers were, of course, typical of their time—a time when it was not imagined that homosexuals could be or should be cast in a positive light, and when no one—certainly no prominent citizen or leader—had spoken in the media to which these writers had access in defense of homosexuality. If something like homophobia was theorized at all, it was theorized (even though the word was not used) as the only appropriate response to what was also unanimously called "perversion." I have used the word "homophobia" throughout this study even though it has no currency during much of the time about which I have written. It can, however, be seen how textual constructions of homosexuals simultaneously constructed homophobia.

After World War II suspicion of homosexuality ignited one of the most appalling public episodes of homosexual persecution and homophobic panic ever to have been seen in America. Between 1950 and 1955 the government investigated its own employees, members of the armed forces, and some people outside the government in an attempt to link their suspected political beliefs with suspicions of homosexuality. Communism or homosexuality—known, suspected, alleged, and often simply fabricated—caused these people to be "security risks." By the time the campaign was finished, the image of the homosexual as dangerous to the state, disloyal to the nation, and a political as well as sexual menace to society was added to all the previous imputations of social undesirability.

In 1950 a *New York Times* article signalled the beginning of the story when it indicated that inquiries were under way to establish just what percentage of government personnel had resigned because of investigation as security risks. The article reported that many who had resigned "were homosexuals." A few weeks later Senator Joseph McCarthy alleged in the Senate that the State Department contained a "flagrantly homosexual" employee who was at risk because of the possibility of blackmail. In April 1950 the *Times* reported that the Republican national chairman asserted that "sexual perverts who have infiltrated our government in recent years" were "perhaps as dangerous as the actual communists" (quoted in Katz 1976, 92). In May a private study by the senators from Nebraska and Alabama alleged that, according to the Washington Vice Squad, more than 3,500 "perverts" were employed by the government. When asked about his sources, the vice officer, Lieutenant Ray Blick, said that his information was a "quick guess" based on his experience that when a homosexual was arrested he would often implicate others whose names were then added to the lists of known homosexuals being kept by the Washington police.

When Blick was later interviewed by Max Lerner in an attempt to pinpoint the accuracy of his estimates, Lerner asked how he arrived at the number. Blick asserted that "since every one of these fellows [arrested] has friends" whose names under pressure they sometimes disclosed, he compiled his list in part by putting on it named friends and in part by multiplying "the list by a certain percentage—say three or four percent." Lerner asked if this meant that his list was under 200 and he multiplied it by 25 or 30. Blick responded that it was larger and said he meant "I multiply my list by 5," to which Lerner responded, "Does this mean your list is a thousand?" Blick could not answer his question. When pressed Blick was unable to justify his estimate. The incredible farce of this account does not mitigate the tragedy that Blick's imaginary numbers would precipitate as the Senate pursued its investigations. As Lerner commented, "This was how a statistic got to be born."

By December 1950 the government issued a document on the "Employment of Homosexuals and Other Sex Perverts in Government." The *Times* described the conclusions of the report, which "labeled sexual perverts today as dangerous security risks and demanded strict control and careful screening to keep them off the Government payroll." The *Times* reported the committee as saying that "the lack of emotional stability which is found in most sex perverts and the weakness of their moral fibre makes them susceptible to the blandishments of foreign espionage agents" and "easy prey to blackmailers."

In 1951 in their muck-raking book *Washington Confidential*, Jack Lait and Lee Mortimer summed up in a chapter called "A Garden of Pansies" the prevailing popular beliefs that could only have become more firmly entrenched by the Washington procedures against homosexuals: "The only way to get authoritative data on fairies is from the other fairies. They recognize each other by a fifth sense immediately. . . . Some are deceptive to the uninitiated. But they all know one another and have a grapevine of intercommunication. Since they have no use for women . . . and are uneasy with masculine men, they have a fierce urge. . . for each other's society. They have their own hangouts . . . and cling together in a tight union of interest and behavior. Not all are ashamed of the trick that nature had played on them. They have their leaders, unabashed, who are proud queens who revel in their realm" (quoted in Katz 1976, 100).

Lait and Mortimer raise here the most frightening characteristic of the homosexual, one that has been hinted at in some earlier texts: though some are obvious, many, perhaps even most, are "deceptive to the uninitiated." Lait and Mortimer also invoke another specter—that of organized homosexuality, which had also been a feature of earlier homophobic constructions. This supposed organization would be dubbed the "homintern," a play on the secret Comintern that was supposed to control the evil empire of communism. The equally "evil empire" of homosexuality, Lait and Mortimer suggest, had spread its tentacles into every corner of the nation: "With more than 6,000 fairies in government offices, you may be concerned about the security of the country" (quoted in Katz 1976, 101).

The authors reported that a Congressman Miller, "author of the District's new bill to regulate homos," assured them that foreign agents were "given a course in homosexuality, then taught to infiltrate in perverted circles." By January 1955 more than 8,000 people were separated from their government jobs as security risks, of which more than 600 were described as being involved in "sex perversion." It was not reported in the *Times* or anywhere else until 1974 that the columnist Drew Pearson mentioned in his diary that Senator McCarthy, whose accusations began the witch hunt, had been linked by rumor to homosexual activity. Roy Cohn, McCarthy's agent provocateur, concealed his homosexuality throughout his life, denying it even in death.

In 1969, on the eve of Stonewall, Sara Harris published a book called *The Puritan Jungle: America's Sexual Underground*. Harris interviewed a cross-section of "lesbians, homosexuals, hustlers, vice cops, alcoholics, sadists, masochists, transvestites, wife swappers, and the wives they swap." In one interview, she asked John Sorenson, a Baptist deacon and former head of the Miami Vice Squad, how he felt about homosexuality. Sorenson replied, "I would rather see any of my children dead than homosexual. . . . I feel there is no cure because of the complete degeneracy of these people. They appear on the surface to be respectable, but they're the lowest forms of people." Homosexuals should be regulated, because no matter what they do in private, Sorenson asserts, sooner or later "they have to come out of that room and they may be school teachers." When asked if the law should include the death penalty for homosexuality, Harris replied with conviction, "If homosexuality could be a reason for the death penalty, you would see almost a stop to the whole thing" (quoted in Katz 1976, 123–24).

Near the end of the witch hunts in Washington articles appearing in journals intended for public and medical consumption suggested that electric shock therapy, castration, aversion therapy, lobotomy, and incarceration in what were still called insane asylums might well control or alter sexual perverts—a group that now included anyone homosexual. The record of experimentation on gay people in America from the early 1920s to the mid-1970s in order to change or cure homosexuality is an appalling, horrific, and criminal episode in the annals of medicine. A moving and horrifying account of the institutional torture visited on one gay man can be discovered in Jonathan Ned Katz's *Gay American History*. There Katz reports the first person account of a young man who was, in 1964, committed to a mental hospital by his parents in order to undergo shock therapy to cure his homosexuality. For two and a half years he underwent the therapy. When he was finally discharged, he was, as he said, subject to "the most severe depression after shock treatment . . . it just seemed so hopeless."

Suffering from loss of memory he "never knew if I would be able to connect my thoughts." Amnesia happened "maybe a thousand times. And you never know how long it will last." The therapy damaged his memory but not his homosexuality or his determination to be what he knew no therapy could change. During a therapy session after the shock treatments he recalls an explosive scene: "At one session they brought up the gay issue. We always went for the main problems we were supposed to be there for. I said it was not a problem for me. They said 'don't you think you're abnormal thinking you can have feelings for males as well as females?' I said 'No. I think you could be subnormal for not being able to have those feelings.' The doctor says, 'I think we got him too late'" (quoted in Katz 1976, 205).

Happily, they did not get him, and as he knew, neither late nor early was the issue. His resounding "No" resonates against Jennie June's brave conviction that the time had come to join an organization of like-minded people to resist homophobia and the "world's bitter persecution." It revivifies the story of other men and women whose resounding "No" informs the history of organized American resistance to homosexual oppression that begins with Jennie June at the birth of the century and comes to a symbolic though ultimately pragmatic climax in the chant that now sounds in unison with the cadenced march at every gay pride parade—a chant that reminds the nation, indeed demands of it, that homophobia has got to go.

chapter 14

INVENTING OURSELVES: GAY AMERICANS
AND GAY AMERICAN LITERATURE, 1924–1969

There is no homosexual problem except that created by heterosexual society.
—Donald Webster Cory (1951)

In 1924 an anthology of homoerotic poetry called *Men and Boys* was announced with a prospectus that declared the book to have been "approved by the American Society for the Study of Sex Psychology." Though there is no record of this group, of its meetings, or its membership, its name echoes that of the British Society for the Study of Sex Psychology that was founded in 1914 with Edward Carpenter as first president; it had probably grown out of the shadowy and certainly homosexual Order of Chaeronea, founded by the homosexual reformer George Ives in the 1890s. It is possible that some of the Americans whose poetry appeared in *Men and Boys* were members of Chaeronea, the British Society, and the American Society, if there was one. The British Society was active in studying and publishing on all aspects of sexuality, especially homosexuality; what the American Society intended to do is unknown. Invisibility does not mean nonexistence, however. If this society did exist, its members may have recognized, as the Cercle Hermaphroditos already had, the need for unity against "bitter persecution."

In 1921 Dr. Perry Lichtenstein asked whether "the fairy or fag" really existed. His answer is affirmative, and he proves it in an article in the *Medical Review of Reviews*. In a subsequent issue a letter appeared from Ralph Werther. This is of course Earl Lind, who points out that he is "the best authority in the United States on androgynism, having associated with fairies to a greater extent than any other writer." Lind argued that it was "only prejudice and bigotry" that marked "ultra-androgynes as a 'menace to society.'" He signed himself "yours for the relief of the oppressed" (quoted in Katz 1983, 403–404).

Relieving the oppressed is the announced mission of the Chicago Society for Human Rights, which is the earliest known officially chartered homosexual group in America. Its charter, granted by the state of Illinois in 1925, says that the purpose of the group was to "protect the interests of people who by reason of mental and physical abnormalities are abused and hindered in the legal pursuit of happiness . . . and to combat the public prejudices against them." Even though the charter accepts and inscribes social and scientific definitions of homosexuals as mentally and physically abnormal, the foundation of the society is still a significant landmark—the official entrance into the American social and political discourse of a group defining itself as homosexual and therefore as oppressed, with a stated intention to "combat" that oppression. This American group assumed, just as had the Order of Chaeronea, that the emancipation of homosexuals must be achieved by homosexuals themselves (Weeks, 127).

The Chicago Society not only intended to resist oppression but to provide information for other homosexuals about its progress. This was to be done in the newspaper—probably the first such American homophile journal—*Friendship and Freedom*, of which two issues were published. From the beginning the group met with opposition. As Henry Gerber, one of the founding members, recalls in a memoir of the group, "The big fearful obstacle seemed always to be the almost willful misunderstanding and ignorance on the part of the general public concerning the nature of homosexuality." Misunderstanding turned to persecution when Gerber was arrested for being a member of a "strange sex cult" as it was described by the *Chicago Examiner*.

Also arrested were three other men, none of whom were with Gerber in his room, but one of whom had a copy of a pamphlet that must have been a copy of *Friendship and Freedom*. Gerber tells the story:

> On Sunday . . . I returned from a visit downtown. After I had gone to my room, someone knocked at the door. . . . I opened up. Two men entered the room. They identified themselves as a city detective and a newspaper reported from the *Examiner*. The detective asked me where the boy was. What boy? He told me he had orders from his precinct captain to bring me to the police station. He took my typewriter, my notary public diploma, and all the literature about the Society and also personal diaries as well as bookkeeping accounts. At no time did he show a warrant for my arrest. At the police station I was locked up in a cell but no charges were made against me. . . . A friendly cop at the station showed me a copy of the *Examiner*. There right on the front page I found this incredible story: "Strange Sex Cult Exposed."

In police court, though still with no charges made, Gerber was confronted by the "evidence" against him and the others that included the pamphlet in which, the *Examiner* alleged, men were urged to "leave their wives and children." In addition, the police produced another piece of evidence:

> The detective triumphantly produced a powder puff which he claimed he found in my room. That was the sole evidence of my crime. It was admitted as evidence of my effeminacy. . . . The young social worker . . . read from my diary out of context: "I love Karl." The detective and the judge shuddered over such depravity. To the already prejudiced court we were obviously guilty. We were guilty by just being homosexual.

Gerber at a later trial was acquitted on the grounds that he had been arrested without a warrant. But "the experience convinced me that we were up against a solid wall of ignorance, hypocrisy, meanness, and corruption." The detective's parting jibe was, "What was the idea of the Society for Human Rights anyway? Was it to give you birds legal right to rape every boy on the street?" This, as Gerber says, "definitely meant the end of the Society for Human Rights" (quoted in Katz 1976, 389–93).

It did not, however, mean the end of attempts to organize against homophobia. In 1932, under the pen name "Parisex," Gerber published an article in the periodical the *Modern Thinker* called "In Defense of Homosexuality." Gerber's essay may be one of the first pro-homosexual essays to appear after Mayne's *Intersexes*. Under his own name in 1934 Gerber wrote several articles, among them "Recent Homosexual Literature" for a mimeographed magazine called *Chanticleer*. Journals like *Chanticleer*, or the journal put together by "Lisa Ben," a lesbian writer in California who between 1947 and 1948 published nine issues of the lesbian oriented *Vice Versa: America's Gayest Magazine*, are small but telling indications that American homosexuals were beginning to see themselves not only as a distinct sexual minority but as a political and social group.

Identification of homosexuals in the armed forces in the late 1940s, when known homosexuals were discharged as undesirable, "marked a new institutional position. For the first time homosexual men and women became a statistically and socially designated minority."[1] With this there began to appear small organizations that were, if not homosexual groups, then sympathetic to what was seen as official persecution of gay people. The Quaker Emergency Committee "was organized to assist gay males arrested in public places" (Licata and Petersen, 166). The Knights of the Clock was formed in Los Angeles to "combat both homophobia and racism." Neither group seems to have had any significant membership, however. Gerber's Chicago Society numbered fewer than a dozen, the Knights no more than 20.

The government investigation of homosexuals as security risks was certainly one of the contributing factors to the modern homosexual movement in the United States. The man Jonathan Katz describes as the "founding father of the American homosexual liberation movement," Henry Hay, describes what led him to conceive of a gay organization:

> The anti-communist witch hunts were very much in operation; the House Un-American activities Committee had investigated Communist subversion in Hollywood. The purge of homosexuals from the State Department took place. The country, it seemed to me, was beginning to move toward fascism and McCarthyism; the Jews would not be used as a scapegoat this time—the painful example of Germany was still too clear to us. The Black organizations were already pretty successful looking out for their interests. It was obvious McCarthy was setting up a pattern for a new scapegoat, and it was going to be us—Gays. We had to organize, we had to move, we had to get started. (quoted in Katz 1976, 408)

In 1950 Hay wrote "Preliminary Concepts" for a group that he then called the International Bachelors Fraternal Order for Peace and Social Dignity, whose purpose was to be "a service and welfare organization devoted to the protection and improvement of society's androgynous minority." Hay was the only member. He soon met "X," however, and they were joined in late 1950 by several others. Discussion groups were formed, and the conclusions of one of them suggests an outline of homosexual self-definition in the 1950s: "Homosexuals are 'lone wolves' through fear of heterosexual society. A homosexual has no one to whom he must account, and in the end . . . he must decide everything for himself. Those in greatest need are sometimes the most reluctant to help each other or themselves, tending to think of personal experiences as things apart from the mutual effort toward betterment."

The identification of homophobia and the fear and social isolation it produces among homosexuals as the chief problem confronting gay people led to the writing of the "Missions and Purposes" of the Mattachine Society in April 1951. The society sought (1) to "unify" those "isolated from their own kind" so that "all of our people can . . . derive a feeling of belonging"; (2) to develop an "ethical homosexual culture" paralleling "the emerging cultures of our fellow minorities—the Negro, Mexican, and Jewish Peoples"; (3) to lead "socially conscious homosexuals" to "provide leadership to the whole mass of social deviates"; and (4) to take "political action" to counter "discriminatory and oppressive legislation" and aid "our people who are victimized daily as a result of our oppression," a "people" who make up "one of the largest minorities in American today" (quoted in Katz 1976, 406–29).

The identity constructed by this document clearly defines homosexuals as a minority not solely by sexual desire but also by cultural sensibilities and political responsibilities. The written purposes of the Mattachine Society also define the labor to be undertaken by the homosexual liberation movement in the years to come. The complex history of the Mattachine Society—including the dissensions that plagued it and the eventual split between East and West Coast chapters—is best approached in accounts by Hay and in several recent discussions of the early gay rights movement like John D'Emilio's *Sexual Politics, Sexual Communities* (1983).

The Mattachine Society impelled the birth of other groups, among them a men's group in Los Angeles founded in 1952 that called itself ONE, and the Daughters of Bilitis, a lesbian organization founded in 1955. By the mid-1960s several Mattachine chapters, notably Mattachine Washington and Mattachine New York, were politically active, aiming their work at fighting discrimination against homosexuals in government institutions. The East Coast Homophile Organization and the Society for Individual Rights were formed. In 1967, in protest against routine violence against homosexuals by the Los Angeles Police Department, demonstrations were held led by a group calling itself PRIDE (Personal Rights in Defense and Education).

Not only did these groups provide social space for homosexuals to meet and together engage in dialogue about identity and oppression, but they also provided the opportunity to create textual sites in which this information and exchange could be put to valuable use. Each of these groups published journals wherein homosexuals were able to define and discover their political, sexual, and cultural identity. In these journals each of these liberationist groups recorded their activities, contributed to the education of homosexuals about the homosexual liberation movement, and to the dissemination of knowledge about the history and literature of homosexuality. Most important, they provided an arena where homosexual writers could for the first time offer to a receptive audience not only fiction and poetry but also speculative essays on literary, historical, sociological, and legal topics.

In 1951 appeared *The Homosexual in America*, written under the pseudonym Donald Webster Cory, which was the first extensive and careful examination of the current state of knowledge about homosexuality, written by a homosexual, to appear in America since Mayne's *The Intersexes*. Cory makes a strong case for the recognition of homosexuals as a minority group whose concerns are similar to those of other oppressed American minorities and argues that discussion of homosexuality should not be part of a moral or medical discourse that demonizes it but rather as part of a larger dialogue concerning civil rights. He surveys and anatomizes aspects of gay culture and in passing begins to establish some useful parameters for the discussion of theoretical concepts of a "gay culture," articulating a liberationist and even revolutionary view of the task of gay people in 1951.

Cory does not view homosexuality as a problem; the real problem is that "anyone taking such an initiative is open to pillory and contumelious scorn." Thus "the homosexual is locked in his present position. If he does not rise up and demand his rights, he will never get them, but until he gets those rights, he cannot be expected to expose himself to the martyrdom that would come should he rise up and demand them." He argues that one answer is to be "found in the liberalization of our newspapers, radio, and theater, so that homosexuality can be discussed as freely as any subject." He insists that "what the homosexual wants is freedom—not only freedom of expression, but also sexual freedom" to use his body as he sees fit "so long as he does not use the force of violence, threat, or superior age, so long as he does not inflict bodily harm or disease upon another person; so long as that other person is of sound mind and agrees to the activity."

Cory speculates that "if only all of the inverts, the millions in all lands, could simultaneously rise up in our full strength" then perhaps the freedom he seeks might be realized. This is speculation, Cory says, but necessity also, for the homosexual "is historically forced to enter the struggle for the widening of freedom of expression . . . he is historically compelled to enlist in the legions fighting for liberalization of the sexual mores of modern civilization." In totalitarian states—he has cited both Nazi and Marxist persecution of homosexuals—"there was no room for a group of people who, by their very sexual temperaments, could never be assimilated, must always remain apart with their own ways of life, their own outlooks, their own philosophies." To homosexuals who fear confrontation or believe it to be a hopeless cause, to homosexuals who prefer to "pass" as heterosexual while staying in the closet, who seek to ameliorate rather than celebrate difference, Cory voices a creed that he believes gives justification to homosexuals to "rise up in our full strength" and demand our rights: "it is this inherent lack of assimilability that is the greatest historic value of homosexuality" (Cory, 228–35).

Cory's book went through six printings between 1951 and 1956, and perhaps its popularity encouraged writers. In 1953 ONE, Inc., began publishing *ONE* magazine, containing articles on all aspects of homosexual culture and politics. The December 1953 issue, for example, described as the "All-Fiction Issue," sold for 25 cents and contained the story "Death in a Royal Family," by James Barr, author of the homosexual novel *Quatrefoil*; poems by Camilla ("Images") and Elizabeth Lado ("Din"); and stories by Smith ("Why Doesn't the Damned Thing Ring!"), Saul K. ("Jingle, You Belles You!"), and Mike Schwartz ("The Voice in the Vase"). Subsequent issues contained not only fiction and poetry but articles, such as one in the April 1956 issue by Lynn Pedersen, entitled "Miami's New-Type Witch-hunt," while later issues published articles from homophile journals in Europe, like Terry David's essay "The Male Homosexual in Black Africa," translated from the French homophile magazine *Arcadie*. Over the years *ONE* reviewed most of the books written by or about homosexuals and "continued to serve as the unofficial voice of the homosexual rights movement until 1972" (Licata and Petersen, 170). At about the same time that *ONE* began to publish, the Mattachine Society began its own journal, the *Mattachine Review*. Similar to *ONE*, it also published a mixture of fiction, poetry, and articles concerning the civil rights of homosexuals, like the April 1956 article by Donald West, "Should the Laws Be Changed?," or Ross Puryear's essay "The Homosexual in Prison" that appeared in June 1956. ONE began to publish *ONE Institute*

Quarterly, devoted to articles that forecast later gay studies concerns such as David Pagari's "Existentialism and the Homosexual Poet"; Noel I. Garde's essay on Xavier Mayne, "The Mysterious Father of American Homophile Literature"; or W. Dorr Legg's "The Sociology of the Homosexual," all of these appearing in various issues in the late 1950s and early 1960s.[2]

The Daughters of Bilitis also published a journal, the *Ladder*, that was instrumental in forming, as one of its correspondents said, the awareness that "our problems as women are profoundly unique" and that "women, like other oppressed groups . . . have had to pay a price of intellectual impoverishment that the second class status imposed on us for centuries created and sustained" (quoted in Katz 1976, 425). When the Society for Individual Rights began publishing its journal, *Vector*, in the 1960s and PRIDE published in 1967 a magazine called the *Advocate* that still publishes today, gay journalism had come of age. These journals became the philosophical and political arena in which writers were able to counter the negative constructions of homosexual identity that had been formed by medical texts and by governmental intervention into the lives of homosexual women and men. They spoke positively about homosexuality, provided access to the history and literature of homosexuality, and, most important, demonstrated what Henry Hay had forecast in 1951—that "some glad day there shall be a body of knowledge which would . . . show that homosexuals . . . have much in common" (quoted in Katz 1976, 412).

After World War I not only did the intensity of the homophobic discourse increase, and not only did America begin to see some token resistance to it, but American writers began to mount what might be called a sustained textual attack on homophobia and an intensive and extensive textual speculation on the nature of homosexual identity. The appearance and intensification of the liberationist movement in American in the middle of this century has had as its great beneficiary the homoerotic text—gay literature—that both reflected and helped to invent emancipation and identity.

POETRY

The poetry anthology *Men and Boys* offers not only a selection of "present-day poets" but also homoerotic poetry from the earliest times to the twentieth century—beginning with the biblical lament of David for Jonathan, Greek and Roman lyrics, Arabic poetry, and Renaissance lyrics and sonnets. It provides brief comments on the works and gives a list of eighteenth-century writers who dealt with homoerotic themes. The Uranians are liberally represented. Of American poets, Bayard Taylor and the pseudonymous and unknown Clement Andrews are represented by more poems than Walt Whitman, though Whitman's "Once I Pass'd through a Populous City" is present in the original text—with masculine, not feminine, pronouns—a text that was only unearthed in 1920. Among "present-day poets" (presumably those living at that time) *Men and Boys* offers writers whose work is now forgotten and whose names remain unidentified, in most instances deservedly so. Known though distinctly minor American writers include Robert Hillyer, Charles Hanson Towne, Burges Johnson, Douglas Malloch, Willard Austin Wattles, and James Fenimore Cooper, Jr., grandson of the novelist.

Some of the American writers in the book were in fact women, and others, as Donald Mader, the editor of the facsimile text points out, may not have been any more homosexual than their verses, some of which have been liberally edited and even rewritten by the compiler of the anthology, who appears in the pages as the poet "Edwin Edwinson" but who almost certainly was Edward Mark Slocum, by profession a chemist. More tantalizing are the unidentified poets, among them the pseudonymous Clement Andrews, the mysterious Fidian, and Sidney Wilmer, especially since these writers' works are among the best in the book.

Most of the poems in the anthology dwell on standard Uranian themes, singing the praises of handsome youths, lamenting their loss, or celebrating love and announcing desire. Their debt to the English Uranians is suggested by Gordon in his poem "Lad's Love" an echo of a thousand Uranian titles and specifically John Barford's *Ladslove Lyrics* (1918). In many of the poems, however, there is a suggestion of more than distant admiration for these young men, as C. Worth suggests in "Possession" in just what way he wants to possess his lover:

> My love I own in his white, white youth,
> For he gave to me his heart of fire
> And fiercely my two strong hands shall keep
> His uttermost desire.
> The swift unsullied lips he bends to me are mine,
> And mine the hands that never tire.
> But oh, his singing self goes free!
> I do not own my lover's soul,
> And all his tinctured dreams I can dimly see
> Inviolate within a crystal bowl.

H. Lange (Hamiel Long) seems to be in no doubt that the love he celebrates is quite natural as he describes "Boy Lovers" who "think no more of love than this / That it is something not amiss," while Giles de Gillies argues that men are disobeying divine ordinance when they condemn homosexual love: "Red mouths of lads for Love God made; / Yet men His kindly will gainsayed!" The last poem of the book, by Douglas Malloch, moves the focus of the collection away from poems celebrating "boyhood" firmly into the erotic arena of "young manhood" as he praises, in a very American locale, "Manly Love":

> Deep in your heart understand
> the love of a man for a man;

He'll go with you over the trail,
the trail that is lonesome and long;
His faith will not falter nor fail,
nor falter the lilt of his song.
He knows both your soul and your sins,
and does not too carefully scan,—
The Highway to Heaven begins
with the love of a man for a man!

As Mader points out, many of these verses tend to cling "tenaciously to a Lyric vein of poetry" that by 1924 was outmoded and that "was being destroyed around them by modern verse." The poet Sidney Wilmer, however, whose "The Mess Boy" is the most arresting poem in the book, engages a more "modern" style and in doing so encapsulates in a few lines a very modern homosexual sensibility that confronts homophobia rather than being debased by it. The mess boy of the title, whose function seems to be both servant and sexual object for sailors is, despite his willing prostitution of his body, both intellectually and spiritually superior to those he services and immune to their homophobic insults:

He had contempt that was divine
For every sailor that he fed,
For while they talked of "Fun" and "Wine"
He read.

He washed their dishes, made their bed,
And gave their bodies joy with grace;
Nor could their insults on his head
Erase

That fine immobile pride of his,—
In the embraces of each man
He was as different as a Kiss
From Pan!

Hart Crane, our greatest homosexual poet after Whitman, published his first poem in 1916 and titled it "C33," the number of Oscar Wilde's cell in Reading Gaol. In another early poem, "Modern Craft," he explores questions about the nature of love and the nature of poetry especially when its muse is constructed to be female rather than male. He ends the poem with the admission that "My modern love were / Charred at a stake in younger times than ours."[3] Both of these references—the one to Wilde's imprisonment and the other to the burning of sodomites—site homosexuality as a subtext in his poetry. Crane's allegiance to Whitman is evidenced throughout his poetry, not only in his epic cycle *The Bridge* but in a number of his early poems, like "Episode of Hands," and the later "Repose of Rivers" from *White Buildings*. Crane's short life—he committed suicide in 1932 at the age of 32—has been unsparingly documented, and his presumed alcoholism and his known homosexuality have not been ignored by recent critics. Thus Wallace Fowlie in 1965 could argue that "sexual aberration and drunkenness were the pitfalls in which his spirit wrestled with a kind of desperation" (quoted in Woods, 140).

The complexity of his poems, attributed by some critics to a desire to inscribe within his texts the homosexuality he would not admit, are also famously recognized as some of the most difficult texts in early twentieth-century American poetry. That same complexity has also been described as a kind of poetic failure and laid at the door of his homosexuality, as critics invoke the idea that the emotional limitation ascribed to homosexuality is mirrored in a consequent emotional limitation in the art. In *Hart Crane and the Homosexual Text* Thomas Yingling offers the best summary of this critical perception and certainly the most profound analysis of the homoeroticism of Crane's poems.

Crane was an obsessive collector of the past, a reader in all eras of poetry, and nowhere did he find a more congenial master than in Whitman. Whitman demonstrated for Crane not only this Americanism, not only special lessons about poetic craft and the uses of language, but just how male-male affection might be inscribed in texts. In a sense Crane chose a tradition for himself, or else he recognized in himself the voice of a tradition that he felt had already possessed him, a tradition at once American, as *The Bridge*, in its visionary record of an American spiritual quest, suggests, and implying the possibility that the love of men for men could be a subject of poetry. That Crane's poetry is complex and allusive and has often been misunderstood and underestimated is without doubt. As Robert K. Martin in *The Homosexual Tradition in American Poetry* and Yingling in his more extensive commentary demonstrate, this misunderstanding and underestimation derive perhaps in large part from the critical erasure of homosexuality as a relevant presence in Crane's poems. Yet that presence has also been accounted as evidence of his failure as a poet or else denied as relevant to his poems.

R. P. Blackmur hinted at the first when he commented that "in Crane the poet succumbed to the man." Though Blackmur does not say that in the man there is the homosexual, he suggests that there was about Crane "the distraught but exciting splendor of a great failure" (quoted in Yingling, 17). That telling "distraught" echoes the "chronic excitation" that Aldridge believed to typically accompany the "minor" homosexual talent, and it is clearly the key to what Blackmur believes to be Crane's failure. Samuel Hazo in 1963 argued the second point, the irrelevance of homosexuality to texts, when he urged that "whatever influence Crane's homosexual relationships . . . may have had on the composition of 'Voyages' [Crane's cycle of poems commemorating his love affair with Emil Opfer] is a point best left to psychological disquisition. There is nothing in the poems that explicitly betrays a perversion of the impulses of love and there is no thematic reason that would lead a reader to relate the love imagery, where it does exist, to a source homosexual in nature" (quoted in Yingling, 92).

In effect, homosexuality does not matter, Hazo seems to be saying. Even if Hazo is technically right—and the poem does not explicitly portray homosexual sex or mention the sex of the lover who is addressed—Yingling demonstrates with finality how wrong he is and points out that what "Voyages" achieves is to "present homosexual desire within the field of language understood now not as a medium of incarnation [i.e., the explicit portrayal of homosexual sex] but as one of difference." As an example of this, in "Voyage V," for example, Crane describes a moment of revelation between the two men. "For we," Crane says,

> Are overtaken. Now no cry, no sword
> Can fasten or deflect this tidal wedge,
> Slow tyranny of moonlight, moonlight loved
> And changed . . . "There's
>
> Nothing like this in the world," you say,
> Knowing I cannot touch your hand and look
> Too, into that godless cleft of sky
> Where nothing turns but dead sands flashing.
>
> "—And never quite to understand!" No,
> In all the argosy of your bright hair I dreamed
> Nothing so flagless as this piracy. (CP, 38)

There are a number of ways to explain these lines, but one inexplicit yet pertinent homosexual text that can be derived lies in the pivotal assertion that even in a moment of homoerotic tenderness Crane feels constrained because the hovering prohibitions of heterosexuality decree that "I cannot touch your hand" and that even in his lover's argosy of bright hair—the ship of their desire—the piracy exercised by the exclusive heterosexualizing of desire—the exclusion of homosexual desire from legitimate paradigms of love—creates a sense of loss and hopelessness. Hazo's assertion of homosexuality as a perversion of love and his demand for its "explicit" presence echoes the homophobic presumption that no homosexuality exists unless it is precisely and sexually resonant. Even then, as both Hazo and Blackmur seem to suggest, it can only be relevant to a text in judging its failure, not its success. Crane's poetry—from "C33" through "Voyages" through the several homoerotic texts to be found in *White Buildings* and *The Bridge* through the "The

Broken Tower"—reveals that homosexuality, in which Crane found both pain and joy, was the defining impulse of his life as well as of his poetry.

In an early poem some sense of the often delicate place of homosexuality in Crane's texts may be seen. In "Episode of Hands," which I quote here in its entirety, Crane's poem speaks directly to the secrecy and signs of homosexual passion just as it also recalls Anderson's story "Hands," in which the homophobic retribution for the expression of homosexual desire is tragically described. Here, however, there is quiet triumph, and the signs of conforming masculinized worlds disappear—"factory sounds and factory thoughts"— banished by the touch of the factory owner's son, whose hands partake not only of conventional images of manhood—iron, leather—but when they touch the worker's hands create images implying difference—wings of butterflies. At the end the factory owner's son and the factory worker are translated out of the ordinary world defined by conventional male relationships into a special world populated only by these two men, and they are given a special language silently imparted by what Whitman called the flash of eyes offering love:

> The unexpected interest made him flush.
> Suddenly he seemed to forget the pain.—
> Consented,—and held out
> One finger from the others.
>
> The gash was bleeding, and a shaft of sun
> That glittered in and out among the wheels,
> Fell lightly warmly down the wound.
>
> And as the fingers of the factory owner's son,
> That knew a grip for books and tennis
> As well as one for iron and leather,—
> As his taut spare fingers wound the gauze
> Around the thick bed of the wound,
> His own hands seemed to him
> Like wings of butterflies
> Flickering in sunlight over summer fields.
>
> The knots and notches,—many in the wide
> Deep hand that lay in his,—seemed beautiful
> They were like the marks of wild ponies' play,—
> Bunches of new green breaking a hard turf.
>
> And factory sounds and factory thoughts
> Were banished from him by that larger, quieter hand
> That lay in his with the sun upon it.
> And as the bandage now was tightened
> The two men smiled into each other's eyes. (CP, 173)

It may be that Crane's attempt to discover the meaning of the homosexual self in poems was never satisfied. In "The Broken Tower," he writes, "I entered the broken world / To trace the visionary company of love, its voice / An instant in the wind." But though "my word I poured . . . / The steep encroachments of my blood left me no answer" (CP, 160).

Crane had read Whitman and must surely have known about Whitman's celebration of the special blood that flowed in the veins of men like him— blood that gave to Whitman at least the imperative command that he must celebrate the love of comrades. Crane, Martin argues, "had significantly enlarged the possibilities of homosexual poetry, by extending it beyond 'mere' subject matter. In Crane the poet's 'sexuality' is rarely the subject of the poem . . . but it nonetheless helps determine the poem's images and even its structural patterns" (Martin 1979, 164). Crane arrived at an uncomfortable truce with homosexuality, and so it cannot be said that his poems celebrate it in ways as directly as some of the poems in Men and Boys or in novels like Imre or in Lind/June's texts, nor as confrontationally as in A Scarlet Pansy. Crane presents the dilemma of the American homosexual poet, being unable to clearly express, as Yingling has said, what he still felt impelled and yet forbidden to say.

In his assessment of "The Bridge" Yingling defines the power of homosexually charged silences in Crane and in homosexual American poetry prior to its explosive appearance in the 1950s: "What we need to see is how the 'not-saids.' . . . [T]hose discourses and knowledges relegated to [the poem's] unconscious, contradict its conscious intentions. Thus, we will often be reading against the poem's desire to present a synthesis of America, a myth for the modern age . . . and will be inspecting the ways in which that consciousness cannot fully elide the counter-discourse and knowledge of the homosexual although it has the power to force it into invisibility" (Yingling, 198).

Invisibility was the situation out of which homosexual texts were emerging, just as it was the situation that homosexuals were also trying to change. Crane was undeniably one of those writers for whom homosexuality was as much a torment as it was a passion. It should not be ignored that his alcoholism can surely have cast a dark shadow on his interior determination of what homosexuality might mean. In 1932 he committed suicide by leaping from a boat bound from Mexico to New York. But Crane's poems, no matter how uncertain he may have been about the daily incidence of homosexual desire (and his letters attest to that incidence), can hardly be judged as either failure or indifferent vehicles for an undifferentiated desire.

Robert Duncan announced his homosexuality in a 1944 essay about Crane: "Crane's suffering, his rebellion, and his love are sources of poetry for him not because they are what make him different from, superior to mankind, but because he saw in them his link with mankind; he saw in them his sharing in universal human experience" (quoted in Katz 1983, 593).

Duncan was convinced that homosexuality was only one of many shared human experiences and felt that what he called the "cult of the homosexual"—the assumed superiority to heterosexuals and the claim to a special knowledge—was not a salutary but a pernicious deployment of difference. In this essay, "The Homosexual in Society," Duncan argued that it was not difference but human community that the homosexual poet ought to emphasize.

Writing in 1944 when constructions of homosexual identity by medical texts and by homosexuals themselves often emphasized the isolation, bitterness, and tragedy of homosexual life, Duncan's call for a rejection of the ghettoized locales often found in homosexual novels and the separatist condescension often to be found especially in urban homosexual enclaves would be shortly supported by some of the normalizing novels, like Vidal's *The City and the Pillar*, that called for homosexual stories about seemingly "normal" American boys who incidentally loved men. The problem for homosexuals, Duncan said, was that

> there is in the modern scene no homosexual who has been willing to take in his own persecution a battle front toward freedom. Almost co-incident with the first declarations for homosexual rights was the growth of a cult of homosexual superiority to the human race; the cultivation of a secret language, the camp, a tone and vocabulary that is loaded with contempt for the human. . . . In what one would believe the most radical, the most enlightened "queer circles" the word "jam" remains, designating all who are not homosexual, filled with unwavering hostility and fear, gathering an incredible force of exclusion and blindness. (quoted in Katz 1983, 592)

Duncan's assessment of the "homosexual situation" at that time is in some sense reasonably accurate. He was perhaps too close in time and physical proximity to recognize what he saw as part of the process of new constructions of difference that were even then growing out of the identities adopted or performed by gay men. What Katz describes as his "disowning of difference" was not only a contradiction in his work, as Katz suggests, but also an indictment that homophobia condemned, as much as homosexuals themselves emphasized, that difference. Duncan argued that the solution for homosexuals was to "face in their own lives both the hostility of society in that they are queer and the hostility of the homosexual cult of superiority." If this were to be done, then the homosexual, as both artist and citizen, must assert "that only one devotion can be held by a human being" who seeks "creative life and expression, and that is a devotion to human freedom, toward the liberation of human love, human conflicts, human aspirations. To do this one must disown all special groups . . . that would claim allegiance" (quoted in Katz 1983, 593).

Duncan's words prophesy in one sense some of the attempts by homosexuals in the 1950s and 1960s to demand that their humanity be recognized and that their human rights be given them. But Duncan's indictment of difference goes against the American homosexual grain, for difference is the essence of homosexual culture as well as the message of the best American homosexual texts. Duncan did not or would not recognize this in his essay. In a 1978–79 interview Duncan revealed the genesis of his words and reveals also something about the very nature of internalized homophobia and the still potent dictates of a masculinized American myth: "'The Homosexual in Society' article of 1944 arose from my reaction to a fashionable gay party and seeing a younger poet, seeing what I feared I might be too, in his affected voice. Hadn't he lost his own natured voice, having lost his manhood essentially?"[4]

In his poetry, however, Duncan's "natured voice" clearly speaks of the kind of manhood he constructed. The disowning of difference is overwhelmed by the sheer celebration of desire and the delight of the flesh made word and the flesh made love. In his poem "Torso" (1968) he describes a sexual epiphany that defines one pathway of homoerotic difference when he describes his lover, whose body "leading into paradise," provokes a "quickening fire in me." In this poem there is no disowning of difference, for he concludes by saying, "Gather in me, you gather / your Self. / For my Other is not a Woman but a man."[5]

In his 1966 collected poems Duncan seems to have come to believe that difference and resistance after all may be the motive force in his texts when he says in describing his first homosexual love and its affect on his poetry: "There had been an awakening of rhythm, the imprint of a cadence at once physical and physiological, that could contain and project the components of an emerging homosexuality. . . . Perhaps the sexual irregularity underlay and led to the poetic; neither as homosexual nor as poet could one take over readily the accepted paradigms and conventions of the Protestant ethic" (quoted in Martin 1979, 174). His polite term for homophobia—"the conventions of the Protestant ethic"—interestingly echoes another kind of religious ethic he identifies in the 1978–79 interview, where he suggests approvingly that "there is a kind of homosexual religion. . . . [T]here is a level in which I think we can identify a kind of religion of the homosexual and also the homoerotic" (quoted in Martin 1979, 171). Duncan's new cult of the homosexual, a post-Stonewall cult, suggests just how far homosexual constructions of difference as a positive rather than negative element of homosexual identities had come.

In that same interview Duncan observed about American homosexual culture and literature that "we have yet to begin to create the psychological and mythological tradition to build the gay culture and gay arts movement that would be needed." To do that he suggests that in America "we have never treated sexuality as language." Perhaps he is suggesting that culture—in part homosexual style—and a language of sexuality will produce the kind of homosexual religion he envisions. In "Night Scene" (1964) he engages a highly eroticized language in which sexuality is firmly inscribed within a poetics of homoeroticism. Stumbling into a room at four o'clock in the morning he imagines himself to be

> a spirit of the hour descending into body
> whose tongue touches
> myrrh of the morgenrot
> and in a cowslip's bell that in a moment comes Ariel
> to joy all around
> but we see one lover take his lover into his mouth
> leaping, Swift flame of
> abiding sweetness is in this flesh.
>
> Fatigue spreading back, a grand chorale
> of who I am, who is he, who we are,
> in which a thin spire of longing
> perishes, this single up-fountain of a
> single note around which
>
> the throat shapes!

It almost seemed, Martin has said, that "in the 1950s . . . the only openly gay poet was Allen Ginsberg" (Martin 1979, 165). This of course was not entirely true. Frank O'Hara was openly gay in the 1950s, as was Duncan and W. H. Auden, who had come to more congenial and perhaps what he felt were more homosexual shores, although he denied the relevance of a specific sexuality to his poems. O'Hara anatomized homosexuality, his own and the idea of it, in "Homosexuality," in which he described as the motive power of his poetry "the law of my own voice," a law derived from desire for homosexual love. In the context of cruising the subways men's rooms and parks of New York, O'Hara sees homosexuals as remarkable creatures whose "delicate feet" may never "touch the earth again," as they—he among them—utter a cry "to confuse the brave": "It's a summer day, / and I want to be wanted more than anything else in the world." O'Hara, like Duncan, engages sexuality as language, and both engage difference as that which makes that language comprehensible.

It was indeed Ginsberg whose poetry, more than that of any American homosexual poet since Whitman, was to take to heart Whitman's injunction not only to celebrate the love of comrades but to write about "the midnight orgies of young men." In the 1950s Ginsberg became the essential homosexual poet, the heir of Whitman, an American celebrant of difference and unabashed homosexual desire. His poem "Howl" asserts that the only way to confront homophobia is to deliberately affront the sensibility that supported it. In a moment Ginsberg banished the simpering pose of the homosexual cult so despised by Duncan. He also left no dogmatic ground for novels like

Vidal's *The City and the Pillar* or for the philosophy of some of the ameliorating homosexual rights movements that tried to reconstruct homosexuality into a version of heterosexuality.

In "Howl" Ginsberg's fairies are as joyful in their sexual experiments as Whitman's 28 bathers or as Whitman in the embrace of his fierce wrestler. In "Howl" they are "fucked in the ass by saintly motorcyclists and screamed with joy." Not since Whitman had an American homosexual poet dared to intimate, let alone announce, that joy, not pain, was the result of homosexual rape and to suggest that sex, not philosophy, might be the most powerful weapon against oppression. Sex becomes for Ginsberg not a furtive or perhaps even anticlimactic conclusion to highly romanticized desire but the point at which desire is liberated from all literary constructions and intellectualization. In "Howl" and later in "Please Master," written the year before Stonewall, Ginsberg's constructions of homosexual identities inscribe homosexual desire most powerfully in scenes of ecstatic homosexual rape and the passive surrender of all remaining emotionally held myths about American manhood to that demanding penetration.

In "A Supermarket in California" (1955) Ginsberg testified to Whitman's influence when he described him as "dear father, graybeard, lonely old courage-teacher." He asked Whitman, "What American did you have when Charon quit poling his ferry and you got out on a smoking bank and stood watching the boat disappear on the black waters of Lethe?" Whitman had, as this book has shown and through no fault of his own, an America in which he felt constrained to redesign his own words and distance himself from the earlier pledge he made to "sing no songs today but those of manly attachment." Ginsberg found an America in the 1950s that was ripe for Whitman's pledge to be reenacted again by sons—and daughters—even then being born.

PLAYS

A 1925 report by the Juvenile Protective Association of Chicago revealed that there were "in certain theaters . . . performances as vulgar and sensual as . . . [any] found in houses of prostitution. The detailed . . . description of performances given in a certain West Side Theatre and witnessed every afternoon and every evening by a large audience of men and boys would . . . be barred from our mails. . . . It was through the investigation of these performances that we found the almost unbelievable situation of little boys, as young as even ten years of age, frequenting certain theatres for the purposes of soliciting men for homo-sexual practices" (quoted in Katz 1983, 423). If Americans did encounter "perversion" on stage it was more likely to reflect lesbian than male homosexuality. In 1921, however, the *New York Times* reviewed a play called *March Hares* by Harry Gribble that the reviewer, Alexander Woollcott, described as a "curiously effeminate comedy" that was quite the opposite of a "Red-Blooded Hundred Per Cent American Play" since it invoked Oscar Wilde and featured "odd folk" who "talked a good deal about one another's sex appeal." Among the odd folk was Geoffrey, "an odd young professor of elocution" who, despite the general innuendo, does the right thing in the end by marrying his fiancée, who he has tried to make jealous by the ruse of inviting a young man home.

Other odd folk who appeared in plays in the 1920s were the women in *The Captive* (1926), who *Times* critic Brooks Atkinson described as being in a "twisted relationship" that led the heroine, who has left her male lover for a woman, to be "crushed by a frightful tyranny beyond her control" that the other woman exercises over her. This reaction to *The Captive* constructs the familiar image of the homosexual as sexual predator preying on the innocent, just as the review of *March Hares* conjures the equally familiar and contradictory construction of the effeminate and trivial homosexual. Social reaction to *The Captive* was not at all trivial, however, for the play was closed by the police, and the controversy "led the New York State legislature to ban 'sexual perversion' as a theme on the state's stages, a law which remained on the books until 1967" (Katz 1983, 428).

Perhaps because of that ban, Mae West's *The Drag* played only in Bridgeport, Connecticut, in 1927. *The Drag* is, as William Hoffman suggests, "the first modern gay play" (Hoffman, xvi). It concerns a gay man, Rollo, who, married and unhappy, falls in love with a straight man, Allen. Allen falls in love with Rollo's wife, Clair, and at a drag party David, Rollo's former lover, murders him, and Rollo's death is covered up by Rollo's influential father as a suicide. West also wrote *The Pleasure Man* (1928), a play with a number of gay characters that played in New York for three performances before it was raided by the police and closed. The reviewer for the *New York Evening Post* found *The Pleasure Man* to be "smeared from beginning to end with such filth as cannot possibly be described in print, such filth as turns one stomach to remembers." If the reader was not sure what the reviewer meant, he makes it clear when he explains that "the most nauseating feature of the evening was the laughter of the audience, or at least that part of it which howled and snickered and let out degenerate shrieks from the balcony" (quoted in Hoffman, xviii).

The ban on portraying "sexual perversion" on the New York stage helps to explain why, between 1933 and the late 1960s, the portrayal of homosexuality in plays was neither so frequent, so intense, or so experimental as it was in the novel during the same period, and when plays with homosexual characters did appear, the theater more often than not simply reflected existing, often homophobic, stereotypes of the homosexual rather than contributing either to new constructions of gay identities or to the destruction of homophobic clichés.

Thomas Dickinson's *Winter Bound* of 1929, which tells of two women who decide to spend the winter in a lonely farmhouse to discover if "women can be true to themselves," was described as a play that "intended to treat of the pathological subject of what must be loosely, vaguely and inaccurately described as decadent love," while *Incubator* (1932), a play set in a boys' school, "for a time . . . threatens to become a shocker dealing with twisted relationships" when "two of the boys develop an unnatural affection" for the hero (quoted in Katz 1983, 471). That lesbian relationships can only inaccurately be described as love is the first reviewer's point, while affection between males is, of course, not only unnatural but a threat to what may have otherwise been a good play seems to be the implication of the other.

Noel Coward's *Design for Living* (1933) is a play of delicious corruption in which an independent "New Woman," shockingly unconcerned with marriage or with conforming to the roles expected of women, lives with two men, an artist and a playwright, whose friendship for each other and mutual attraction to the heroine is equally unconventional. The resulting triangle, richly and suggestively sexual, has, as the *Times* reviewer hinted, "a constant odor of sin." As the reviewer points out, in the play, Leo, talking with Gilda, "succinctly describes the plot: 'I love you. You love me. You love Otto. I love Otto. Otto loves you. Otto loves me'" (quoted in Katz 1983, 473). When Mordaunt Shairp's *The Green Bay Tree* opened in New York in 1933, the *Times* reviewer described it as the story of "a relationship between Mr. Dulcimer, a rich hot-house sybarite, and Julian Dulcimer, whom he adopted at a tender age and has reared in emasculating luxury. The relationship is abnormal, since Mr. Dulcimer with all his petty sensuousness is an abnormal person. But there is nothing in the play to indicate that the relationship is more than passively degenerate" (quoted in Katz 1983, 488). The language of this review invokes nearly every cliché associated with homosexuality, from imputations of excessive and possibly depraved sensuality—"hot-house sybarite"—to the suggestion of child molestation—at a "tender age"—to unmanly weakness—"petty sensuousness and emasculating luxury"—and a depraved but nevertheless inadequate and sterile sexuality—"passively degenerate."

In 1934 another major American writer turned her attention to the effects of homophobia and the destruction caused by innuendo about sexual orientation when Lillian Hellman wrote *The Children's Hour*, in which two women are forced into social isolation and finally death because of rumors about the nature of their relationship. If Hellman's play taught that imputations of homosexuality whether true or not in a homophobic society can victimize and lead to tragedy, then *Wise Tomorrow*, which opened in New York in 1937 and was described by Brooks Atkinson of the *Times* as "the story of an evil minded and treacherous old actress who falls in love with an attractive young actress and wrecks her life," reinforced stereotypes about homosexuals who victimize the innocent. The homosexual monster was again summoned in a review of Jean-Paul Sartre's *No Exit* in 1946, when the *Times* reviewer described one of the characters as a "loathsome homosexual who has poisoned and destroyed the life of a married woman of whom she has been enamored" (quoted in Katz 1983, 610). That plays—more often about lesbians than about homosexual men—constructed and supported these stereotypes suggests that the drama was not a site wherein homosexuals might hope to find positive or tolerant portrayals of their lives or sympathetic constructions of identity.

In 1947 Tennessee Williams allowed the spectral offstage presence of a dead homosexual to inform the ambiance and the essence of *A Streetcar Named Desire*. When Blanche DuBois describes the literal death of love, Williams enshrines in the mythology of the American stage the tortured and doomed homosexual whose identity is shaped by and hangs in the balance between the unspoken and unspeakable promptings of desire and the dogmatic imperatives that define what men ought to be. Williams constructs also that other peculiarly American character, the doomed women who desperately love men like this—women who will often in one form or another populate his plays and whose hopeless love for men whose desires lie elsewhere mirrors some perhaps as yet undefined truth about both American men and American women. Blanche says in scene 6, "There was something different about the boy, a nervousness, a softness and tenderness which wasn't like a man's, although he wasn't the least bit effeminate looking—still that thing was there. . . . He came to me for help. I didn't know that. I didn't find out anything until after our marriage, when . . . all I knew was I'd failed him in some mysterious way. . . . He was in the quicksands clutching me. . . . Then I found out. In the worst of all possible ways. By coming suddenly into a room that I thought was empty—which wasn't empty, but had two people in it . . . the boy I had married and an older man who had been his friend for years."

Though Williams's female characters are not, as is often suggested, homosexual men in disguise, they do encapsulate both homosexual and heterosexual myths. Williams's men, like Brick in *Cat on a Hot Tin Roof*, Sebastian in *Suddenly Last Summer*, Kilroy in *Camino Real*, and Val Xavier in *Orpheus Descending*—all doomed—are also ultimately unobtainable, and sometimes actually homosexual. The women who want them desire them in part because they are unobtainable and because they believe that they can in some way save them—a hope implicit in Williams's portrayal of heterosexual women who love homosexual men. But Williams also seems to believe that homosexual love is itself doomed though eternally desirous, always looking for the damaged youth to heal, for the unobtainable hero to win and love or lose, for a difference sometimes concealed beneath a veneer of irreproachable heterosexuality. If this is so—at least it is for alcoholic Brick and for Blanche's dead husband and for Sebastian—then Williams's women also seek the damaged and even emotionally emasculated American male that waits beneath the surface of an ostensibly American masculinity—"he wasn't the least bit effeminate"—at once man and boy. In this sense Williams writes a devastating critique of American gender-bound society, and sad and brave Blanche can reach out to brave Fay Etrange and Maggie to Myra Breckenridge, and they all may know that they are in some way sisters.

In 1953 Robert Anderson's *Tea and Sympathy* gave homosexuals a high camp line to use at parties—"In years to come when you think of me, and you will, be kind"—but gave nothing to the sensitive young man who is accused of being homosexual by a schoolmaster (who himself is probably homosexual) and finds heterosexual salvation in the arms of an older woman. Homosexuality is vaguely suggested though never outwardly stated in several plays written in the 1950s—for example, those of William Inge are populated with handsome young men whose ultra-virility and tight jeans are often equally admired by both men and women and whose sexuality is curiously and sometimes ambiguously presented. Homosexual stereotypes, usually negative, people other plays of the 1950s, from the effeminate queens of Wolcott Gibb's *A Season in the Sun*, set at Fire Island, to the thoroughly hateful homosexuals in Meyer Levin's dramatization of the Leopold-Loeb murder case. In 1960, in *The Best Man*, Gore Vidal took up the theme of victimization, and his homosexual character is destroyed by rumors about his homosexual past.

The 1960s did, however, see an increasing number of homosexuals portrayed on stage. Edward Albee's *Zoo Story* (1959) has a strong homosexual subtext that conflates homosexuality, violence, and death, just as does LeRoi Jones's *The Toilet* (1964), though a violent encounter between a black and a white youth ends in an evocative moment of homoerotic tenderness. A number of critics have sought to read homosexuality into Albee's *Who's Afraid of Virginia Woolf?* (1962). If this is so, then the overwrought bitchiness of the play, with its high camp yet deadly dialogue, its witty and slashing denigration of heterosexual stereotypes, the presence of an imaginary child to unite the "sterile" couple George and Martha, and the aggressive sexuality of Martha, whose male-hungry forays recall Fay Etrange and predict the intense masculine desire portrayed satirically in *Myra Breckenridge* and fantastically in *City of Night*, may well suggest that homosexual viewers and homophobic critics alike found enough in it to fuel their speculations that Albee had written a play that not only critiques the poverty of heterosexual marriage but also the masks behind which homosexuals were still forced to appear.

In 1967, a play imported from Canada, John Herbert's *Fortune and Men's Eyes*, made no pretense that its characters were anything but homosexual when it examined homosexuality in prison and presented a gallery of homosexual stereotypes—the effeminate Mona, the violent and homophobic Rocky, and Smitty, whose American good looks are the object of everyone's desire but who falls in love with Mona. By the mid-1960s the American theater was beginning to consider the possibility that homosexuality might be portrayed on stage sympathetically if not daringly or originally. Because the commercial Broadway stage was not yet ready for any full-scale sympathetic portrayal, however, it was left to Off-Broadway and small experimental theaters to produce plays like Lanford Wilson's *The Madness of Lady Bright* and Robert Patrick's *The Haunted Host*, which were among the first to present homosexual characters that broke out of stereotypical molds.

Still, stereotypes were what the theater in large part most effectively employed. Mart Crowley's *The Boys in the Band* (1968) gathered together in one room every version of mid-twentieth-century gay identity. The play allowed straight America to imagine that what it had always suspected was true—that homosexuals were self-hating, pitiable and pitiful, though incredibly funny, promiscuous, alcoholic, drug-taking, and ultimately trivial denizens of a minority culture, some of whom, the play shows, attempted to "pass" as straight, while others "allowed" themselves to be freaks, while still others more properly saw the true nature of their sickness but were unable because of their disability to find a "cure." Audiences could be comforted by the surface text, however, that suggested that the impact on society of these creatures as a minority was probably negated by their sheer unimportance to anything that America really valued. The play was sad enough, funny enough, and daring enough, with an appropriate moral conclusion in which the young men, each more or less damaged but none destroyed, disappear into the morning light to live another day with Michael's grim admonition "If you show me a happy homosexual I'll show you a gay corpse" echoing in their ears. This allowed straight America to see, as one reviewer said, that "the 'boys' in Mart Crowley's band are human beings" who, as *Time* noted, just "happen to be deviates."

The Boys in the Band also bore witness to what gay America not only enacted and invented but loved and embraced, hated and rejected; Crowley's version of gay life was far too precisely on-target to be only a fiction and far too accurately reflective of a certain kind of urban gay sensibility to be dismissed as mere sensation. Many gays left the play convulsed by laughter and also uncomfortably shocked by recognition and not a little touched by anger. Gay people seeing it loved the camp humor and witty repartee, the subversive and impudent effrontery of Emory, at once brave and nelly, who had the guts to love a black man, and the sheer magnificent bitchiness of Harold, whose Jewish shtick meshed so perfectly with grand queen malevolence. Attractive, vaguely winning and winsome, and blurry but cuddly was the all-American Donald; honest, decent, caring, and appealing was the normal Hank; excitingly promiscuous, handsome, and slightly sinister was Larry. All these men looked like what every all-American homosexual thought heterosexuals wanted homosexuals to look like. For comic relief there was the hustler, Cowboy, dumb and hot and the stuff on which dreams though not relationships are made, and finally the monstrous, self-hating old-style sickness of Michael, trapped by the twin addictions of religion and booze, a figure whose passion for sweaters and whose outrageous and very American viciousness was so perfectly conflated with Emory's camp and Harold's lyrically destructive soliloquies that it created on stage an absolutely perfect-pitch rendition of 1960s gay talk and gay style.

The Boys in the Band, more than any other play—indeed, probably more than any other work of literature in the twentieth century to that time—publicized a fully formed catalog of gay identity. Produced on the eve of Stonewall, *The Boys in the Band* opened the closet for homosexuality to come out into the mainstream of heterosexual American life, but out of that closet came a group of men whose identities mirrored both stereotypes and reality but who all, only a year later, would be given the opportunity to confront the world that Stonewall promised, a world wherein Bernard would no longer be a token, Cowboy no longer merely an object; a world where Donald, Hank, and Larry would no longer feel constrained to pose as heterosexualized homosexuals, where Alan might come out, and Emory, Harold, and even Michael might be given the chance to redirect their subversive sensibilities and laserlike perception of social reality away from self-hatred and internalized homophobia toward affirmation and liberation.

NOVELS

Between the publication of *Imre* in 1906 and *A Scarlet Pansy* in 1932, nine novels with homoerotic themes were published in America, according to Roger Austen in *Playing The Game: The Homosexual Novel in America* (1977); to this count James Levin in *The Gay Novel in America* (1991) adds one or two more. Bruce Kenilworth's *Goldie*, Charles Henri Ford and Parker Tyler's *The Young and the Evil*, and Richard Meeker's *Better Angel* appeared in 1933 and implied a positive ending for a homosexual character.

Still, with these few positive novels came even more homophobic depictions of gay men. In Hemingway's fiction—from his 1938 short story "The Mother of a Queen" to the homosexuals in *The Sun Also Rises*—gays are pansies and effeminate. In the works of Thomas Wolfe and F. Scott Fitzgerald homosexuals pass through on the edges of life—mysterious, always effeminate, distanced from the reality of the heterosexual characters. John Dos Passos in *U.S.A.* creates a considerable gallery of gay characters, almost none sympathetic, while in James Cain's tough-guy thrillers there was often a fairy to beat up or put down.

Mrs. Blair Niles's *Strange Brother* (1931) is the first of a series of books written after 1930 that demonize homosexuality under the guise of "sympathy" and "compassion" and that purport to confront homosexuality as a "problem." The *New York Times* reviewer who described the "groaning shelf" of homosexual fiction published after 1930 might have listed many books of this kind. Their titles—*Twilight Men, Butterfly Man, Shadows Flying, The Divided Path, The Dark Tunnel, Dark Desires*—indicate the melodramas of sexual anxiety and homophobia played out in their pages and also indicate the psychoanalytic theories that inform many of them when psychiatric and psychoanalytic theory dominated the medical construction of "the homosexual" identity. In these books the causes of homosexuality are often laid to the absence of a father and a domineering or effeminizing mother. The homosexual men, as a presumed consequence, are usually effeminate or at the best sensitive, and if not that then villains and sexual predators. They are all lonely, self-absorbed, isolated, and incapable of love. They frequent a gay underworld that is often luridly and stereotypically described, and their usual end is suicide or death by violence. If these men are left alive they are promised nothing but isolated celibacy, which is, many of these books insist, the only real "cure" for homosexuality, usually diagnosed as social and a personal illness that damages creativity and emotional growth and reflects a seriously arrested development.

Strange Brother can represent them all, for in it Mark, who will eventually commit suicide, can bear his difference no longer because, as he explains to a close woman friend, he is "what you might call a half man." In New York he encounters other "outcasts" like himself but, fearing that he cannot control his passion, determines to reject sex. But retribution stalks him, and when he is threatened with blackmail he kills himself. The cover of the book shows a fine-featured man with black and narrowed eyes, darkly shadowed. He supports his head with a thin and fine long-fingered hand that rises from a bent wrist. He stares painfully out at the reader, and the red tie he wears picks up the deep red of his full and sensuous lips.

In the provocative and prophetically entitled 1949 essay "Preservation of Innocence: Studies for the New Morality," James Baldwin argues that both the source and the curse of American constructions of manhood are to be discovered in the American male's obsession with a masculinity that is founded "in the most infantile and elemental externals" that cause his attitude toward women to be a "wedding of the most abysmal romanticism and the most implacable distrust." Baldwin further argues that the American hatred of the homosexual and "our present debasement of and our obsession with him corresponds to the debasement of the relations between the sexes; and that his ambiguous and terrible position in our society reflects the ambiguities and terrors which time has deposited on that relationship." In the American novel, especially the novel by or about homosexuals, Baldwin asserted, brutality "rages unchecked," and the death visited on so many homosexual characters is not only a function of some novelistic bias but a mirror of American homophobia, which is "compelled by a panic which is close to madness. These novels are not concerned with homosexuality but with the ever-present danger of sexual activity between men" (quoted in Katz 1983, 647–50).

The 1940s saw the publication of Christopher Isherwood's *Berlin Stories* (1946), John Horne Burns's *The Gallery* (1947), and Gore Vidal's *The City and the Pillar* (1948), the last of which sets out to prove that effeminacy and homosexuality do not need to occupy the same conceptual space and that homosexuality can be almost as normal and ordinarily American as football. Vidal's novel was the "most forthright" gay novel, as Austen describes it, to have been published in America to that time. As Vidal explained, "I decided to examine the homosexual underworld . . . and in the process show the 'naturalness' of homosexual relations. . . . In 1946 . . . it was part of the American folklore that homosexuality was a form of mental disease, confined for the most part to interior decorators and ballet dancers. Knowing this to be untrue, I set out to shatter the stereotype by taking as my protagonist a completely ordinary boy of the middle class and through his eyes observing the various strata of the underworld" (quoted in Austen, 119).

Vidal's novel carried the normalizing of homosexuality into respectable fiction and in turn would be the model for much of the normalizing fiction to follow. Despite his desire to shatter stereotypes, however, Vidal still ends the novel with a murder when his ordinary American boy, Jim, kills the thing he loves, Bob, the man with whom Jim had his first homosexual experience. This is the ending of the 1948 version of the book as published. Vidal had originally ended the book with violence, but with retributive violence against straight stereotypes, for when Jim meets Bob again after many years and tries to make love to him again, Bob in a fit of homosexual panic and disgust rejects Jim. Jim then rapes Bob. Vidal's publisher, according to Levin, changed the ending to the even more violent one. Vidal restored the ending in his revision of the book in 1965 (Levin, 76).

In 1948 also appeared Tennessee Williams's homoerotic stories in his collection *One Arm*, and in the next year Burns's second novel, *Lucifer with a Book* (1949), and Truman Capote's *Other Voices, Other Rooms* (1949). After 1950 and before Stonewall Levin and Austen discuss nearly 100 homosexual novels of varying kinds and quality, including James Barr's *Quatrefoil* (1950), one of a number of novels set in the military that seemed to resist the idea that homosexuality was incompatible with military service; Fritz Peters's *Finistere* (1951); and Williams's second collection of stories, *Hard Candy* (1954). In James Baldwin's *Giovanni's Room* (1956), perhaps the most famous of all American gay novels, Baldwin presents a love story between two men, one an American, set in Paris. The book suggests that unless America rejects its puritanical homophobia homosexual love can never flourish on American soil; at the novel's end both men, the American David and his lover Giovanni, are driven to different kinds of desperation— Giovanni to murder and David to what Baldwin hints will be a lonely and futile life of sexual searching and unhappiness.

William Burroughs's *Naked Lunch* (1959) represented the most daring if unsatisfying experiment with homoerotic sexual and sadistic fantasy yet attempted in the American novel. Burroughs uses a strategy initiated by *A Scarlet Pansy* and *The Young and the Evil*. He writes into American fiction the worst fears of American heterosexuals concerning homosexuals. In Burroughs's novels and in works soon to follow (like *Last Exit to Brooklyn* and *City of Night*) America's nightmares about transvestite homosexuals, sexual predators, and insatiable seducers of boys are offered as a version of homosexual reality but without apology, and sometimes without explanation. Charles Wright's *The Messenger* (1963) and Hubert Selby's *Last Exit to Brooklyn* (1964) present especially grim pictures of the homosexual underworld of hustlers and drag queens, while in John Rechy's *City of Night* (1963) the social transgression signaled by the giddy drag and masquerade of *A Scarlet Pansy* is transformed into a new American homosexual transgressive genre—the supersexual masquerade of the macho gay male whose clones will dominate 1960s style.

Levin suggests that Rechy's book is marred by acquiescence to the "psychoanalytic viewpoint" and "infers that the extremes of gender role playing, hypermasculinity and effeminacy, are just two different sides of a similar pathology" and sees Rechy's construction of a version of homosexual identity as homophobic and self-hating.[6] However useful or correct this analysis may be, *City of Night*, because of its daring and often nearly lyric evocation of sex, holds an original and influential place in the inventive and transgressive tradition of American gay confrontational fiction. The political and cultural differences between the straight world and the gay are subsumed in the novel in the highly charged atmosphere of sexual difference and homosexual desire, for though the hustlers nearly all swear allegiance to the peculiar masculinized construction of American heterosexual values, their every act is informed by a politics of power, of dominance and subordination, that is entirely defined in homosexual terms.

James Baldwin's *Another Country* (1962) not only positively presented homosexuality as an ethically superior kind of love, described its rituals and lovemaking in some of the finest lyric prose yet written about male-male love in the twentieth century, but defined, effectively for the first time in American fiction, its troubled association with race. The novel did not avoid the complication of race and homosexuality as did *Giovanni's Room*. Instead, Baldwin weaves a drama in which homophobia and racism are conflated and in which homosexual love becomes the potential instrument that might destroy racial barriers.

Christopher Isherwood's *A Single Man* (1964) and Sanford Friedman's *Totempole* (1965) positively portray the lives of ordinary gay men. Isherwood's novel offers a finely drawn picture of what was and would continue to be an unusual character in a gay fiction often devoted to young men—a middle-aged gay male. Isherwood neither apologizes for nor explains the homosexuality of his hero; homosexuality is a given that neither inhibits nor especially enhances life. In 1966 a work of homosexual pornography, Richard Armory's *The Song of the Loon* (which became an underground bestseller), returned to American fiction some of the exotic, sexually charged, and satiric euphoria that had entered the mainstream of fiction with *A Scarlet Pansy* and *The Young and the Evil* but had been submerged by the often homophobic problem novels of the 1940s and 1950s, attempts to normalize or anatomize homosexuality in the works of Vidal and Baldwin, and attempts to sensationalize it in the works of Rechy, Selby, and Wright.

The first American homosexual fiction forecasts the concerns of what will follow, whether it is to construct homosexuals as "normal" or even extra-manly men who happen to love other men, as tormented outcasts trapped by desires that they would gladly reject if only they could, or as campy and effeminate queens or deliberate transgressive challengers to social and sexual normality. Indeed, the "problem" novel that constructed twilight identities in the 1930s and 1940s, though having lost any real reason for continued existence after Stonewall, still persisted as a form well into the 1970s. Hobson's *Consenting Adult*, for example, appeared four decades after Niles's *Strange Brother*. Both books were written by a nonhomosexual writers. The book jacket for *Strange Brother* describes the story as "a daring adventure into the heart of that which until recently has been forbidden territory to even the most advanced of the sex novelists," and later calls it "a brave and daring novel" and "a sympathetic statement of the genuine problems that confront the sensitive intermediate" a book with "a delicate theme" that Mrs. Niles handles with "perfect taste" and with "courage, tact and broad human understanding."

The jacket of Hobson's book suggests that over four decades there has been little change: it is "a novel of sensitivity and perception" written with a "warmth of human feeling and understanding" about the problems of a mother whose son has come out. But when she offers "him all the supporting love and strength that she can" she discovers that "he doesn't want that kind of love and strength"—what amounts to heterosexual condescension freighted with vague notions involving cure or closeted deception—and that he "fiercely rejects it from the start," preferring to become "out" and activist. Book jacket writers are finely attuned to the telling cliché that lets the public know what they already think, and so it is nothing if not discouraging to see that in 1931 and 1975 the broad "human understanding" apparently possessed in full measure by nonhomosexual writers is a necessary condition for dealing with sensitive inverts or obstreperous faggots, both of whom, despite the good intentions of the authors, still seem to be portrayed between the lines as perhaps a little less human than the writers whose "good taste" so sensitively draws them.

The heterosexualized homosexuals of 1948 and of the 1970s novels of Particia Nell Warren, such as *The Front Runner* (1974), turn up again as good straight boys—no more different from the boy next door except that it is the boy next door they want to sleep with—even in such recent family-oriented homosexual fiction as David Leavitt's. It remains to be decided whether fantasies of masculinity that in effect heterosexualize gay men and submerge difference in a normalizing and heterosexualizing text are becoming, like the dark and punitive books of the 1940s and 1950s, a disappearing strain in homosexual fiction, or whether this form will be renegotiated by parody or comedy, as in David Feinberg's *Eighty-sixed*, or in Michael Chabon's turncoat novel, *The Mysteries of Pittsburgh*, in which the nice gay boy becomes more or less a nice straight boy at the end, or by reassignment to other genres, like Joseph Hansen's grim tough-gay novels.

If *A Scarlet Pansy* was the first novel to predict the gender transgression, eroticized fantasy, and style-as-subject-and-manner in certain American homoerotic texts, it also introduces into what it is probably now correct to call American gay fiction the giddy experimentation of high-camp style and the creation of literary sites within which homoerotic fantasy deconstructs sober homophobic reality. As a title *A Scarlet Pansy* resists, confronts, and challenges and it will not be equalled in its transgressive directness until Burroughs's 1950s novel, *Queer*, Burt Hansen's *Known Homosexual* (1968), or Larry Kramer's *Faggots* (1977). *A Scarlet Pansy* stands at the head of a genealogy of the most transgressive and socially destabilizing of our great gay male texts written before Stonewall: Ford and Tyler's *The Young and the Evil*, John Horne Burns's *The Gallery*, Rechy's *The City of Night*, the work of William Burroughs, Allen Ginsberg, Tennessee Williams, and James Purdy, and it forecasts Vidal's *Myra Breckenridge*, a book that completes for American fiction what *A Scarlet Pansy* had begun—the translation of homosexuality from its position as a diseased and effeminate subversion and inversion of American manhood and morality and a sublime affront to and an interrogation of heretofore unquestioned assumptions concerning the nature of gender, sex, and desire, and a speculation about heretofore unimagined possibilities inherent in the fluid reinterpretations of gender, sex, and desire.

Myra Breckenridge recalled American gay fiction to its great project, and on the eve of Stonewall it was one of the funniest, most remarkable, and most transgressively destabilizing novels of the decade. In it Vidal demands, delivers, and initiates a serious and provocative (if campy) fantasy concerning the indeterminacy of gender and sexuality and the radical irrelevancy of sex-object choice—the very discussion that is so much a part of our own negotiations with concepts of sex, sexuality, gender, and sexual politics.

If Vidal in *The City and the Pillar* can be credited with writing the first American gay novel that normalizes homosexuality, he can also be credited with writing the first in *Myra Breckenridge* that forced a reevaluation of the very canons of enforced heterosexuality that in *The City and the Pillar* he had applied to homosexual lives. Myra Breckenridge, once Myron Breckenridge and now postoperatively a transsexual, sets out to revenge herself on American manhood, which, when she was Myron, made him the object both of sexual and personal humiliation. She chooses as the symbolic object of her revenge the handsome Rusty, a prefect heterosexual, who she eventually rapes with an artificial instrument of truly American proportions, causing Rusty to eagerly embrace homosexuality. Myra also takes revenge on an exemplary flower of American heterosexual womanhood—Rusty's girlfriend, Mary Ann, who falls in love with Myra. Mary Ann fears a sexual encounter with Myra, but when Myra is, as it were, reengendered once more into Myron, Mary Ann marries him, despite his lack of certain key endowments, and the union of the heterosexual woman and the homosexual male becomes an occasion for a satiric celebration of what Vidal sees as the peculiarly American ignorance about and confusion over sexuality, gender, and sexual object choice.

The reinterpretation of and speculation about gender, sexuality, and identity has been the vital project of gay literature since Stonewall. If the term "queer," a linguistic weapon of homophobia, has been deliberately co-opted in our time to refashion the homosexual body and the homosexual imagination into what Frank Browning in *The Culture of Desire* calls "the body of subversion"—in which queerness refuses "to be imprisoned by heterosexual conventions about what is male and what is female"—then queer theorists need to look to Fay Etrange as an undoubted fairy godmother and Myra Breckenridge as our defining sister *and* brother. Between 1930 and the eve of Stonewall, homosexuality was to become in American literature one of the "great subjects," as Henry James might have said—one that, like all great literary subjects, was and still does generate excitement, experimentation, anger, anxiety, rejection. It introduced into our literature as well as into our lives the ineradicable presence of difference and the now undeniable influence of homosexual desire and homoerotic texts that have forced a renegotiation, no matter how uncomfortable, and how inconclusive, of every propriety.

This road to Stonewall has been traveled by a brave pilgrim band, heroes of our history, whether writers of texts or inhabitants of them. With words as their weapons, they are heroes indeed, with a thousand faces and as many names—sodomite, molly, Uranian, invert, pervert, homosexual, fairy, pansy, queer, gay, and queer again. They have constructed not one unchanging identity but many over time. Like all heroic stories, theirs is one filled with dangerous feats, threatening locales, and hostile peoples, and like all heroic stories the hero has ever a single quest—to slay the monster and then to find himself. The Dragon Homophobia still lives, cunning, deadly, insidious, but the travelers to whatever Stonewall may next rise on the horizon no longer seek their destiny alone or in small, devoted bands. Armies of lovers, as Whitman had foreseen, now let the world know that we are everywhere.

Homophobia has always been the shadow text of homosexual literature, and its text is now and has always been a condemnation of that vice not fit to be named. Naming ourselves with names of our own choosing, emptying the silence imposed on us of its oppressive content, and filling that silence with our own voices has been the project of our texts. The assertion that the free use of the body is essential to all freedoms, and the deployment of the free body as a resistant text, derives from that first defiant cry in the eighteenth century and echoes from the first shouts of defiance at Stonewall, when the descendants of a hundred identities and textual enactments determined to put into life what poems, plays, novels, and essays had been for so long inventing. Homosexuality, homotextuality, homoerotic desire—whatever is chosen to denominate the many variations of Whitman's need of the love of comrades—has joined with resistance to homophobia to create famous victories in the work of all those who enact in texts the dizzying, exhilarating, exorbitant, and dangerous demands of the homosexual, the homoerotic, the gay—the queer—imagination.

NOTES AND REFERENCES

INTRODUCTION

1. William Hoffman makes this point in *Gay Plays: The First Collection* (New York: Avon, 1979), xxix.

2. Quoted in Byrne Fone, ed., *Hidden Heritage: History and the Gay Imagination* (New York: Avocation Press, 1979), 320; hereafter cited in text.

3. Martin Duberman, *Stonewall* (New York: Dutton, 1993), xv.

4. Quoted in Frank Browning, *The Culture of Desire: Paradox and Perversity in Gay Lives Today* (New York: Crown, 1993), 35; hereafter cited in text.

5. Donald Webster Cory, *The Homosexual in America: A Subjective Approach* (New York: Greenberg, 1951), 228; hereafter cited in text.

6. Quoted in Roger Austen, *Playing the Game: The Homosexual Novel in America* (New York: Bobbs-Merrill, 1977), 57–58; hereafter cited in text.

7. John W. Aldridge, *After the Lost Generation: A Critical Study of the Writers of Two Wars* (1951; New York: Noonday Press, 1958), 101–2; hereafter cited in text.

8. See Robert K. Martin (*The Homosexual Tradition in American Poetry* [Austin and London: University of Texas Press, 1979], 4; hereafter cited in text) on Holloway's willingness to adduce heterosexuality from the later published version of an earlier manuscript in which the pronouns were changed from masculine to feminine.

9. Quoted in Martin Duberman, *About Time: Exploring the Gay Past* (New York: Gay Presses of New York, 1986), 87; hereafter cited in text.

10. Gay Wilson Allen, *The Solitary Singer: A Critical Biography of Walt Whitman* (New York: Macmillan, 1955), 222ff; hereafter cited in text.

11. William White, "Walt Whitman in the Eighties: A Bibliographical Essay," in *Walt Whitman Here and Now*, ed. Joann P. Krieg (Westport, Conn.: Greenwood Press, 1985), 223; hereafter cited in text.

12. David S. Reynolds, *Beneath the American Renaissance: The Subversive Imagination in the Age of Emerson and Melville* (Cambridge, Mass., and London:

Harvard University Press, 1988), 328; hereafter cited in text. Reynolds's important book has no indexed entry on homosexuality, and the index entry for Whitman's "sexual orientation" leads us only to Reynolds's unwillingness to come to any conclusion.

13.   See Martin 1979, 33ff, on "adhesiveness."

14.   John Snyder, *The Dear Love of Man: Tragic and Lyric Communion in Walt Whitman* (Boston, 1975).

15.   David S. Leverenz, *Manhood in the American Renaissance* (New York, 1989), 30.

16.   Joan Acocella, "Perfectly Frank," *New Yorker*, 19 July 1993, 78; hereafter cited in text.

17.   Thomas Yingling, *Hart Crane and the Homosexual Text* (Chicago and London: University of Chicago Press, 1990), 16; hereafter cited in text.

CHAPTER 1

1.   Quoted in Michel Rey, "Police and Sodomy in Eighteenth-Century Paris: From Sin to Disorder," in *The Pursuit of Sodomy: Male Homosexuality in Renaissance and Enlightenment Europe*, ed. Kent Gerard and Gert Hekma (New York and London: Harrington Park Press, 1989), 136; hereafter cited in text.

2.   Robert Oresko, "Homosexuality and Court Elites of Early Modern France: Some Problems, Some Suggestions, and an Example," in Gerard and Hekma, 106.

3.   See L. J. Boon, "Those Damned Sodomites: Public Images of Sodomy in the Eighteenth-Century Netherlands," in Gerard and Hekma, 245.

4.   No man who loved or made sexual overtures to another man in 1730 or in 1830 would have described himself as "homosexual," as the term was invented in 1869; nor, of course, would they have thought of themselves as "gay." By the mid-nineteenth century (though possibly earlier) the phrase "gay lady" had entered into the argot of male prostitution, but it was not to come into its current use until the early part of this century. The term "molly," prevalent in the seventeenth and eighteenth century and remaining in use into the nineteenth, denoted an effeminate transvestite homosexual. "Sodomite" was both the legal and the most popular appellation.

5.   G. S. Rousseau, "The Pursuit of Homosexuality in the Eighteenth Century: 'Utterly Confused Category' and/or Rich Repository," in *Eighteenth-Century Life: Unauthorized Sexual Behavior during the Enlightenment*, vol. 9, ed. Robert P. Maccubbin, n.s., 3 (May 1985): 147.

6.   Boon, 239; Rousseau, 154; and Louis Crompton, *Byron and Greek Love* (Berkeley: University of California Press, 1985), 16; hereafter cited in text.

7.   James D. Steakley, "Sodomy in Enlightenment Prussia: From Executions to Suicide," in Gerard and Hekma, 171.

8.   Randolph Trumbach, "Sodomitical Assaults, Gender Roles, and Sexual Development in Eighteenth-Century London," in Gerard and Hekma, 110–13.

9.   Quoted in *Don Leon: A Poem* (London: Fortune Press, n.d.), 58; hereafter cited in text by line number(s). *Don Leon* has also been printed in a facsimile of the Fortune Press edition in *A Homosexual Emancipation Miscellany, ca. 1835–1952*, in the series Homosexuality: Lesbians and Gay Men in Society, History, and Literature,

ed. Jonathan Katz (New York: Arno Press, 1975). This Arno edition, like the Fortune Press book, is out of print.

10.   Dirk Noordam, "Sodomy in the Dutch Republic, 1600–1725," in Gerard and Hekma, 215–16.

11.   G. S. Rousseau, "'In the House of Madame vander Tasse, on Long Bridge': A Homosocial University Club in Early Modern Europe," in Gerard and Hekma, 314.

12.   Randolph Trumbach, "London's Sodomites: Homosexual Behavior and Western Culture in the 18th Century," *Journal of Social History* 11, no. 1 (1977): 1–33; hereafter cited in text.

13.   Theo van der Meer, "The Persecutions of Sodomites in Eighteenth-Century Amsterdam: Changing Perceptions of Sodomy," in Gerard and Hekma, 288.

14.   Wayne Dynes and Warren Johansson, "London's Medieval Sodomites," *Cabirion and Gay Books Bulletin*, no. 10 (Winter–Spring 1984): 5ff.

15.   Quoted in Rictor Norton, *Mother Clap's Molly House: The Gay Subculture in England, 1700–1830* (London: Gay Men's Press, 1992), 55.

16.   Tobias Smollett, *Roderick Random* (New York: Signet, New American Library, 1964), 223–27; hereafter cited in text.

17.   Quoted in Michael S. Kimmel, ed., *Love Letters between a Certain Nobleman and the Famous Mr. Wilson* (New York: Harrington Park Press, 1990), 2–3; hereafter cited in text.

18.   See Randolph Trumbach, "Sodomy Transformed: Aristocratic Libertinage, Public Reputation, and the Gender Revolution of the 18th Century," in Kimmel, 105ff, on the rake, beau, and fop.

19.   See Trumbach in Kimmel, 106. If this is so, then Whiffle is a recognizable portrait of at least one aspect—and a significant one at that—of what is understood as and has been practiced as modern homosexual style, familiar to us not only in the aestheticism of the 1980s but from gay style that preceded the ultra-masculine "clone" look of the 1970s and that now exists again in tandem to the activist style of the 1990s—namely, a sexual style in which homosexual desire is maintained and practiced while social style demands a mannered and stylized effeminacy and identification with women, though not necessarily the actual practice of cross-dressing.

20.   Louis Crompton, "Jeremy Bentham's Essay on 'Paedersty': An Introduction," *Journal of Homosexuality* 3 (1978): 384–85. The text of Bentham was first published here.

CHAPTER 2

1.   I will use "sodomite" here as a more historically appropriate term than "homosexual." Although Byron was probably "a sodomite," the very specificity of "sodomite" militates against the broader categories that Byron seems to be theorizing—categories that seem to move toward later theorizations of the "homosexual" and the "homoerotic." The author of *Don Leon* suggests the practice, since he uses "sodomite" only once, and that to point out that "sodomite or saint" can contract disease, saving the use of "sodomy" for a powerful political statement. In a text that attempts to erase the stigma from sodomitical acts the erasure of the word itself is a powerful deployment of the principle that language does indeed precede and empowers action.

2. Michel Foucault, *The History of Sexuality*, vol. 1, *An Introduction* (New York: Vintage Books, 1980), 43; hereafter cited in text.

3. Brian Reade, *Sexual Heretics: Male Homosexuality in English Literature, 1850–1900* (New York: Coward McCann, 1970), 362; hereafter cited in text. Reade's anthology gathers most of the texts pertinent to this period, and I quote from them in their location in Reade.

CHAPTER 3

1. Jonathan Ned Katz, *Gay/Lesbian Almanac* (New York: Harper & Row, 1983), 40; hereafter cited in text.

2. Jonathan Katz, *Gay American History* (New York: Thomas Y. Crowell, 1976), 26; hereafter cited in text.

3. Robert K. Martin, "Knights-Errant and Gothic Seducers: Representations of Male Friendship in Mid-Nineteenth-Century America," in *Hidden from History: Reclaiming the Gay and Lesbian Past*, ed. Martin Duberman, Martha Vicinus, and George Chauncey, Jr. (New York: New American Library, 1989), 170; hereafter cited in text.

4. Michael Moon, "Disseminating Whitman," in *Displacing Homophobia*, ed. Ronald Butters, John M. Clum, and Michael Moon (Durham, N.C.: Duke University Press, 1989), 250.

5. Quoted in Milton Hindus, *Whitman: The Critical Heritage* (London: Routledge & Kegan Paul, 1971), 244–45; hereafter cited in text.

6. Walt Whitman, *Leaves of Grass*, ed. Sculley Bradley and Harold Blodgett (New York: W. W. Norton, 1973), 739; hereafter cited in text as *LG*.

7. Ralph Waldo Emerson, *The Journals and Miscellaneous Notebooks of Ralph Waldo Emerson*, ed. William H. Gilman, Alfred R. Ferguson, George P. Clark, and Merrell R. Davis (Cambridge, Mass.: Belknap Press of Harvard University, 1960), 1: 353; hereafter cited in text.

8. Henry David Thoreau, *The Journal of Henry David Thoreau*, ed. Bradford Torrey and Francis H. Allen, 14 vols. (Cambridge, Mass.: Riverside Press/Houghton Mifflin, 1906), 1: 94; hereafter cited in text.

9. Quoted in Katz 1976 from Perry Miller, *Consciousness in Concord: The Text of Thoreau's Hitherto "Lost Journal," 1840–41, Together with Notes and Commentary* (Boston: Houghton Mifflin, 1958). All quotations in this paragraph are from pp. 176–77 of this text.

10. Quoted in Katz 1976 from Miller, 176–77.

11. Quoted in Byrne Fone, *Masculine Landscapes: Walt Whitman and the Homoerotic Text* (Carbondale: Southern Illinois University Press, 1992), 226; hereafter cited in text.

12. Jay Leyda, *The Melville Log: A Documentary Life of Herman Melville* (New York: Gordian Press, 1951), 211.

13. Robert K. Martin, *Hero, Captain, Stranger: Male Friendship, Social Critique, and Literary Form in the Sea Novels of Herman Melville* (Chapel Hill: University of North Carolina Press, 1986), 16; hereafter cited in text.

14. See Byrne Fone, "This Other Eden: Arcadia and the Homosexual Imagination," in *Literary Visions of Homosexuality*, ed. Stuart Kellog (New York:

Haworth Press, 1983), 13–34.

15. Herman Melville, *Typee* (Garden City: Doubleday, 1961), 52–53; hereafter cited in text.

16. Bayard Taylor, "The Poet's Journal," in *The Poetical Works of Bayard Taylor* (Boston: Riverside Press, 1883). All quotations are from this edition.

17. Walt Whitman, *Notebooks and Unpublished Prose Manuscripts*, vol. 1, ed. Edward F. Grier (New York: New York University Press, 1984), 177; hereafter cited in text as *NUPM*.

18. Bayard Taylor, *Poems of the Orient* (1854), in *The Poetical Works of Bayard Taylor*. All quotations are from this edition.

CHAPTER 4

1. Ralph Waldo Emerson, "Friendship," in *Essays*, first series (1841; New York: A. S. Barnes, n.d.), 65.

2. Walt Whitman, *The Early Poems and Fiction*, ed. Thomas L. Brasher, in *The Collected Writings of Walt Whitman* (New York: New York University Press, 1963), 74; hereafter cited in text as *EPF*.

3. The story was first published in the *New World* in November 1841 and was reprinted as "The Child and the Profligate," *Columbian Magazine*, October 1844, and again in *Brooklyn Eagle*, January 1847. There are variations among the texts, but the most significant variations occur when Whitman published the story in the *Complete Prose Works* in 1892. There his radical later revisions nearly nullify and conceal the implied homoerotic text of the original tale. It is the first version, however, that I would like to address here.

4. Walt Whitman, *Daybooks and Notebooks*, vol. 3, ed. William White, in *The Collected Writings of Walt Whitman* (New York: New York University Press, 1978), 740–41; hereafter cited in text as *DN*.

5. Walt Whitman, *Prose Works 1892*, vol. 2, ed. Floyd Stovall, in *The Collected Writings of Walt Whitman* (New York: New York University Press, 1964), 414–15; hereafter cited in text as *PW*.

6. Quoted in Oscar Lovell Trigg, "Variorum Readings of *Leaves of Grass*," in *Leaves of Grass*, ed. Emory Holloway (inclusive edition) (New York: Doubleday, Doran, 1928), 568.

7. Although the *Calamus* poems were published as part of *Leaves of Grass*, here I treat them as a collection unto itself and identify them by their numbering in the 1860 edition.

8. Quoted in *Whitman's Manuscripts: "Leaves of Grass,"* ed. Fredson Bowers (1860; Chicago: University of Chicago Press, 1955), 13, 34–35.

CHAPTER 5

1. Richard Dellamora, *Masculine Desire: The Sexual Politics of Victorian Aestheticism* (Chapel Hill: University of North Carolina Press, 1990), 86–93; hereafter cited in text.

2. *The Memoirs of John Addington Symonds*, ed. Phyllis Grosskurth (New York: Random House, 1984), 189; hereafter cited in text.

3. Quoted in *Re Walt Whitman*, ed. Horace L. Traubel, Richard Maurice Bucke, and Thomas B. Harned (Philadelphia: David MacKay, 1893), 3.

4. Edward Carpenter, *My Days and Dreams* (1916), vol. 1 of *Edward Carpenter: Selected Writings* (London: Gay Men's Press, 1984), 84; hereafter cited in text.

5. Quoted in Horace Traubel, *With Walt Whitman in Camden*, vol. 1 (London: Gay & Bird, 1906), 159–60; hereafter cited in text.

CHAPTER 6

1. Quoted in Timothy d'Arch Smith, *Love in Earnest: Some Notes on the Lives and Writings of English Uranian Poets from 1889 to 1930* (London: Routledge & Kegan Paul, 1970), 58; hereafter cited in text.

2. See Jeffrey Weeks, *Coming Out: Homosexual Politics in Britain from the Nineteenth Century to the Present* (London: Quartet Books, 1977), 14–15; hereafter cited in text. See also Dellamora, 200.

3. E. M. Forster, *Maurice* (1913; New York: New American Library, 1971), 159; hereafter cited in text.

4. John Addington Symonds, "A Problem in Modern Ethics" (1891; London, 1896), 3; hereafter cited in text.

5. See Gregory Woods, *Articulate Flesh: Male Homoeroticism in Modern Poetry* (New Haven and London: Yale University Press, 1987), 7–123.

6. Bayard Taylor, *Joseph and His Friend* (1870; New York: G. P. Putnam & Sons, 1882), 217.

7. Plato, *Symposium*, trans. Walter Hamilton (New York: Penguin, 1951), sec. 211a; hereafter cited in text.

8. Havelock Ellis, *Sexual Inversion* (1897), vol. 1 of *The Studies in the Psychology of Sex* (Philadelphia: F. A. Davis, 1901). I cite case numbers referring to this edition in the text.

9. *Sins of the Cities of the Plain* (1881; New York: Masquerade Books, 1992).

10. *Teleny* (North Hollywood, Calif.: Brandon House, 1967); hereafter cited in text.

CHAPTER 7

1. Quoted in Phyllis Grosskurth, *The Woeful Victorian: A Biography of John Addington Symonds* (New York: Holt, Rinehart & Winston, 1964), 277; hereafter cited in text.

2. John Addington Symonds, *Studies of the Greek Poets* (London: A & C. Black, 1920); hereafter cited in text.

3. John Addington Symonds, "A Problem in Greek Ethics" (1883; London, 1901), 1; hereafter cited in text.

4. John Addington Symonds, "The Dantesque and Platonic Ideals of Love" in *The Key of Blue* (London, 1893), 84; hereafter cited in text.

5. Carl Westphal, "Die contrare Sexualempfindung, Symptom eines

neuopthischen (psychopathischen) Zustandes," *Archiv fur Psychiatrie und Nevenkrankheitien* 2 (1870): 73–108. Quoted in David M. Halperin, *One Hundred Years of Homosexuality and Other Essays on Greek Love* (New York and London: Routledge & Kegan Paul, 1990).

6. Quoted in Brian Masters, *The Life of E. F. Benson* (London: Chatto & Windus, 1991), 75

CHAPTER 8

1. Edward Carpenter, *The Intermediate Sex* (1908), in *Edward Carpenter: Selected Writings*, 1: 185.

2. Edward Carpenter, "Homogenic Love" (1894), quoted in Reade, 324ff. The essay was later incorporated into *The Intermediate Sex* (1908) as the section "The Homogenic Attachment."

CHAPTER 10

1. See Weeks (118–27) for the best discussion.

2. See Jeffrey Meyers, *Homosexuality and Literature, 1890–1930* (London: University of London/Athlone Press, 1977), 101; hereafter cited in text.

3. See Ian Young, *The Male Homosexual in Literature: A Bibliography* (Metuchen, N.J.: Scarecrow Press, 1975), 155.

CHAPTER 11

1. Earl Lind, *Autobiography of an Androgyne* (1918) and *The Female Impersonators* (1922), 24–25. These books have been reprinted in the series Homosexuality: Lesbians and Gay Men in Society, History and Literature, ed. Jonathan Katz (New York: Arno Press, 1975). Hereafter cited in text.

CHAPTER 12

1. See Katz (1976, 629) for the identification of Peirce.

2. Xavier Mayne, *The Intersexes* (Naples, 1908), 367; hereafter cited in text.

3. Derrick Bailey, *Homosexuality and the Western Christian Tradition* (New York: Archon Books, 1975), 8.

4. Xavier Mayne, *Imre* (Naples, 1906), 107; hereafter cited in text.

5. Henry Blake Fuller, *Bertram Cope's Year* (Chicago: Alderbrink Press, 1919), 116; hereafter cited in text.

6. Sherwood Anderson, "Hands" (1919), reprinted in *Calamus: Male Homosexuality in Twentieth-Century Literature: An International Anthology*, ed. David Galloway and Christian Sabisch, 93–100 (New York: Quill, 1982); hereafter cited in text.

7. Carl van Vechten, *The Blind Bow-Boy* (New York: Alfred Knopf, 1923), 56; hereafter cited in text.

8. Robert McAlmon, "Miss Knight" (1925), reprinted in *There Was a Rustle of Black Silk Stockings* (New York: Belmont Books, 1963), 50; hereafter cited in text.

9. George Chauncey, Jr., "Christian Brotherhood or Sexual Perversion? Homosexual Identities and the Construction of Sexual Boundaries in the World War I Era," in Duberman 1989, 316. George Chauncey vastly enlarges his study of pre–World War II homosexual life in *Gay New York: Gender, Urban Culture, and the Making of the Gay Male World, 1890–1940* (New York: Basic Books, 1994).

10. Robert Scully, *A Scarlet Pansy* (New York: William Faro, 1933); hereafter cited in text.

CHAPTER 13

1. La Forrest Potter, *Strange Loves: A Study in Sexual Abnormalities* (New York: Padell, 1933), 5; hereafter cited in text.

2. George Henry, *Sex Variants: A Study of Homosexual Patterns* (1941; New York: Paul B. Hoeber, 1948), ix; hereafter cited in text.

CHAPTER 14

1. Salvatore Licata and Robert Petersen, eds., *The Gay Past: A Collection of Historical Essays* (New York: Harrington Park Press, 1985), 166; hereafter cited in text.

2. See *ONE Institute Quarterly*, Fall 1958, 94, for Garde; Fall 1963, 46 and 58, for Pagari and Legg.

3. *The Complete Poems of Hart Crane*, ed. Marc Simon (New York and London: Liveright, 1986); hereafter cited in text as *CP*.

4. *Men and Boys: An Anthology*, ed. Donald Mader (1924; New York and London: Coltsfoot Press, 1978), xlvii.

5. *Gay Sunshine Interviews*, vol. 2, ed. Winston Leyland (San Francisco: Gay Sunshine Press, 1982), 90; hereafter cited in text.

6. James Levin, *The Gay Novel in America* (New York: Garland Publishing, 1991), 198; hereafter cited in text.

BIBLIOGRAPHIC ESSAY

Over the past two decades lesbian and gay studies have produced an impressive library of critical texts, research tools, and theoretical discussions of which the following are only a small and recent sampling.

For American studies I direct the student's attention to the following: Jonathan Ned Katz's two ground-breaking books—*Gay American History* (New York: Thomas Y. Crowell, 1976) and *Gay/Lesbian Almanac* (New York: Harper & Row, 1983)—provide access to rare homosexual texts and the homophobic counter-texts from our American past. Another seminal and wise book is Roger Austen's *Playing the Game: The Homosexual Novel in America* (New York: Bobbs-Merrill, 1977). This is complemented by James Levin, *The Gay Novel in America* (New York: Garland Publishing, 1991). Robert K. Martin's *The Homosexual Tradition in America Poetry* (Austin and London: University of Texas Press, 1979) was the first important study of homoeroticism in American poetry. Thomas Yingling's *Hart Crane and the Homosexual Text* (Chicago and London: University of Chicago Press, 1990), Michael Moon's *Disseminating Whitman: Revision and Corporeality in "Leaves of Grass"* (Cambridge, Mass., and London: Harvard University Press, 1991), my own *Masculine Landscapes: Walt Whitman and the Homoerotic Text* (Carbondale: Southern Illinois University Press, 1992), and Gregory Woods's *Articulate Flesh: Male Homoeroticism in Modern Poetry* (New Haven, Conn., and London: Yale University Press, 1987) all provide useful analysis of the homosexual component of major American poets.

For the study of nineteenth-century English homoerotic texts, the following should be consulted by any student: Timothy d'Arch Smith's *Love in Earnest: Some Notes on the Lives and Writings of English Uranian Poets from 1889 to 1930* (London: Routledge & Kegan Paul, 1970), Brian Reade's *Sexual Heretics: Male Homosexuality in English Literature from 1850 to 1900* (New York: Coward McCann, 1970), Louis Crompton's *Byron and Greek*

Love: Homophobia in Nineteenth-Century England (Berkeley: University of California Press, 1985), Jeffrey Weeks's *Coming Out: Homosexual Politics in Britain from the Nineteenth Century to the Present* (London: Quartet Books, 1977), and Richard Dellamora's *Masculine Desire: The Sexual Politics of Victorian Aestheticism* (Chapel Hill: University of North Carolina Press, 1990).

Useful for eighteenth-century English sodomitical history is Kent Gerard and Gert Hekma's *The Pursuit of Sodomy: Male Homosexuality in Renaissance and Enlightenment Europe* (New York and London: Harrington Park Press, 1989), which includes essays by Randolph Trumbach, G. S. Rousseau, Dennis Rubini, and Stephen O. Murray. A lively study is Rictor Norton, *Mother Clap's Molly Houses: The Gay Subculture in England, 1700–1830* (London: Gay Men's Press, 1992).

Valuable texts for periods I do not address in my text are Derrick Bailey, *Homosexuality and the Western Christian Tradition* (New York: Archon Books, 1975); K. J. Dover, *Greek Homosexuality* (Cambridge: Harvard University Press, 1978); David M. Halperin, *One Hundred Years of Homosexuality and Other Essays on Greek Love* (New York and London: Routledge & Kegan Paul, 1990); John Boswell, *Christianity, Social Tolerance, and Homosexuality: Gay People in Western Europe from the Beginnings of the Christian Era to the Fourteenth Century* (Chicago and London: University of Chicago Press, 1980); John Boswell, *Same-Sex Unions in Premodern Europe* (New York: Villard Books, 1994); James M. Saslow, *Ganymede in the Renaissance: Homosexuality in Art and Society* (New Haven and London: Yale University Press, 1986); Bruce R. Smith, *Homosexual Desire in Shakespeare's England* (Chicago and London: University of Chicago Press, 1991); Alan Bray, *Homosexuality in Renaissance England* (London: Gay Men's Press, 1982); and Gregory W. Bredbeck, *Sodomy and Interpretation: Marlowe to Milton* (Ithaca, N.Y., and London: Cornell University Press, 1991).

For theoretical discussions—social construction versus essentialism, gay and queer theory— I direct the reader to Edward Stein, *Forms of Desire: Sexual Orientation and the Social Construction Controversy* (New York and London: Routledge, 1990), a collection of essays that pursues the debate that asks whether gay people—in terms of style and social substance—have existed throughout history in much the same way we imagine ourselves now to be, or whether homosexuality and homosexual style is, instead of being a constant and "essential" element of human nature, instead a "social construction," an invention of recent times. David Greenberg's *The Construction of Homosexuality* (Chicago: University of Chicago Press, 1988) exhaustively also addresses the topic. Frank Browning in *The Culture of Desire: Paradox and Perversity in Gay Lives Today* (New York: Crown, 1993) considers significant social questions.

Collections of essays valuable for looking at the range of gay and queer studies are Stuart Kellog, ed., *Literary Visions of Homosexuality* (New York:

Haworth Press, 1983); Salvatore Licata and Robert Petersen, eds., *The Gay Past: A Collection of Historical Essays* (New York: Harrington Park Press, 1985); Martin Duberman, *About Time: Exploring the Gay Past* (New York: Gay Presses of New York, 1986); Martin Duberman, Martha Vicinus, and George Chauncey, Jr., eds., *Hidden from History: Reclaiming the Gay and Lesbian Past* (New York: New American Library, 1989); Ronald Butters, John M. Clum, and Michael Moon, eds., *Displacing Homophobia: Gay Male Perspectives in Literature and Culture* (Durham, N.C., and London: Duke University Press, 1989); John D'Emilio, *Making Trouble: Essays on Gay History, Politics, and the University* (New York: Routledge & Kegan Paul, 1992); David Bergman, ed., *Camp Grounds: Style and Homosexuality* (Amherst: University of Massachusetts Press, 1993); and Moe Meyer, ed., *The Politics and Poetics of Camp* (London and New York: Routledge, 1994).

Founding texts in gay and queer theory are Eve Kosofsky Sedgwick, *Between Men: English Literature and Male Homosocial Desire* (New York: Columbia University Press, 1985), and Sedgwick's *Epistemology of the Closet* (Berkeley: University of California Press, 1990). In addition, Joseph A. Boone and Michael Cadden, *Engendering Men: The Question of Male Feminist Criticism* (New York and London: Routledge & Kegan Paul, 1990), and Diana Fuss, *Inside/Out: Lesbian and Gay Theories* (New York and London: Routledge & Kegan Paul, 1991), address questions of theory.

The history of Stonewall has been definitively addressed in Martin Duberman, *Stonewall* (New York: Dutton, 1993), and the history of the gay civil rights movement in Barry D. Adam, *The Rise of a Gay and Lesbian Movement* (Boston: Twayne, 1987). A special study is George Chauncey, Jr., *Gay New York: Gender, Urban Culture, and the Making of the Gay Male World, 1890–1940* (New York: Basic Books, 1994).

Indispensable for research are Wayne Dynes, *Homosexuality: A Research Guide* (New York: Garland Publishing, 1987), and Wayne Dynes et al., eds., *Encyclopedia of Homosexuality* (New York: Garland Publishing, 1990).

INDEX

THE AUTHOR

Byrne Fone is professor of English at the City College of the City University of New York, where he taught the first gay literary studies course the college offered. He is the author of *Hidden Heritage: History and the Gay Imagination* and *Masculine Landscapes: Walt Whitman and the Homoerotic Text*. As Ron Denby he is the author of the novel *American Lives*. He is currently at work on an anthology of literary texts illustrating desire, sex, love, and friendship between men from the earliest times to the present.